THE CANADIAN WAY OF WAR

THE CANADIAN WAY OF WAR

Serving the National Interest

Edited by
Colonel Bernd Horn

DUNDURN PRESS
TORONTO

Editor: Michael Carroll
Copy-editor: Nigel Heseltine
Design: Jennifer Scott
Printer: Tri-Graphic Printing Limited

Library and Archives Canada Cataloguing in Publication

The Canadian way of war: serving the national interest / edited by Bernd Horn.

Includes bibliographical references and index.
ISBN-10: 1-55002-612-7
ISBN-13: 978-1-55002-612-2

1. Canada--Military policy--History. 2. Canada--History, Military.
3. National interest--Canada--History. I. Horn, Bernd, 1959-

UA600.C368 2006   355'.03357109   C2006-905102-X

1   2   3   4   5   10   09   08   07   06

  Conseil des Arts   Canada Council
du Canada   for the Arts   Canadä

We acknowledge the support of the **Canada Council for the Arts** and the **Ontario Arts Council** for our publishing program. We also acknowledge the financial support of the **Government of Canada** through the **Book Publishing Industry Development Program** and **The Association for the Export of Canadian Books**, and the **Government of Ontario** through the **Ontario Book Publishers Tax Credit program**, and the **Ontario Media Development Corporation**.

Care has been taken to trace the ownership of copyright material used in this book. The author and the publisher welcome any information enabling them to rectify any references or credits in subsequent editions.

J. Kirk Howard, President

Printed and bound in Canada.
Printed on recycled paper.

www.dundurn.com

Dundurn Press	Gazelle Book Services Limited	Dundurn Press
3 Church Street, Suite 500	White Cross Mills	2250 Military Road
Toronto, Ontario, Canada	High Town, Lancaster, England	Tonawanda, NY
M5E 1M2	LA1 4XS	U.S.A. 14150

Contents

FOREWORD
by Major-General (Retired)
Lewis W. MacKenzie

Canadians are known as a tolerant and peaceful people. We pride ourselves on our multiculturalism and humanitarian outlook. In fact, much of our identity has been shaped by the peaceful settlement of our frontier and our willingness to maintain justice and to do what is right — to help bring peace to those far and near. This goal has never been easy. It has been expensive in blood and dollars, yet this is the role that history has bestowed upon us. For the past half-century we have defined ourselves as a culture and society largely by our efforts at peace rather than war.

Nevertheless, although not a warlike or militaristic people, Canadians have earned a reputation as brave and capable soldiers. This recognition was achieved through the toil and sacrifice of those Canadians who served their country under arms since our nation's birth. From the hardy and intrepid colonists of New France to the well-trained professional soldiers who deployed to Afghanistan, one constant has always remained — their courage, tenacity, and capability on the battlefield. Canadians have always been a welcomed ally and a dreaded foe. But our commitments have come with a considerable cost. Contemplating the loss of life within the span of our human memory tells a compelling story. Of the 620,000 who served in World War I, 60,000 were killed and another 172,000 were wounded. Twenty years later, World War II prompted the entire nation to mobilize. An incredible 1.1 million Canadians served in uniform, of which 42,042 were killed and 54,414 wounded. Five years later, 26,971 Canadians volunteered to fight again, this time in Korea. Once again, the price paid was 516 killed and 1,072 wounded. But the cost did not end there. Canadian involvement in peace support operations since 1956 has cost the lives of approximately 130 personnel, as well as permanently transforming the lives of thousands of others — in and out of uniform. As lamentable and painful as the sacrifice was and continues to this day, we as individuals and as a nation realize the importance of Canada's contribution to international peace and security.

Consistent with Canada's participation in homeland defence or international security has been an identifiable Canadian way of war. We, as a nation, have evolved certain cultural and philosophical approaches to warfare that form a common thread throughout our colourful and dramatic history. This book articulates those timeless themes. As such, it fills an important gap in our military history. Aptly written by military and civilian members of the Department of National Defence, all with links to the Royal Military College of Canada, their collective contribution to our understanding of a proud and complex past is commendable.

Lewis W. MacKenzie, OstJ, OOnt, MSC, CD
Major-General (Retired)

Acknowledgements

$\mathbf{A}$ny project of this magnitude owes its existence to a myriad of supporters. As such, initially, I must thank all the contributors who made this volume possible. Their efforts represent a collective attempt to explain an important and often misunderstood aspect of Canada's military history and continued existence as a nation. In addition, I would like to thank the Academic Research Program (ARP) for their generous support. Without their assistance, the final product would never have been as complete or timely.

Furthermore, as with any project of this scope, there is an inordinate debt owed to countless individuals who contributed their expertise, memories, resources, and time. Collectively, our sincere thanks are extended to all those who assisted, directly or indirectly, with this book Although it would be impossible to acknowledge everyone individually, the significant contributions of some oblige me to make special mention of their efforts. In this regard, I wish to convey my sincere gratitude to Chris Heffernan, Dr. Michael Hennessy (RMC), Christopher Johnson, Denise Moffat (RMC), "The Old Guard," Silvia Pecota, and Suzanne Surgeson (Parks Canada).

I must also make special mention of the selfless effort and enormous support provided by the staff of the DND Directorate of History and Heritage, Library and Archives Canada, the Royal Military College of Canada, and the Fort Frontenac Army Library in Kingston.

Colonel Bernd Horn
Kingston, Ontario
June 2006

INTRODUCTION
by Bernd Horn

Writing about Canada's military history and its "way of war" calls to mind the observation that Canadians perceive themselves to be a peaceful people. Moreover, they take great pride in their reputation as "peacekeepers." In fact, a mythology has evolved of Canadians as reluctant warriors — destined to fulfill a role to bring peace to others in a hostile and unstable world. This popular image is not entirely new. "We are first of all a peace-loving people," espoused T.S. Sproule, the Member of Parliament for East Grey, in the House of Commons in May 1899.[1] Several months later, the prime minister, Sir Wilfrid Laurier himself, exclaimed, "The cause for which you men of Canada are going to fight [in South Africa] is the cause of justice, the cause of humanity, of civil rights and religious liberty." He added, "This is not a war of conquest."[2] Five decades later, renowned Canadian historian C.P. Stacey echoed those exact same sentiments. Canada "struck good blows for the good cause," proclaimed Stacey.[3] He observed that "Canada is an unmilitary community." And went on to explain, "Warlike her people have often been forced to be, military they have never been."[4]

This theme was repeated half a century later in 2001 by Adrienne Clarkson, the governor general of Canada and commander-in-chief of the Canadian Armed Forces.[5] She described Canada as "a peaceable kingdom" and asserted that Canadians "are basically a forgiving and compassionate people."[6] In the wake of the tragic terrorist attack on the twin towers of the World Trade Center in New York on September 11, 2001, she commented on "our ability to maintain justice and do what is right, to bring peace to those far and near." She went on to say that this "is difficult. It is trying. This is a role which history has allotted us."[7]

More recently, Major-General Andrew Leslie, the deputy commander of the International Security Assistance Force (ISAF) in Afghanistan and the top Canadian serving in that theatre at the time, posed the rhetorical question, "Is Canada still willing to pay the price of its soldiers' blood in Afghanistan?" He replied, "I suspect it is, because if Canadian soldiers weren't here a whole bunch of innocent people would die and we are a helping nation so arguably this is what we do."[8]

This flattering image of a benevolent country that dispatches its reluctant warriors throughout the world to do good is somewhat simplistic and naïve. Often, Canadians have taken up arms and employed military forces internally to resolve domestic problems, as well as externally to assist with global stability. These forces were most often drawn from volunteer soldiers; however, the government resorted to conscription when necessary. Throughout, the rationale for the use of force was always to fight the good fight. The use of military force was always cast in an unselfish light. It was always necessary to ensure survival, to further national unity, or as a contribution of a sovereign nation to the greater good.

Nonetheless, regardless of how it was packaged, war, conflict, and the military itself have made an indelible impression on Canada and its society. Similarly, the nature of the country and its society has had a similar impact on our "way" of war. Quite simply, the approach a nation takes to war is based on its geography, governance, and history, as well as its societal makeup and culture. All these factors determine how a nation interprets the use of force for their own growth and well-being. These elements have also shaped how nations understand strategy. Strategy, in turn, is directly related to a nation's policy, namely how it chooses to mobilize its resources and power. In the end, it is government policy that dictates the strategy that will be followed.

As such, war, conflict, and the military have been important components in forging this nation and creating a national understanding of who we are as a society and people. In fact, this experience has shaped a distinct Canadian way of war — or in simple terms, a methodology whereby the nation structures and uses the military to further its national interests and fight its wars.

In essence, Canadians are a product of their experience and circumstances. From the very beginning, they were but one small and very junior component of a larger empire, originally French and later British. In either case, they could expect only limited assistance. Resources, particularly personnel and defence spending, were always at a premium. Debate over responsibility for defence — should it fall to French or British regulars, or Canadian Militia — and who should pay, regardless of the enemy (Iroquois, English, American, Russian), was always a sore point.

Not surprisingly, Canada, militarily, particularly in light of the perennial debate over funding, as well as its distance from Europe, its small population base, and its vast, untamed, and harsh environment, was always in a position of relative weakness. As a result, military operations had to be limited — in essence they were largely tactical, most often attempting to capitalize on economy of effort and alliances to achieve an influence greater than Canada's military, economic or political strength would normally allow. This philosophical and practical approach to war was already present in New France. The custodians of the fledgling nation developed a methodology for survival that included alliances and a manner of fighting that met its needs, capability, economic capacity, and the temperament of its people. As such, the violent and bitter experience of *la petite guerre* and many of those principles that served New France so well represented a strategy of survival, many elements of which continued to resonate throughout the Canadian military experience.

In fact, many attributes and themes would continue throughout Canada's participation in conflict and war, none more than its experiential baggage and cultural norms. After all, "Canadians," proclaimed the influential British *Army and Navy Gazette*, "are largely offspring of old military stock of two famous fighting nations, the British and French, consequently their qualities for soldiering cannot be doubted."[9] Paradoxically, Canadians, were loathed and admired by their imperial regular officers. Free-spirited, independent, and difficult to control, they were also courageous, hardy, intelligent, and brimming with initiative.

Normally, in the final analysis, their strong qualities won out. A British general observing the Canadians during the attack at Paardeburg later exclaimed, "Those men [Canadians] can go into battle without a leader — they have intelligence and resourcefulness enough to lead themselves."[10] Similarly, a journalist in the Boer War was struck by the ability of Canadian soldiers to think on their own. Canadians, he noted, who relied on their "own resources" were able to take their "place along with the British man of the line, and not only equal but surpass in nearly every way the average Tommy."[11] This was no surprise to Lieutenant-General Sir Arthur Currie, the commander of the Canadian Corps during World War I, who described the "rugged" Canadians that served him so well as "vigorous, clean-minded, good-humoured, unselfish, intelligent, thorough … wide awake, and full of intelligent initiative."[12]

But, as effective as the nation's soldiers have been, they have largely been used at the tactical level of war. As the junior member in alliances and coalitions, Canada has rarely been able to have a great impact at the operational or strategic level of decision making. But then again, militarily Canada's leaders have always seemed content to perch under the protective wing of a senior ally and allow the arduous task of determining strategy to be addressed by someone else. After all, as a small player in big alliances, the nation could reap the security benefits of its more powerful protector and needed only to react to the doctrine of its primary ally, first Britain and later the United States. At the same time, it could always use its junior position, lack of economic and military resources, as well as its independence and sovereignty, to plead exemption to the larger strategic decisions that did not resonate well with Canadians.

This relationship and approach was continually deemed by Canada's politicians to be best suited for the nation. It allowed for defence on the cheap. Someone else, whether Britain's Royal Navy and garrisons in North America, or later the Americans, would ultimately ensure Canadian security and pay the enormous bills that inherently accompany potent military capability. The nation's political leaders were always risk averse (for example, they feared becoming embroiled overseas in a conflict that may be high in casualties, and thus, potentially cause a political backlash, enormous costs, or in the worst instance conscription and the resultant challenge to national unity and political control) and conscious of the deep cultural and political chasm in Canada, particularly in regards to supporting overseas conflict in support of "imperial" ventures whether British or American. It was often a question of political will. Not surprisingly, they realized that the tactical approach served the nation's interests best.

Quite simply, the nation could meet its strategic ends with tactical means. In the end, it came down to functionalism and saliency — what can we realistically do (or more accurately what are we willing do)?[13] The answer to this question also had to be balanced with saliency — Canada had to make an important or notable contribution to any alliance or coalition effort. Importantly, it had to be recognized as such by its partners. And so, the nation has consciously and consistently used military force in support of the national interest to further its security, as well as its economic and political well-being. But it has done so in a deliberate manner to reduce its costs, liabilities, commitments, and risks to the lowest possible level. However, Canada's military and political leadership has rarely failed to realize that the use of military force is an important tool in an unforgiving global environment where *realpolitik* is the real foundation of action regardless of whatever "humanitarian" facade is presented to the general public.

And so, this philosophical, as well as practical methodology of war has woven its way through the entirety of the Canadian military experience. In its examination, it becomes evident that two strong conclusions can be drawn. First, Canadians have always been willing and highly capable soldiers. They have consistently proven that they are second to none. Their tenacious spirit and endurance made them valued combatants whether in the colonial period against the Iroquois, British, and later Americans, or in later centuries during overseas deployments in South Africa, Europe, and no matter where else in the world they found themselves.

The second conclusion that can be drawn is that the military and military force has always been wielded deliberately for practical purposes, specifically to serve the national interest. "The best defence for Canada," asserted General Rick Hillier, former commander of the Canadian Army, "is a good offence." He added, "We must play a significant part in the world to prevent that violence and conflict coming home."[14] This concept of forward defence is well rooted in Canadian military history.[15] Undoubtedly, the use of the military in that role has been beneficial to others, particularly to assist in global stability. However, that force has always been wielded consciously and in keeping with the Canadian way of war to attain the greatest possible effect with the least amount of cost and risk. As General Hillier has repeatedly stated, "When a Canadian soldier walks on foreign soil all Canadians walk on foreign soil. Canadian soldiers are our credentials."[16] Furthermore, the use of military force has always served a specific national interest greater than mere humanitarianism. Simply put, the Canadian way of war has been a critical element in the maturation, development, and continued strength of our nation as an advanced, affluent, industrial democracy in a very competitive and dangerous world.

This volume explores elements of Canada's military experience and touches on components of the Canadian way of war. Whether through outright action by Canada, or the failure thereof, or reticence on its part to develop a doctrine or strategy of its own, a generally consistent philosophical and practical approach to the use of the military or military force, to further national interests is always discernable. Moreover, it has always been driven by circumstance and political will. In this vein, the themes articulated earlier resonate throughout the chapters. However, as always in historical debate, varying interpretations provide food for thought, discourse, and further discussion and investigation. Nonetheless, in the end, what becomes clear is the fact that the Canadian military experience has been integral to creating the strong nation that exists today. Undeniably, despite the popular mythology of humanitarian "do-gooding," Canadian national interest has actually been best served by the hard edge of military participation in alliance and coalition operations. In so doing, amazingly, Canada has consistently achieved, for the most part, its strategic goals with tactical means.

NOTES

1. *Debates of the House of Commons of the Dominion of Canada* (henceforth *Debates*), Vol. 48, May 1, 1899, 2347.
2. Quoted in Robert Page, *The Boer War and Canadian Imperialism* (Ottawa: Canadian Historical Association Historical Booklet No. 44, 1987), 13.
3. C.P. Stacey, *The Canadian Army 1939–1945* (Ottawa: DND, 1948), 312.
4. C.P. Stacey, *Six Years of War: The Army in Canada, Britain and the Pacific* (Ottawa: Queen's Printer, 1955), 3. A few years prior, Prime Minister W.L. Mackenzie King stated, "We are fighting to defend democratic and Christian ideals" and "we have transformed one of the least military peoples on earth into a nation organised for modern war." W.L. Mackenzie King, "The Message of Canada," *Hutchinson's Pictorial History of the War*, No. 1, Series 13, July–December 1941, 199.
5. The anti-militaristic image is arguably perpetuated in the actual name of the Canadian Armed Forces. The "Armed" was dropped in the 1980s in favour of a more palatable and less aggressive and more "public friendly" Canadian Forces. However, the Canadian defence act still refers to the Canadian Armed Forces.
6. Her Excellency the Right Honourable Adrienne Clarkson, governor general of Canada, convocation address at Royal Military College of Canada, May 18, 2001.
7. "Clarkson says Canada a nation of peacekeepers," *Calgary Herald*, October 16, 2001, A7. Almost three years later she stated, "Canadians have always answered the call when asked to defend freedom and democracy around the world. Whether in battle, on peacekeeping missions or delivering humanitarian aid, the brave Canadians who serve in our military are willing to give their own lives if necessary to defend the values we cherish most." Adrienne Clarkson, "Governor General's CF Day Message," *The Maple Leaf*, June 2, 2004, 16. In regard to the death of Corporal Jamie Murphy in Afghanistan, the Honourable David Price, parliamentary secretary, stated, "Let this tragedy be a reminder to all Canadians that Corporal Jamie Murphy made the ultimate sacrifice in an effort to make the world in which we live a safer place." "Statement from Associate Minister of Defence and Parliamentary Secretary," January 27, 2004, *http://www.forces.gc.ca/site/newsroom/view_news_e.asp? id=1297*, accessed January 28, 2004.
8. "Soldiers Keeping Thousands of People Alive," *Kingston Whig-Standard*, November 24, 2003, 12.
9. "The Royal Canadians," *Army and Navy Gazette*, Vol. 61, No. 2098, April 7, 1900, 343.
10. Stanley McKeown Brown, *With the Royal Canadians* (Toronto: The Publishers' Syndicate, 1900), 138.
11. *Ibid.*, 136–137.
12. Colonel George G. Nasmith, *Canada's Sons and Great Britain in the World War* (Toronto: Thomas Allen, 1919), introduction by Currie, v, vii–viii.

13. See Sean M. Maloney, "The Canadian Tao of Conflict," in Bernd Horn, ed., *Forging a Nation: Perspectives on the Canadian Military Experience* (St. Catharines, ON: Vanwell, 2002), 271–286.
14. General Rick Hillier, Strategic Planning Session 7, Cornwall, November 29, 2003.
15. And it remains so. The most recent government security policy, *Securing an Open Society: Canada's National Security Policy*, published in April 2004, states that "our forces must ... address threat to our national security as far away from our borders as possible." *Securing an Open Society: Canada's National Security Policy* (Ottawa: PMO, April 2004), 49.
16. General Rick Hillier, CLS Orientation, Ottawa, September 11, 2003.

PART I

Establishing a Distinct Canadian Way of War

CHAPTER 1

La Petite Guerre: *A Strategy of Survival*
by Bernd Horn

Experience is a powerful force, and historical experience is even more so. Its influence is pervasive and is often the driving factor behind the behaviour and actions of individuals, institutions, nations, and cultures. In short, we are all, to some degree or other, prisoners of our own experience. Within this context, arguably, it was the brutal struggle for survival in New France that developed a distinct Canadian strategy of survival based on circumstance, geography, and political will. For that reason many tenets of the strategy adopted would resonate throughout Canadian military history.

From necessity the intrepid leaders and settlers of New France realized that survival lay in the adoption of a number of basic principles. First, alliances for economic benefit and military cooperation were critical to counterbalance economically and/or numerically superior antagonists and neighbours. They were fundamental for survival in a hostile world. Second, subordinate stature as a distant wilderness colony in a larger empire limited New France's population and resource base. These principles determined how much of its treasury France was willing to deplete in defence of its untamed colony, guaranteeing that New France would largely live or die by its ability to protect itself.

Such realities quickly dictated a distinct approach to war — adapt to the surroundings and circumstances of the colony and use those methods that would ensure survival and maintain the balance of power within North America. Given this largely tactical focus, strategic decisions and initiatives were simply beyond the scope and ability of New France. War, as such, had to be conducted on the cheapest possible footing, since New France was a distant theatre and the limited Canadian economy could not afford a protracted conflict, nor would the colony's inhabitants tolerate one. Moreover, as circumstances eventually bore out, France was also unwilling to risk its position on the European continent, or in any of its more lucrative colonies, in defence of New France.[1] Therefore, support and supply from outside would be and was exceedingly limited.

As a result, the inhabitants of New France focused on, and practised, a way of war that developed from their experience and was driven by necessity. Their way of war also needed to be limited and cost-effective — both fiscally and in regards to resources and personnel — particularly in casualties. Furthermore, *les habitants* practised war in a manner that was distinct to their abilities and temperament and that counterbalanced their weaknesses. In short, they adopted *la petite guerre*. Although not unique to North America or its Native peoples, the wilderness, terrain, and weather etched a distinct New World meaning to the concept.

La petite guerre was, in essence, small-scale irregular warfare.[2] Key to its success was the selection of limited objectives that could be easily overcome. Stealth and surprise were of the utmost importance, ambushes and raids were the preferred method of attack, and lightning-quick strikes were always succeeded by immediate withdrawals. There were no follow-on attacks or campaigns, and rarely were any of the tactical operations capable of achieving a larger strategic value other than pre-empting, delaying, or disrupting possible enemy offensive action.

This form of warfare became ideally suited to the Canadians. For much of their early history they were the target of Iroquois war parties that were highly adept at this method of war making. But for an equally long period of time the colonists were the eager apprentices of their Native allies. From their aboriginal friends, they learned how to dress, fish, hunt, travel, navigate, and flourish in the North American wilderness. Moreover, survival necessitated that they also learn the Native manner of fighting. The Canadians soon became skilled practitioners of the art. In later years the practice and methodology of *la petite guerre* became as much identified with the Canadians as it did with their Native allies. In the end, *la petite guerre* became a strategy for survival.

This approach was rooted in a bitter struggle of survival and conflict that transcended generations. It was the result of hard-won, if not bloody, experience and adaptation to a hostile, savage environment. The harsh climate, seemingly impenetrable wilderness, and bellicose Natives, most notably the Iroquois, proved too much for most Europeans. Initially, few settlers ventured to the New World. By the middle of the seventeenth century only about 2,500 Europeans lived in New France. Many of these were explorers, fur traders, and missionaries. Nonetheless, the lure of freedom, opportunity, and, especially, wealth was enough of an impetus to spur growth, and the French established settlements and a series of forts, predominately for fur trading.[3]

However, economic prosperity, if not survival, necessitated alliances. For this reason Samuel de Champlain, the first governor of New France, entered into treaties of friendship and trading partnerships with a number of northern tribes for example, the Abenakis, Algonquin, Huron, Montagnais, and Outaouais. But many of these tribes were locked in conflict with the far more aggressive Iroquois Confederacy.[4] Champlain understood that his choice of allies would alienate the Iroquois and possibly cause conflict. Of greater consequence, though, was his decision to actively support the war efforts of his newfound friends. On July 20, 1609, Champlain led the first combined French, Algonquin, and Huron force against the Iroquois at a site near present-day Ticonderoga, New York. Armed with an arquebus, Champlain felled two Iroquois chiefs and injured a third warrior with his first shot. His two French companions were also equipped with firearms, and they opened fire from the flank. This onslaught, particularly because of the new weaponry involved, caused panic among the Iroquois, and they fled the field of battle.

In June 1610, Champlain accompanied another expedition that expelled an Iroquois war party from the Richelieu Valley.[5] These humiliating defeats inflicted on the Iroquois were not soon forgotten. The consequences of these events would rock the colony for generations.

Library and Archives Canada C-6643

The governor of New France, Samuel de Champlain, with allied Natives defeating the Iroquois near the present town of Ticonderoga, New York, July 30, 1609.

The Iroquois Confederacy became the intractable enemy of the French. "Between us and them," conceded an intendant of New France, "there is no more good faith than between the most ferocious animals."[6]

In 1615 the repulse of Champlain and his Algonquin and Huron allies in their ill-fated bid to invade Iroquoia buoyed the confidence of the Iroquois, who then carried the war to the northern tribes, as well as to the French. A bitter war of annihilation ensued that lasted almost a century. At its peak it threatened the very survival of New France. By 1627 the Iroquois had become a constant terror to the settlers in Canada. "Conscious of their strength, the natives became daily more insolent; no white man could venture beyond the settlement without incurring great danger," wrote one early Canadian historian. "Buildings languished, and much of the cleared land remained uncultivated."[7]

From 1648 to 1649, the Iroquois mounted a major offensive that culminated in the destruction of Huronia.[8] Subsequently, they focused their attacks on the French settlements in the St. Lawrence Valley. "They are everywhere," wrote one French governor. "They will stay hidden behind a stump for 10 days, existing on nothing but a handful of corn, waiting to kill a man, or a woman." He lamented, "It was the cruellest war in the world," and that the Iroquois "were not content to burn the houses, they also burn the prisoners they take, and give them death only after torturing them continually in the most cruel manner they can devise."[9]

The Iroquois war parties were extremely effective. They forced the colonists to remain barricaded in cramped stockades, only venturing out to tend their fields in large armed groups that even then were no guarantee of survival. "The Iroquois used to keep us closely confined," conceded one Jesuit missionary, "that we did not even dare till the lands that were under the cannon of the forts."[10]

Even the anemic infusion of colonial troops from 1604 to 1663 did little to ease the perpetual menace. Although they provided limited garrisons in some locations, they were too few to cover the entire colony and were incapable of matching the Iroquois on their own terms.[11] The Iroquois control over the French was such that one sachem boasted: "We plied the French homes in the war with them that they were not able to go out a door to piss."[12]

His taunt was no idle bluster. "The Iroquois," decried King Louis XIV, "through massacres and inhumanities, have prevented the country's population from growing."[13]

The constant hardship and terror inflicted on the Canadians shaped their collective experience and outlook. It tempered a stoicism and

courage, if not contempt for danger, as well as a ruggedness and fortitude that enabled them to withstand the rigours of the North American
wilderness. It also ingrained in them a level of ferocity and savageness
in conflict that recognized no mercy and gave no quarter. The
Canadians adopted a Native manner of making war — a tactical outlook that was dependent on the clever use of ground and cover, the element of surprise, sudden ambushes, swift raids, and engagement in
combat only when the likelihood of success was high and the possibility of casualties was low.

This evolutionary process was born out of necessity. The tutelage by
Native allies, as well as a study of the enemy, provided the colonists with
the necessary knowledge to overcome the problem. Pierre Boucher, the
governor of Trois-Rivières, studied the Iroquois manner of war and
concluded the Natives were very competent at war fighting, and always
demonstrated a preference for quick hit-and-run attacks that enabled
them to achieve maximum shock and surprise against their victims.[14]
He also deduced they would never fight if they were outnumbered, or
could not achieve a decisive advantage. Boucher further recognized that
the Canadians could only survive if they became capable of taking the
initiative and fighting on the same terms. He argued that the only way
to destroy the Iroquois was to take offensive action with the assistance
of a large force of 800 or 900 regular soldiers.[15]

Although for decades pleas for relief from the Iroquois scourge in
New France fell largely on deaf ears at the Royal Palace and the Ministry
of Marine in France, finally some respite was promised. In 1664 the
French court informed the leaders in the colony that "The principal
menace to the inhabitants being the Iroquois, who at all moments attack
the French ... and massacre them cruelly ... the King has resolved, if it is
necessary, to send next year some regular troops to the country."[16]
Subsequently, in the spring of 1665, approximately 1,200 men of the
Carignan-Salières Regiment departed La Rochelle for New France.[17] In
addition, Lieutenant-General Alexandre de Prouville de Tracy and a further 200 soldiers were dispatched from Guadeloupe to Quebec to assist
in vanquishing the Iroquois menace.

It took Tracy less than a month to decide on a plan of action. After
determining the details of the threat and the Native manner of making
war, he decided the first step was to deny the Iroquois, most notably the
Mohawks, access to the vital waterways that led into New France. As
such, he decided to build forts at strategic locations to close off the
Richelieu Valley from Lake Champlain to the St. Lawrence River.[18] Once

completed, these forts served a multitude of functions. First, they filled an important economic and political purpose by controlling access to major waterways and acting as trade outlets. In this vein they reinforced French territorial claims and power, and provided a presence within the wilderness that was recognized and accessed by the various Native nations. This became a key factor in the French hold on their Native allies.[19]

Second, the strategic locations of the fortifications denied the Iroquois easy access into New France, particularly the use of the Richelieu Valley waterway. By garrisoning these positions, they could possibly intercept Iroquois war parties going to, or from, their forays against the colony. At a minimum they would force the enemy to seek alternate routes by either land and/or water, thereby extending the distances that had to be

Carignan-Salières Regiment, 1665 by Derek Fitzjames copyright © Parks Canada

A soldier from the Carignan-Salières Regiment, circa 1665. Many of these soldiers decided to stay in Canada after their tour of duty, thus increasing the pool of colonists with military experience available for raiding operations.

travelled and the time needed to execute attacks on the settlements. In essence, they represented the first line of defence for New France — a defence that was based on fighting on the outer frontier of the colony or beyond it.

Finally, the forts provided the French forces with a secure forward operating position. They could now function more easily at a distance from the settled areas and attempt to contain the violence and destruction to the frontiers. More important the forts acted as launching pads to conduct offensive operations. They provided assembly points and supply depots before setting off into enemy territory. At long last the French and Canadians could conduct war elsewhere — they could fight away to protect their home.

Instead of just suffering through a gruelling and demoralizing defensive war with all the human and material destruction while hoping to beat off the Iroquois, Canadians could make war. The offence could now be practised as the most effective form of defence. It was a positive activity and a psychological sign that something more could be done. Moreover, by ensuring the enemy was preoccupied with defending their own territory, they would have little time or resources for a strike at New France. By fighting elsewhere, the Canadians hoped to find some peace and stability for their settlements. Importantly, the initiative no longer rested solely with the enemy.

Theory and practice did not take long to converge. By January 1666, Tracy authorized the first French expedition to attack the Iroquois in their own territory. Here began a tradition ruthlessly practised by the succeeding leaders in New France. The seminal decision was not without risk, as the expedition was launched at the height of the vicious North American winter. However, although the 300 regular troops may not have been inured to the difficulty, they marched with approximately 200 Canadians and a number of friendly Natives who were. In fact, Daniel de Rémy de Courcelle, the governor of New France and leader of the expedition, became deeply impressed by the abilities and fortitude of the Canadians. He quickly realized that they were at home in the woods and capable of the Native method of war.[20] Rémy de Courcelle made great use of them, notably as the vanguard during the approach and as the rearguard during the return to French territory. In subsequent expeditions, as a point of principle, large contingents of Canadians were always included.

Nonetheless, the expedition did not attain the lofty aims intended. It failed to destroy or humble the Iroquois.[21] Its brief and inconclusive encounter with Mohawk warriors occurred on the outskirts of the Dutch-Anglo settlement of Schenectady, the sovereign territory of another European power. In addition, French casualties were heavy because of the severe winter conditions and were exacerbated by the poorly equipped regular troops who lacked adequate clothing, shoes, or supplies, and who were not versed in survival in the bitterly cold North American wilderness.

However, the excursion represented a turning point. It demonstrated that expeditions were possible, even at the worst time of the year, when neither side normally conducted operations. Moreover, elements of the French expedition, namely the Canadians, proved to the French leaders and regulars, as well as to the Iroquois, a mastery of travelling, surviving, and fighting in the trackless forest. Of significance to all, the Iroquois now became the hunted. The expedition had violated the sanctity of their territory. The initiative no longer rested with them. And no doubt spirits among all in New France were given a boost by the fact that war could be carried to the enemy.

The next French foray took place in autumn of the same year. Peace overtures were suspended when a series of Iroquois raids in the spring and summer of 1666 killed a number of French soldiers. Tracy was now intent on another expedition. The inclusion of Canadians necessitated a fall operation since the harvest was of primary importance and no one could be spared until this critical task was completed. This time the force was substantially larger — made up of approximately 600 regulars, an equal number of Canadian volunteers, and about 100 Natives.[22]

It was also more successful. Although the two-month operation failed to bring the Mohawks to decisive battle, the French did march a large force into the heart of Mohawk territory and destroy four villages, their crops, and stored foodstuffs estimated at sufficient quantities "to nourish all Canada for two entire years."[23] The action condemned the Iroquois to a possible slow death by starvation and exposure over the winter, or the humiliating prospect of begging for subsistence from other tribes, or their English allies. Importantly, the objective was achieved — the bold strikes brought their enemies to the negotiating table and allowed for an era of prolonged peace.[24]

To summarize, the expeditions had an significant psychological effect on the Iroquois and the French. Both realized the initiative had irrevocably shifted to the French. Resources, a string of fortifications, discipline, firepower, and a willingness and ability to fight in the wilderness made the French and Canadians a more imposing foe. The expeditions also underlined to the Canadians the importance and effectiveness of offensive action. They also inculcated volunteers with military experience and regulars with wilderness indoctrination. Of greatest consequence, the expeditions highlighted the inherent strength of utilizing the Canadians who were adept at living, travelling, and fighting in the Native fashion in North America. In short, it was the practical and functional aspect that gave the Canadians a martial value and field skills.

Not surprisingly, in April 1669, King Louis XIV ordered Governor Courcelles to organize a Canadian militia and to ensure that the men between 15 and 60 years of age "always be well armed and always have the powder, lead, and fuses necessary to use their arms when needed."[25] With the Iroquois threat quelled, the Carignan-Salières Regiment was redeployed to France in 1668, and the defence of New France was once again largely left in the hands of a few scattered regular and colonial troops, and the French Canadian settlers.

However, this time it was different. First, confidence and experience provided strength. Jacques de Meulles, the intendant of New France in 1683, wrote: "They [Iroquois] have two thousand six hundred good soldiers, and are well seasoned for war. But our youth is hardened and quite used to the woods." He added: "Besides, we make war better than they do."[26] Second, a core of regulars chose to remain in Canada.[27] The benefit was enormous. It provided a nucleus of military experience, which when added to exposure and knowledge of the Native way of war created unrivalled irregular fighters for *la petite guerre.*

This capability was increasingly demonstrated, much to the misery of the English and to some degree their Iroquois allies to the south. Raids against the English in Hudson Bay in 1686, the Seneca in New York in 1687, the Iroquois in 1693 and 1696, and a number of devastating strikes against English settlements such as Casco, Deersfield, Haverhill, Salmon Falls, and Schenectady during a succession of wars from 1688 to 1748 refined the French Canadian practice of *la petite guerre.*[28]

Many French and Canadian leaders, particularly those with extended exposure to the North American manner of war, or those born and raised in Canada, came to believe that the optimum war-fighting strategy was achieved by a mixed force. This force would combine the military strengths of regulars (courage, discipline, and tactical acumen) with those of volunteers and Natives (endurance, marksmanship, and familiarity with wilderness navigation and travel), who relied more on initiative, independent action, and small-unit tactics than on rigid military practices and drills — in simple terms the Native way of war.

The Native way of war was fundamental to the practice of *la petite guerre* in North America.[29] Distinctly and diametrically opposed to the conventions of warfare at the time, it stood in stark contrast to the European emphasis on mass, rigid discipline, and volley fire. Instead it placed great reliance on cunning, furtiveness, the use of cover, and, especially, marksmanship.[30] "So stealthy in their approach, so swift in their execution, and so expeditious in their retreat," noted a Jesuit missionary, "that one commonly learns of their [Indians] departure before being aware of their arrival."[31]

Colonel Henry Bouquet, a recognized expert at the time on light infantry tactics and Native fighting, concluded that Native warriors were "physically active, fierce in manner, skilful in the use of weapons, and capable of great guile and stealth in combat." He considered them formidable opponents. "Indian tactics in battle," Bouquet explained, "could be reduced to three principles: surround the enemy, fight in scattered formation, and always give ground when attacked."[32] Colonel Isaac Barre, another officer who served in colonial North America, felt that the Natives were, as enemies, "the most subtle and the most formidable of any people upon the face of God's earth."[33]

The Native manner of warfare also took full advantage of their innate mobility and their knowledge of the terrain and forests. "The woods," wrote Jesuit missionary Pierre Roubaud, "are the element of the Savages; they run through them with the swiftness of a deer."[34] They used cover well to avoid presenting themselves as obvious targets. The Natives said they gained great advantage because they "always took care in their marches and fights not to come too thick together; but the English always kept in a heap together [so] that it was as easy to hit them, as to hit a house."[35] Similarly, prisoners released from capture reported that Native "young men from their past observations express no very respectable opinion of our manner of fighting them, as, by our close order, we present a large object to their fire, and our platoons do little execution as the Indians are thinly scattered, and concealed behind bushes or trees."[36]

The effectiveness of their method was evident. "In all the time," recounted one lucky survivor of Major-General Edward Braddock's defeated force at the Monongahela River in 1755, "I never saw one nor could I on Enquiry find any one who saw ten [Indians] together." He added "If we saw five or six at one time [it] was a great sight."[37] Another soldier at the same battle reported, "The Indians ... kept an incessant fire on the Guns & killed ye Men very fast. These Indians from their irregular method of fighting by running from one place to another obliges us to wheel from right to left, to desert ye Guns and then hastily to return & cover them."[38] Years later, during a small skirmish, an English captain conceded that "It is estimated that though [the Indians] were but five, they killed about 20, not counting the wounded."[39]

Much of this success derived from the emphasis placed on achieving tactical surprise, mobility, and marksmanship. Some contemporary writers felt that it was the unerring fire of the Natives that made them such a threat.[40] Although initially their proficiency with weapons was superior on the whole to that of the Europeans, soon the colonists, particularly those who engaged in war, became equally adept. As a point of principle, they aimed at single targets, specifically at officers who were easy to identify by their dress and position on the battlefield.[41] Captain Pierre Pouchot, a member of the French Béarn Regiment that fought with

Soldier, Compagnies Franches de la Marine by Michel Pétard copyright © Parks Canada

A colonial soldier, circa 1745.

distinction in North America, wrote in his memoirs that the Natives were excellent marksmen who "very rarely fail to shoot their man down."[42]

But it was not just fieldcraft or marksmanship that set the Natives apart from the Europeans. There was a cultural and philosophical component that was not always understood. For the Native warriors, "taking up the hatchet" or going to war, was largely a personal endeavour meant to prove a warrior's courage and skill and offer opportunities for prestige through achievement in combat. The individual warrior was subordinate to no other. Natives saw neither shame nor dishonour in abandoning the field if the odds of easy success were against them.[43] Moreover, if individuals tired of the campaign or simply failed to support a plan of action, their departure was seldom condemned by their peers.[44] They were not interested in a fair fight, but only one in which they could achieve their aims with a minimum of casualties. Ambush, raids, and terror were the preferred methods of conducting war. In short, the Natives practised what some contemptibly called the "skulking way of war."[45]

But the Natives, as well as the Canadians, did not see it as that. "The art of war," declared Tecaughretanego, a Kahnawake chief, "consists in ambushing and surprising our enemies, and in preventing them from ambushing and surprising us."[46] Similarly, Jesuit missionary Father Nau observed, "Their mode of warfare is but stratagem and surprise."[47] Abbé H.R. Casgrain, the prominent nineteenth-century French Canadian chronicler of the Seven Years' War, explained that "For them, withdrawal was not a flight, nor a disgrace, it was a means of falling back to occupy a better position."[48]

The Canadians ably practised the Native way of war and adopted many of the cultural and philosophical aspects, as well. In fact, during the contest for North America between the French and the English, the practice of the Native way of war, or *la petite guerre*, was associated as much with the Canadians as it was with the Natives. The English often referred to their opponents as "our cruel and crafty enemy the French."[49] One participant conceded in his diary that "I can't but take notice of ye cruel nature of our Indians, I look on'm not a whitt better than ye Canadians."[50] One American summed up the sentiment of many when he wrote: "Canadians delight in blood; and in barbarity exceeding if possible, the very savages themselves."[51]

However, the skill and effectiveness of the Canadians was also recognized. Major-General James Wolfe felt that "Every man in Canada is a soldier."[52] Other contemporary English accounts echoed with the lament that the Canadian woodsmen and *coureur de bois* "are well known to be the most dangerous enemy of any ... reckoned equal, if not superior in that part of the world to veteran troops."[53] Even the French regulars, who despised the Canadians and Natives, had to concede that they contributed distinct skills and capabilities to campaigns. "God knows," wrote Colonel Louis-Antoine de Bougainville, "we do not wish to disparage the value of the Canadians.... In the woods, behind trees, no troops are comparable to the natives of this country."[54] Casgrain described them as "the elite Canadians and Indians," who "glide from tree to tree, stump to stump," from which they maintain an accurate and incessant fire.[55] The official journals kept by Major-General Louis-Joseph de Montcalm's army also revealed, "The Canadians ... certainly surpass all the troops in the universe, owing to their skill as marksman."[56]

But the Canadian's distinct North American manner of fighting should not be surprising. It was born from harsh reality and bitter experience. Furthermore, it suited their circumstances, their resources, their alliances, and their temperament. Moreover, the Canadian strategy and method of warfare continually proved both efficient and effective. It bestowed on New France greater influence and power than its actual military strength would warrant. This tendency was demonstrated again on July 9, 1755. Faced by the imminent attack of a much larger English force, the commander of Fort Duquesne in the Ohio Valley decided to practice the methodology of *la petite guerre* in an effort to pre-empt the strike against him. With 36 officers and cadets, 72 colonial regulars, 146 Canadian militia, and 637 Natives, Captain de Beaujeu, a colonial officer of the Troupes de la Marine, engaged approximately 1,200 British regulars and 800 provincials.[57] Although Beaujeu was killed in the opening moments of the battle, his force inflicted a crushing defeat on the English that seemed to exemplify the effectiveness of the Canadian way of war.

It also proved to be a fatal lesson on warfare in North America for Major-General Edward Braddock. His 45 years of service had predictably endowed him with a deep-rooted comprehension of warfare that was reinforced by his own experience. He accepted as truth that the more disciplined and well-drilled force would normally emerge victorious. In fact, Benjamin Franklin, writing 15 years after the event recorded that Braddock dismissed the threat posed by irregular troops or Natives. "These savages may, indeed, be a formidable enemy to your raw American militia," declared Braddock, "but upon the King's regulars, it is impossible they should make any impression."[58]

He was sadly mistaken. Lieutenant William Dunbar recounted the harrowing slaughter of Braddock's forces. "We had not marched above 800 yards from the River," he wrote: "when we were allarmed by the Indian Hollow [battle cry], & in an instant, found ourselves attacked on all sides, their methods, they immediately seize a Tree, & are certain of their Aim, so that before the Genl [General] came to our assistance, most of our advanced Party were laid sprawling on the ground." Dunbar revealed:

> Our Men unaccustomed to that way of fighting, were quite confounded, & behaved like Poltrons, nor could the examples, nor the Intreaties of their officers prevail with them, to do any one what was ordered. This they denied them, when we begged of them not to throw away their fire, but to follow us with fixed Bayonets, to drive them from the hill & trees, they never minded us, but threw their fire away in the most confused manner, some in the air, others in the ground, & a great many destroyed their own Men & officers. When the General came up to our assistance, men were seized with the same Pannic, & went into as much disorder, some Part of them being 20 deep. The officers in order to remedy this, advanced into the front, & soon became the mark of the Enemy, who scarce left one that was not killed or wounded.[59]

Another British officer conceded, "By the particular disposition of the French and Indians it was impossible to judge of the numbers they had in the field that day."[60] Conversely, the French forces had excellent fields of observation and fire. From their covered positions they stealthily advanced very close, and observed that the British ranks reloaded to ordered drumbeats and commands. Therefore, they carefully sniped the officers and drummers creating even greater confusion and panic. Then they continued to pour an unrelenting fire that mercilessly cut swaths into the British ranks.

Braddock's failure, or inability, to adjust his European mode of combat resulted in the destruction of his army. In the end, Braddock's courage and steadfast belief that inevitably the undisciplined, motley opponents that faced his troops would break, combined with the training and discipline of his regulars to stand their ground regardless of the chaos that engulfed them, led to their ruin. Once ambushed, the closely packed troops were impossible to miss and they suffered horrendous casualties. Ironically, the provincials, particularly the Virginians, immediately sought cover and began to return fire against their phantom antagonists. Their actions provided some hope of staving off defeat. However, Braddock, incensed at this lack of courage and discipline, ordered them back into line using both oaths and the flat of his sabre.[61] But it was for naught. The contrast in dialectic between the European and Native ways of war was never sharper. Tom Faucett, a bitter veteran who served with the Provincials, scathingly reminisced: "We was cowards, was we, because we knowed better than to fight Injuns like you red-backed ijits across the ocean is used to fight: because we wouldn't stand up rubbin' shoulders like a passel o' sheep and let the red-skins made sieves outen us!"[62]

And so, despite the exhortations of the officers and the discipline of the regulars, as the ranks were continually thinned by a steady and deadly fire, from an antagonist that could not be seen, the regulars lost their steadiness and eventually succumbed to an uncontrollable panic. "And when we endeavored to rally them," recounted George Washington, then a young officer assigned to Braddock's staff, "it was with as much success as if we had attempted to stop the wild bears of the mountains."[63] The cost of the debacle was enormous. The French lost approximately 5 percent of their engaged force. The British lost 70 percent of theirs, including 60 out of 86 officers.[64]

Although the British regulars were slow to appreciate the wilderness tactics, the victory over Braddock, in the eyes of the French and Canadians, seemed to underscore the superiority of their manner of combat. They also had a pragmatic reason to support it — they were economically and numerically inferior to the British in regular military forces, civilian population, and material wealth and resources. This stunning victory by such a small irregular force against a much larger regular army, at a great distance from home, and at such low cost, validated the practice of *la petite guerre*.

Not surprisingly, this latest success reinforced the belief held by the governor of New France, Canadian-born Pierre de Rigaud de Vaudreuil, in the Canadian way of war. He continued the traditional policy — a series of fortifications on the frontiers of the colony to control access to waterways leading into New France. As already mentioned, these strategically positioned forts were symbols of power, as well as economic centres. More important, they were imposing barriers that provided a buffer between hostile territory and the French settlements. Their strategic locations allowed a relatively small force to be capable of delaying, or stopping altogether, a much larger and stronger antagonist. In addition, these wilderness sentinels forced would-be invaders to lengthen their lines of communication and supply, and thus expose themselves to constant attack by irregulars.

They were also key to Vaudreuil's strategy of pre-emption and terror, by acting as springboards for offensive action.[65] Although many French

Library and Archives Canada C-3708

officers felt that Vaudreuil and the rest of the Canadians believed that the English would not dare, or at least were incapable of, conducting operations against New France, they failed to realize that the governor did not base his perception on hope. He clearly understood a hard-earned lesson rooted in generations of struggle, which said an opponent who is focused on defending his home, is less apt and less able to conduct mischief elsewhere.[66] Vaudreuil knew that he could mobilize a series of devastating raids faster than the English could organize an invasion.

Pierre de Rigaud, the marquis de Vaudreuil and governor of New France, relied heavily on the Canadian way of war to maintain the security of New France despite its demographic, economic, and military inferiority vis-à-vis the British colonies.

As such, the fortifications located at strategic points on the fringes of French territory were key.[67] They were important economic, political, and social centres that cemented Native alliances. Equally significant, they acted as staging posts for offensive strikes deep into the territory of their enemies. The forts allowed for forward defence, namely, a fight-away policy. From these bastions, raiding parties could be sent to devastate the New England frontier and strike terror in the hearts and minds of their antagonists. "It was from [Fort St. Frederic]," wrote Major-General William Shirley, a former commander-in-chief of British forces in North America, "that all those parties which during the late war ravaged and laid waste to many towns and settlements upon the Frontiers of New York and the Massachusetts Bay were fitted out; and so great was the influence which the French had over the Five Nations of Indians by means of this fort, so great were their apprehensions of the mischief, which it was in the power of the French to do them, that it was not till late in the war and not even without great difficulty and still greater expense that they were prevailed upon to take up the Hatchet."[68]

Major-General Jeffery Amherst concurred with the assessment of the importance of the French fortifications. Upon hearing of the capture of Fort Niagara, he wrote: "His Majesty's subjects on the Mohawk River will be thereby as effectually freed from all inroads and scalping parties of the enemy as I may say the whole country ... is by the reduction of [Fort] Ticonderoga."[69]

But in keeping with the theory of *la petite guerre*, the savage tactical manner of warfare that the Canadians and Natives practised against their enemies from these strategic positions was not intended to seize strategic points or terrain. The objective was not to capture territory or destroy the enemy's army. Rather, it was to terrorize the enemy population into seeking peace as the only alternative, as well as to disrupt and pre-empt the abilities of the English to invade or strike at New France. It was a cost-effective strategy to maintain the balance of power in North America and protect the French settlements from the ravages of war. It was a strategy derived from relative position of weakness.

However, the weakness was mitigated by the clever, ruthless manner of fighting. As such, raids were central to the Canadian way of war. "Nothing," wrote Vaudreuil, "is more calculated to discourage the people of these [English] colonies and make them wish for the return to peace."[70] The Canadians and Natives earned a reputation for barbarity and savageness. The English targeted Vaudreuil himself as the architect of their wanton violence.[71] Regardless, his strategy was effective. The deep strikes into English territory during the Seven Years' War consistently disrupted British campaign plans and kept them on the defensive from the summer of 1755 until 1758. Moreover, it ravaged frontier settlements, economies, and public morale.

"We are under the utmost fear and consternation," complained one English colonist, "upon accounts of the Indians having again began their murders and massacres in the province of Pennsylvania, upon the River Delaware adjoining to this province.... These fresh depredations have so terrified us that we dare not go out to our daily labour, for fear of being surprized [*sic*] and murdered by the Indians."[72] Similarly, an English officer angrily decried, "nothing is to be seen but desolation and murder, heightened with every barbarous circumstance, and new instances of cruelty — They, at the instigation of the French with them, burn up the plantations, the smoke of which darkens the day and hides the mountains from our sight."[73] These laments were widespread.

Although it was distasteful, the strategy was carried out year-round and was both inexpensive and extremely successful. It was clearly an economy of effort. Small parties of Canadians and Natives, who disliked the European manner of war, could in their own way make an effective contribution to the war effort.[74] The raids terrorized the frontier and tied down large numbers of troops for rear security. The political leaders of the English colonists could not ignore their plight. The incursions into Virginia alone caused the governor there to raise 10 militia companies, or 1,000 men, for internal defence. Similarly, Pennsylvania raised 1,500 provincial troops and built a string of forts extending from New Jersey to Maryland in an attempt to try to impede the raiders.[75]

Moreover, the English militiamen were reluctant to undertake campaigns when they felt their families were at risk. Furthermore, the destruction of settlements, farms, and livestock, as well as the murder or capture of settlers, ate away at the economy of the English colonies. Crops could not be sown or harvested. Grains could not be stored for the winter, or used to feed the army on campaign. This harassment created privations for both soldier and citizen alike. The impact on the frontier was simply devastating.[76]

Although an effective strategy for the outnumbered French, the attacks were only successful as a delaying action. It did not bring the English to the peace table as Vaudreuil had hoped.

Nonetheless, of great importance, raiding was effective and relatively cheap. It required limited resources. Small parties of tactically competent warriors, led by French or Canadian officers and consisting of Natives and militia skilled in the Native way of war, could wreak havoc far more than their size and tie up considerably larger enemy forces committed to protecting settlements from enemy incursions. But much like the early Canadian experience, to surrender the initiative and remain on the defensive is inefficient and condemns a people to suffer war. For it is near impossible to protect everyone, everywhere, all the time. "What can one do against invisible enemies who strike and flee with the rapidity of light?" questioned Bougainville rhetorically. "It is," he asserted, "the destroying angel."[77] Critical for the Canadians, they could choose when and where to strike, thus tying down large enemy forces while ensuring that adequate numbers of workers were available for the vital fall harvesting period.[78]

Equally important to Vaudreuil's or the entire Canadian strategy were strong alliances with the various Native tribes. This realization permeated the Canadian philosophy from the beginning. Social and economic ties with the Natives were key to the survival and growth of New France.[79] As early as 1667, the secretary of state for the colonies, Jean-Baptiste Colbert, instructed the Intendant of New France: "You must try to draw these [Native] peoples, and especially those who have embraced Christianity, into the neighbourhood of our settlements and, if possible, intermingle them there so that, with the passage of time, having but one law and the same master [the king] they will form thereby a single people of the same blood."[80] This attitude, bolstered by the large number of *coureur de bois* and soldiers serving at frontier outposts, and intermingling or living with the Natives, fostered acceptance and tolerance towards the Natives and their culture that did not exist between the English and the Amerindians.

However, the issue of racial tolerance is not the point. Quite simply, a reliance on alliances was a cornerstone of New France's long-term policy and survival. Its small population base put it at a distinct disadvantage. With only 60,000 people, New France faced the danger of being engulfed by its larger neighbour to the south, namely the English colonies with approximately 1.5 million inhabitants.[81] As such, the Native alliance represented an effective means of adding personnel to their military. Furthermore, Natives were proficient practitioners of *la petite guerre* — expert bush fighters who were at home in the wilderness and knew its myriad of trails and waterways.

For the French and Canadians, the Natives became a vital source of strength. In 1710 mission Natives alone could provide the French with 600 skilled warriors.[82] Forty years later the number of warriors in tribes north of the Ohio River friendly to the French was approximately 16,000.[83] This pool of warriors provided Vaudreuil, who fully appreciated how terrified the Natives made the English, with a powerful weapon to keep them off balance and on the defensive. When conflict loomed, Vaudreuil never failed to unleash raiding parties, which were always readily available because of the historical alliances, the provision of presents and supplies, and the promise of plunder.[84]

Remarkably, through this strategy and methodology of warfare, the French and Canadians were able to maintain a balance of power and influence greater than their military or economic power should have warranted.[85] However, their distinct approach to war differed dramatically from the accepted European model. The influx of a relatively large number of French regular soldiers following the commencement of the Seven Years' War, and the eventual arrival of Major-General Montcalm in 1756 as the field commander of French forces in North America, exacerbated the clash in cultures.[86]

Although Montcalm was subordinate to Governor Vaudreuil, his contempt for the governor, the Canadians, the Natives, and the Canadian way of war was pronounced and was shared by his French officers. Montcalm, known as a vain, opinionated, and stubborn officer with a quick temper, believed that the Canadians were an undisciplined rabble of little to no military value who had an inflated opinion of themselves. "The Canadians thought they were making war," he quipped, "when they went on raids resembling hunting parties."[87] Bougainville's disdain for the Canadian approach is also clearly discernable in his journal: "to leave Montreal with a party, to go through the woods, to take a few scalps, to return at full speed once the blow was struck, that is what they called war."[88]

Montcalm and his officers neither hid their prejudices, nor concealed their criticisms of Vaudreuil's strategy and method of war fighting. Quite simply, the Canadian way of war was anathema to them. Montcalm's predisposition to the European model of warfare caused him to often complain of the "petty means" and "petty ideas." He contemptuously discounted the value of taking "a few scalps and burning a few houses." Montcalm quickly discerned that the Canadian method of warfare could not inflict a lasting defeat on the English. He was convinced that against British regulars the only hope lay in a static defence. The French general believed that the dispersion of scarce personnel among the western outposts was perilous. As such, Montcalm was adamant that the only hope of saving New France was to concentrate as much force as possible at the critical point — Quebec.[89]

The divergence of ideas could not have been greater. The differing views on strategy were exacerbated by the petty jealousy over authority and the desire for recognition and reward. Perhaps a touch of national jealousy and disdain was involved, as well — Vaudreuil was Canadian-born, Montcalm was French.

By virtue of his position Vaudreuil was the senior appointment. As such, he maintained his strategy of extended defensive lines, and was intent on "contesting the ground on our frontiers inch by inch with the enemy."[90] Vaudreuil relied on the ingrained lesson that offence was the only practical defence for New France. "The Marquis de Montcalm," wrote an exasperated Vaudreuil in September 1758, "is not ignorant that superiority of numbers being on their side, I dare not promise myself any success unless I can surprise them by an attack in the inclement season."[91]

Louis-Joseph Marquis de Montcalm despised the Canadian militia and colonial troops and sought to fight a defensive war based on interior lines rather than Governor Vaudreuil's strategy of forward defence.

Vaudreuil's approach was logical. It had also proven to be successful in the past. Furthermore, the traditional policy allowed him to use to the best advantage the varied troops at his disposal. For, as he claimed, the Canadians and colonial troops of La Marine "knew how to make bloody war on the British, while Montcalm's French Regulars fought in too gentle a manner."[92] In addition, in what would become a recurring theme in Canadian history, Vaudreuil also informed Paris that the Canadians and the savages did not operate with the same confidence under the command of officers of the French regular army as they did under the control of their own Canadian officers.[93]

Significantly, the struggle between the two rival leaders and their divergent philosophies, if not cultures, took a fateful turn. Montcalm's stunning victory at Fort Ticonderoga in July 1758 became a catalyst for dramatic change. Outnumbered almost four to one, with only 3,600 troops, primarily French regulars, Montcalm routed Major-General James Abercromby's army of 6,000 regulars and 9,000 provincials, the largest force ever assembled in North America to date.[94] "This brilliant victory," wrote a jubilant Brigadier-General François-Gaston Chevalier de Lévis, "saved Canada."[95] Once again, any English hope of launching an invasion against New France was thwarted in the distant backwaters of the wilderness.

However, Montcalm used his latest victory, achieved without the assistance of Canadians or Natives, to make his point that a concentration of force in the heart of the colony was the best strategy to defeat the British. His representations to Paris carried by letter and an envoy (Bougainville) in the autumn of 1758 bore fruit. The French government was in disarray and already skeptical of the regime in New France.[96] Not surprisingly, particularly after such a convincing victory at Ticonderoga, Montcalm was promoted to lieutenant-general, a grade that outranked that of a colonial governor. As a result, Montcalm was given the command of all military forces in Canada. More important, Montcalm's strategy was accepted — the ministers of war and the marine hoped for an encore performance of Ticonderoga, but this time at the gates of Quebec.[97]

So as the British resumed their offensive in 1759, the French frontier forts pulled back when they came under pressure, and Montcalm achieved his desire: he concentrated his forces in Quebec. To alleviate his shortage of personnel he drafted colonial troops and the fittest of the Canadian militia into his line battalions.[98] As far as Montcalm was concerned, war would now be fought as he knew it in Europe.

In the early-morning hours of September 13, 1759, he was given his wish. Wolfe had managed a surprise landing at Anse au Foulon and mere hours later had approximately 4,500 troops on the Plains of Abraham. Montcalm rashly rushed those troops immediately available to him out onto the plain, fearing incorrectly that any delay would only serve to strengthen the British. The French deployed towards the British lines, and once within range, began to fire volleys. However, the deployment became ragged as Canadians, recently drafted into the ranks of the regulars, with little training and a stronger inbred experience with their own way of war, threw themselves to the ground to reload. Others bolted for the cover of trees to join other Canadians who had been kept as irregulars to snipe from the flanks. The Canadians used to swell the ranks of the regulars, complained Captain Pouchot, are "only suited to petite-guerre ... [and they] were a hindrance to the operation." He explained that lacking experience with "European tactics," notably the British volley, "the Canadians, who had little experience of being under fire without cover" lost their nerve and "broke ranks & fled."[99]

Needless to say, these actions caused disarray and confusion in the French ranks.[100] And if the deadly British volley had not been enough, the subsequent battle cry and sight of British regulars with gleaming bayonets and kilted Scotsmen with claymores turned the confusion into utter panic, and the French streamed from the battlefield hotly pursued by the British.

Ironically, it was the very troops — the Canadians, who were chastised for their "cowardice" and failure to maintain formation during the initial confrontation — who now saved the French regulars from complete annihilation. Fighting as they had always practised from behind cover as irregular fighters the Canadians saw their courage and marksmanship come to the fore. Their galling fire necessitated that the British redirect their focus to clear them out of the woods. This relieved pressure and allowed the escape of Montcalm's regulars, though at great cost in Canadian blood.[101]

Despite the Canadian efforts, the battle, if not the contest in North America, had already been determined. By the following spring, the remaining French forces in North America were defeated and control of Canada fell to the British. Would a continuation of Vaudreuil's strategy of *la petite guerre* have made a difference? Quite simply, no. Although his strategy was effective for generations and helped maintain the balance of power in North America by 1758 circumstances had changed and total defeat was only a matter of time.

The British, under the stewardship of William Pitt, the secretary of state, decided to make the contest in North America their primary focus. As a result, in contrast to the French, they now made the necessary resources available.[102] The Royal Navy controlled the seas, as well as the St. Lawrence River, and the British regular army was assembled in numbers hitherto unheard of in North America.[103] No amount of raids or pre-emptive strikes could hold off the avalanche of force that was arrayed against Canada on so many fronts.

But the outcome of the contest did not detract from the Canadian experience that was etched through generations of conflict and toil. Major-General Abercromby later wrote: "The Canadians are a hardy race of people and have been accustomed to arms from their infancy ... those people are certainly the properest kind of troops to be employed in an Indian War."[104]

Ironically, although now under a different king, many of the problems that faced New France remained. Arguably, not much had changed. Canada was still a distant subordinate colony, a small player in a much

This painting, Council with the Allies *by Robert Griffing, depicts a meeting between Montcalm and his Native allies near Carillon on the shore of Lake Champlain.*

larger empire, bordered by a neighbour to the south who would soon be hostile again. Not surprisingly, the Canadian way of war would once again become relevant and continue to burn itself into the psyche of Canadians.

Quite simply, Canadians became a product of their experience and circumstances. They were but one small and junior component of a larger empire. As such, they could expect only limited assistance. Resources, particularly soldiers and defence spending, were always at a premium. Debate over responsibility for defence — British regulars or Canadian militia — was always a sore point. Militarily, Canada was always in a position of relative weakness. As a result, military operations had to be limited. In essence, they were largely tactical, most often attempting to capitalize on economy of effort and alliances to achieve an influence greater than Canada's military, economic, or political strength would normally allow. In many ways, *la petite guerre* allowed the Canadians for decades to gain a strategic end by a tactical means. These principles that served New France so well would continue to resonate throughout the Canadian military experience.

NOTES

1. For example, in 1758, Colonel Louis-Antoine de Bougainville was dispatched to Versailles by Pierre de Rigaud de Vaudreuil, the governor of New France, and Major-General Louis Joseph de Montcalm, the French field force commander in Canada, to plead the case for a large number of reinforcements. However, the minister of marine, reflecting the dire strategic situation of France at the time, bluntly told him "When the house is on fire, you don't worry about the stables." Edward P. Hamilton, ed., *Adventures in the Wilderness: The American Journals of Louis-Antoine de Bougainville, 1756–1760* (Norman, OK: University of Oklahoma Press, 1990), 322–323.

2. The literal translation is small war. European understanding of "petite guerre" is "carried on by a light party, commanded by an expert partisan ... separated from the army, to secure the camp or a march; to reconnoiter the enemy or the country; to seize their posts, convoys and escorts; to plant ambuscades, and to put in practice every stratagem for surprising or disturbing the enemy." M. Pouchot, *Memoirs on the Late War in North America Between France and England* (originally Yverdon, 1781; reprint Youngstown, NY: Old Fort Niagara Association, Inc., 1994), 242. See also Hew Strachan, *European Armies and the Conduct of War* (New York: Routledge, 1983), 30–37; and Ian McCulloch, "Within Ourselves ... The Development of British Light Infantry in North America During the Seven Years' War," *Canadian Military History*, Vol. 7, No. 2, (Spring 1998), 44–45.

3. The allure of the wilderness and the freedom it ingrained in the inhabitants remained a constant irritant to French administrators and regular officers. The Canadian traits criticized the most by French administrators were idleness, indiscipline, and insubordination. Peter N. Moogk, *La Nouvelle France: The Making of French Canada — A Cultural History* (East Lansing: University of Michigan Press, 2000), 144. Colonel Louis-Antoine de Bougainville, an aide to Montcalm stated, "In all ways they are, most of them, more undisciplined, more lazy than the Indians." He added, "Canadians, breathing an air permeated with independence, work indolently." Hamilton, ed., *Adventures in the Wilderness*, 51, 195, 259.

4. Bruce G. Trigger, "The French Presence in Huronia: The Structure of Franco-Huron Relations in the First Half of the Seventh Century," *Canadian Historical Review*, Vol. 49, No. 2, June 1968, 118. The Iroquois confederacy (Five Nations) consisted of the Cayuga, Oneida, Onondaga, Mohawk and Seneca tribes. The Tuscarora joined the confederacy in the first quarter of the eighteenth century. The Huron viewed the Iroquois as "devil men, who needed nothing, and were hard to kill." George T. Hunt, *The Wars of the Iroquois: A Study of Intertribal Trade Relations* (Milwaukee: University of Wisconsin Press, 1967), 93. See also William R. Nester, *The Great Frontier War: Britain, France, and the Imperial Struggle for North America, 1607–1755* (Westport, CT: Praeger, 2000), 96; Robert A. Goldstein, *French-Iroquois Diplomatic and Military Relations, 1609–1701* (Paris: Mouton, 1969), 29–47.

5. W.J. Eccles, *The French in North America 1500–1783* (Markham, ON: Fitzheny & Whiteside, 1998), 21–23; and Marcel Trudel, "Samuel de Champlain," in George Brown, ed., *Dictionary of Canadian Biography, Vol. 1* (Toronto: University of Toronto Press, 1966), 186–199. See also W.J. Eccles, *France in America* (Markham, ON: Fitzhenry & Whiteside, 1990), 103; and Goldstein, 48–54.

6. Statement by Jean Talon in 1667, Quoted in Hunt, 135. Jesuit missionary Jean de Lamberville wrote in 1682, that the Iroquois "are ready to fall upon Canada on the

first occasion that shall be given to them." Reuben Gold Thwaites, ed., *The Jesuit Relations and Allied Documents: Travels and Explorations of the Jesuit Missionaries in New France, 1610–1791*, Vol. 62 (New York: Pageant Book Company, 1959), 14.

7. *The Conquest of Canada, Vol. 2* (New York: Harper & Brothers, 1850), 93.

8. Hunt, 92; Trudel, 31; René Chartrand, *Canadian Military Heritage, Vol. 1, 1000–1754* (Montreal: Art Global, 1993), 55–56.

9. Letter, Vaudreuil et Raudot au Ministre, November 14, 1708, quoted in W.J. Eccles, *The French in North America*, 41. There were major similarities in torture between most Indian tribes — running the gauntlet, slow burning, application of a necklace of hot tomahawks, piercing of flesh, slicing pieces of flesh for consumption/cannibalism, feeding captive his own fingers and ears, mutilation, sticking burning torches into flesh, scalping prisoners before death, pouring live coals and hot sand onto scalped head, dissection of body after death, fastening to a stake, and torture of both sexes and all ages. See Raymond Scheele, "Warfare of the Iroquois and their Northern Neighbours," unpublished PhD (Political Science) Thesis, Columbia University, 1950, 100–101; Charles Hamilton, ed., *Braddock's Defeat: The Journal of Captain Robert Cholmley's Batman; The Journal of a British Officer; Halkett's Orderly Book* (Norman, OK: University of Oklahoma Press, 1959), 30; Frederick Drimmer, ed., *Captured by the Indians: 15 Firsthand Accounts 1750–1870* (New York: Dover Publications Ltd., 1961), 9–104; Andrew Gallup, ed., *Memoir of a French and Indian War Soldier [Jolicoeur Charles Bonin]* (Bowie, MD: Heritage Books, 1993), 115–17; Letter, Father Pierre Roubaud, Missionary, October 21, 1757, in Thwaites, Vol. 60, 123–128; Letter from Father le Petit, Missionary, July 12, 1730, Thwaites, Vol. 68, 167 and 169; Letter, Father Jean de Lamberville, in Thwaites, Vol. 62, 71–77; Captain John Knox, *An Historical Journal of the Campaigns in North-America for the Years 1757, 1758, 1759, and 1760*. Vol. 1 (London: 1769), 232; and William M. Osborn, *The Wild Frontier* (New York: Random House, 2000), 37.

10. W.J. Eccles, *Canada Under Louis XIV* (Toronto: McClelland & Stewart, 1964), 46. From 1633 until the end of the century the Canadians realized less than 15 years of peace. Between 1608 and 1666, 191 settlers were killed by the Iroquois out of a population that numbered 675 in 1650 and 3,035 in 1663. Eccles, *The French in North America*, 40–41.

11. Drafts normally numbered from 50 to 200 at a time for short durations.

12. Quoted documents, display, Fort Chambly National Historic Site of Canada, Chambly, Quebec. Accessed August 23, 2001.

13. *Ibid.*

14. See Pierre Boucher, *Histoire veritable et naturelle des moeurs et productions de la Nouvelle-France vulgairement dite le Canada* (Paris: Florentin Lambert, 1664), National Library of Canada, Rare Books Collection. See also Michel Wyczynski, "New Horizons — New Challenges: The Carignan-Salières Regiment in New France, 1665–1667," in B. Horn, ed., *Forging a Nation: Perspectives on the Canadian Military Experience* (St. Catharines, ON: Vanwell, 2002), 18–19.

15. Wyczynski reveals that "The information provided by Boucher and by others was regrettably never passed along to the French administrators overseeing the outfitting phase of the Carignan-Salières Regiment. Many factors contributed to this lack of foresight: Winter warfare was not part of the French army's doctrine; the cost factor to provide winter clothing and required equipment was prohibitive; both the French and New France administrators were operating with limited budgets; and since the King had agreed to send a regiment, it was expected that the colony provide supplies and equipment during the troops operations in the colony." *Ibid.*

16. Matthew Dennis, *Cultivating a Landscape of Peace: Iroquois-European Encounters in Seventeenth-Century America* (New York: Cornell University Press, 1993), 212.

17. See Jack Verney, *The Good Regiment: The Carignan-Salières Regiment in Canada, 1665–1668* (Montreal: McGill-Queen's University Press, 1991), 3–17; Wyczynski, 21; and Goldstein, 90–91. The colony's newly appointed governor, Daniel Rémy de Courcelle and the Intendant Jean Talon both sailed with the Carignan-Salières Regiment to New France. Chartrand, *Canadian Military Heritage, Vol. 1*, 54.

18. This was not the first fort to be built on the Richelieu River. In 1642, Governor Montmagny, with a recently arrived contingent of 40 soldiers built a fort at the mouth of the Richelieu River in the present day city of Sorel. See Chartrand, *Canadian Military Heritage, Vol. 1*, 54.

19. "Look about you and see!" exclaimed a Native chief, "You have no fortifications; no, not even in Quider (Albany). It is but a step from Canada hither, and the French may come and turn you out of doors ... Look at the French; they are men! They are fortifying everywhere. But you are all like women, bare and open, without fortifications!" Extract from response by Six Nations to a speech by the lieutenant-general of New York, at Albany, July 2, 1755, in Armand Francis Lucier, ed., *French and Indian War Notices Abstracted from Colonial Newspapers, Vol. 1: 1754–1755* (Bowie, MD: Heritage Books, 1999), 272; and Pichon's "Memoires du Cap Breton, 1760," quoted in Gerald E. Hart, *The Fall of New France, 1755–1760* (New York: G.P. Putnam's Sons, 1888), 10.

20. See Verney, 42–43; Chartrand, *Canadian Military History, Vol. 1*, 68; and Goldstein, 93–95.

21. They failed to locate any Mohawk villages and only destroyed a few outlying cabins. Furthermore, they only killed four warriors and wounded six others at the cost of approximately 400 of their own. An approximate casualty count is given as 400 by Verney. Most of these are attributed to hypothermia and starvation. Only seven French were killed and four wounded in the skirmish with the Mohawks. Verney, 50, 52; Goldstein, 98–99.

22. Thwaites, Vol. 50, 140; Verney, 43, 72; and Dennis, 217. This reality demonstrates one characteristic of *la petite guerre*, namely the citizen/soldier makeup is closely wedded to the land and to civilian needs. It is both a great strength and weakness. But it also shows the very "practical" and "functional" characteristic inherent in how these people think.

23. Thwaites, Vol. 50, 143; Dennis, 217; and Verney, 79. For a detailed account of the expedition see Verney, 71–84 and Wyczynski, 33–36.

24. *Conquest of Canada, Vol. 2*, 290; Hunt, 135; and Verney, 90; and Edward P. Hamilton, *Fort Ticonderoga: Key to a Continent* (Ticonderoga, NY: Fort Ticonderoga,1995), 33.

25. Eccles, *France in America*, 73; and Chartrand, *Canadian Military Heritage, Vol. 1*, 74. All men between the ages of 16 and 60 who were fit to bear arms were compelled to join the Militia. Companies were based on the same framework as a regular company — each was commanded by a captain, assisted by a lieutenant and an ensign, as well as a number of non-commissioned officers (corporals and sergeants) and a body of soldiers. The companies were approximately 50 men strong. Each parish provided a company, or more depending on its size.

26. Letter, De Meulles to Seignelay, 1683, in Richard A. Preston and Leopold Lamontagne, *Royal Fort Frontenac* (Toronto: University of Toronto Press, 1958), 147; and Eccles, *France in America*, 95.

27. Of the 1,200 members of the Carignan-Salières Regiment that landed in 1665, 446 settled in Canada and 200 returned to France. Wyczynski, 37. Intendant Jean Talon

stated: "integrate the soldiers and the settlers so that they can teach each other how to farm and help defend themselves in times of need. Letter, Talon au ministre, Québec, October 27, 1667, LAC, MG 1, Series C11A, Vol. 2, folio 308, microfilm F–2.

28. Notably: King William's War (War of the Grand Alliance), 1688–1697; Queen Anne's War (War of the Austrian Succession), 1740–1748; and King George's War (War of the Austrian Succession), 1740–1748. See Robert Leckie, *A Few Acres of Snow* (New York: John Wiley & Sons, 1999) and Ian K. Steele, *Guerillas and Grenadiers* (Toronto: Ryerson Press, 1969); and Goldstein, 148–154. For example, on January 25, 1693, 100 Troupes de la Marine, 200 Natives, and 325 Canadians left Montreal to strike at the Mohawk. They torched three villages, destroyed their winter food supply and took 300 prisoners. W.J. Eccles, "Frontenac's Military Policies, 1689–1698 A Reassessment," *Canadian Historical Review*, Vol. 37, No. 3, September 1956, 208. The infamous attack on Deerfield, Massachusetts, on March 16, 1704, by 200 Indians and 50 Canadians destroyed the town, killed 47 inhabitants, and resulted in 111 others being carried away as captives. Dale Miquelon, *New France, 1701–1744* (Toronto: McClelland & Stewart, 1989), 40.

29. The use of Natives, however, had its drawbacks. Tribalism, the influence of sachems, superstition, personal and band rivalry, the practice of torture and barbarity, and the cultural difference in the methodology in conducting war all created tension between the Europeans and their Native allies. Bougainville confided to his journals, "They gather together in mobs, argue among themselves, deliberate slowly ... Between the resolution made and the action taken there passes considerable time, sometimes one nation stops the march, sometimes another. Everybody must have time to get drunk, and their food consumption is enormous. At last they get started, and once they have struck, have they taken only a single scalp or one prisoner, back they come and are off again for their villages. Each one does well for himself, but the operation of the war suffers, for in the end they are a necessary evil." Hamilton, *Adventure in the Wilderness*, 59–60.

30. This is not surprising, because traditionally these attributes were required to be successful on the hunt. To ensure game was killed required exceptional fieldcraft skills. The more clever and stealthy the hunter, the greater were his chances of success. Firearms merely provided a more efficient and lethal weapons technology with which to kill. Clearly, all these skills were transferable to war making.

31. K.L. Macpherson, *Scenic Sieges and Battlefields of French Canada* (Montreal: Valentine & Sons Publishing Company, 1957), 4.

32. Charles E. Brodine, "Henry Bouquet and British Infantry Tactics on the Ohio Frontier, 1758–1764," in David Curtis Skaggs and Larry L. Nelson, eds. *The Sixty Years' War for the Great Lakes, 1754–1814* (East Lansing: University of Michigan, 2001), 46. Another contemporary officer wrote, "They are an active hardy People, capable of fatigue, hunger, and cold and know perfectly the use of arms. And tho' their number nor their valour may not make them a formidable enemy, their little wood skirmishing, and bush fighting will always make them a very troublesome one." Canada Archives, *The Northcliffe Collection* (Ottawa: King's Printer, 1926), 70.

33. Quoted in *The Conquest of Canada, Vol. 2*, 18.

34. Letter, Father Pierre Roubaud, Missionary, October 21, 1757, in Thwaites, Vol. 60, 121.

35. Thomas Church, *The History of Philip's War* (Exeter, NH: J & B Williams, 1829; reprint Bowie, MD: Heritage Books, 1989), 108–109. One survivor of Braddock's defeat reported "They continually made us Retreat, they haveing always a large marke to shoute [shoot] at and we having only to shoute at them behind trees or on their Bellies." Hamilton, *Braddock's Defeat*, 28–29.

36. Jeremy Black, *War: Past, Present and Future* (New York: St. Martin's Press, 2000), 127. The Indians did acknowledge "our troops thereby show they are not afraid, and that our numbers would be formidable in open ground, where they will never give us an opportunity of engaging them."

37. Hamilton, *Braddock's Defeat*, 29; and Fred Anderson, *Crucible of War* (New York: Vintage Books, 2001), 100. The veteran also recalled: "they Either on their Bellies or Behind trees or Running from one tree to another almost by the ground." At the battle at Lake George, in early September 1755, Baron Dieskau's French regular officers and men, who remained in the open, suffered horrendous casualties against the New England men that fired from behind logs. They lost nearly all their officers and approximately half of their soldiers. Conversely, the French Canadians and Indians on their part remained behind cover and suffered negligible losses. Anderson, 158–159.

38. Hamilton, *Braddock's Defeat*, 50.

39. *The Northcliffe Collection*, 216.

40. Carl Benn, *The Iroquois in the War of 1812* (Toronto: University of Toronto Press, 1998), 71; and Patrick M. Malone, *The Skulking Way of War* (Lanham, Maryland: Madison Books, 1991), 59–60.

41. The Natives often carved grooves into the stocks of their weapons so that they could take better aim by being able to align their eyes along the barrels of their muskets and in line with their targets. This was because neither the French Charleville .69 caliber musket, nor the British .75 caliber "Brown Bess" musket had rear sights as the Europeans felt this was unnecessary due to the perceived inaccuracy of the smooth bore musket and the reliance on volley fire. The North Americans believed otherwise. A Native veteran observed that in combat "the right men [Indian leaders] concealed themselves, and are worst clothed than the others." Leroy V. Eid, "American Indian Military Leadership: St. Clair's 1791 Defeat," *Journal of Military History*, Vol. 57, January 1993, 81.

42. Pouchot, 160 and 476.

43. Colonel Bouquet observed: "They seldom expose themselves to danger, and depend entirely on their dexterity in concealing themselves during an engagement, never appearing openly, unless they have struck their enemies with terror, and have thereby rendered them incapable of defence." *Warfare on the Colonial American Frontier: The Journals of Major Robert Rogers and an Historical Account of the Expedition Against the Ohio Indians in the Year 1764, Under the Command of Henry Bouquet, Esq.* Reprinted from an original 1769 Edition (Bargersville, IN: Dreslar Publishing, 2001), Bouquet's Account 52.

44. See Nester, *The Great Frontier War*, 91; and Robert F. Berkhofer, "The French and Indians at Carillon," *The Bulletin of the Fort Ticonderoga Museum*, Vol. 9, No. 6, 1956, 137–138 and 147; D.P. MacLeod, *The Canadian Iroquois and the Seven Years' War* (Toronto: Dundurn Press, 1996), 21; Osborn, 45; Benn, 82; Eid, 81; and Martin L. Nicolai, "A Different Kind of Courage: The French Military and the Canadian Irregular Soldier During the Seven Years' War," *Canadian Historical Review*, Vol. 70, No. 1, 1989, 60. Jesuit missionary, Father Roubaud, asserted that "the Savage is his own Master and his own King, and he takes with him everywhere his independence." Letter, Father Pierre Roubaud, Missionary, October 21, 1757, in Thwaites, Vol. 60, 137. The Natives recognized "only voluntary submission."

45. For example, Lieutenant-General Jeffrey Amherst described them as "These little skulking men ..." Jeffrey Amherst, *Journal of William Amherst in America, 1758–1760* (London: Butler & Tanner Ltd., 1927), 20. Captain John Knox described them as "these skulking wretches," although he did include that they "are so hardy,

that scarce pass one day [in February 1758] without scouring the environs of this fortress." Knox, 102. See also Malone, *The Skulking Way of War.*

46. MacLeod, 34–35.

47. He added, "Their encounters are mere attempts at assassination. They fight bravely then only when they know that the sole alternative lies between victory or death." Letter from Father Nau, missionary, in Thwaites, Vol. 68, 275.

48. H.R. Casgrain, *Montcalm et Lévis — Les Français au Canada* (Québec: Maison Alfred Mame et Fils, undated), 43.

49. Letter to Boston Gazette, June 13, 1757, quoted in Armand Francis Lucier, ed., *French and Indian War Notices Abstracted from Colonial Newspapers, Vol. 2: 1756–1757* (Bowie, MD: Heritage Books, 1999), 256. During King William's War, a Canadian scouting party ran into English troops and fought like Natives. The "New England men taunted them as cowards who would never fight except under cover." Journal extract quoted in Ian K. Steele, *Guerillas and Grenadiers* (Toronto: Ryerson Press, 1969), 30.

50. "The Journal of Dr. Caleb Rea written during the Expedition against Ticonderoga in 1758," *Historical Collections of the Essex Institute*, Vol. 43, April–January 1881, No. 4–6, 109.

51. Quoted documents, display, Fort Chambly National Historic Site of Canada, Chambly, Quebec. Accessed August 23, 2001. "Some of the French subjects," wrote one English colonist, "always go with the Indians, on these incursions, and are both privy in, and instigators of, their robberies and murder." Letter, gentleman in Virginia to friend in Annapolis, January 16, 1754, quoted in Lucier, Vol. 1, 1.

52. Letter, Major-General James Wolfe to William Pit, quoted in A. Doughty, *The Siege of Quebec and the Battle of the Plains of Abraham*, Vols. 1–6 (Quebec: Dussault & Proulx, 1901), 65.

53. Impartial Hand, *The Contest in America Between Great Britain and France with Its Consequences and Importance* (London: Strand, 1757), 128. The writer also notes that the Natives and Canadians, who travel without baggage, support themselves with stores and magazines, and maintain themselves in the woods "do more execution ... than four or fives time their number of our men." *Ibid.*, 138. See also Eccles, *French in North America*, 208.

54. Hamilton, *Adventures in the Wilderness*, 333. Even Montcalm, who particularly disliked the Canadians, wrote after his victory at Fort Ticonderoga in July 1758, "The colonial troops and Canadians have caused us to regret that there were not in greater number. Chevalier Levy under whose eyes they fought speaks highly of them." Quoted in Andrew Gallup and Donald F. Shaffer, *La Marine: The French Colonial Soldier in Canada, 1745–1761* (Bowie, MD: Heritage Books, 1992), 42. One early Canadian historian concluded, "For scouting harassing the enemy, fighting under cover of wood or earthworks, the undisciplined native American soldier whether French or English could not be equalled by any regulars." Doughty, 52.

55. Casgrain, *Les Français au Canada*, 87.

56. Quoted in Abbé H.R. Casgrain, *Wolfe and Montcalm* (Toronto: University of Toronto Press, 1964), 196–197. Casgrain, a renowned expert on this period of North American history wrote "These Canadians seasoned and skillful hunters, do not waste a single bullet and create gaps in the ranks of the enemy." *Ibid.*, 60.

57. Paul E. Kopperman, *Braddock at the Monongahela* (Pittsburgh: University of Pittsburgh Press, 1977), 30; George F. Stanley, *Canada's Soldiers: The Military History of an Unmilitary People* (Toronto: Macmillan of Canada, 1960), 65; Noel

St. John Williams, *Redcoats Along the Hudson: The Struggle for North America 1754–63* (London: Brassey's Classics, 1998), 76; Anderson, 96–97; and Strachan, 28. Brumwell gives the British strength at 1,469. Stephen Brumwell, *Redcoats: British Soldiers and War in the Americas, 1755–63* (Cambridge, Eng.: University of Cambridge Press, 2002), 16. Increasingly, Canadians began to serve as officers in the Compagnies Franches de la Marine. The colonial troops offered little upward mobility for regular French officers (since each company was only commanded by a captain). Therefore, positions were often difficult to fill. As such, vacancies were given to individuals from the Canadian gentry or to families of French officers who remained in Canada. This became common practice. See Chartrand, *Canadian Military Heritage, Vol. 1*, 84–85; and Eccles, *The French in North America*, 173–174.

58. Benjamin Franklin, *Autobiography* (New York: E.P. Dutton, 1937 ed.), 168. See also Anderson, 95; Thomas Fleming, "Braddock's Defeat," *Military History Quarterly*, Vol. 3, No. 1, Autumn 1990, 90; and Nicolai, 60. Captain Pouchot later reflected, "If, on terrain without real problems, such a disaster could happen to brave & well-disciplined troops, through an inability to direct fire & ignorance of the nature of the enemy they were engaging, then this provides a good lesson that these two aspects of warfare should receive close attention." Pouchot, 83.

59. John Keegan, *The Book of War* (London: Penguin Books, 1996), 92–93.

60. Letter from an officer, dated Fort Cumberland, July 18, 1755, in Lucier, Vol. 1, 251.

61. Francis Parkman, *Montcalm and Wolfe* (New York: The Modern Library, 1999), 111and 117–118; Robert Leckie, *A Few Acres of Snow: The Saga of the French and Indian Wars* (Toronto: John Wiley & Sons, 1999), 284–285; Anderson, 102–103; and Kopperman, 79. Tragically, as the provincials moved forward to take cover and engage the enemy in the woods they were cut down by volleys from the British regulars, who seeing the smoke of discharges coming from the brush at the side of the road mistook them for enemy.

62. Kopperman, 139 and Annex E. See also Hamilton, xvii.

63. Stanley, 66; and Kopperman, 70.

64. Strachan, 28; Anderson, 105; and Stanley, 66. Actual numbers vary. Pouchot recorded in his journal that the casualties were approximately 1,300 for the English and 11 killed and 29 wounded for the French. Pouchot, 82–83. A more accurate count of the English casualties is given at 977 men, 500 of which were killed. French losses were 23 dead (three officers, two men, three militiamen, and 15 Natives) and 16 wounded. Chartrand, *Canadian Military Heritage, Vol. 2* (Montreal: Art Global, 1993), 20. Benjamin Franklin gave the English casualties as 63 out of 86 officers killed or wounded, and 714 men killed out of 1,100. Franklin, 170. Brumwell states that two thirds of the 1,469 British troops or approximately 979 were either killed or wounded. Brumwell, 16. William Weir places them at 456 killed and 421 wounded of 1,459 engaged for the English and eight French or Canadians killed, six wounded and 27 Indians killed or wounded. William Wier, *Fatal Victories* (Hamden, CT: Archon Books, 1993), 111.

65. One contemporary commentary stated, "They are in possession of all the frontiers of our colonies, and can at any time pour in their irregulars, Coureurs de Bois, and Indians into them; by which our people dare not stir nor march to Crown-Point, or any where else but are obliged to stand upon their defence at home." Impartial Hand, 125. The Natives also castigated the English for their lack of fortifications.

66. Louis de Courville, *Mémoires sur le Canada depuis 1749 Jusqu'à 1760* (Quebec City: Imprimerie de Middleton and Dawson, 1873), 116.

67. Vaudreuil believed that the French regular troops should be used to garrison the forts and the Canadians and their Native allies should be used for raids against the English colonies.

68. "Remarks on the Fort built by the French at Crown Point in North America," LAC, Colonial Office (CO), Microfilm B–25, Vol. 13, 157. Major-General James Wolfe recognized the importance of offensive action. He wrote, "An offensive, daring kind of war will awe the Indians and ruin the French. Blockhouses and a trembling defensive encourage the meanest scoundrels to attack us." Quoted in Casgrain, *Wolfe and Montcalm*, 74–75. Similarly, in 1758, Johnson wrote to Abercromby that "the inactivity of that year's [1757] campaign on our side not only produced additional dread of the enemy upon the afore said nations but greatly cool'd what ardor there was towards our cause in the rest of the Six Nations." Letter, William Johnson to Major-General Abercromby, March 17, 1758. PRO, WO 34/39, Amherst Papers.

69. Letter, Amherst to Brigadier-General Gage, Camp at Crown Point, August 14, 1759. PRO, WO, 34/46a.

70. Quoted in Stanley, 72.

71. Horace Warpole confided to his diary, "Had he [Vaudreuil] fallen into our hands our men were determined to scalp him, he having been the chief and blackest author of the cruelties exercised on our countrymen." George M. Wrong, *The Fall of Canada: A Chapter in the History of the Seven Years' War* (Oxford: Clarendon Press, 1914), 59.

72. Extract from a letter dated April 28, 1757, quoted in Lucier, Vol. 2, 233. By the spring of 1756, raids by Canadians and Natives organized by Captain Dumas had resulted in 700 deaths or captures. By the end of the summer operations had extended as far south as the Carolinas. One report noted, "All these provinces are laid waste for forty leagues from the foot of the mountains, in the direction of the sea. The number of prisoners in these territories since last April [1756] is estimated at about three thousand — men, women and children, in addition to thirteen hundred horses." Steele, *Guerillas and Grenadiers*, 97–98. In the spring of 1758, in an approximate three-month period, raiding parties delivered to Fort Duquesne alone, 140 prisoners or scalps. H.R. Casgrain, ed., *Journal du Marquis De Montcalm durant ses Campagnes en Canada de 1756–1759* (Quebec City: L.J. Demers & Frère, 1895), 357.

73. Letter from an officer, dated Fort Cumberland, October 6, 1755, in Lucier, Vol. 1, 329. The effect was clearly explained in yet another letter, "The barbarous and bloody scene which is now opened it the upper parts of Northamton County, is the most lamentable that perhaps ever appeared ... There may be seen horror and desolation; populous settlements deserted; villages laid to ashes; men, women and children cruelly mangled and massacred." *Ibid.*, 353.

74. This functionalism is what gave the contemporaries relevance and most likely kept Paris involved in far away Quebec. In later years "making yourself useful" becomes a Canadian way both in war and diplomacy. It is associated with functionalism — a longtime Canadian practice only articulated by Prime Minister Mackenzie King in World War II.

75. Letter from General Shirley to Major-General Abercromby, June 27, 1756, PRO, War Office 1/4, Correspondence, 1755–1763.

76. Claude-Godefroy Coquart, a priest, wrote his brother, "Our Indians have waged the most cruel war against the English ... Georgia, Carolina, Marrelande, Pensilvania, are wholly laid waste. The farmers have been forced to quit their abodes and to retire into the town. They have neither plowed nor planted." Robert C. Alberts, *The*

Most Extraordinary Adventures of Major Robert Stobo (Boston: Houghton Mifflin, 1965), 152. See also Anderson, 637; Leckie, 101; Letter From William Shirley (New York) to Principal Secretary of War, December 20, 1755, PRO, War Office 1/4, Correspondence, 1755–1763; Parkman, 173; H.R. Casgrain, ed., *Lettres du Chevalier De Lévis concernant La Guerre du Canada 1756–1760* (Montreal: C.O. Beauchemin & Fils, 1889), 75; Steele, *Guerillas and Grenadiers*, 24; Casgrain, *Journal du Marquis De Montcalm*, 110–111; Le Comte Gabriél de Maurès de Malartic, *Journal des Campagnes au Canada de 1755 à 1760* (Paris: Librairie Plon, 1902), 52–53; Kopperman, 232; O'Meara, 161; Gavin K. Watt, *The Burning of the Valleys* (Toronto: Dundurn Press, 1997), 73; and Don R. Gerlach, "The British Invasion of 1780 and 'A Character ... Debased Beyond Description,'" *The Bulletin of the Fort Ticonderoga Museum*, Vol. 14, No. 5 (Summer 1984), 311.

77. Alexander, *Adventures in the Wilderness*, 191.

78. Ensuring the Canadians returned from campaigns in time to harvest their crops was critical to the economy of New France. It was often a point of contention between Vaudreuil and Montcalm. H.R. Casgrain, ed., *Lettres du Marquis De Vaudreuil au Chevalier de Lévis* (Quebec City: L.J. Demers & Frère, 1895), 52. See also A. Doughty, *The Siege of Quebec*, Vol. 1, 158.

79. Scholar Fred Anderson in his seminal work *Crucible of War* concluded, "France maintained its empire in America for more than a century despite the steady increase of British power and population because the governors of Canada had generally sponsored cordial relations with the Indian peoples of the interior. Trade was the sinew of these intercultural relationships, which in time of war became the military alliances that made the frontiers of the British colonies uninhabitable and rendered a successful invasion of the Canadian heartland impossible." Anderson, 454.

80. Quoted in Moogk, 21.

81. Stanley, 61; Eccles, "French Forces ," xx; Leckie, 103; Doughty, Vol. 1, 158; Nester, *The Great Frontier War*, 54; and Fleming, 87. The scale of the threat was enormous. During the French and Indian War, the English colonies outnumbered New France in manpower by nearly 25 to one. The supply of foodstuffs appeared limitless. In 1755, the governor of Pennsylvania asserted that he alone could produce food for an army of 100,000 men. In addition, the colonial iron industry was able to compete effectively with that of Britain. See Steele, *Guerillas and Grenadiers*, 74. "What a scourge!" exclaimed Bougainville, "Humanity shudders at being obliged to make use of such monsters. But without them the match would be too much against us." Hamilton, *Adventure in the Wilderness*, 191.

82. Moogk, 42.

83. Steele, *Guerillas and Grenadiers*, 66.

84. Alliances with the Natives came at a price. European commanders characterized the Natives as an unwanted burden, if not a nuisance. "They drive us crazy from morning to night," exclaimed one senior French officer. "There is no end to their demands," he added, finally concluding, "in short one needs the patience of an angel with these devils, and yet one must always force himself to seem pleased with them." A. Doughty, *The Siege of Quebec*, Vol. 2, 202; *The Northcliffe Collection*, 138; and Berkhofer, 146. Bougainville bemoaned, "One must be the slave to these savages, listen to them day and night, in council and in private, whenever the fancy takes them, or whenever a dream or a fit of vapors, or their perpetual craving for brandy, gets possession of them; besides which they are always wanting something for their equipment, arms, or toilet." Hamilton, *Adventure in the Wilderness*, 133. In an attempt not to aggrieve the

Natives the most wanton outrages were often accepted. One French officer decried the tolerance shown to their Native allies. "You could see them running throughout Montreal," he recorded, "knife in hand, threatening and insulting everyone." Courville, 97; Doughty, 202–203; and Benn, 136. Governors of New France, particularly Vaudreuil, were constantly criticized for their leniency towards the Natives. Of 76 Natives accused of disorderly conduct, assault, or murder in the Montreal District alone from 1669 to 1760, only one was actually prosecuted. The rest were released without charge. The rationale was simple, though unpalatable for the French and Canadians — the authorities feared that the application of the harsh justice demanded by the French criminal code would alienate the Indians and cause them to defect to their enemies. See Moogk, 43–45; and Gallup, 142. Their behaviour on campaigns was little better. Montcalm confided to his journal that "[the Indians] feeling the need we have of them, are extremely insolent; they wish our fowls this evening. They took with force some barrels of wine, killed some cattle, and it is necessary to endure all." Casgrain, *Journal du Marquis De Montcalm*, 385. French officers claimed that it proved very expensive to maintain their Native allies because they "exhausted so much provisions" and "could not be stinted to allowance taking everything at pleasure and destroying three times the Quantity of Provisions they could eat." The Natives had no sense of rationing and would consume a week's allocation of provisions in three days and demand additional replenishment. Consistently, the Europeans denounced the Natives as disruptive to their campaigns and a drain on valuable resources. Ian K. Steele, *Betrayals: Fort William Henry and the Massacre* (New York: Oxford University Press, 1990), 132–133; Parkman, 238; Berkhofer, 156; and Robert S. Allen, *His Majesty's Indian Allies* (Toronto: Dundurn Press, 1992), 144. "One is a slave to Indians in this country," lamented Bougainville, but he also added that, "they are a necessary evil." Hamilton, *Adventure in the Wilderness*, 171.

85.   This was so only as long as the Americans were unwilling to overcome their parochial regional interests and bickering, which consistently resulted in a failure to present a unified front against the French. It was also a function of the unwillingness and/or inability to permeate in numbers through the Appalachian Barrier into the Ohio Valley. That is what happened by 1754, and the Anglo-Americans and British were increasingly unremitting in their will to occupy that new territory.

86.   The North American component of the Seven Years' War, often referred to as the French and Indian War, is generally accepted to have spanned the period 1754 (confrontation at Fort Necessity) to 1760 (surrender of remaining French forces in Canada at Montreal). Six of France's 395 existing infantry battalions were dispatched to Canada to bolster French garrisons at Louisbourg, Cape Breton Island, and Quebec in May 1755. These troops were under the command of Major-General Baron Jean-Armand Dieskau who was subordinate to the governor of New France. However, his defeat and capture at the hands of Major-General William Johnson's forces at Lake George on September 8, 1755, necessitated his replacement, Montcalm who arrived on May 13, 1756. Montcalm, like Dieskau, was subordinate to Vaudreuil in everything. He was responsible only for the discipline, administration and internal ordering of the army battalions. He was strictly the commander in the field and was responsible for obeying the orders of the governor. See *Dictionary of Canadian Biography, Vol. 3, 1741–1770* and *Vol. 4, 1771–1800* (Toronto: University of Toronto Press, 1974/1979), 458–459 and 660–671.

87.   Quoted in C.P. Stacey, *Quebec, 1759: The Siege and the Battle* (Toronto: Robin Brass Studio, reprint 2002, Donald Graves, ed.), 33. Montcalm wrote, "They know neither discipline nor subordination, and think themselves in all respects the first

nation on earth." Letter, Montcalm to the Minister of War, September 18, 1757, quoted in Francis Parkman, Montcalm and Wolfe (New York: The Modern Library, reprint 1999, 231.

88. Alexander, *Adventure in the Wilderness*, 252.

89. See H.R. Casgrain, ed., *Lettres et Pièces Militarires: Instructions, Ordres, Mémoires, Plans de Campagne it de Défense 1756–1760* (Quebec City: L.J. Demers & Frère, 1891), 45; Anderson, 346; Steele, *Guerillas and Grenadiers*, 108–110; Eccles, *The French in North America*, 210–211; Pouchot, 171; Martin L. Nicolai, "A Different Kind of Courage: The French Military and the Canadian Irregular Soldier during the Seven Years' War," *Canadian Historical Review*, Vol. 70, No. 1, 1989, 59–64; and Richard Preston, and Leopold Lamontagne, *Royal Fort Frontenac* (Toronto: University of Toronto Press, 1958), 277. Despite Montcalm's virulent dislike for Vaudreuil, the Canadians, Natives, and guerrilla warfare, he did see the usefulness of harassing the enemy. He believed that successful raids, particularly while besieged at Quebec, lowered enemy morale, bolstered that of the Canadians, and maintained the offensive spirit in his troops.

90. Quoted in Steele, *Guerillas and Grenadiers*, 109.

91. Vaudreuil's Observations on Montcalm's Memoir on Lake Ontario, Montreal September 12, 1758, document included in Preston and Lamontagne, 277.

92. Quoted in Gallup, *La Marine*, 16. Vaudreuil complained that Montcalm and his "troops of the line wish only to preserve their reputation and return to France without having experienced a single check; they think more seriously of their private interests than of the safety of Canada." Quoted in Steele, *Guerillas and Grenadiers*, 109–110.

93. Letter, Vaudreuil to Ministry of Marine, October 30 1755, *Extraits des Archives des Ministéres de la Marine et de la Guerre A Paris — Canada — Correspondence Générale — MM. Duquesne et Vaudreuil Gouverneurs-Généraux, 1755–1760* (Quebec City: L.J. Demers & Frère, 1890), 107.

94. The British suffered 1,944 casualties, 1,610 of those regulars. The French suffered only 377. See René Chartrand, *Ticonderoga 1758 — Montcalm's Victory Against All Odds* (London: Oxford University Press, 2000); *Dictionary of Canadian Biography, Vol. 3*, 462; Noel St. John Williams, *Redcoats Along the Hudson: The Struggle for North America 1754–63* (London: Brassey's Classics, 1998), 143–145; and Anderson, 240–249.

95. H.R. Casgrain, *Lettres du Chevalier De Lévis,*199. Brigadier-General Lévis was Montcalm's second in command.

96. See Leckie, 319–331; Anderson, 237–339; Parkman, *Montcalm and Wolfe*, 359–360. Approximately 400 Canadians and Natives were present, however, they were positioned to cover Montcalm's right flank and played no significant role in the actual defeat of the British. In fact, at one point, they refused orders to sally forth and attack the attacking British forces.

97. The French government was neither willing nor able to spare French regulars for North America. The control of the seas by the Royal Navy alone reasoned against the gamble of sending scarce troops away from the continent. In addition, Montcalm's own defeatist analysis of the situation in Canada argued against investing further resources. Anderson, 239; C.P. Stacey, *Quebec, 1759: The Siege and the Battle* (Toronto: Robin Brass Studio, reprint 2002, Donald Graves, ed.), 39–40; and Parkman, *Montcalm and Wolfe*, 346.

98. The French officer Malartic stated that each line battalion had received a draft of 108 Canadians. The Canadian historian George Stanley asserts that since "no battalion at

the Plains had more than 350 men the proportion of Canadians was undoubtedly high." Stanley, 91.

99. Pouchot, 242.

100. Doughty, *The Siege of Quebec*, Vol. 3, 159. See also Leckie, 363; and Nicolai, 69.

101. Doughty, *The Siege of Quebec*, Vol. 3, 126. One account is telling from the extract of a journal kept at the army commanded by the late Lieutenant-General de Montcalm quoted in Doughty: "The rout was total only among the regulars; the Canadians accustomed to fall back Indian fashion and to turn afterwards on the enemy with more confidence than before, rallied in some places, and under cover of the brushwood, by which they were surrounded, forced divers corps to give way, but at last were obliged to yield to the superiority of numbers." *Ibid.*, 165. Townshend's report on the Battle of the Plains of Abraham stated, "The enemy lined the bushes in their front with 1,500 Indians and Canadians & daresay most of their best Marksmen which kept up a very hot tho' irregular fire upon our whole line." *The Northcliffe Collection*, 419–420. See also Eccles, *The French in North America*, 229; *The Conquest of Canada*, Vol. 2, 218–219; and Nicolai, 69.

102. Anderson, 219–231.

103. By 1758, Britain's total forces for their offensive campaigns numbered 44,000 — half of which were British regulars. This compares to 11,000 troops in 1755, one in seven a British regular. Steele, *Guerillas and Grenadiers*, 114 and 123.

104. Letter, Abercromby to Amherst, January 10, 1764. Quoted in Chartrand, *Canadian Military Heritage, Vol. 2*, 49.

CHAPTER 2

"They Really Conducted Themselves Remarkably Well": Canadian Soldiers and the Great War, 1783 to 1815
by John R. Grodzinski

On October 26, 1813, a force of 1,700 Canadians defeated an army of 3,764 Americans at the Battle of the Châteauguay, just southwest of Montreal in Lower Canada. As the Canadian defensive position was set in five successive lines, only those in the forward most positions, as well as a group farther to their south, across the Châteauguay River, totalling some 339 men, actually saw action against the vastly superior American Army. They were led by Lieutenant-Colonel Charles-Michel d'Irumberry de Salaberry. A Canadian, he was, somewhat uniquely for the time, a professional soldier, and was once described as "*le diable au corps.*" The battle itself is noteworthy as it was the sole encounter during the War of 1812 where the Americans were defeated by an almost exclusively Canadian force. Problems in the American camp aside, the Canadian victory achieved operational success by stopping one of two American armies that invaded Canada during the fall of 1813 — the largest American operation of the war, aimed at capturing Montreal.[2]

The War of 1812 was the culmination of a complex period of Anglo-American relations following the American War of Independence and British global operations during the French Revolution and Napoleonic Wars. The Americans, motivated perhaps more by pride than sound policy, sought to secure, and in some cases expand, their frontiers bordering British, Native, and Spanish colonies. The British, occupied in Europe and elsewhere, first considered North America as a sideshow, but by late 1814, dispatched a considerable portion of its army and naval forces to British North America.

To understand fully the British approach and the Canadian connection, it is important to examine the period from the end of the American Revolution, in 1783, to the end of the War of 1812, in 1815. Since Canada was a British colony, a colonial governor ruled the country, who received his instructions on foreign policy and defence matters from several ministries and departments in Britain. "Canadian" authority on military matters was limited to a narrow range of administrative authority granted to provincial assemblies and legislative councils over the militia. Without an army and more important, with limited responsibility for defence, Canada would be expected to have had little share in the regional conflicts of the time, but in reality, "Canada" contributed far more soldiers and formed military units than is generally recognized. Moreover, on occasion, employment of Canadian forces exerted operational influence.

Although the "militia" is generally subject to derisory commentary, it was in reality a tiered organization composed of units with varied training and capabilities. Furthermore, there were some regular troops stationed in Canada, who were as well trained and equipped as their British counterparts. The diversity and complexity of this system is best demonstrated at the Battle of Châteauguay, where the Canadian Militia included four types of corps — a "provincial" unit, select embodied militia, sedentary militia, and Natives. Each had differing terms of service, discipline, motivation, and fighting skills that produced units with combat capabilities ranging from the most fundamental (for example, the sedentary militia) to the more advanced such as that of the select embodied militia and the provincial units, which were on par with British regular units.

British decision-making was clearly influenced by the overall threat environment within North America and the evolving military problem of defending Canada. In turn, these factors affected the nature of the forces raised here and their eventual employment. The primary threat to Canada at this time was the United States. As British North America had no permanent standing army, other than its British garrison, its defence was obviously dependant upon British forces. The British, short of personnel because of priorities in Europe and elsewhere, required support from Canadian militia, permanent units and Native allies. As such, Canadian soldiers played a significant role in several important operations, and in some cases provided the majority of troops employed, and by their presence and performance, as already mentioned, influenced operational outcomes.

A Powder Keg Waiting to Explode:
The Frontiers of British North America

Within British North America,[3] decisions regarding defensive plans, garrison locations, fortifications, and logistics were left to the governor-in-chief and his military staff, with final approval resting in London. To one degree or the other, this system would dominate Canadian defensive issues until the twentieth century. Although France, Spain, and even Russia challenged Canadian security during this time, the primary threat to British North America was the fledgling United States of America. Another war with the southern neighbour was considered inevitable. Although British planning was defensive in nature, eventually land and naval forces based in Canada began conducting offensive operations into French territories in North America and later, on a much larger scale, into the United States. Between 1791 and 1815, Britain, France, Spain, Russia, and the United States all held or controlled territories on the North American continent. As competition between them for additional territory continued, the chances of open war increased.

Of these, Spain and Russia posed the least threat. Russia, interested in exploiting the wealth of the Pacific coast north of Mexico, planned to claim sovereignty over the entire territory north of the Queen Charlotte Islands, but was diverted by a war with Turkey and Sweden.[4] Between 1774 and 1790, competing British and Spanish claims to Vancouver Island almost led to war, but ended in a negotiated peace.

The most serious problem occurred in 1789, when Spain established a post at Nootka, which it eventually garrisoned with regular troops armed with artillery. Then the Spanish commander exceeded his authority and seized three British vessels causing both countries to mobilize their fleets. However, the prospect of war over "some far away island" ended when France, now in revolution, refused to assist Spain. A negotiated settlement was reached in October 1790 that recognized the claims of both empires to the Vancouver Island area.

Four years later, Spain found herself allied with Britain against France. Threatened by France at home, Spain withdrew from Nootka, leaving that territory to the British, who now fostered the belief that they controlled the western coast from California to Alaska, an idea the United States would be quick to challenge.[5]

The United States also benefited from the decline of Spanish power in North America and actively sought to gain its colonies. After a brief period of Spanish control, Louisiana returned to France at the end of 1800.

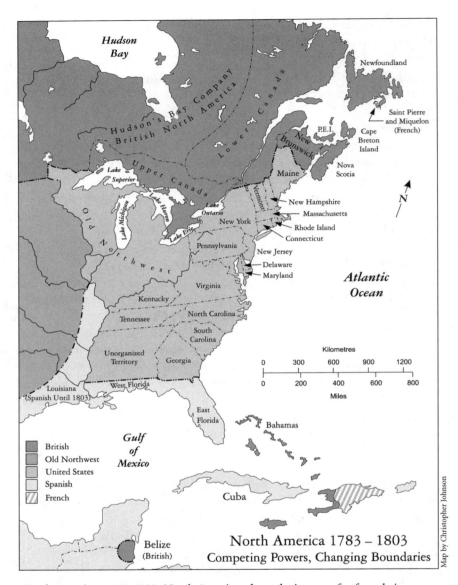

Labels on map:

Hudson Bay

Newfoundland

Hudson's Bay Company
British North America

Saint Pierre and Miquelon (French)

Lower Canada

P.E.I.

Cape Breton Island

Lake Superior

New Brunswick

Nova Scotia

Upper Canada

Maine

Lake Michigan

Lake Huron

Lake Ontario

Vermont

New Hampshire

Lake Erie

New York

Massachusetts

Rhode Island

Connecticut

Old Northwest

Pennsylvania

New Jersey

Delaware

Maryland

Virginia

Atlantic Ocean

Kentucky

Tennessee

North Carolina

South Carolina

Unorganized Territory

Georgia

Louisiana (Spanish Until 1803)

West Florida

East Florida

Bahamas

Gulf of Mexico

Belize (British)

Cuba

N

Kilometres
0   300   600   900   1200
0   200   400   600   800
Miles

British
Old Northwest
United States
Spanish
French

North America 1783 – 1803
Competing Powers, Changing Boundaries

Map by Christopher Johnson

North America 1783–1803. North American boundaries were far from being finalized after the American War of Independence, and competition between the British and several European powers and the United States continued throughout the eighteenth and nineteenth centuries. Eventually, France and Spain gave up all or most of their continental holdings, leaving the British and Americans. By 1871, Great Britain was no longer a power in North America.

The following year, President Jefferson offered to buy it, which the French surprisingly agreed to, perhaps to reduce the chance of an Anglo-American alliance against France. The Americans took possession of Louisiana on April 30, 1803, effectively doubling the size of their territory.[6]

That same year, the Americans shifted their efforts towards Spanish Florida, against the Red Sticks, members of the Creek Native tribe, who were sympathetic to the British and responsive to Tecumseh's call for Native unity against the Americans. However, Britain's alliance with Spain in 1808 soon increased tensions between Britain and America since the British now had a stake in maintaining the integrity of Spain's colonies. In 1810, American forces occupied portions of western Spanish Florida, which the American Congress incorporated into the Mississippi Territory. Next, American troops illegally moved into East Florida. The following year Andrew Jackson led a campaign against the Creeks that ended successfully on March 27, 1814. The territory was then secured by the United States.[7]

Farther north, there had been boundary issues and problems with the Natives along the frontier separating British North America from the United States. These had generally been resolved with the signing of the "Treaty of Amity, Commerce and Navigation," or Jay's Treaty, in London on November 19, 1794. As a result of this treaty, several forts that remained within American territory and that were to have been surrendered following the American War of Independence in 1783, but remained in British control, (for example, Oswegatchie [Ogdensburg], Oswego, Niagara, Presque Isle [Erie], Sandusky, Detroit, and Michilimackinac) were finally abandoned by the British.

Aside from limiting American access northward, these forts had been traditional meeting points where British Indian Department officials conducted their annual transactions with allied Natives. Handing over the posts effectively terminated British control of the St. Lawrence and Great Lakes, but was seen as a necessary step to avoid another American War.[8] The transfers were largely completed by June 1, 1796.[9]

The surrender of forts and territory also effectively ended plans to cement the British-Native military and commercial alliance by creating an Native State in the Michigan territory that aimed to deter American incursion into the region and act as a buffer between Britain and the United States.[10] The implementation of the treaty also affected British military power as 8,000 of a potential 10,000 Native allies now found themselves in American territory, which meant that Canadians would be expected to play a greater role in the defence of their homeland.[11]

The Defence of the Canadas

Like their predecessors, British authorities faced a number of significant challenges in planning the defence of British North America. First, there was the difficulty in defending a large territory with a small, dispersed population. Second, the infrastructure was limited and most manufactured goods, including war stores, had to be imported.[12] Third, if British attention was on Europe or elsewhere, intervention by other European countries in North America, as had occurred during the American Revolution, could be repeated. Fourth, it was perceived to be unfeasible to control the interior lakes and rivers, because rapids in the Upper St. Lawrence River stopped the Royal Navy from moving vessels west of Montreal. As naval power was the foundation of British doctrine, any policy advocating the defence of Upper Canada was considered impossible since the Royal Navy could not support it.[13]

Nonetheless, two different defensive concepts emerged after 1784. The first was a defence in depth, perhaps best expressed in Sir George Prevost's estimate of the military problems in defending the North American provinces. Written in early 1812, at the request of the secretary of state for war and the colonies, the report included a general assessment of each province along with comments on specific stations (military fortifications and posts). As such, this document offers insight into the intent of the commander-in-chief of British North America and the state of the defences in the spring of 1812.[14]

In general terms, Upper Canada was "the most contiguous to the Territory of the United States" and in the "event of war, more liable to immediate attack." Overall, the posts in Upper Canada were poorly fortified, lightly garrisoned, isolated, and consequently, exposed. The most critical point was Kingston, as it was "open to sudden attack, which if successful, would cut off the communication between the Upper and Lower Province and deprive us of our naval resources." The proximity of several potential American bases on Lake Ontario "with good Harbours" posed an immediate threat to Kingston. In order to preserve communications between Upper and Lower Canada, a strong contingent of regulars supported by militia would be needed there.

Moving to the western end of the province, Fort St. Joseph was also poorly fortified. Abandoning it was out of the question, as its position along the communication link between Lake Huron and Lake Superior was necessary to support the Northwest fur trade. Like Fort Amherstburg farther to the south, it was point of assemblage with friendly Natives, a factor of considerable importance. Fort Amerherstburg also had a dock-yard and naval station.[15]

The situation was much the same on the north shore of Lake Ontario, where York was poorly fortified but offered a good harbour. Prevost believed that its "retired situation from the American frontier makes it a position particularly desirable ..." for a naval base and arsenal. Southeast of York, along the Niagara River, Forts George, Chippawa, and Erie were contiguous to American territory. In the event of war, the capture of Fort Niagara, across the Niagara River from Fort George was deemed crucial to securing communication along the Niagara frontier.[16]

In Lower Canada, the outline defensive plan was clear. The security of Quebec, with "the only permanent fortification in the Canadas," and Montreal, as "the principal commercial city in the Canadas," were paramount. Protecting both depended on an "impenetrable line on the South Shore . . . with a sufficient flotilla to command the Rivers St. Lawrence and the Richelieu." Montreal would be the first object of any attack, while Quebec was "the key to the whole and must be maintained." The fortifications needed improvement to withstand a "vigorous and well conducted siege" and await reinforcement from Britain.[17]

Prevost stressed that "it would be in vain ... with the hopes of making an effectual defence of the open country [for example, Upper Canada], unless powerfully assisted from Home." With the limited resources that might be added to his already paltry forces in wartime, Prevost concluded "the preservation of Quebec as the first object, and to which all others must be subordinate." As defective as the fortifications at Quebec were, it could not be surrendered as "the door of entry for that Force the King's Government might find it expedient to send for the recovery of both, or either of these provinces." Britain's commitments elsewhere might not "allow the sending of that force which would defend both" reinforcing the importance of Quebec.[18] Sir George understood the difficulty of attacking Canada and rightly predicted, "All predatory or ill conceived attacks undertaken presumptuously and without sufficient means, can be resisted and repulsed."[19]

Like so many military plans, this outline for the defence of Canada was not new. In December 1807, Prevost's predecessor, Lieutenant-General Sir James Craig explained the instructions he had received for defending Canada to the lieutenant-governor of Upper Canada, Francis Gore. Craig's letter could well have served as a template for Prevost's report in 1812, as Craig wrote:

> The preservation of Quebec is the object of my first and principal consideration, and that to which all others must be subordinate. It is the only post, defective as it is in many respects, that can be considered tenable for a moment ... [it affords] the only door for future entry of that force which it might be found expedient, and which the King's Government might be then able to send for the recovery of both [Upper and Lower Canada] or either ... for if the Americans are really determined to attack these provinces ... I fear it would be in vain for us to flatter ourselves with hopes of making any effectual defence of the open country, unless powerfully assisted from home.[20]

In reality, the plan described by Craig and repeated by Prevost first appeared in 1793, when Lord Dorchester, the governor of Canada wrote to John Graves Simcoe, his subordinate in Upper Canada. Dorchester observed that "should hostilities commence, the War cannot be confined to Upper Canada, and the greatest part of the Forces may eventually be drawn from thence, whatever may be the inconvenience of that Province."[21]

There were simply too few soldiers and other resources to defend all of Canada against the Americans. The best the British could achieve, with the limited resources they had, would be to hold Quebec, await reinforcements, and regain Upper Canada at some later date.

While one school focused their ideas on retaining Quebec and Montreal, another group held that Upper Canada could be defended. John Graves Simcoe first outlined this idea in response to Dorchester's claim that Upper Canada would have to be abandoned. He believed that by improving the militia, redistributing the garrison, enhancing fortifications, developing better relations with the Native nations on the River Thames and maintaining "command of the water," the existing forces could "act with an efficacy more than adequate to their insufficient numbers."[22] It seemed a replay of the dilemmas and similar solutions faced by Governor Vaudreuil and the marquis de Montcalm a half-century earlier in their attempts to defend New France.

Although Colonel Isaac Brock eventually advocated this approach, he initially supported the views of Craig and Prevost that Quebec was the vital point of Canada.[23] However, in the fall of 1811, less than two months after assuming command of Upper Canada, and having had an opportunity to tour the province, he radically altered his perspective. Not only did he agree that Upper Canada could be defended, he developed the side of the debate by arguing that any American attack could be completely disrupted by taking to the offensive on the western frontier, a vulnerable point for the Americans. An aggressive stance by the British would divert American attention away from both Upper and Lower Canada, saving both provinces. Brock advocated the venerable Canadian way of war — the concept of forward defence, strong usage of his Native allies and the disruption of the enemy's offensive capabilities.

The records do not completely explain the basis for this bold strategy but it may be partially attributed to a study of earlier Canadian history, as well as Brock's character. Any notion of passivity or surrendering the initiative to the Americans was anathema to him.[24] He believed that if the western Natives were armed and encouraged to fight and conduct raids, and if Michilimackinac and Detroit could be taken immediately upon declaration of war, the American forces destined for Upper Canada would probably be diverted westward. If the British maintained their naval superiority on Lake Ontario and Lake Erie, the only other place left for an American attack would be the Niagara region, which he believed should be strongly reinforced.[25] Prevost agreed with Brocks proposals, but could not approve them, because his instructions from London, where there was still hope that war could be avoided in North America, did not authorize the type of bold offensive operations Brock advocated.[26]

The defence of the St. Lawrence River figured prominently in these discussions. As the only means of reinforcing and supplying Upper Canada, it would likely be a primary objective for the Americans. If the portion of the St. Lawrence that was accessible from Lake Ontario at Kingston, was fortified, it would "prevent the Subjects of the United States bordering upon the Lakes from entertaining the most distant hopes of carrying into execution their claim to pass down the River St. Lawrence."[27] Simcoe argued that by not making any preparations in Upper Canada and concentrating regular troops and resources at Montreal and Quebec, the Americans would do exactly what the British feared most and sever communications along the St. Lawrence or even send an army down the river, making the fall of Upper Canada a self-fulfilling prophecy.

Simcoe also understood the difficulties of protecting the St. Lawrence. In his correspondence with Dorchester, he emphasized that no one position "near the entrance of that River, can effectually unite all the necessary requisites for its protection."[28] Initially at least, nothing could prevent the Americans from moving down the river with a superior force. Defence of the St. Lawrence therefore lay not at its mouth, with its numerous channels, but lower down, where the channel narrows. The past, once again cast a shadow — once again, the strategy of an outer crust of defence was needed to hold the enemy at a distance while opening him up to predatory raids.

Quite simply, if a series of blockhouses armed with heavy artillery were placed successively along the St. Lawrence at the many points where its channels narrowed, the Americans could effectively be halted. Once stopped, troops and boats could fall on the enemy's rear, cutting off communication and supplies. While gunboats and rowboats harassed them, friendly troops could be concentrated before making a decisive attack with regular troops. The proposed system of blockhouses also offered the militia a useful mission. Simcoe held that establishing a base at York was critical to this plan, since its central position would allow support to be given not only to the St. Lawrence, but to the Niagara River, as well.[29]

Military matters remained paramount, and when Quebec split into Upper and Lower Canada in 1791, they were divided into four military districts. Lower Canada had two, one of which covered the line of communication from Montreal to Coteau-du-Lac on the St. Lawrence. A third district, Kingston, included the dependencies of Carleton Island and Oswegatchie and the fourth district consisted of the four westernmost outposts of Oswego, Niagara, Detroit, and Michilimackinac.[30] Following the signing of Jay's Treaty, the four western posts were transferred to the Americans, while Oswegatchie was handed over "without ceremony," on July 1, 1796.[31]

As the summer of 1812 approached, the likelihood of a successful defence of Upper Canada seemed poor. The improvements needed were clearly understood, but little was done, other than reinforcing certain posts. No new fortified posts were established and no existing posts improved between Kingston and Montreal. With few British regulars available, the initial burden to defend Canadian territory would fall upon the militia. Pre-war planning assumptions held that any enemy would be of comparable strength and skill to the British regulars. This added to the challenges the militia would face. Fortunately, for the British, the American preparations were not much better. Their strategy would prove fragmented, and their army suffered from inferior training and leadership.

Nonetheless, the reliance on the Canadian Militia, which did not amount to much, seemed tenuous. Serious reform in legislation and training practices were necessary to enhance its capabilities. However, to understand the reform it is important to examine the evolution of the militia, as well as the immediate military experience of Canadians.

Canada and the French Revolution:
A Theoretical Construct for Mobilization

On February 1, 1793, following the execution of Louis XVI by the government of the new French Republic, Great Britain declared war on France. In British North America, the French threat to Canadian security was taken seriously and several changes were made to defence organizations. Upper Canada and New Brunswick passed their first militia acts, while other colonies, such as Lower Canada and Nova Scotia, sought to improve existing acts. The provincial militias were set on wartime footing through the provision of additional funding, improvements in discipline and enhanced training for the sedentary militia. In Halifax, the militia increased parades[32] to twice a week, rather than once or twice a year.

The outbreak of war also had regular units on the move as three line regiments in Nova Scotia and a portion of the naval squadron departed for the West Indies, a deployment that seriously weakened the garrison, leaving the poorly manned 4 Regiment of Foot and three under strength companies of 65 Regiment of Foot behind. As no replacements were forthcoming, a number of provincial units were raised in Atlantic Canada to oppose any possible French attack on the east coast, while in Upper and Lower Canada, where the possibility of war with the United States loomed, other units were formed to protect the western frontier.

Each province was responsible for raising at least one permanent corps, while other elements of the militia were to be readied, as best as they could, for active service. Local defensive plans were also prepared, again placing reliance on the militia. These measures achieved some success. For instance, within several weeks, Governor Wentworth of Nova Scotia could report the ability to muster some 1,500 militiamen within two hours following a notice of a French landing and over 9,000 more, if given a few more days. In short, the militia of the Atlantic colonies was mobilized.[33]

The provincial units in Atlantic Canada were recruited for the duration of the conflict and subject for service anywhere in the province they were raised, or in "any of His Majesty's provinces in North America." This allowed detachments or entire regiments to be shifted wherever the threat was greatest. For example, detachments of the Royal Nova Scotia Regiment served in St. John's, mainly to drill recruits of the Royal Newfoundland Regiment, during 1794 and 1795, while members of the Royal Newfoundland Regiment also served in Halifax. They were even joined by one British provincial regiment, the Loyal Surrey Rangers, who served in Halifax between 1800 and 1802.[34]

During the first year of the war, the perceived threat fueled public support. This brought increased defence expenditures and a swell of willing recruits for the militia. Some 400 Acadians also came forward, causing Governor Sir John Wentworth to comment that the old wounds of the deportation may have healed for the moment. The arrival of a large French naval squadron with 2,400 troops off New York in July 1793 (which also began recruiting Americans to join them) hastened preparations, including the construction of bat-

A soldier of the Royal Canadian Volunteers, circa 1798, as depicted by Charles Stadden. One Anglo and one Franco battalion of this regiment were recruited in Lower and Upper Canada between 1795 and 1802. They served along the Canadian-American frontier during a period of increased tension with the United States, and also against potential hostilities with Spanish troops based in Louisiana.

teries and defensive works and the purchase of arms. It was the fear that the French might use the islands of Saint-Pierre and Miquelon as bases for French naval squadrons and for mounting raids that led to immediate action. These islands had already created a problem as hundreds of residents took refuge on Cape Breton Island and the Magdalen Islands to escape the effects of the Revolution.[35]

British authorities moved immediately and on May 14, 1793, succeeded in the bloodless capture of the islands using a 400-man force, drawn from the Halifax garrison and accompanied by members of the Nova Scotia Regiment. While it was believed that the French garrison numbered 30 to 45 men from the Compagnies Franches de Saint-Pierre-et-Miquelon, as well as a French frigate, the victorious British actually found 120 soldiers and 16 pieces of artillery. Fortunately, the French gave up without a fight and the British returned to Halifax on June 11, along with prisoners, captured ordnance, and 450 fishermen. A garrison of 160 men from 4 Regiment of Foot was left at Saint-Pierre to guard the newly won possessions.[36]

In 1796, a combined French-Spanish squadron of 20 vessels, carrying 1,500 regular troops appeared off the coast of Newfoundland, predicating another crisis. At St. John's the local garrison of the Royal Newfoundland Regiment, the Royal Artillery, the Royal Newfoundland Volunteers, aided by most able-bodied men, established a camp atop Signal Hill at the beginning of September. A boom was constructed across the harbour and three fire ships prepared. Tradition has it that the French commander, Admiral Joseph de Richery, decided not to land after he saw this force. After hovering in the area for several days, Richery chose instead to land at Bay Bulls, 18 miles south of St. John's, on September 4. He remained there for four days and the French troops spent most of their time looting. After taking 61 prisoners, he then sailed to Saint-Pierre and Miquelon, which were held by the British at that time, and remained near the islands for two weeks, taking on water and preparing for the voyage back to France.[37]

In the interior of the country, the militia also filled an important role. The Queen's Rangers played a deterrence role against American incursion into Upper Canada. The potential for conflict was real here as well, since territorial aspirations, mutual suspicion, and an ongoing war between the Americans and Natives could expand into a full-blown war with Britain. True to form, Lieutenant-Governor John Graves Simcoe advocated an aggressive defensive posture that relied heavily on the Queen's Rangers to defend outposts at Detroit, Niagara, York, Gloucester, Long Point, and London. He also intended to employ them in guarding the critical lines of communication along the Upper St. Lawrence River.

Simcoe feared the removal of forces from Upper Canada for service elsewhere. When added to the difficulty of bringing remaining regiments up to strength, he realized that in such a situation Upper Canadians would have to face "the peculiar horrors of Indian Warfare as well as that of the United States." Nevertheless, he remained prepared "to resist any attempt of the Armies of the United States to pass" into "His Majesty's settlement." Plans were also developed to employ gunboats to cooperate with the militia.[38]

During the early 1790s, the British garrison in Upper Canada consisted of scattered company or smaller-sized posts. Many of these companies were under strength. The militia had 16 battalions totalling 4,716 men. About 1,000 were located along the Detroit and Niagara border regions, the focal point of any future war with the United States.

To augment the regulars, the British raised two new battalions during 1794 and 1795. These were 1 and 2 Battalions of the Royal Canadian Volunteers, raised respectively in Lower and Upper Canada. Each had a complement of 750 officers and men divided into 10 companies. Problems plagued the raising of the second battalion and Simcoe regretted the "slow progress made" in its recruitment. In a terse letter to Dorchester he wrote: "the raising of the Canadian Corps has not facilitated what I consider to be so necessary a measure."[39]

An interesting precedent was also established in raising 1 Battalion, which was made up of French Canadians. This was noteworthy because, under the French Regime, "the authorities had no success in their attempts to incorporate Canadians as regular soldiers." Both battalions garrisoned forts in both provinces, and in 1796 and 1797, the second battalion was alerted when a Spanish invasion from Louisiana was feared.[40]

The Peace of Amiens in March 1802 brought a brief peace to Europe and with that the need for the various units that were raised disappeared. As a result, the Royal Canadian Volunteers, Queen's Rangers, Royal Newfoundland Regiment, Royal Nova Scotia Regiment, the King's New Brunswick Regiment, and the His Majesty's Corps of St. John's Volunteers were disbanded that year.

Confronted more with scares than actual threats, these units demonstrated the feasibility of raising provincial units led by Canadian officers. Their continual deployment as independent detachments demonstrated the flexibility and adaptability of the officers and the men. Certainly, there were many shortfalls, in some cases similar to those of the British line regiments, such as desertion, sickness, and other problems common to every regiment. The Royal Newfoundlander Regiment did experience a minor mutiny, while the Island of Saint John Volunteers encountered problems with sedition. Not all these units were equal replacements for British regular battalions and many personnel and training shortfalls occurred. Nonetheless, calling upon the residents of British North America to defend their homeland "created the firm basis for an effective and well-organized militia system complete with headquarters staff," and built upon the considerable military experience of the Loyalists. Fear of war with France or America proved a stimulus to recruitment, even for those considered reluctant to join the colours, demonstrating Canadians could serve alongside British regiments as an effective deterrent.[41]

The Defenders of Canada: The British Forces

British North America included two commands: Canadian Command and Atlantic Command with the commander-in-chief of British North America responsible for military matters in both. Canadian Command included Upper and Lower Canada while New Brunswick, Nova Scotia, Cape Breton Island and Prince Edward Island formed Atlantic Command. Newfoundland lay outside of this structure and Bermuda was added in 1811.[42]

The commander-in-chief and head of the civilian government from 1811 to 1815, was Lieutenant-General Sir George Prevost,[43] who was subordinate to the secretary of state for war and the colonies, who transmitted the wishes of the government. For routine army matters such as discipline, organization, and promotion for cavalry and infantry units,[44] Prevost's dealings lay with the Horse Guards,[45] while matters concerning the Royal Artillery and Royal Engineers were referred to the Board of Ordnance.[46]

Lord Dorchester estimated that a proper defence of Canada required 4,000 to 5,000 infantry, 700 to 800 seamen, and 10 or 12 ships of 150 tons each on the lakes.[47] At the commencement of hostilities in June 1812, Prevost had under his command 5,720 effective "serjeants," trumpeters, drummers, and rank and file. These included 420 gunners of the Royal Artillery, five battalions of British infantry, and four Canadian fencible[48] units. Two of the British battalions were scheduled to move to Europe, and a third from Canada to Nova Scotia. Of the troops in Upper Canada, a handful was at Fort St. Joseph, 120 at Fort Amherstburg opposite Detroit, 400 at Fort George, and others scattered along the Niagara River at Fort Chippawa and Fort Erie. Three companies were at York and four at Kingston. Moving east, the next garrison down river was Montreal, where 49 Regiment was stationed.[49]

As stated, the Canadian Militia could provide the only augmentation to this force, at least until matters in Europe were settled. The state of the militia was deplorable. That in Lower Canada was the most efficient with the population reflecting "some continuing interest in and support for the militia." In fact, in 1812, it had some 49,532 men able to bear arms. In Upper Canada, only 200 of a potential 8,600 men were trained. Nova Scotia had a paper force of some 10,000 militiamen, but insufficient arms and poor training reduced the effective numbers to equal those in Upper Canada. Prince Edward Island and Cape Breton were dependent on a "small and dispers'd body of unarm'd and undisciplin'd Militia," while

New Brunswick had 5,000 poorly armed and trained men. Improvement was desperately required, particularly in Upper Canada, which, in a conflict with the United States, would be an important theatre.[50]

When Upper and Lower Canada were created by the Constitutional Act of 1791, each province was left responsible "for the regulation of its militia,"[51] which resulted in some variation between the two.[52] The first Militia Act in Upper Canada was passed on March 31, 1793, and the Upper Canada Militia Department was established on July 9, 1793.[53] Universality of service was the basic principle upon which the militia was founded, and the entire white male population between 16 and 50 were expected to serve.[54] Organizational division was by county, of which there were 13 within the province. By 1794, the militia numbered 4,716 personnel with 40 percent or 1,902 of this total residing in six counties from Kingston to the inter-provincial boundary.[55] Exemptions and a general lack of interest in the militia resulted in shortfalls and the upper age limit was increased in 1794 to 60.[56] Personnel were normally paraded one day annually on the king's birthday.

By 1808, the number of British regulars in Canada had declined, while tensions with the United States increased. This led to improvements in the militia in Upper Canada as a new act consolidated the various amendments enacted between 1794 and 1808. Each county was now organized in battalions of between eight and 10 companies, each company being between 20 and 50 men.[57] If too few men came forward to form battalions, then independent companies would be raised. As the population increased, regimental boundaries were divided and additional units created. One significant change was that during war, rebellion, or an emergency, the Upper Canadian militia could serve anywhere in Canada or beyond its borders when pursuing an enemy or attacking someone preparing to invade the province. This eliminated the need to request that a militia serve beyond the provincial or international boundary and thus made its employment more responsive to defence requirements. The maximum period of continuous service was six months.[58]

Acknowledging that the training and size of the sedentary militia[59] limited its employment, Brock continued improving it and introduced several important supplementary clauses to the Militia Act that were passed on March 6, 1812. These authorized the formation of voluntary or "embodied" units, and the addition of two flank or service companies within each militia battalion, recruited to established strength, fully equipped, and paraded six times per month. Brock hoped this measure would raise 1,800 soldiers, who by having their loyalty attested, would provide "a better trained, loyal, and dependable core in each militia regiment … that could be called upon to give effective support to his [Brock's] all too few regulars."[60]

In a circular letter to all commanding officers, Brock explained the role of the flank companies was "to have in constant readiness, a force composed of loyal, brave and Respectable Young Men, so far instructed to enable the government, on any emergency, to engraft such portions of the Militia as may be necessary."[61] Individual companies would be embodied when required, and if necessary, might have their service extended two months beyond the normal six-month limit. Generally speaking, at the completion of six months service, one third of the company would be discharged, followed by a second third the next month, and last third after eight months, ensuring an experienced cadre was always at hand. Discharge depended on relief personnel coming forward.[62] The flank companies of every sedentary regiment were to be completed to the required establishment by the end of April 1812.

These changes proved successful, and the flank companies proved to be backbone of the militia during the war, with several participating in a number of engagements.

Because of the various pre-war improvements, the Upper Canadian militia had grown to 11,650 personnel by 1812.[63] Impressive as this growth was, American immigration to Upper Canada led authorities to question their loyalty as noted by Prevost's oft-quoted observation that "it might not be prudent to Arm more than 4,000."[64] While the loyalty of almost all the militia may have been in question, most of them also belonged to the least useful component, namely the sedentary militia, an organization based on universal and not voluntary service.

Support of the war was not universal, a common enough phenomenon in any conflict. Participation varied among English and French Canadians and Acadians. Some men avoided conscription, deserted, refused to fight or even joined the forces of the enemy. However, many did serve in the provincial, volunteer, and sedentary units of the militia, or supported the war effort by farming, trade, and other activities. Problems with recruitment and retention were not limited to Canadians, the Americans had them, as well, and it remains important to note that 4,000 militiamen *did* volunteer for the flank companies, embodied, incorporated, and provincial corps during the course of the war.

In July 1812, 720 militiamen belonging to 14 different flank companies from six different counties were serving at Kingston.[65] By June 1813, there were 11 embodied companies totalling 451 men from five counties serving there.[66] At any one time, approximately 400 embodied militiamen from Eastern, Johnston, and Midland Districts were in Kingston, while the less skilled sedentary militia were employed on improving fortifications.[67]

The militia's "Incorporated" units generally drew their personnel from the flank companies.[68] The incorporated militia was permanently embodied and paid by the British Army, but subject to the Militia Act. The "Provincial Corps" were regularly enlisted and attested — meaning that they were liable, by Martial Law and subject to the regulations of the British Army, to serve under any officer in His Majesty's Service.[69]

The distinctions between the incorporated militia and the provincial corps were not always clear in their names or records, sometimes making it difficult to trace their history. Suffice to say, that the incorporated and provincial units were to all intents and purposes the closest approximation to a professional Canadian force raised in Upper Canada during the war. These units were among the most effective. Whether referred to as incorporated or provincial troops, recruitment of the first three "permanent" Canadian units commenced in 1803. Another two were raised in 1812, and all five served throughout the war. The last was disbanded in 1816 and they all appeared on the Army List at one time.[70] The province of Lower Canada also raised four battalions of embodied militia in May 1812, and thus added some 2,000 to 3,000 regular troops to the British garrison throughout the war.[71]

Canadian Participation in the War

The intent of this chapter is not to provide a complete overview of Canadian operations during the War of 1812. Rather, it will focus on several specific operations to demonstrate that while "Canada" or "Canadians" had no role in the development of defensive strategy or operations during the conflict, they did make a definite contribution to the war and the protection of their homeland. The examples that will be discussed are the two battles for Ogdensburg in the Upper St. Lawrence theatre, the amphibious operations against Sackets Harbor, and the defence of Montreal in the fall of 1813.

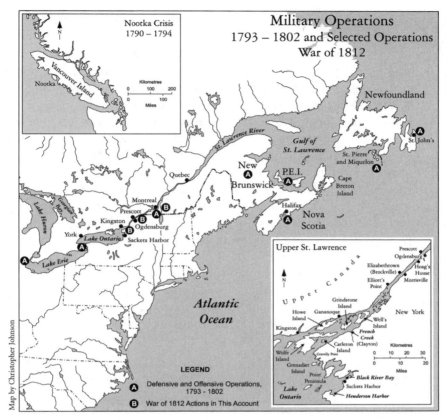

Map by Christopher Johnson

Military Operations 1793–1802 and Selected Operations, War of 1812. With focus resting on events in Europe during the French Revolution and the Napoleonic Wars, it has generally been forgotten that between 1793 and 1802, a number of defensive measures and military operations were undertaken in British North America in response to potential attacks from France or the United States. During the War of 1812, the Northern Theatre, encompassing the area around Lake Ontario and along the Upper St. Lawrence River, was the most important of the war. All these events contributed to the development of the Canadian Militia and were an important part of Canada's military development.

The St. Lawrence Theatre of Operations

British control of the Upper St. Lawrence River between Montreal and Kingston was paramount to the successful defence of Upper Canada. The only means of moving troops, seamen, stores, and the supplies necessary to Upper Canada was by water to Kingston, which was the hub from which the lifelines to other western posts radiated. The Upper St. Lawrence was unique in the annals of military history in that it represented at the same time a front, a supply line, and a flank, some 253 kilometres long.[72] Upper Canada's security, therefore, rested on keeping navigation of the St. Lawrence open, which, in a war with the United States, meant achieving naval supremacy on Lake Ontario.[73]

As such, the Upper St. Lawrence theatre was a primary objective for the Americans and as Simcoe had stated, if Upper Canada were not properly defended, this would invite the Americans to send their army down the St. Lawrence River and the fall of Upper Canada would then become a self-fulfilling prophecy. If the St. Lawrence was fortified, or at least its access from Lake Ontario at Kingston, this would "prevent the Subjects of the United States bordering upon the Lakes from entertaining the most distant hopes of carrying into execution their claim to pass down the River St. Lawrence."[74]

On the Upper St. Lawrence, the sedentary militia participated in at least seven minor and one major action between September 1812 and February 1814,[75] while the flank companies and provincial units also fought in a number of actions. While the British undertook some 13 predatory attacks (that is against communities along the frontier) along the upper river between June 1812 and February 1813, only one, the attack on Ogdensburg, New York, in February 1813, was decisive and merits discussion.

Unlike the other actions, which were more akin to raids, Ogdensburg pitted relatively larger numbers of British regulars and Canadian units against American regulars and militia. Some scale of the effort is noted in comparing the British amphibious attack against Sackets Harbor in May 1813, a major undertaking by North American standards, where approximately 700 British and Canadian personnel embarked,[76] while at Ogdensburg, 480 British regulars and Canadian militia were employed. However, there were two battles of Ogdensburg of which the first proved disastrous.

A Tale of Two Battles: The Attacks on Ogdensburg

From the outset, the British defensive strategy sought to avoid provoking the Americans to more severe action, hoping the war might still be ended diplomatically. General Prevost's instructions to Colonel Robert Lethbridge, commanding at Kingston, urged him not to "engage in active hostilities or provoke them on the part of the enemy."[77] However, finding himself with a respectable little force at Prescott, the British commander hoped to end the harassment of the bateaux convoys by conducting his own raid on Ogdensburg. Calling in the local militia, by October 3, 1812, he assembled 600 members of 1 Regiment of Glengarry Militia, 1 Regiment of Dundas Militia, and 2 Regiment of Grenville Militia.[78] Across the river, the American commander, Brigadier-General Jacob Brown watched these preparations with great interest.[79]

The next day, accompanied by two companies of Glengarry Light Infantry with 125 soldiers and the 600 militiamen, Lethbridge's force set off in 25 boats and two gunboats to attack Ogdensburg.[80] Across the river, the morning parade had just been dismissed when the boats were noticed. A brass 6-pounder and an iron 12-pounder were quickly manned and the 1,200 men of the garrison readied. Fire from the Canadian shore covered the boats, but once halfway across the river, American guns were able to put heavy fire down on the flotilla. One boat was disabled, another sunk, and several men killed and others wounded. American troops then returned musket fire. As the disabled boat turned to go back, several others followed while others were scattered. None got within a quarter of a mile of the American shore.[81] The attack had failed, Lethbridge was sent back to Montreal, and the Americans continued raiding the Canadian shore and harassing convoys.

In early February 1813, Colonel Thomas Pearson, the British commander at Prescott, was ordered to a new post at Kingston. His replacement at Prescott would be his second-in-command Major George Macdonnell of the Glengarry Light Infantry who was given the local rank of lieutenant-colonel.[82] Pearson and Macdonnell, like Lethbridge, wanted to eliminate the American garrison at Ogdensburg. An opportunity to do so came on February 21 during a stopover at Prescott by Prevost, who was en route to Kingston. Prevost immediately rejected the proposal to attack Ogdensburg, thinking it might cause the Americans to expand their raids along the frontier.[83] That evening, Macdonnell repeated his request, adding a warning that two American deserters indicated the Americans knew of Prevost's presence and his safety might be threatened. Macdonnell offered to create a diversion out on the ice the next day, allowing Prevost continue his journey.[84] Prevost agreed and departed the next morning with Pearson. Reaching Brockville, Prevost had second thoughts and felt it necessary to remind Macdonnell not to exceed his authority, writing that "unless the imbecile conduct of your enemy should offer you an opportunity for his destruction and that of his shipping, batteries and public stores,"[85] otherwise, Macdonnell might be inviting a revival of predatory warfare.[86]

At Ogdensburg, the American forces under Major Benjamin Forsyth included a company from the United States Regiment of Riflemen, a small detachment from an artillery company of Albany volunteers[87] and volunteers who operated the guns. Forsyth had arrived at Ogdensburg during the summer of 1812 with 150 soldiers from the Regiment of Riflemen, the first regular troops in the region.[88] Forsyth was an experienced officer who had served with his regiment since 1808 and his aggressive spirit inspired numerous raids that changed the conduct of the war along the St. Lawrence frontier.[89] His soldiers carried rifles[90] giving them a distinct tactical advantage over the smooth-bored musket armed British and Canadian troops.

The defences at Ogdensburg included several small works, the remnants of the old French fort and artillery pieces. In the town, there was one iron 12-pounder and one brass 6-pounder both on wheeled carriages; and an iron 12-pounder mounted on a sled in a wooden breastwork. Along the shore was a brass 9-pounder on a sled carriage and to the rear of the garrison were two iron 6-pounders. In front of the gateway, between two stone buildings belonging to the garrison, were a brass 6-pounder and an iron 6-pounder, both on sleds. A number of guns also lay frozen in the ice, having been left by gunboats at the end of the season. Below the town was an incomplete redoubt that was not yet occupied.[91] The garrison itself occupied a barracks and fort on the western edge of Ogdensburg.[92] In the town was a large warehouse belonging to David Parish, a civilian trader.

Macdonnell, who intended to disregard Prevost's orders, formed his men up on the ice at approximately 7:00 a.m. — just one hour before Prevost's reminder not to act brashly arrived from Brockville. The Americans took no action since the garrison regularly drilled on the ice. Macdonell had 480 regulars and militia who split into two columns, each supported by guns on sleighs. The right column, under Captain John Jenkins of the Glengarry Light Infantry, was to check the enemy's left and interrupt his retreat. His force included the Glengarry flank company and 70 militiamen. On the left, the main column under Macdonnell with 120 men from 8 Regiment, 40 of the Royal Newfoundland Regiment, and 200 militiamen advanced towards the town, above the stone garrison.[93] Realizing this was no parade, Forsyth drew up his men at the rear of the garrison, facing Macdonnell's approaching column.[94]

The river was about one mile wide and the ice and snow impeded the movement of both columns. As in the previous attack, once halfway across the river, the columns came under artillery fire, but on this occasion, they did not stop or turn. Returning fire with his guns, Jenkins's slow moving column then came under a prolonged crossfire[95] from two American guns, leading some of the militia to return to the Canadian side of the river.[96] Jenkins attempted to take the guns, but the heavy snow made the approach slow and difficult. His left arm smashed by a grape shot, Jenkins continued to press his men on until he fell, unable to move. Lieutenant Macaulay took over, but too few able men remained to continue the slow charge.

Macdonnell's column faced less resistance. With the Newfoundlanders and some militia leading, the column came under fire from two guns. One stopped firing and the other was captured. Three more guns quickly fell with little or no resistance. Members of 8 Regiment succeeded in turning the Americans right flank and forced them through the town. Several riflemen reached the fort. Macdonnell wanted to storm the fort, but as the men were exhausted from marching through the snow and fighting, they held their ground while two men went forward under a white flag to request the American's surrender. Hearing that Forsyth's refused "without more fighting" to capitulate,[97] Macdonnell drew his men up in two ranks in preparation for the assault but fell back following the discharge from an American gun. The Americans suffered few casualties to this point, but as the British took up fire positions, their losses increased. A detachment of 8 Regiment and a Highland company of militia under Captain Eustace stormed into the fort but to their surprise, found it empty. Forsyth saw he was outnumbered and had ordered his men to flee through another exit and make for a tavern on Black Lake eight miles away.[98]

With the enemy gone, the final reduction of the military post at Ogdensburg was now undertaken. The schooners and gunboats trapped in the frozen ice were put to flame and the military stores, 11 guns and other public property were either destroyed or taken to Prescott. Four officers and 70 men were taken prisoner.[99] British losses were not accurately recorded, but appear to have included seven killed and between 34 and 48 wounded;[100] among the latter were Macdonnell and Jenkins.[101] Prevost heard of the victory that evening and was so elated that he sent a note of congratulations to Macdonnell, despite his having "rather exceeded my orders."[102]

In his report, Forsyth stated that his position became untenable and he was forced to make "a saving retreat" of about eight or nine miles. About

20 men were killed or wounded in the attack and another 70 taken prisoner. Undeterred, he claimed that with a resupply of ammunition and provisions plus 300 reinforcements, he could not only retake Ogdensburg, but capture Prescott, as well.[103] No assistance was forthcoming, so Forsyth continued to Sackets Harbor.[104] Forsyth's superiors chose not to blame him, as no significant stores were lost.[105] Nonetheless, 800 regular and militia reinforcements were dispatched as reinforcements.[106]

However, none of these reinforcements, or any of the other troops called out, reached Ogdensburg as the Americans were convinced Sackets Harbor was the next target. Wild estimates again circulated on the forces collected at Kingston for this task.[107] As a result, nothing more happened. The British achieved lasting success by forcing the withdrawal of the primary threat to their communication and security on the Upper St. Lawrence and Ogdensburg was left without a garrison for the balance of the war. The Canadian provincial troops and militia had provided a significant reinforcement to the small number of British troops and by doing so, helped achieve a significant victory, guaranteeing British dominance of the Upper St. Lawrence for the remainder of the war.[108]

The Raid on Sackets Harbor: 1813

During the winter and spring of 1813, the Americans developed plans to sever the St. Lawrence at Kingston to isolate Upper Canada and take Montreal. If Kingston were captured, the British would be "deprived thus of the water communications, the enemy could retain no position to the westward, because neither reinforcements nor supplies could reach them."[109]

Eventually, a sequenced plan was developed to strike at "Kingston and Prescott and the destruction of the British ships," followed by an attack on York where the frigates under construction in the dockyard would be destroyed, followed by attacks on the final objectives, "the two forts in the Niagara."[110] A good campaign plan was quickly unravelled when faulty intelligence estimates concluded there were anywhere from 1,000 to 6,000–7,000 troops at Kingston, half of them regulars.[111]

In response to the intelligence, the Americans outwitted themselves as they now made Kingston "the last object instead of making it the first."[112] In reality, Kingston was not as formidably prepared as the Americans believed. In June 1813, there were 451 members of the Embodied Militia at Kingston, of which about 267 were immediately available for duty,[113] while the defences boasted only 14 mounted pieces of ordnance.[114]

The Americans commenced their revised strategy on April 27, 1813, when 15 vessels carrying 1,700 troops conducted the largest American joint operation to date by landing near York.[115] Weakly defended, York quickly fell and for several days was occupied and pillaged by the Americans. Casualties reduced the American land force to 1,000 effectives. That reality and poor weather forced them to return to Sackets Harbor before continuing with the next phase of their strategy.[116]

The next month, another major amphibious operation led to the capture of Fort George at the northern end of the Niagara Peninsula, and the British were forced to evacuate the Niagara region, retiring towards Burlington Bay. The British rushed additional troops and supplies around the Head of the Lake and collected more in Kingston.[117]

General Prevost also moved to Kingston to direct operations and in a bold decision, announced that with the American fleet absent from Sackets Harbor, he would attempt "a diversion in Colonel [John] Vincent's [commander in the Niagara] favour by embarking the principal part of the garrison ... and proceed with them to Sacket's Harbor."[118]

The British had considerable experience with amphibious operations, conducting some 68 major landings and dozens of smaller ones during the Napoleonic Wars. They were common enough in North America where a number of major attacks and raids were mounted from the sea and inland lakes. These were complex operations involving a landing force of army troops and marines, transported on naval vessels and required considerable planning, preparation, rehearsal, and coordination of land and naval forces. The most difficult landing operations were those against a major enemy naval base, which were usually fortified with strong garrisons. British success against such targets was mixed as "in practice, such operations were never as successful as hoped, and ended in recriminations, and suggestions that opportunities had been missed." Such would be the case at Sackets Harbor.[119]

Prevost's decision to attack Sackets Harbor was bold and mounted quickly. The time between conception, reconnaissance, loading, and sailing was only a few hours. There were a number of significant risks. Prevost intended to employ the bulk of the Kingston garrison. This left the city open to attack should Commodore Isaac Chauncey suddenly appear off Kingston. The Royal Navy had just taken over control of the Provincial Marine squadron at Kingston and had little time to complete crews, or gain familiarity with the vessels and conditions on the lake.

Lastly, surprise would be difficult and the Americans ashore would undoubtedly be ready for the attack. The British would therefore have to rely on the haulage capacity of the fleet and the supporting firepower the ships' guns could provide.[120] The total assault force collected numbered 800 men, most of which, some 500, were Canadians.[121]

Early on the morning of May 29, 1813, the landings commenced just west of Sackets Harbor on Horse Island. Following a brisk firefight, the assault force reached the mainland and began marching eastward to the harbour, with the intent of destroying the barracks, works, stores and a ship that was under construction. The Americans had anticipated the location of the British landings and prepared their defences accordingly. As they advanced, the British moved into the strongest point of the American position, doing so without any artillery support, because the two artillery pieces could not be unloaded from the naval vessels. The only support came from one gunboat and the schooner *Beresford*, armed with 12 of the 92 guns in the naval squadron.[122]

Despite these disadvantages, the combined Canadian/British assault force managed to reach the barracks just short of the harbour around 7:00 a.m. and cleared out one of the buildings. An American gun was captured and turned on the other barracks. The moment of decision appeared to be coming. On the American side, Chauncey's brother, seeing American militia fleeing, ordered the dockyard storehouse and the frigate under construction to be put to the torch. It was now anyone's battle.[123]

Then, General Prevost, who had gone ashore, mistook the dust columns in the distance as American reinforcements en route to the barracks, rather than militia running away, and the rising smoke as proof of success. Taking account of British losses so far and fearing that Chauncey might appear at any moment, he ordered the attackers to withdraw, despite arguments to the contrary by several of his subordinate officers. Once ordered back, the troops conducted an orderly withdrawal.[124]

In the end, Prevost may have been right as Captain Jacques Viger of the Canadian Voltigeurs later recalled: "We could hardly expect to take [the strong works] except with the help of heavy artillery." Without this critical support, it was impossible to advance farther.

Upon hearing of the raid, Commodore Chauncey broke off support to the troops ashore and attempted to intercept the British squadron. Staying briefly off Kingston, he then returned to Sackets Harbor, where he saw little consequence to the lost stores and was relieved to find the frigate safe. He chose to remain at his base until the new ship was fitted

The Provincial Corps of Light Infantry (Canadian Voltigeurs) in bivouac as portrayed by G.A. Embleton. This light infantry battalion was raised in March 1812 and saw extensive service in Upper and Lower Canada, playing a particularly distinguished role in the 1813 battles of Châteauguay and Crysler's Farm. The Voltigeurs were disbanded in 1815.

and added to his squadron, which meant that for the months of June and July 1813, the Royal Navy was allowed to roam Lake Ontario freely, one of the most significant developments in the war.[125]

On June 3, 1813, Commodore Sir James Yeo left Kingston to reinforce Vincent at Burlington Heights. Reaching Burlington Bay on June 8, reinforcements were landed and the squadron operated in conjunction with the ground forces, harassing the Americans who were now retreating to Fort George after the Battle of Stoney Creek. Thereafter, the British squadron conducted a number of raids along the southern shore of Lake Ontario.[126]

Although a tactical defeat, the attack on Sackets Harbor resulted in unexpected operational gains on Lake Ontario. By remaining at his base after the raid, Chauncey handed control of Lake Ontario to the British, allowing them to follow up their success at Stoney Creek, while Chauncey's willingness to provide the army with naval support began to wane. Prevost's decision to attack Sackets Harbor was bold, and it was the ability to quickly collect an assault force, largely of Canadians, that allowed this success. The arrival of the companies of the 104 Foot, recently arrived from Lower Canada, and a portion of the surviving garrison from York, along with the Canadian and British units in Kingston, gave Prevost a ready-made assault force, all of whom were well-trained grenadier or light troops.

Most of them saw their first combat at Sackets Harbor, and despite spending almost two days on the boats, without surprise or adequate artillery support and facing strong American resistance, they acquitted themselves well. Although they did not have any role in planning this operation, Canadians helped secure an operational success for British arms.[127]

Defending Montreal: 1813

The significance of the Battle of the Châteauguay has already been mentioned. During the final American campaign against Canada in 1813, Canadians assumed a key role in defending Montreal, the objective of a two-pronged American invasion during October and November 1813. Since Montreal lacked any permanent fortifications and many of the regulars had been sent into Upper Canada, Prevost believed the defence of the "principal commercial city in the Canadas ... depended on our being able to maintain an impenetrable line on the South Shore, extending from La Prairie to Chambly."[128]

Facing simultaneous attacks from two directions, Prevost covered the southern approaches to Montreal with two lines — a forward position along the Châteauguay River, and a second line behind it, just south of Montreal. These were known as the reserve and advanced positions. The former was commanded by Major-General Sir Roger Sheaffe, the latter by Major-General Louis de Watteville. Under the direction of de Watteville, de Salaberry took responsibility for the defences along the Châteauguay River.

Both positions included British regulars, and relied on a strong presence of sedentary and embodied militia, provincial corps, and Natives. Most of the troops in the advanced position were Canadian, including the Canadian Light Infantry, Canadian Voltigeurs, Canadian Battalion of Light Infantry and 1 and 2 Battalions of Embodied Militia, which had been brigaded since May 1813. All were generally well trained and equipped. British regular troops were largely based at Montreal, where they would be augmented by whatever aid could be provided from Upper Canada once American intentions were confirmed.[129] A brigade composed of three battalions of town militia and volunteer companies was also formed in Montreal. The southern defences included 3,000 British troops, nearly 8,000 sedentary militia, and five battalions of Select Embodied Militia, 2,400 strong.[130]

A largely Canadian force opposed the American Army under Major-General Wade Hampton when it commenced its march north from New York State. Hampton was checked at the Châteauguay, while a second American army that had proceeded down the St. Lawrence River was defeated at Crysler's Farm on November 11, 1813. With these two defeats, the largest American operation mounted in the northern theatre had failed, due not only to some bold and decisive British leadership, but also because of the presence and skill of Canadian provincial and incorporated troops supported by the militia.

Canadian Troops and the British: The Balance Changes

Canadian provincial and incorporated units proved such an important addition to the British garrison during 1812 and 1813, a time when numerically, the American regular army outnumbered the British regular troops in North America. By December 1814, following the end of the war in Europe, this balance changed because 44 artillery, cavalry, and infantry units were moved to Canada, the Maritime Provinces, or occupied American territory. At the end of 1814, there were over 48,000 British soldiers in North America with 30,728 serving in the Canadas and the Old Northwest. Contrary to the popular view, less than half of them were from Wellington's Peninsular Army.[131]

This influx of regulars meant that the role and importance of the experienced Canadian units diminished, although they still carried out operations, particularly when Prevost was instructed to destroy Sackets Harbor and the American naval establishments on Lake Erie and Champlain, and occupy Detroit and the Michigan country.[132] No further orders were issued before the cessation of hostilities in early 1815, leaving us only to wonder what the Canadians might have achieved.

The defensive requirements in different regions of British North America varied considerably during the War of 1812. The Atlantic Provinces provided a vital base of operations for expeditionary warfare against the United States and French holdings in the Caribbean. The defence of this Royal Navy base was paramount. British regulars, provincial troops from Newfoundland and Nova Scotia, and Nova

Scotian militia fulfilled that responsibility. Key to the retention of British North America was the Quebec — Montreal Corridor, which was closely guarded by troops from throughout British North America. The cockpit proved to be Upper Canada, which witnessed many of the major campaigns in the Northern Theatre and which despite pre-war concern to the contrary, proved capable of defending itself.

Connecting these three areas was the St. Lawrence, the only means of moving men and supplies to and from the interior. British control of this waterway proved vital to their success, and Canadians played important roles. They helped operate the transportation system, defend the waterway during the construction of fortifications, garrison the forts, and fight the battles.

Conclusion

In British North America, the period between 1783 and 1815 was one of continued military crisis. The War of the American Revolution was followed by the scare of the French Revolution, then the Napoleonic Wars, and finally the War of 1812. There was also the territorial expansion of the United States, which helped fuel tensions with Great Britain. To the British, the years between 1793 and 1815 were known as "The Great War," until a later conflict took that name.

This first "Great War" engulfed every continent. British North American military institutions, still in their infancy and of little real value, evolved as administration was improved, training enhanced, and units integrated into defensive plans, campaigns and other work. It was not perfect, but nonetheless, great strides were made. Examples included improvements to the sedentary militia, and the formation of the active flank companies, which culminated in the creation of five embodied corps that served with distinction throughout the war.

More often than not, the embodied corps "fought in the open," that is, in line, facing their opponent, without the aid of defensive works, demonstrating their fine training, motivation, leadership, fire discipline, and above all, resolve. Like those who followed them, Canadian soldiers demonstrated they could fight well if well led.

The idea of how Canada could be defended also changed during the war. Brock disrupted American strategy in 1812 with his quick and decisive attacks, leaving his opponents plans for a quick victory in ruin.[133] His pre-emptive strikes and use of Native allies proved to be reminiscent of

Soldier of 10 Battalion Royal Veterans, 1812, as depicted by Charles Stadden. This unit was raised in 1806 after a suggestion by Colonel Isaac Brock that such a unit could aid the small British garrison in Canada by manning posts along the frontier with the United States. It was made up of men from existing veteran battalions, discharged soldiers still fit for service, and re-enlisted personnel. Originally formed for frontier duty, the battalion served in Lower and Upper Canada and the North-West between 1812 and 1815.

an earlier era and in consonance with the Canadian way of war. So too was the use of tactical victories to achieve strategic gains.

As such, it becomes clear that certain tenets of warfare in North America, as well as the cultural and experiential disposition of its people, provided a philosophical and practical outlook on conducting war. Undeniably, from a purely Canadian standpoint, the provision of troops was not only valuable to the war effort but the Canadian soldiers made several key contributions to the war's outcome by increasing the options available to British commanders.

Furthermore, this period witnessed the revitalization, or maintenance, of a budding military professionalism that was derived from the experience of units called up during the period of crisis from 1793–1802, and the War of 1812, as well as from those individuals who served in the British Army and the Royal Navy. To a degree, this set the stage for the next 90 years, and the calling up of units, in some cases for several years, provided a useful contribution to Canadian defence. Another tradition established in the 1990s was the perpetual attempts to improve the militia, which in many ways, much as today, kept going round in circles without seemingly achieving a fundamental improvement.

The strategic environment played a crucial role in this evolution as threats first came from overseas and then from a number of powers within North America. Ultimately, the security environment was dominated by problems with a single country, the United States, which was a threat, but nowhere close to being a "power" at this time. Simcoe, whose writings demonstrate a clear understanding of the military problems of the period, offered solutions of how to overcome them. Yet no one today really acknowledges his influence in saving, and then developing Canada.

Then there were the Natives, who by 1815 lost much of their military and political influence. In trying to sum up their overall effect, one has difficulty divining their legacy. As the War of 1812 progressed, the irregular tradition of the previous two centuries, never really translated into any concrete methodology or means of conducting war, increasingly giving way to traditional European doctrine. Stephen Brumwell[134] was correct to argue that during the Seven Years' War (1754–1760 in North America), irregular warfare as employed by the Natives was an important part of North American warfare, but it did not eclipse the need for well-trained soldiers employing modern (not traditional) European tactics. The irregular troops and the Natives helped their forces get through the wilderness to face their opponents, but in the end, regular European doctrine won the battle.

Canada did not produce general officers or military theorists, however, several officers were notable tacticians and proved their tactical acumen in raising, training, and commanding units in battle and in employing the latest doctrinal concepts. Perhaps the best known of these men was Charles de Salaberry, who had served with the British 60 Regiment of Foot since 1799, raised and trained the Canadian Voltigeurs as light infantry, demonstrating that he was a leader in light infantry tactics. His conduct in the defence of the area south of Montreal during 1813 and 1814 proved him a capable field commander. In many ways, he and several other Canadian officers continued the tradition established by their predecessors in New France, such as the tactician Françoise Hertel de Routel.[135]

Military service by Canadians had to be balanced with economic matters, leading to a continual struggle between the need to secure enough men for military service and leave adequate numbers for farming. There were simply not enough to satisfy the demands of both. The dismissal of the last militia troops following the first campaign season in November 1812, demonstrated the defence of Upper Canada required "a great proportion of the male population was necessarily brought forward to aid His Majesty's troops."[136] Many men were absent from their farms during the late summer months and fall, leaving few hands for the harvest. They returned home only to find much of their produce lost and many of their families in distress.[137] A noticeable decline in the harvest occurred in areas

The sedentary militia, portrayed here by Barry Rich, circa 1813, was made up of all able-bodied men, aged 16 to 60 years, who, before the War of 1812, paraded but once a year. During the war, several units volunteered for service or were embodied briefly and were generally the least effective of the Canadian units employed.

where men were called out to repel the American invasions, thus complicating the work of the Commissariat.[138]

Similar conditions existed in the Atlantic Provinces. New Brunswickers provided over 1,300 men to 104 Foot and the New Brunswick Regiment of Fencible Infantry, straining the economy and prompted the Provincial Assembly's refusal "to accept any further disruptions to the province's labour force. Some relief came from the raising of a second provincial unit in New Brunswick, negating the need for the embodied militia, which was soon disbanded.[139]

It would be foolish to claim that Canadians won the War of 1812. That honour lay with the British regular. However, Canadians played a key role in all aspects of operations, particularly during the years preceding the abdication of Napoleon, when British reinforcements were limited. Canadians established their military prowess and fought in many conventional and amphibious battles, demonstrating they could meet all the challenges warfare in this period provided. In this, they established a tradition that would serve those who followed.

Appendix: A Canadian Provincial Unit

The record of the Glengarry Light Infantry provides a good example of the quality of the provincial units raised during the War of 1812 and the commitment made by Canadians to defend their homeland and the service they provided. The Glengarrys were to have been attired in Highland dress and recruited exclusively from Glengarry County in Upper Canada, but as war seemed inevitable, these plans were changed. The unit was raised to battalion status as a "fencible" (raised for the duration of a war or crisis) regiment of the regular British Army and designated as the Glengarry Light Infantry Fencible Regiment, or more popularly as the Glengarry Light Infantry or simply the Glengarrys. Highland dress was discarded and recruitment extended to an expanded geographic area, including Glengarry County, Montreal, and the Eastern District of Upper Canada to all of Upper and Lower Canada, Nova Scotia, and Prince Edward Island.[140]

Between 1812 and 1816, when it was disbanded, 1,400 men served in the ranks of the Glengarrys, one-third of them becoming casualties. As period casualty reports were notorious for being incomplete, it is estimated that at least 53 died from battle injuries, a further 165 wounded in action, 140 lost to disease, another 48 captured, and 17 missing in action. Of those soldiers whose origin is known (about 50 percent of the total), the majority came from Lower Canada, while the number of foreign-born personnel reflects percentages found in other British regiments, with Englishmen, Irish, and Scots and others born in the United States, Italy, Ireland, German, Poland, and at least a dozen other countries. Many of its officers and non-commissioned officers came with experience from campaigns in Europe and elsewhere.[141]

The Glengarrys participated in several major actions in the northern theatre of operations including Ogdensburg, York, Fort George, the raid on Sackets Harbor, Lundy's Lane, Fort Erie, and Cook's Mills. Individual officers and detachments also fought in other actions. The Glengarrys' most significant actions occurred during the 1814 Niagara Campaign, an intensive 125-day struggle that witnessed several major battles, a number of minor actions, and a siege that tested the fighting skill and administrative machinery of both opponents. For this campaign, the Americans fielded what were probably their best regular troops of the war. The Glengarrys fought in the line and were often employed as screening or reconnaissance troops for the British Right Division. The culminating action was the Battle of Lundy's Lane, on July 25, 1814, where 5,300 British, Canadian, and American troops, along with their Native allies, fought a desperate action that raged into the night. With 376 officers and men, the Glengarries formed a significant portion of the Light or 2 Brigade under Colonel Thomas Pearson, made up mainly of Canadian "regulars" and militia.[142] At one point they manoeuvred at a right angle to the British line and effectively harassed Brigadier-General Winfield Scott's First Brigade in the flank. When Lieutenant-General Gordon Drummond, commanding the forces in Upper Canada, ordered realignment, poor light conditions, and identification problems because of their green uniforms, resulted in the Glengarrys coming under fire from two British units, 103 and 104 Regiments — ironically, the latter regiment had also been recruited in Canada.[143]

A private in DeMeuron's Regiment, 1813, as illustrated by G.A. Embleton. This "foreign" corps was originally a Swiss regiment recruited for Dutch colonial service, entering British service in 1795. It arrived in Canada in 1813, and after taking part in several operations, it was disbanded in 1816. Some 353 members of the regiment chose to stay in Canada, many of whom were eventually recruited for service in the fledgling settlement of Red River.

American troops respected the Glengarrys' fighting skill and as one American at Lundy's Lane observed, the Glengarrys were "scattered according to the practice of irregular warfare, taking ev'ry advantage of which the open nature of the ground would admit." Their last engagement was a small action at Cook's Mills, on October 24, 1814, where they fought alongside elements of 6, 8, 82, and 100 Regiments of Foot, and managed to turn back the American advance. Shortly thereafter, General Drummond concluded the unit was worn out and ordered it into winter quarters at Kingston, and early in 1815, the war ended.[144] Later, the Glengarry Light Infantry received a unusual distinction, when it was granted the Battle Honour "Niagara" for its "unshaken firmness and gallantry" in the 1814 campaign, making it the only Canadian provincial unit to receive such an award. This not only acknowledged their skill in the Niagara, but also the superb record of the regiment or its detachments at many key actions in the northern theatre of operations.[145]

NOTES

1. Captain Andrew Gray writing to Colonel Edward Baynes, November 23, 1812, on the conduct of the Glengarry Light Infantry at the attack on French Mills, New York, November 22, 1812, RG 8 Vol. 729, 22–25, Library and Archives Canada (henceforth LAC).
2. Donald E. Graves, *Field of Glory: The Battle of Crysler's Farm, 1813* (Toronto: Robin Brass Studio, 1999), 94, 351, 354.
3. British North American included the provinces of Upper Canada, Lower Canada, New Brunswick, Nova Scotia, Cape Breton, Prince Edward Island, Newfoundland, and Bermuda.
4. René Chartrand, *Canadian Military Heritage, Vol. 2, 1755–1871* (Montreal: Art Global, 1995), 77–82.
5. Chartrand, *Canadian Military Heritage, Vol. 2*, 80–82.
6. Robin Reilly, *The British at the Gates: The New Orleans Campaign in the War of 1812* (Toronto: Robin Brass Studio, 2002), 182.
7. Reilly, 43, 44, 103, 105, 112. Jerry Keenan, *Encyclopaedia of American Indian Wars, 1492–1890* (New York: W.W. Norton and Company, 1999), 56.
8. J. Mackay Hitsman, *The Incredible War of 1812: A Military History* (Toronto: Robin Brass Studio, 2000), 22.
9. Hitsman, *Incredible War of 1812*, 3; Text of Jay Treaty at *www.yale.edu/lawweb/ avalon/diplomacy/britain/jay.htm*.
10. Robert S. Allen, *His Majesty's Indian Allies: British Indian Policy in the Defence of Canada* (Toronto: Dundurn, 1993), 58, 61, 76.
11. *Ibid.*, 121.
12. Kingston was 290 kilometres from Montreal, York (later renamed Toronto) another 257 kilometres distant, Amherstburg 688 kilometres farther and St. Joseph's Island almost 1,216 kilometres away. *Saint Lawrence River Pilot: Quebec Harbour to Kingston Harbour* (Ottawa: Canadian Hydrographic Service, 1955), ix.
13. Gerald S. Graham, *Sea Power and British North America, 1783–1820* (London: Cambridge-Harvard University Press, 1941), 93.
14. The complete document is Prevost to Liverpool, Quebec, May 18, 1812, CO 42/146, 197–202, Royal Military College (RMC).
15. *Ibid.*, 197.
16. *Ibid.*, 197, 198. In late 1813, the British would actually implement this strategy and continue to hold both forts for the remainder of the war.
17. *Ibid.*, 198, 199.
18. *Ibid.*, 200
19. *Ibid.*, 200.
20. Craig to Gore, December 6, 1807, CO 42/136, 154, RMC.
21. Dorchester to Simcoe, October 7, 1793 in E.A. Cruikshank, ed., *Documentary History of the Campaigns Upon the Niagara Frontier in 1812 to 1814*, nine volumes (Welland, 1896–1908), Vol. 2, 84. Hereafter this reference will be referred to as "DH" followed by the volume number.
22. Simcoe to Dorchester, December 2, 1793 in E.A. Cruikshank, ed., *The Correspondence of Lieut. Governor John Graves Simcoe, 1789–1793 in Six Volumes* (Toronto: Ontario Historical Society, 1923), Vol. 2, 112. Hereafter this publication will be referred to as Cruikshank, *Simcoe Papers*, followed by volume number and page.
23. Hitsman, *Incredible War of 1812*, 8, 14; A.M.J. Hyatt, *Brock and the Defence of Upper Canada in 1812*, Unpublished Master's Thesis, Carleton University, June 1961, 49.

24. Hyatt, *Brock and the Defense of Upper Canada in 1812*, 49, 50, 51; Hitsman, *Incredible War of 1812*, 41.

25. Hitsman, *Incredible War of 1812*, 41.

26. Prince Regent to Prevost, October 22, 1811, CO 42/43, 117, RMC.

27. Simcoe to Dundas, February 23, 1793, in Cruikshank, *Simcoe Papers*, Vol. 1, 158.

28. Simcoe to Dorchester, *ibid.*, in Preston p. 235–236; Simcoe to Dundas, February 23, 1794, in Cruikshank, *Simcoe Papers*, Vol. 2, 160.

29. *Ibid.*, 237; Ross Mackenzie, *The Naval Business: Point Frederick and the Provincial Marine*, unpublished manuscript in the author's possession, 59.

30. Clarke to Dundas, Quebec, May 25, 1793, in Cruikshank, *Simcoe Papers*, Vol. 1, 335.

31. Carleton Island was to have been transferred also, but its status remained unchanged for several more years. Richard A. Preston, ed., *Kingston Before the War of 1812* (Toronto: Champlain Society, 1959), lxxix, n. 57.

32. These parades were not for ceremonial purposes but to conduct training or do other work critical to local defence.

33. Captain Ernest J. Chambers, *The Canadian Militia: A History of the Origin and Development of the Force* (Montreal: L.M. Fresco, n.d.), 33, 44, 76, 77; David Facey-Crowther, *The New Brunswick Militia, 1787–1867* (Fredericton: New Brunswick Historical Society, 1990), 11.

34. David A. Webber, *Skinner's Fencibles: The Royal Newfoundland Regiment, 1795–1802*, (St. John's, NF: Newfoundland Naval and Military Museum, 1964), 17; Harry Piers, "The Fortieth Regiment, Raised at Annapolis Royal in 1717; and Five Regiments Raised Subsequently in Nova Scotia," *Collections of the Nova Scotia Historical Society*, Vol. 21, 170, 171; Captain W.B. Arrnit, RCN, *Halifax 1749–1906: Soldiers Who Served and Founded a Garrisoned a Famous City* (no data), 344.

35. Chartrand, *Canadian Military Heritage Vol. 2*, 88, 89; Facey-Crowther, *The New Brunswick Militia*, 11; David Webber, *A Thousand Young Men: The Colonial Volunteer Militia of Prince Edward Island, 1775–1874* (Charlottetown: Prince Edward Island Museum and Heritage Foundation, 1990), 28.

36. J.W. Fortescue, *A History of the British Army, Vol. 4, 1789–1801* (London: Macmillan and Company, 1906), 134; J. Mackay Hitsman, *Safeguarding Canada, 1763–1871* (Toronto: University of Toronto Press, 1968), 56; Chartrand, *Canadian Military Heritage Vol. 2*, 88. J. Mackay Hitsman, "Capture of Saint-Pierre-et-Mequelon, 1793," *Canadian Army Journal*, Vol. 13, No. 3, July 1959, 79, 80.

37. Colonel G.W.L Nicholson, *The Fighting Newfoundlander: A History of the Royal Newfoundland Regiment* (St. John's, NF: Government of Newfoundland, n.d.), 18, 19; Chartrand, *Canadian Military Heritage, Vol. 2*, 91.

38. Lieutenant-Colonel H.M. Jackson, *The Queen's Rangers in Upper Canada, 1792 and After* (Montreal: Industrial Shops for the Deaf, n.d.), 41, 41; Simcoe to Henry Dundas, December 15, 1793, Cruickshank, *Simcoe Papers*, Vol. 2, 122. Simcoe to Dorchester, March 14, 1794, *Simcoe Papers*, Vol. 2, 179; Dorchester to Simcoe, April 16, 1794, *Simcoe Papers*, Vol. 2, 206.

39. Simcoe may actually have been exaggerating due to his frustrated attempts to retain a larger garrison of troops within the province.

40. Chartrand, *Canadian Military Heritage Vol. 2*, 90. Stations of the British Army in Canada, 1794, Simcoe Vol. 2, 197, General Return of the Militia, Province of Upper Canada, 293; Simcoe to Portland, February 17, 1795, Cruikshank, *Simcoe Papers*, Vol. 3, 300; Simcoe to Dorchester, December 9, 1795, *Simcoe Papers*, Vol. 3, 156.

41. Webber, *A Thousand Young Men*, 27, 28. Facey-Crowther, *The New Brunswick Militia*, 17.

42. *Ibid.*, 28.

43. Prevost's staff included an adjutant general (responsible for the supervision of personnel, discipline, and returns), quartermaster general (operational matters, quartering, and movement) and the military secretary (conduit for all correspondence to the commander-in-chief). Other officials were responsible for barracks, medical matters and other administrative duties.

44. During this period, the land forces of Britain were divided into two separate parts. The Horse Guards was responsible for the cavalry and infantry, recruiting and training the troops and for commissioning and promoting the officers, while the Royal Artillery and Royal Engineers came under the Board of Ordnance, which functioned like a ministry of supply, providing much of the material to the army including the weapons and ammunition for the infantry and cavalry and the navy. See Stuart Sutherland. *His Majesty's Gentlemen: A Directory of British Regular Army Officers in the War of 1812* (Toronto: Iser Publications, 2000), 28–31.

45. Stuart Sutherland. *His Majesty's Gentlemen: A Directory of British Regular Army Officers in the War of 1812* (Toronto: Iser Publications, 2000), 28–31.

46. Carol M. Whitfield, *Tommy Atkins: The British Soldier in Canada, 1759–1870* (Ottawa: Parks Canada, 1981), 11.

47. Dorchester to Dundas, October 25, 1793, in Graham, *Sea Power and British North America*, 80.

48. Fencible units were raised for limited service, such as within a defined geographic region, and for a limited time, such as the duration of a war or crisis. See Charles James, *A New and Enlarged Military Dictionary* (London, 1802), entry for Fencible.

49. Monthly Returns, Canada, 1812, June 25, 1812, WO 17/1516, p. 66, LAC.

50. Luc Lépine, *Les officiers de milice du Bas-Caada, 1812–1815* (Montreal: Société Généalogique Canadienne-Française, 1996), 28; Facey-Crowther, *The New Brunswick Militia*, 19.

51. Chambers, *The Canadian Militia*, 33.

52. Joseph Bouchette, *A Topographical Description of the Province of Lower Canada with Remarks Upon Upper Canada* (London: W. Faden, 1815), 24.

53. Chambers, *The Canadian Militia*, 33; Frederick H. Armstrong, *Handbook of Upper Canadian Chronology* (Toronto: Dundurn Press, 1985), 43.

54. Chambers, *The Canadian Militia*, 35.

55. General Return of the Militia, Province of Upper Canada, June 23, 1794, Cruikshank, *Simcoe Papers*, Vol. 2, 293.

56. Chambers, *The Canadian Militia*, 35.

57. "Statutes of His Majesty's Province of Upper Canada, An Act to explain, amend and reduce to one Act of Parliament the several Laws now in being for the raising and training of the Militia, passed March 16, 1808," 6, LAC.

58. *Ibid.*, 4, 7, 8.

59. The sedentary militia included all able-bodied men between 16 and 60, who trained once a year. See William Gray, *Soldiers of the King: The Upper Canadian Militia, 1812–1815* (Toronto: Stoddart, 1995), 32.

60. Brock to Prevost, April 22, 1812, DH III, 57: Gray, *Soldiers of the King*, 85.

61. Brock to Butler, April 8, 1812, in Hitsman, *Incredible War of 1812*, 40.

62. "An Act to Amend the Militia Act, March 6, 1812," DH IV, 9, 10.

63. William Gray, *Soldiers of the King*, 33.

64. Prevost to Liverpool, May 18, 1812, CO 42/146, 199, RMC. Prevost noted in the same letter that elements of provincial units were either in the process of forming, training or moving to Upper Canada for the Marine Service and other work.

65. General Return of the Flank Companies Stationed at Kingston in the Province of Upper Canada, Kingston, July 16, 1812, RG 9 IB7 Volume 10, p. 25, LAC.

66. Weekly State of the Embodied Militia Stationed at Kingston Under Command of the Honourable Colonel Cartwright, June 5, 1813, RG 9 IB7 Vol. 10, p. 27, LAC.

67. Return of Drafted Militia from 15 Regiments in the Eastern, Johnston, and Midland Districts to do Duty at Kingston from the 10 Instant, RG 9 IB7, Vol. 10, p. 7, LAC.

68. Chambers, *The Canadian Miltia*, 41.

69. *Ibid.*, 41.

70. These units were the Royal Newfoundland Fencible Infantry, the Nova Scotia Fencible Infantry, the Canadian Fencible Infantry, the Glengarry Light Infantry Fencibles and the New Brunswick Regiment of Fencible Infantry. The last of these was the second regiment to bear that name, the first being raised in 1803 and brought into the line as 104 Regiment of Foot on September 11, 1810. Another regiment, raised in Lower Canada and paid for by the provincial government were the Voltigeurs Canadiens. Facey-Crowther, *New Brunswick Militia*, 19, 32, 33; W. Austin Squires, *The 104th Regiment of Foot (The New Brunswick Regiment), 1803–1817* (Fredericton: New Brunswick Press, 1962), 81.

71. Chartrand and Graves, *The United States Army*, 31, 32.

72. Simcoe to Dundas, February 23, 1794, E.A. Cruikshank, *Simcoe Papers*, Vol. 2, 157.

73. C.P. Stacey, "Naval Power on the Lakes, 1812–1814" in Phillip P. Mason, ed., *After Tippecanoe: Some Aspects of the War of 1812* (East Lansing, MI: Michigan State University Press, 1963), 50.

74. Simcoe to Dundas, February 23, 1793 in Cruikshank, *Simcoe Papers*, Vol. 1, 158.

75. These included Toussaint's Island, Ganonoque, Ogdensburg, Salmon River (all 1812), Brockville, Ogdensburg, Hoople's Creek, Crysler's Farm (all 1813) and Salmon River (1814). For a discussion of these actions, see John R. Grodzinski, "The Vigilant Superintendence of the Whole District: The War of 1812 on the Upper St. Lawrence," Royal Military College of Canada (RMC) War Studies MA Thesis, 2002.

76. Canadians made up two-thirds of the attack force. See Patrick A. Wilder, *The Battle of Sackets Harbor, 1813* (Baltimore: The Nautical and Aviation Publishing Company, 1994), 72.

77. E.A. Cruikshank. "Militia in the Eastern District," 76.

78. L. Homfrey Irving, *Officers of the British Forces in Canada During the War of 1812* (Langley, BC: Western Canadian Distributors, 1992), 41, 45, 49.

79. Hitsman, *Incredible War of 1812*, 108.

80. Franklin B. Hough, *A History of St. Lawrence and Franklin Counties* (New York: Regional Publishing, 1970), 625.

81. *Ibid.*, 625.

82. General Order Quebec February 8, 1813, DH V, 60.

83. Hitsman, *Incredible War of 1812*, 132.

84. Lieutenant-Colonel W.S. Buell, "Military Movements in Eastern Ontario During the War of 1812," *Ontario Historical Society, Papers and Records*, Vol. 10, 1913, 152.

85. Prevost to Macdonnell, February 22, 1813, in Philatheles [pen name for Macdonnell], "The Last War in Canada," *Journal of the United Services Institute, 1848*, 436, 437.

86. *Ibid.*, 437.

87. Hough, *History of St. Lawrence and Franklin Counties*, 625.

88. J.A. Morris, *Prescott, 1810–1967* (Prescott: Prescott Journal, 1967), 25.

89. John C. Frederickson, *Green Coats and Glory: The United States Regiment of Riflemen, 1808–1821* (Youngstown, NY: Old Fort Niagara Publications, 2000), 28; and Daniel

S. Heidler and Jeanne T. Heidler, eds. *Encyclopedia of the War of 1812* (Santa Barbara, CA: ABC-CLIO, 1997), 191.

90. The Model 1803 Rifle, due to its rifling, was far more accurate than any comparable smooth bore weapon. While the British Baker Rifle had similar characteristics, it was not used in the Canadas.

91. Hough, *A History of St. Lawrence and Franklin Counties*, 627, 628.

92. Hitsman, *Incredible War of 1812*, 132.

93. Macdonnell to Baynes, February 22, 1813, DH V, 74, 75; Hough, *A History of St. Lawrence and Franklin Counties*, 629.

94. *Ibid.*, 629.

95. Macdonnell to Baynes, February 22, 1813, DH V, 75.

96. Hough, *A History of St. Lawrence and Franklin Counties*, 629.

97. Fredricksen, *Green Coats and Glory*, 33.

98. Hough, *A History of St. Lawrence and Franklin Counties*, 630; Fredricksen, *Green Coats and Glory*, 33.

99. Macdonnell to Baynes, February 22, 1813, DH V, 74.

100. Both Hitsman and Hough agree on numbers, while the document Cruikshank presents has the lower figure. See Hitsman, *Incredible War of 1812*, 132; Hough, *A History of St. Lawrence and Franklin Counties*, 633 and Cruikshank, DH V, 76.

101. "Return of Killed and Wounded in the Action of 22 February, 1813, at Ogdensburg," DH V, 76.

102. Prevost to Macdonnell, February 22, 1813, in Philatheles, "The Last War in Canada", 438.

103. Forsyth to Macomb, February 22, 1813, DH V, 74.

104. Fredrickson, *Green Coats and Glory*, 33.

105. Macomb to Dearborn, February 23, 1813, DH V, 77.

106. Dearborn to Secretary of War, February 25, 1813, DH V, 78.

107. Hitsman, *Incredible War of 1812*, 134.

108. This was actually challenged in the fall of 1813, ending with disaster for the Americans at Crysler's Farm. Regardless, a sizable American garrison never reappeared on the frontier.

109. *Ibid.*, 136.

110. *Ibid.*, 137.

111. Chauncey to Secretary of the Navy, January 21, 1813, in William S Dudley, ed., *The Naval War of 1812: A Documentary History, Vol. 2* (Washington, DC: Naval History Centre, 1992), 418. Dearborn to Armstrong, March 9, 1813, DH V, 101, 102.

112. Armstrong to Dearborn, March 29, 1813, DH V, 140, 141.

113. Weekly State of the Embodied Militia Stationed at Kingston Under Command of the Honourable Colonel Cartwright, June 5, 1813, RG 9, 107, Vol. 10, p. 27, LAC.

114. Return of Guns and Ammunition in the Batteries and Blockhouses at the Port of Kingston, June 4, 1813, LAC, RG 8 C, Vol. 688c, 96.

115. By standards of the time, the carrying capacity of the fleet was good. While the normal large-sized British expedition numbered 10–15,000 men, the average soldiers landed was around 5,000. See Michael Duffy, "'Science and Labour.' The Naval Contribution to Operations Ashore in the Great Wars with France, 1793–1815," Captain Peter Hore, ed., *Seapower Ashore: 200 Years of Royal Navy Operations on Land* (London: Chatham Publishing, 2001), 39.

116. Robert Malcomson, *Lords of the Lake: The Naval War on Lake Ontario, 1812–1814* (Toronto: Robin Brass Studio, 1998), 110.

117. General Order Kingston, June 6, 1813, DH VI, 4, 5.

118. Prevost to Bathurst, June 1, 1813, DH VI, 3.
119. Brian Lavery, *Nelson's Navy: The Ships, Men and Organisation, 1793–1815* (London: Conway Maritime Press, 1989), 312, 313.
120. *Ibid.*, 212, 214; and Duffy, "Science and Labour," 43.
121. The assault force was comprised of the following units: Royal Artillery, two guns; Native contingent, 1 Battalion, 1 Regiment of Foot (one company), 1 Battalion, 8 Regiment of Foot (two companies), 100 Regiment of Foot (one company), 104 Regiment of Foot (four companies), the Royal Newfoundland Regiment of Fencible Infantry (one company), the Glengarry Light Infantry (one company), and the Voltigeurs Canadiens (two companies). See Donald E. Graves, *The Attack on Sackets Harbor, 29 May 1813: The British/Canadian Side*, unpublished documentary collection produced at the Directorate of History, Ottawa, Appendix: British Order of Battle.
122. John D. Morris, *Sword of the Border: Major General Jacob Jennings Brown, 1775–1828* (Kent, OH: Kent State University Press, 2000), 42, 43.
123. Baynes to Prevost, May 30, 1813, DH V, 276, 277.
124. Donald E. Graves, ed., *Merry Hearts Make Light Days: The War of 1812 Journal of Lieutenant John Le Couteur, 104 Foot* (Ottawa: Carleton University Press, 1994), Entry from May 29, 1813, 117; Wilder, *Sackett's Harbor*, 118.
125. Jacques Viger, "Diary of 1812 Battle," *Waterton Daily Times, 28 May to 4 June, 1963*, entry for May 29, 1813; Malcomson, *Lords of the Lake*, 138, 141; and Wilder, *Sackett's Harbor*, 109.
126. Malcomson, *Lords of the Lake*, 146, 147; Yeo to Croker, 29 June 1813, Dudley, *Naval War of 1812, Vol. 2*, 498.
127. Chauncey to Jones, June 24, 1813, Dudley, *Naval War of 1812, Vol. 2*, 487.
128. Victor J. Suthren, "The Battle of Châteauguay," *Canadian Historic Sites: Occasional Papers in Archaeology and History, No. 11* (Ottawa: National Historic Sites Service, 1974), 103.
129. Graves, *Field of Glory*, 82, 83.
130. *Ibid.*, 83, 84, Suthren, "The Battle of Châteauguay," 105, 106, 107. General Order Kingston, May 19, 1813, LAC, RG 8 C I C3502, Vol. 1170, 212, 213.
131. Donald E. Graves, "The Redcoats are Coming! British Troop Movements to North America in 1814," *Journal of the War of 1812*, Vol. 6, No. 3 (Summer 2001), 15, 16.
132. Bathurst to Prevost, June 3, 1814, printed in Hitsman, *Incredible War of 1812*, 289, 290.
133. At the beginning of hostilities in 1812, he quickly seized the initiative and captured Michilimackinac and Detroit. These early victories were instrumental in buoying the confidence of the outnumbered British colony. See Hitsman, *Incredible War of 1812*, 62–84.
134. For a lively discussion of this subject, see Stephen Brumwell, *Redcoats: The British Soldier and War in the Americas, 1755–1763* (London: Cambridge University Press, 2002). Chapters 6 and 7 are particularly noteworthy.
135. Lepine, *Les officers du milice*, 44. Chartrand, *Canadian Military Heritage, Vol. 2*, 91.
136. Sheaffe to Bathurst, December 31, 1812, DH IV, 338.
137. *Ibid.*, 338.
138. Steppler, "A Duty Troublesome Beyond Measure," 56.
139. Facey-Crowther, *New Brunswick Militia*, 33.
140. Winston Johnston, *The Glengarry Light Infantry, 1812–1816*, Charlottetown, Benson Publishing, 1998), 6. Charles James, *Military Dictionary* (London: T. Egerton, 1802), entries for "fencible" and "incorporated."
141. *Ibid.*, 26, 27, 33, 178, 179.

142. The Light Brigade included 115 British Regulars, 742 Canadian Regulars, and 300 Canadian Militia. See Donald E. Graves, *Where Right and Glory Lead: The Battle of Lundy's Lane, 1814* (Toronto: Robin Brass Studio, 2000), 261, 262.

143. Johnston, *Glengarry Light Infantry*, 145–149.

144. On October 24, 1814, the total strength of the Glengarries was 405 all ranks, with 253 serving with the regiment and the remainder scattered among 10 posts in Canada and several sick personnel in England. *Ibid.*, 166.

145. The 104 Foot, recruited in Canada, also received the same battle honour. *Ibid.*, 145, 167, 212; Hitsman, *Incredible War of 1812*, "Appendix 8: British and Canadian Battle Honours, Medals and Awards of the War of 1812," 312.

CHAPTER 3

A Modicum of Professionalism:
The Canadian Militia in the Nineteenth Century
by John R. Grodzinski

*If a country should maintain in time of peace, the military
establishment only which is required in time of peace, it would
keep up no military force at all. A military force is maintained in
time of peace as a preparation against a possible war, and it is an
admitted axiom that the most effective preparation against such
an emergency is to maintain in peace the skeleton of an army
which can be filled in and augmented when the occasion arrives.
A skeleton force representing a large army is far more valuable as
a precautionary measure in peace and at the same time far less
costly than a small army complete in all its parts would be. Of
such a skeleton army the General Staff and the officers form at
once the most essential and the least costly parts. Hence at the
termination of a war the reduction of expenditure is achieved
principally by the reduction of the rank and file; in a very small
degree only by the reduction of the Staff and Officers.*

— Colonel Patrick MacDougall,
Adjutant-General of the Canadian Militia, 1868

The spring and summer of 1815 were notable for the celebrations
throughout the provinces of British North America. In March of that
year, news of the negotiated end to the War of 1812 was confirmed,
while during the summer came the joyful news that allied forces under
the command of the duke of Wellington had defeated Napoleon
Bonaparte once and for all at Waterloo. At Montreal and the few other
major centres, victory parties, dinners, and balls were held.[1]

For the British and Canadian Regulars in Canada came the opportunity to ponder the return to peace, demobilization, and the civilian life,
following a quarter-century of war. Their fame was lost in the shadows
of Waterloo, "the greatest action of modern time," which likely made

them feel much like the soldiers of a future world war, the "D-Day Dodgers" of Italy, or the forgotten army of Burma. One regimental surgeon wryly wrote in his diary "thank God he [Wellington] managed to do without us."[2]

Despite hopes to the contrary, the end of the Great War of 1793–1815 did not bring a prolonged peace. Over the next ninety years, British troops found little rest as a series of minor crises and wars around the world kept them busy. This was also true in Canada, where invasion, threats of war, internal dissension, uprisings, and efforts to establish national authority not only kept the redcoats preoccupied, but the militia, as well. As British defensive strategy evolved during the century, Canada took increasing responsibility for its own defence and its militia was thrust into the forefront of complicated and difficult military operations that demanded professionalism.

The militia could hardly be called a professional force. Nonetheless, during the incremental transformation of Canada from colony to state, it transformed from a sedentary foundation to a volunteer force with a balanced all-arms structure under national authority capable of undertaking prolonged operations in Canada. Moreover, it grew to the point that it was on the cusp of raising expeditionary forces to aid the empire.

Several factors contributed to these changes, most notably the changing strategic and threat environment. British strategy underwent two dramatic changes. First, the War of 1812 demonstrated that the complexities of modern warfare allowed insufficient time to prepare defences once hostilities commenced, so huge sums were invested in Canada to build fortifications and improve communication. The second strategic element was the formation of a "Canadian" defence policy prompted by the withdrawal of British troops west of Halifax in 1871, followed by the remainder from Halifax in 1906. In negotiating the Treaty of Washington in 1871, Britain may have finally accepted the Canadian position that the United States no longer posed a threat to the colony. As such, it left the North American sphere at a time when Canada was facing a multitude of internal and external threats that required a well-trained militia that could conduct sustained operations. Along with this, came the rise of imperial defensive strategy, where Canada was now regularly prompted to send forces abroad.

Somehow, while battling the pulls and pushes of domestic and imperial defence and the ups and downs of political and fiscal apathy, the militia achieved a modicum of professionalism, achieving more spectacular successes than it did failures, culminating in the creation of several contingents for service overseas in South Africa. Despite the presence and assistance of the British Army in Canada until 1871, this important stage in the development of the Canadian Army could only be achieved once Canada was on its own.

A New Strategy for British North America

The Treaty of Ghent ended the War of 1812 without any resolution to the quarrels that caused the war. There were no significant territorial gains for either side, although the Americans gained control over territory accorded them by the Treaty of Paris (1783), and thereby ended British plans for a Native confederation in the Old Northwest. The continued tensions between Great Britain and the United States, periodically spiked by various crises, led those in authority to conclude that a third war between the two states was inevitable and that preparations for it would have to be made.

British authorities, armed with the experience and lessons of the last conflict, reflected on their North American strategy. In 1816 work on fortifications was halted, and for the next two years, various proposals were examined in light of a critical and long-standing limitation: fiscal restraint. For the British, spending in the colonies was never popular and after 25 years of war, there was great pressure to limit expenditures, especially for defence. In 1792, £4.5 million was expended for defence in North America and by 1815 this amount had grown to £58 million.[3] Montreal lacked defences, the line of communication between Upper and Lower Canada was a weakness requiring correction, and many fortifications constructed hastily during the War of 1812 were more ruins than defensive works and desperately needed improvement.[4]

Diplomacy also conflicted directly with new plans for Canada. In essence, any new military projects were seen as in conflict with efforts to improve relations with the United States,[5] particularly since contact between British North America and the United States continued to grow, and trade soared following the end of the War of 1812.[6]

Study of the problems of defending Canada began in 1815, with an examination of the problems posed by the state of the line of communications between Montreal and Kingston. Commodore William Owen's report recommending the construction of an alternate water route was followed by another prepared by the Commanding Royal Engineer in Canada, E.W. Durnford, but little resulted from their work. In 1818, the new governor general, the duke of Richmond,[7] had several proposals on communications and fortifications combined into a comprehensive broad defence plan:

> In the defence of Canada, the primary objects appear to be the preservation of Quebec, Kingston, and Montreal, the first two as being the keys to their respective Provinces, and the last, as the Depot of the Arms and Ammunition for the Militia of that part of the Country, of those Stores which must be sent to Upper Canada, and as absolutely necessary to preserve the Communication between the Provinces.[8]

Despite having a powerful ally in the duke of Wellington, Richmond's clearly formulated plan only received support for the most critical works at Kingston, Quebec, Île-aux-Noix, and for the construction of canals.

A commission headed by Sir James Carmichael-Smyth, which studied the defence problem for the entire colony, made better progress. The report of the Carmichael-Smyth Commission, published in 1825, recommended the construction of 21 different works, ranging from major fortresses at Montreal, Kingston, Niagara, and Halifax; the canalization of the Ottawa and Rideau Rivers, and other lesser defensive works at key bases or along the likely avenues of approach, with the aim of making any American penetration difficult.[9] The commissioners estimated the cost of these works at £1,646,218, a sum laughed at by Parliament. In the end, only £56,000 was authorized for the construction of the Rideau Canal, far short of the original estimate of £156,000.[10]

Despite efforts to limit spending in British North America, the sum allocated for the Rideau Canal marked the beginning of a huge investment. Not only did the ridiculously low estimates ran into cost overruns, but periods of increased tension with the United States led to Parliament authorizing the construction of additional fortifications, leaving Canada with a formidable chain of defence works.[11]

Although one would expect this investment to enhance the defensive position vis-à-vis the United States, it actually became worse, due mainly to the growing military power of the United States, particularly at the end of the American Civil War. Money and a larger British garrison were recommended by an 1862 commission, while an 1864 report written by William Drummond Jervois, concluded "an American invasion could not be successfully resisted,"[12] and the most appropriate defensive strategy would be for British troops to take refuge in the citadels and forts and await help from Europe.[13]

The British were slowly coming to understand the growing military power of the United States and their own limitations. Whereas Britain could at one time easily engage in wars in both North America and Europe, it was, in the 1860s, having considerable difficulty in collecting forces for potential operations in Europe and looked to its garrisons for help. Overseas commitments left two-thirds of the British Army stationed in foreign garrisons. This limited the government's ability to intervene in Europe. Thus, proposals were made to return all British troops in Canada home, or alternatively, empty Upper Canada of troops and concentrate them at Montreal and Quebec.

Once again the issue of protecting the key part of Canada, much like the debates of the 1790s and early 1800s, emerged,[14] but this time, Canada was called on to take a share of the defensive bill, not only with money, but also by providing soldiers.[15] However, at this time Canada was not interested in offering any money, and its militia, at best capable of being an auxiliary to the British Army, was incapable of conducting military operations on its own.

In January 1869, there were 16,185 British soldiers in Canada, representing a significant proportion of the 50,025 allotted to the colonies. The British intended to reduce their overseas garrison to 12,000 all ranks and recalled 4,000 soldiers from Canada, noting that further reductions would come.[16] European events interceded again and when the possibility of intervening on that continent arose during the Franco-Prussian War, the safety of Britain gained primacy over defence of the colonies, and the government continued to plan reductions.

When the last two British units[17] left Quebec in 1871, the defence of the Dominion passed to the officers and men of "A" Battery, School of Gunnery based at Kingston and "B" Battery, School of Gunnery at Quebec, with 143 and 166 officers and men respectively.[18] Some regulars were also detached to Toronto, St. Helen's Island, and Lévis and the volunteer militia garrisoned several sensitive frontier posts, such as at Fort Wellington at Prescott, Ontario. When the 200 British regulars marched out of that fort, only 24 Canadian volunteers replaced them.[19]

There was little elsewhere, as the government had decided that the meagre force of regulars were sufficient, and could be supplemented by the volunteer militia in times of crisis. During the 1860s, there were on average a dozen British artillery batteries in Canada, now there were only two, supported by the militia.[20] The only other body of professional soldiers was at Halifax, where 1,500 British troops protected the naval base.[21]

The same policies cost Newfoundland its garrison, as well. Although the threat from the United States was far less than that faced by central Canada, the Newfoundland government found itself, like the government of Canada, forced to become increasingly responsible, as it was unable to count on the imperial garrison to maintain social order or defend its territory.[22]

Before these reductions transpired an important event occurred that had a significant influence on the question of Canadian defence. In 1865, a deputation led by Sir John A. Macdonald, secured British approval for the completion of several outposts at British cost, as well as assurances that the imperial government "fully acknowledged ... defending every portion of the Empire with all the resources at its command." This guarantee came with a price, however, as Canada was expected to "devote all her resources both in men and money to the maintenance of her connexion with the Mother Country."[23] This agreement appealed to both governments and was viewed as a particular success in Canada as one member of the Macdonald's delegation wrote:

> We have received strong assurances that all the troops at England's disposal & the whole navy of Gt. Britain will be used for the defence of every portion of Canada in the event of war. We have got quit of the burden of five million dollars for works of defence. We have choked off the cry that we will do nothing towards defence.[24]

And thus a framework governing Canadian defence was born. The government would find however, that it would be unable to "do nothing towards defence," as security threats and domestic problems caused it to spend money on the military.

The Militia

The backbone of the defence of Canada rested with the British garrison, supported by the Canadian Militia, which, in time of war, would be called up to augment the regular troops. The term *militia* identified all Canadian land forces until 1940, when the designation *Canadian Army* was officially adopted. Before that date, *militia* referred to all elements of the military, the status of each component further identified as volunteers, administrative, active, sedentary, provisional, or simply *militia* to denote their status as permanent or regular troops and reserve or part-time soldiers. Unlike the period before 1815, the importance of Native contingents diminished as the dissolution and eventual termination of the British-Native military alliance ended the military role of Natives and their influence on doctrine.[25]

Before Confederation, each province in British North America had its own. The Militia Act of 1868 brought four separate organizations from Canada (Ontario and Quebec), Nova Scotia, and New Brunswick,[26] which were joined by the militia of Prince Edward Island, when it became a province in 1875. Furthermore, the formation of the North-West Mounted Police (NWMP) in 1873, organized on military lines, provided the government with a paramilitary presence in the Northwest and another source of officers and soldiers, particularly during the South African War.[27]

The provinces of Lower and Upper Canada played a central role in the development of the Canadian Militia. When the Militia Act of 1846 amalgamated both their militia forces, Upper Canada boasted a sedentary militia of 248 battalions with 117,000 men, while Lower Canada had 178 battalions with 118,000 men.[28] This paper army was virtually unchanged from the late 1700s and was untrained and unequipped, thus "offering little in the way of a concrete defensive force."[29] The new act did little to modernize or improve the training or organization of the militia. The impetus for change came within a few years stemming from the Crimean War, a recognition that Canada should play a greater role in its defence and, surprisingly, American influence.

The 1850s witnessed the continual depletion of the British garrison in both Canada and the Maritimes, which accelerated during the Crimean War. Whereas in 1851, British troops in both regions stood at 6,106 and 2,697 respectively, by 1855 there were only 1,887 troops left in Canada and 1,397 in the Maritimes.[30] A Canadian commission was appointed in 1855 to study the issue. It called for a continuation of the compulsory sedentary system, but advocated the creation of a new force of approximately 4,000 *uniformed* soldiers with an adequate proportion of cavalry, artillery, and infantry, and sufficient arms and equipment. In a significant departure from the past, the commission recommended that soldiers "carry out a course of prescribed training."[31]

The volunteer movement eventually displaced the sedentary militia, placing voluntary above compulsory service. In time it offered uniforms, equipment, pay, and annual training camps. The volunteer force was initially structured on that in Britain, but drew greater influence from several American states such as New York, Massachusetts, and Connecticut.[32] The volunteer movement was the foundation of the modern Canadian Militia.

Following the commission, the Militia Act of 1855 introduced professionalism into the militia and began its transformation from an auxiliary force to an instrument of national defence. It included two divisions, the "sedentary" and "active" militia. The sedentary militia had two classes, divided into several categories based on marital status. The first included "service men," who attended muster once a year and "reserve men," who were exempt from muster or service. By 1856, the muster day was abandoned, ending compulsory service and further emphasizing the volunteer basis of the Canadian Militia.

The "active" or "volunteer" militia had actually been introduced in the 1846 act, but received little official encouragement.[33] The new act gave it new life and allowed the organization of up to 16 troops of cavalry, seven field batteries, five foot companies of artillery, and 50 companies of riflemen, totalling 5,000 men (tactical grouping of these subunits into battalions, regiments, and brigades[34] would soon follow and many contemporary units owe their origin to these humble beginnings). They were allowed 20 days of training annually — at public expense — 10 of which had to be continuous.[35] Enlistment was voluntary, and the general principles of providing pay for parading, proper dress, weapons,[36] and equipment, as well as offering adequate training, proved sound inducements to recruiting and retention, then as they do now. This was reflected in the 1857 Militia Report, which stated: "as soon as an opportunity to form Volunteer Corps, and the people generally satisfied that good Arms and Accoutrements would be given to those volunteering, there was no lack of Men to wield them."[37] Within two years of the passage of the bill, the Canadian Active Militia had an effective strength of 188 officers and 3,464 men.[38]

A similar approach was taken in the Maritimes and each province created its own volunteer system while maintaining an enrolled sedentary force. In 1865, the New Brunswick Militia reported a volunteer force of 1,791 officers and men,[39] while in Nova Scotia an act similar to that in Canada was passed in 1855. The Trent Affair stimulated recruiting, and in 1862, the province boasted 2,500 members in its active militia, largely from the Halifax area, but an increase of 1,000 from the previous year.[40]

Confederation brought the end of provincial "control of its citizen soldiery" as responsibility was transferred to the new Dominion. On March 31, 1868, a new militia bill was introduced aimed at unifying the militias of Canada, New Brunswick, and Nova Scotia, creating a militia, that if mobilized, could provide upwards of 700,000 men, a number representing more soldiers than the Southern Confederacy raised during the American Civil War.[41]

Central Canadian practice dominated the new bill and lineage within the new militia, creating some dissatisfaction, as authorities in Ottawa refused to acknowledge the lineage of several Maritime units. The Halifax Volunteer Battalion is one example. Much to the surprise of the Nova Scotia militia staff and unit officers, it was allocated the number 63 on the Canadian Militia List. Having been formed on May 14, 1860, they felt the unit was "entitled to the third place in the roll of regiments of the Active Militia of Canada." Inquiries as to why this happened and how more recently formed units were placed higher on the list were met with silence and the reasons as to "how the battalion came to be called 63 Regiment has never been satisfactorily explained."[42]

The formation of the active component gave the militia a semi-professional cadre that was further improved by the establishment of the permanent force in 1870. Nonetheless, the proportion of arms was poorly balanced. In 1868, three-quarters of the militiamen belonged to the infantry, while there were only 10 field batteries, and 1,500 cavalrymen. The Militia Act did provide for engineers, "a military train, and a medical staff, as well as commissariat, hospital, and ambulance Corps," but these would only be "formed whenever the exigencies of the service may require, the same."[43] Aside from a few stretcher-bearer elements and engineer companies, none of these important corps were ever formed and until the early years of the twentieth century, the militia consisted only of cavalry, artillery, and infantry units. In the early 1900s engineer, signal, transportation, medical, ordnance, and pay services were formed, giving the militia a modern structure that could potentially conduct formation level operations for sustained periods, as it began doing in 1914.

Anglophones also dominated positions of authority during this period. The Lower Canadian Militia was first formed in 1663 and after the Conquest it continued as an important social institution, which on more than once occasion helped to save Canada. As the 1800s progressed, vestiges of the former system disappeared as it became increasingly difficult for the French bourgeois to obtain commissions and impossible to raise French units. French county names were even anglicized. As the officer corps in Lower Canada became Anglophone in composition and the soldiers in the main, French, the sensitive issue of French as a language of command was debated. Despite a significant number of Francophones serving in the militia, the creation of some 16 French-speaking militia units during the latter 1800s, efforts to increase usage of the French language, and the production of some bilingual manuals, French was barely tolerated and Francophone presence in positions of authority was virtually eliminated.[44] By 1830 so many French Canadians had turned away from the militia that French Canadian participation was virtually wiped out. Having lost control of an organization that was dear to their hearts, the resulting discontent helped fuel the fires of rebellion in 1837.[45]

As the nineteenth century progressed and improvement was made in the organization and training of the militia, an interesting phenomenon emerged that changed the basis of Canadian defence. The Canadian government had earlier accepted responsibility for defending its territory. Simply put, the militia served two primary domestic roles, that of homeland defence and that of maintaining social order. No other role was ever envisioned for it, until the British and Canadian governments entered into discussions on "Imperial defence."

After years of defending colonial territories, Britain now expected help from the colonies. Initially, Canadian officials thought this to mean the replacement of British garrisons at Halifax and Esquimalt by Canadian troops, thus, releasing them for service elsewhere. Such a possibility was proposed during the Anglo-Russian scare of 1877–1878. The difficultly lay in the possibility of a crisis arising with the United States while Britain, and its imperial garrisons, were occupied elsewhere. British planners feared that with the small Canadian permanent force dispersed between Kingston, Montreal, Halifax, and perhaps, Esquimalt, and a paltry number of British regulars left behind, Canada would be exposed to attack. The Canadian government did not consider this a possibility, as it believed the United States was no longer a threat to Canada.[46]

More significantly, although not yet apparent, was the possibility of providing Canadian troops for service abroad; but until 1898, there was no real need for such a contingency. Sir John A. MacDonald, flatly refused any suggestion that the militia aid the garrison at Halifax,[47] but eventually, this did occur, as did the creation of a unit to replace a British battalion there. For the government, maintaining a small permanent force had certain advantages, as it could only provide limited assistance to British troops in Canada and its meagre size all but eliminated the possibility that Canada could contribute troops to an overseas war. For now at least, Canadian resources would not be locked into any overseas plans.

Command and control of the militia also evolved during this period, as authority for the militia passed from British to Canadian governments. However, its professional leadership remained largely British. After considerable political haggling, a general officer commanding (GOC) of the Canadian Militia, responsible to the minister of militia and charged "with the command and discipline of the Militia,"[48] with the local rank of major-general, was appointed in 1874. British officers held this post until 1904, and each generally experienced sour relations with the minister of militia, while facing challenges to their authority from the general officer commanding at Halifax, who technically outranked his counterpart in Ottawa. Personality played an important role as noted by the rift created between the two when Colonel Robertson Ross commanding the Canadian Militia, bluntly refused to acknowledge any role of his "superior" in Halifax, Sir Hastings Doyle, with Canadian security issues in 1870.[49]

When the British proposed amalgamating the two positions, the Canadian government surprisingly took a firm stand on its responsibility for defence and rejected it outright, as the loyalty of the GOC of the Canadian Militia had to be above all else to the Canadian government and not imperial authority.[50] Thus, for the first time in its history, the Canadian government claimed responsibility for military operations, albeit through a British officer appointed by London.

Imperial Defence in Nova Scotia and Esquimalt

The continued presence of the British garrison provided the Halifax Militia with opportunities for training that were impossible elsewhere in Canada. The withdrawal of British troops from all points *west* of Halifax left that city and its harbour as an Imperial Station, and the sole British garrison in Canada until Britain assumed responsibility for Esquimalt in 1893.[51] The British would remain in both stations until "a second and more complete withdrawal from Canada" occurred in 1906.[52]

The possibility of an attack from land or sea and the nature of Halifax harbour and surrounding terrain created a complex military problem demanding coordination of both army and naval elements over a large area. These planning efforts resulted in a series of "Defence Schemes" written between 1887 and 1906. These documents, each averaging over

120 pages, demonstrate the complexity of joint military planning of the period. As with earlier defensive plans, British troops provided the bulwark of the defences, while specific tasks were assigned to the militia from the Halifax area, whose services "would on any emergency be available for the defence of their town" even if schemes to "affiliate the Militia of the town with the garrison ... had not yet been approved."[53]

For example, a 1901 plan called for 617 Canadian gunners and two militia battalions[54] to reinforce fire command posts or gun detachments at 12 locations, 284 militia infantry to augment two posts, and 651 others to join the field force. In this scheme, the Canadian contribution of 1,552 soldiers was, on paper, a significant addition to the garrison of 1,824 British troops. Like the above plan, in almost every plan published between 1890 and 1901, Canadian troops provided, at least on paper, almost half those necessary to implement the plans. The difficulty was that deficiency of numbers meant the actual numbers of militia soldiers "barely sufficed for the out-post line," and if they were employed in secondary tasks there would be "no men whatever to occupy and watch our main position." A lack of regular troops forced the British commander to rely on the militia, but their limited training, which was just 12 days a year, negated whatever augmentation to his numbers they may have brought.

In time of war, wrote one general officer, the "value of the troops will be evident," leading to appeals to Britain for another regular infantry battalion and gunners. For in 1890, despite all attempts at reform and efforts at professionalization, the Canadian Militia, many believed, did not count for much.[55] Paradoxically, somehow, Canada was able to contribute to imperial defence, while not really contributing at the same time.

Nonetheless, a curious relationship developed between the garrison and the militia. Having too few troops and faced with stony silence to his demands to attach the militia to the garrison, the general officer commanding at Halifax, Sir John Ross, decided to act. In 1888 he arranged for the regulars and militia to work together in imaginative fortress manoeuvres demanding marching, manoeuvre, and the employment of marital skill against amphibious assaults that ensured "the militia always got into the thick of action."[56] Lacking actual authority over the Halifax Militia and the ability to offer pay, the general officer commanding Halifax could only ask for volunteers, which he did: in 1888, 800 out of 900 available troops showed up for exercises.[57]

By 1890, these joint imperial-militia schemes received support from Major-General Ivor John Hebert, commanding the Canadian Militia, whose policy of integrating[58] Canadian and British units, and the combined efforts of the two British general officers, almost resulted in the Halifax Militia being placed under imperial command. Unity did not prevail between the British generals in Canada and on one occasion, the commander in Halifax sought authority over all imperial officers in Canada.[59] While events in Halifax could be labelled as imperial politicking, Britain was making serious efforts to make the Canadian Militia "something it had never been: a strong fighting force able quickly and independently to take to the field."[60]

Thus, in the twilight of the British presence in Canada, officers such as Major-General Edward Hutton, the general officer commanding the Canadian Militia, sought to reassert the militia in Canadian defence and create a "Canadian Army." Well trained, with a balance of arms and support services, it would have the potential to become a Canadian expeditionary force available for despatch overseas in the event of large imperial war.[61]

The Militia and Military Operations

Military operations varied and included responding to border threats, invasions, domestic disturbances, and outright rebellion. The first major confrontation after the War of 1812 resulted from domestic political problems rather than a direct military threat. The Patriot War or Rebellion Crisis of 1837–1841 owes its origins to a reform movement that sought greater democratization in Upper and Lower Canada, initially through peaceful means. When this proved difficult, the reformers formed secret paramilitary associations, secret societies, and political clubs, transforming their movement into an armed rebellion aimed at creating an American style republic. Tensions rose in both Lower and Upper Canada through the 1830s and in 1837, in anticipation of an armed rising, the British garrison of Montreal was placed on high readiness. Fighting broke out that fall and several sharp encounters took place between British and *Patriote* forces in Lower Canada. Moreover, a complete breakdown of order seemed possible following the British defeat at St. Denis. Volunteers were called out to restore order in Montreal, setting the largely Anglophone militia against the *Patriotes*, but the rebellion was finally crushed at Saint-Eustache.[62]

Meanwhile, the Patriot Hunters, a clandestine organization based in the United States, and composed largely by Americans, viewed this turmoil as an opportunity to invade Canada, throw off British rule there

The Battle of Saint-Eustache on December 14, 1837, was the last campaign of the 1837 Rebellion. During the battle, 1,200 British troops with 220 volunteers attacked a group of Patriotes *at Saint-Eustache northwest of Montreal. After four hours of fighting, 70* Patriotes *lay dead compared to only three British. After nightfall, a terrible sacking and pillaging of the town occurred, which was described by one British officer as being equal to, if not surpassing, that by the British Army at Badajoz in 1812.*

and create a republican state. Several comic encounters, such as the skirmish at Montgomery's Tavern,[63] ended with the Patriots dispersing after the first shots were fired. However, general panic spread and the British garrison was quadrupled, while 6,200 volunteers were called out in Lower Canada and another 3,500 in the Upper province. A similar rising the following year resulted in an even greater mobilization as 19,318 active volunteers were employed throughout the colony and another 2,800 embodied in four battalions and a cavalry company.[64] In 1838, operations were conducted along the Niagara Frontier, at Windsor and Prescott, where in November, a four-day battle was fought at "the Windmill," against Patriot insurgents from the United States.[65]

The effects of the rebellions were markedly different in each province and had a lasting effect on Anglo-Franco relations. In Upper Canada, the insurrection was relatively bloodless and led to slight recrimination, whereas in Lower Canada, where a number of bloody encounters were fought, retribution was swift as villages and farms were burned and repression traumatized the population.

Generally, the militia performed well under these circumstances, apparently eager to defend their homes against invasion. The Patriot War led to increased tension with the United States and the possibility of yet another war. There were also several incidents along the border regions, including the undeclared Aroostook War, along the New Brunswick-Maine Boundary. The Royal Navy, absent from the Great Lakes for a number of years, returned and the dockyard at Kingston once again witnessed naval activity.

But cross border forays did not flow in only one direction. During the American Civil War, a group of American southerners based in Montreal, staged a raid into Vermont during 1864, creating havoc in the small town of St. Albans. Outraged that Canada could be used as a base for raids, a number of states were mobilized and stationed along the frontier with Canada. For the first time since the 1837–38 rebellions, 2,000 Canadian volunteers were called up to form three administrative battalions based in Windsor, the Niagara, and La Prairie whose role was to protect the frontier and prevent the recurrence of events similar to the St. Albans raid. These three units were disbanded in March 1865, just two weeks prior the end of the American Civil War.[66]

The first major test of the volunteer system came in the spring of 1866, as a different external threat, again based in the United States, emerged. The American wing of the Irish Republican Brotherhood, known as the Fenian Brotherhood, originally promoting the cause of Irish independence, became militant and sought to strike the British Empire anywhere, including British North America. Armed with intelligence of the Fenian preparations from British diplomats in the United States, the British and Canadian governments called out the militia to stem the threat of a Fenian invasion. Some troops were called out in November 1864 to garrison Prescott, Niagara, Windsor, and Sarnia. Then, in March 1866, 10,000 troops, later raised to 14,000, were positioned along the border.[67]

In April, the Fenians staged a minor raid against Campobello Island in New Brunswick, and in Nova Scotia, British troops occupied various posts around the province. In addition, 700 soldiers from the Halifax garrison were sent to New Brunswick. Before they left, 600 Halifax Militia gunners were called up to strengthen the depleted garrison. Although there were no encounters, the crisis demonstrated the importance of the militia as an auxiliary to the British garrison, and dramatically illustrated "the need for the British North American colonies to unite to defend themselves effectively."[68]

Eventually, the Fenians cobbled together a campaign plan that involved a three-prong invasion of Canada. Two wings would strike Canada West (Ontario), while the main wing would move from Vermont and New York into Canada East (Quebec) with a view to capturing Montreal and Quebec City. An Irish republic in exile would be carved out of the Eastern Townships to serve as a bargaining chip that could hopefully be exchanged for Irish independence.

Fanciful as these plans might appear today, they were taken seriously at the time. Possessing some 10,000 Springfield rifles and 2.5 million rounds of ammunition, 10,000 Fenians were concentrated along the border. They were organized and had many members with considerable military experience. The existence of this formidable army-in-exile, created as one veteran noted, "a period of great peril to this rising young Nation … which might possibly have ended in the severance of Canada from British dominion."[69] Many members of the

British volunteer cavalry withdrew after a sharp engagement with Fenian forces near Freleysburg, Canada East, on April 15, 1867. The decade following Confederation was a turbulent one. The most serious threat was posed by the Fenians, who conducted a number of raids into Canada between 1866 and 1870, serving to demonstrate the inadequate training of the militia.

Library and Archives Canada C-011731

brotherhood chose not to come forward when they were called up in May 1866, but 5,000 of them were concentrated in the Buffalo area. The reduced numbers resulted in a change of plans, and the invasion of Canada West was limited to the Niagara frontier, where, it was intended to seize the area east of the Welland Canal and River, cut the canal and rail lines, disrupt an important part of the Canadian economy, while humiliating the British and Canadian governments.[70] Without any opposition in the immediate area, it would take several hours to counter the invasion, giving the Fenians an opportunity to consolidate and prepare for a set piece attack by the Canadians and British forces.

Fortunately for Canada, the Fenian plans were plagued with problems, the most important being the lack of American support. While taunting the British lion might have appealed to some in Washington the prospect of war against the British Empire did not, and American units quickly stopped the Fenians. Nonetheless, some 850 of them managed to cross the Niagara River on June 1, 1866, and after securing Fort Erie, moved farther inland. The militia staff fulfilled its role admirably, and aided by modern methods of communication and transportation such as the telegraph and railway, had 20,000 Canadians under arms within three days.

The only significant encounter occurred at Ridgeway, on June 2, 1866, when the Fenians soundly defeated an ad hoc Canadian brigade led by Lieutenant-Colonel Arthur Brooker, commanding officer of 13 Battalion from Hamilton. Clearly, several factors could be blamed for the defeat, such as poorly trained Canadian officers leading "raw troops in battle without the benefit of training, experience or staff,"[71] and the tactical mistakes of the British commander of Canada West and his subordinates. In the end, this encounter demonstrated that leadership, training, and experience were crucial and could not be made up for in the field on short notice before the first encounter.

A host of other problems plagued the militia, ranging from basic weapons handling, shortage of staff, and the lack of adequate commissariat, transport, and medical services. When the Canadian Militia was employed not as an auxiliary to British forces, as was intended, but in a primary combat role, the effect of these shortfalls was multiplied and proved disastrous.[72] As impressive as the militia mobilization appeared, the expulsion of the Fenians from Canada, into the arms of waiting American law officials on June 3, 1866, owed little to Canadian martial skill. More significant was a cool military decision by the opposing commander, who, because of Ridgeway, understood he was unable to continue with his plan, but could claim the only victory for the Irish Independence movement between 1798 and 1919.[73]

Therefore, it may not be a surprise that on the eve of the Fenian Raid of 1866, few officers were qualified for their posts. Of the 961 officers in Canada, 224 held certificates qualifying them to command a battalion, while 183 were certified for company command.

This was the first occasion where training in company and battalion drill and administration at an established training centre were mandatory prerequisites for commission and command of a battalion.[74] Given the limitations of the period, one might assume that having just less than half of the officers qualified was a significant achievement, particularly given the numbers of officers holding the battalion command qualification. However, selection for training and testing was based largely on personal preferment. Also, continual changes to the training syllabus and the gradual withdrawal of the British garrison, who provided the instructors and members of the examination boards, meant the "system of military education was neither uniform nor universal," leaving the successful candidates with a general familiarity of military duties rather than the skills to lead men into battle.[75]

Nonetheless, there was remarkable progress over the next several years and a concerted effort was made to overcome the most important shortfalls resulting from Ridgeway, namely the training of officers and men. Compounding the need for reform was the final withdrawal of the British garrison. With their departure went the nucleus of the training centres, and mixed field brigades consisting of British and Canadian units, which provided valuable training experience, became impossible. As the militia moved from being an auxiliary to the British Army to forming the first line of defence, its exposure to credible training was reduced.

This created huge problems. Volunteers were now selected to run the training camps and there were obvious limitations to their abilities to instruct drill and tactics, and examinations were held before a board of officers of mixed ability and experience. The situation was far worse for the soldiers. Their camps now became little more than "military picnics," interest declined, and attendance dwindled.[76] The militia was in a sorry state and efforts to improve it were further hampered by another consequence of the British departure — it was given increased responsibility for domestic order.

In 1868, before the departure of the British garrison, the militia, which would now be the force of last resort,[77] received the added responsibility of maintaining law and order. In short, "The Active Militia, or any

Library and Archives Canada C-2769

This painting depicts the Battle of Ridgeway on June 2, 1866, the Fenian charge that precipitated a withdrawal by the Canadian Militia, providing the only victory in the Irish independence movement between 1798 and 1919.

corps thereof, shall be liable to be called out for active service with their arms and ammunition, in aid of the civil power in any case in which a riot, disturbance of the peace or other emergency requiring such service occurs … or … is anticipated as likely to occur…."[78]

For the government, the militia was also an auxiliary police force to maintain order and counter threats to it, placing the militia in a difficult situation. To many militiamen, confronting Orangemen or strikers meant battling their neighbours or friends, demanding impartiality on their part. As Colonel W.D. Gordon of the Montreal Militia reminded his soldiers in 1903, "you are not going there to fight unions, but to protect the freedom of all citizens without any distinction whatsoever," whereas in 1906, Lieutenant-Colonel Septimus Denison had no difficulty in saying "give it to them, boys," when his unit charged a crowd after it had been read the riot act.[79]

For a government official calling out the militia was less expensive than forming a local police force. In many cases, municipalities simply refused to pay and the federal government did not bother to collect or take retaliatory action, as in any case the militia was legally bound to respond to orders.

Between 1876 and 1914, the militia was called out to the aid of the civil power 48 times.[80] Although most of these were in response to civil disturbances, strikes, natural disasters, and elections, the Red River Expedition of 1870 was a major military operation.[81] Indeed, the militia played a significant role in the establishment of government authority in the Northwest, proving its importance in the development of Canada, a importance that is often wrongly accorded to the North-West Mounted Police.

The Northwest:
The Militia Establishes Peace and Security

Lawlessness was a regular feature in the early history of the Red River settlement in the Northwest. In 1816, the first Red River Expedition[82] was dispatched there when fighting broke out between Nor'Westers and the Métis. Faced with a difficult crisis, the governor of Manitoba, Lord Selkirk, chose not to wait for Canadian troops and engaged veterans of the War of 1812. Technically not soldiers, these 100 men-at-arms were allowed to wear their uniforms, received firearms, and were promised land upon arrival at Fort Garry. Within a few months, peace was restored and the "unit" disbanded.

Problems between the Natives, white settlers, and Métis continued as the population of the Red River settlement increased. In 1835, the governor of the Hudson's Bay Company, Sir George Simpson, ordered the formation of the Red River Volunteers, a unit of 60 men to defend and police the colony. Each member agreed to "well and truly serve the same double office of Private in the Volunteer Corps and Peace Officer." As a militia unit, the Red River Volunteers lacked uniforms, probably used personal hunting weapons, and would most likely have served much use in a major crisis.[83]

In 1846, a 383-strong detachment (including women and children) of 6 Foot with an 8-pounder and three 6-pounder guns proceeded to Fort Garry by way of Hudson Bay as a show of sovereignty against American infringement on British territory. They remained in the Northwest until sent back to Britain in 1847, at which time a garrison was maintained in the form of 56 enrolled pensioners. With little equipment, training, and relatively poor health, they proved useless. In 1857 the presence of American cavalry on the southern frontier of the Red

River settlement brought 100 members of the Royal Canadian Rifles[84] there from Montreal for three years.

These continual problems resulted in attempts to form a militia from the settlers and the Métis, however, the authorities in Britain, in particular the duke of Wellington, were horrified at this prospect, as they were uncertain of the loyalty of the population and the plan went nowhere.

Unrest between the white settlers and the Métis prompted the return of a largely British contingent in 1870. In June, a field force of 87 officers, 1,048 men, 256 voyageurs, and 15 guides left Canada for the Red River Colony under the command of Colonel Garnet Wolesley.[85] Included were two corps of riflemen, each of 21 officers and 350 men, recruited from Ontario and Quebec[86] for a period of one year. When the force finally arrived at Red River that August, the Métis and their leader were gone. Wolseley and most of the British troops were withdrawn that October, but the two Canadian battalions remained behind as a garrison. In May 1871 the two battalions were reduced and reorganized as a provisional battalion with two service companies.

In 1871 a Fenian sortie into Manitoba from Minnesota ended quickly, but the raids exposed the limited effectiveness of the militia, while demonstrating a certain level of skill on the part of the Department of Militia in raising contingents. Within nine days, 200 troops were documented, examined, and equipped and arrangements for their movement were complete.

Meanwhile, the reinforced battalion was redesignated as the Provisional Battalion of Rifles, "infantry" later replacing the rifle designation. To all intents and purposes it was a regular unit. Its duties included guarding public buildings, patrolling the streets of Winnipeg by night, and showing the flag throughout the region. As terms of service expired, replacement contingents were drawn from Canada East and Canada West. In 1872 a third rotation[87] was recruited, and the process continued until 1877 when the battalion was finally disbanded.[88] The defence of the province now rested with the militia companies.

In 1870, the Manitoba Constabulary was formed under the command of Captain F. Villiers, from 2 (Quebec) Battalion of Riflemen.[89] Recruitment from the local population proved so poor, that the military authorities were asked to detach personnel from the two battalions and transfer them to the police. When their terms of service ended the following spring, many of these men exchanged their military uniforms for police ones.

The "B" Battery School of Gunnery, Royal Canadian Artillery, stationed at St. Helen's Island, Quebec, in 1873. The withdrawal of the British garrison from all points west of Halifax in 1870 and 1871 prompted the government to form the first two permanent units of the Canadian Militia, which provided a meagre replacement to the garrisons of Kingston, Quebec, and several other smaller stations.

By this time, the government realized that a more effective military organization was needed in Manitoba, so upon achieving provincial status, Manitoba became subject to the Militia Act, but no steps were taken until 1872 to establish militia units there. In October 1871 the Department of Militia established a new military district, No. 10 in the province and authorized one half-battery of field artillery, two troops of cavalry, and nine companies of infantry.[90] In his first report, Lieutenant-Colonel Osborne Smith, commanding the district wrote the efficiency of these units was increasing, but they were incapable of defending the large territory encompassing the district. The lack of physical obstacles or fortifications meant that a mobile defence was suitable, leading Smith to suggest mounted infantry as the correct arm for this role.

The Riel Rebellion provided a major test for the reformed militia and the permanent force. It was also the last major military campaign conducted by the militia in Canada, employing the latest form of British tactical doctrine. It was the first occasion when the militia "went into action under the centralized, direct control of an agent of the Canadian government."[91] The entire force was drawn from Canadian cavalry, artillery, and infantry units in the Maritimes, the Northwest, and the NWMP. The campaign demanded the establishment of long lines of communication requiring not only an organization to account for, move, and issue supplies, but to protect it, as well. The movement of the force by rail and foot gave the militia staff some taste of strategic movement and sustainment, as the field force was moved some 3,000 kilometres by rail, broken by many incomplete sections, and a 560-kilometre march by trail.[92]

From the beginning Sir John A. Macdonald felt that a Canadian presence and security for the region would best be served not by the military, but by a police force. His dream was interrupted by the reality of the instability in the Northwest. A small band of police officers could not correct Métis disaffection, Native problems, and illegal trade. Without dismissing his dream, Macdonald used the military option, but with the proviso that once it had established order, the militia would disappear and be replaced by police. History has supported the view that the Northwest was pacified by the police, and aside from the two field forces of 1870 and 1885, the story of the Provisional Force and the early militia of Manitoba has been largely forgotten.

Eventually, Canada needed a permanent solution to the security problem in the Northwest. Wary of the American example of using expensive military forces, the Canadian government at first thought that the simple presence of a constabulary would secure Canadian sovereignty and maintain good order. It quickly learned that this could only happen once peace was established. It stuck to this agenda but ensured that for the first few years of the existence of the NWMP, that quasi-permanent troops were available in Winnipeg to meet any large problems. Once order was more or less established the provisional troops were disbanded.

The Culmination of Imperial Defence: The Anglo-Boer War

While questions regarding command, control, and responsibility over Canadian soldiers employed overseas are among the first to be asked today, they appear to have been of little concern in 1899. The Anglo-Boer War of 1899–1902 brought to a conclusion the imperial defence question of the proceeding two decades. The matter had been debated without resolution and it came to a head abruptly on June 8, 1899, when the British commander-in-chief told the secretary of state for war that along with help from the Australian colonies, "Canada should furnish two battalions of foot."[93] The Canadian prime minister, Wilfrid Laurier, initially rejected the call, because he feared political problems based on French Canadian opposition to the war and lacked the conviction that Canadian help was needed. As time passed and the debate continued in Cabinet and Parliament, sentiment grew in English Canada, and in the other colonies, to send soldiers. With chaos at home, and individuals wiring the British government directly with offers of raising volunteers to fight overseas, a decision was needed. The break came as a compromise: the government offered to assist anyone anxious "to serve in the British Army now operating in South Africa," by recruiting, equipping, and transporting a maximum of 1,000 men, who would then be paid, maintained, and returned to Canada by the War Office.[94]

While Laurier held the costs borne by Canada to be minimal, he did not address any questions regarding the legal status of the contingents or jurisdiction over them in the field. For example, it was anticipated that the first contingent, which included 2nd (Special Service) Battalion, Royal Canadian Regiment of Infantry, would "be kept together as much as possible," but the employment, composition, and disposition of the unit was left entirely to the War Office and the commander-in-chief.[95]

While cost was a parliamentary issue, there was an important moral question about the use of Canadians overseas that government did not appear to consider a Canadian concern. Parliamentary authority was not requested for the raising of the contingent, suggesting Laurier may have operated on the assumption that if the monarch could call out troops for service overseas, then the government could, as well. Yet the question of protecting their citizenry against judicial abuse or arbitrary treatment does not appear to have been addressed.[96]

This problem did not likely weigh heavily on the minds of Canadian officers and soldiers, whose performance during the war was exemplary. Canadian heroism on the field was evident and acknowledged by the award of 55 honours and decorations, including four Victoria Crosses.

The Canadian contingents consisted of new recruits and members of the various elements of the militia. For instance, the recruiting for both 2 Battalion, Canadian Mounted Rifles (2 CMR), and Lord Strathcona's Horse occurred in the same region. As such, it is interesting to compare the make up of both. Like 2 CMR, the Strathconas tended to be more British, older, and more Anglican than the other contingents. British born recruits made up approximately half of each unit, while policemen, ranchers, ranch labourers, and farmers made up 75.6 percent of 2 CMR, but only 56.9 percent of the Strathconas. Rather, the Strathconas included a greater share of blacksmiths, engineers, prospectors, clerks, and hunters. Finding good men was more difficult for the Strathconas, as many had already gone to 2 CMR. Preference was given to those with military or NWMP experience, but only 44 people with police experience joined the Strathconas as compared to 127 with 2 CMR. Most surprising is that 86.3 percent of the Strathconas had no military experience, while almost half of 2 CMR did.[97]

In all, the North-West Mounted Police provided 245 of its members to the various contingents, including a sizable portion of the officers within the mounted units, in particular Strathcona's Horse, which drew nine of its officers from the force. The NWMP also played an important role in the enrollment and concentration of men in the Northwest and in the provision of mounts.[98] The war also provided a test for the Royal Military College of Canada (RMC) as 158 of its graduates, with either pre-war or wartime commissions, served in the British Army in South Africa.

Canadians were also involved in the establishment of internal social order beginning in December 1900, when 1,248 officers and men were recruited for the South African Constabulary, a permanent mounted force created in October of that year, to maintain order and public security in the Orange River Colony and the Transvaal. Originally detailed to form one of the four divisions of the South African Constabulary, the Canadians soon found themselves distributed among all the divisions.

Between 1899 and 1902, the various contingents of troops formed for service in South Africa, totalled over 8,000 men and women, costing Canada some 224 war dead, 252 injured, and $2,830,000. About 3,000 actually took part in active operations.[99]

Training in the Post-War Militia and Permanent Force

Beginning in 1906, the non-permanent militia was organized into 20 infantry brigades and seven mounted or cavalry brigades.[100] In April 1911, to meet the needs of mobilization plans, the four commands in Ontario, Quebec, and the Maritimes were reconstituted as six divisional areas, providing six infantry divisions and four cavalry brigades.[101] If mobilization proved necessary, these units would provide elements to an expeditionary division and a mounted brigade.

The divisional areas maintained the responsibilities of the previously established Commands while the brigades and units within them were regrouped to reflect the new structure. Each division[102] had three infantry brigades, each of three or four regiments,[103] and divisional troops. Cavalry brigades included three cavalry regiments, a horse battery, ammunition column, a troop of engineers, wireless telegraphic detachment, company army service corps and a cavalry field ambulance. Due to funding, personnel or equipment shortages, some headquarters and units within each division and cavalry brigade were not organized.

Annual training was conducted for a period of about two weeks at camps of instruction, in locations such as Goderich, Niagara Camp, and Kingston in Ontario; La Prairie, Three Rivers (Trois-Rivières), and Lévis in Quebec; and Sussex, Aldershot or Charlottetown in Nova Scotia and Prince Edward Island. Each camp included a commandant, staff, and a number of brigade staffs and units for training. Training included a course of instruction and provided "sufficient drill and manoeuvre to enable troops to cooperate and act together in the field"[104] — this was unit level training and formation level, collective training as we know today never occurred. Cavalry and artillery training was handicapped by the size of the training camps, while the quality of training was generally reported to be unsatisfactory.

Training in the tiny Permanent Force was not much better and only three concentrations occurred between 1894 and 1914. The first two were the concentration of a single unit, while the final one included most of the permanent force. Permanent Force regiments and corps had sub-units scattered across the country, and in 1894 included the Royal Canadian Dragoons, the Royal Regiment of Canadian Artillery, and the Royal Canadian Regiment of Infantry, totalling 904 all ranks. The Royal Canadian Regiment accounted for 395 of these personnel.[105] In 1901 the Royal Canadian Mounted Rifles were formed in Winnipeg (in 1909 they became Strathcona's Horse) and in the early 1900s a number of support corps were formed. By March 31, 1910, the Permanent Force had grown to 206 officers and 2,591 men, with the Royal Canadian Regiment now having 944 personnel, more than the entire permanent force in 1894.[106]

The first concentration came in 1894 when the dispersed companies of the Royal Canadian Regiment of Infantry were brought together,[107] followed by another concentration beginning on July 14, 1899, when the four companies of the Royal Canadian Regiment were again concentrated, this time at Rockcliffe, near Ottawa, to conduct battalion level training.[108] The battalion commanding officer was Lieutenant-Colonel W.D. Otter and the syllabus included battalion attack and defence of defiles, wood, and bridges; actions against cavalry and artillery; escorts to guns and convoys; musketry and drills, and included the first night exercise conducted in Canada. While calling the exercise as an unqualified success, the final report noted the "want of care in methodically arranging for and carrying out the formation of the columns for assault by the whole brigade before moving to the assault" was wrong and that the guiding principle for night attacks should be a clearly defined and carefully marked alignment.[109] Training continued until the end of August.[110]

In June and July 1907 practically the whole of the Permanent Force was assembled at the recently opened camp at Petawawa. Included were both squadrons of the Royal Canadian Dragoons; "A" and "B" Batteries, Royal Canadian Horse Artillery, a heavy battery, Royal Canadian Garrison Artillery; No. 2 Company, Royal Canadian Engineers; eight companies of the Royal Canadian Regiment, and detachments of the Permanent Army Medical Corps, Permanent Army Service Corps and Canadian Ordnance Corps. Due to their distance from Petawawa, the Royal Canadian Mounted Rifles in Winnipeg did not attend.

The first object of the exercise was to allow units to complete their annual squadron, battery or company training on ground suitable for up to date training, something that was impossible at their own stations. For example, this was the first occasion that two batteries of horse artillery were able to function in an artillery brigade organization. This was followed with combined training and field operations that had previously been impossible. Other activity included reconnaissance and scouting by cavalry and infantry, convoys and marches (including marches by units from their garrison location to Petawawa), fire-discipline, and field operations of all arms in combination, and field firing operations with all arms.[111] The commandant appointed for the exercise was Brigadier-General W.D. Otter, with Lieutenant-Colonel W.G. Gwatkin, a British officer serving in Canada, as chief staff officer.

Collective training was considered essential, and it was anticipated these exercises would become an annual event, although it was expected that Winnipeg based units would never be able to train with other permanent units.[112] Plans were developed for the Permanent Force to undergo yearly progressive training beginning in September, culminating with combined training in a central camp in August.[113] Unfortunately, planned celebrations for the tercentenary of the founding of Quebec in 1908, and funding limitations precluded any collective training, while other reasons made this impossible until 1914.

Conclusion

Between the celebrations marking the end of the War of 1812 and the Anglo-Boer War, the Canadian Militia underwent a revolutionary transformation from a sedentary, mandatory service organization that was virtually untrained, to an all arms volunteer force capable of operations anywhere in Canada and on the verge of contributing an expeditionary force in support of imperial objectives.

What does this period demonstrate about the Canadian military experience? First and contrary to conventional wisdom, the militia played a significant role in national development. For most of the nineteenth century, the militia was concerned with providing demonstrations of force along the frontiers, repelling invasions or dealing with rebellions and threats to the national fabric of Canada. This resulted partly from the possibility of war between Britain and the United States, but more from the threat posed by the irregular forces (such as the Fenians) based in the United States, similar to some of the "homeland" security threats North America faces today.

Although the British Army and Royal Navy ensured the continued existence of Canada between 1759 and 1870, the militia assumed this role with meagre preparations when they were unavailable. While its performance was sometimes poor, such as when it opposed the Fenians in 1866, the militia could have moments of success such as when it established security in Manitoba, thus allowing the North-West Mounted Police to start its work. The militia also showed that was a reliable force of last resort during the North-West Rebellion, particularly as the NWMP was unable to deal with the crisis.

In addition, the defensive plans after 1815 were premised on the lessons of the War of 1812. As such, huge sums of money went into the constructions of citadels, forts, blockhouses, and waterway communications. The British Army and the Royal Navy provided the front line of defence, and like earlier wars on the continent, the Canadian Militia afforded an auxiliary service. Surprisingly, British plans did not include the creation of any sedentary or embodied militia as they had during the last war against the United States. Instead, a series of progressive reforms, through legislative acts, provision of training opportunities alongside British regulars, and the dogged efforts of a number of British and Canadian officers, slowly enhanced both the fighting capability and structure of the militia.

Initially, the presence of a large garrison allowed the establishment of schools and camps to improve the efficiency of the militia allowing it

French's Scouts at Fish Creek, Saskatchewan, during the North-West Rebellion in 1885. This unit was one of several small special ones raised in western Canada under Captain John French, an ex-North-West Mounted Police officer who provided scouts for one of the three columns organized for the North-West Field Force.

the potential to become a more credible force. The end of that threat, defined by the rapid growth of economic and military power of the United States, increased British focus on Europe, and other factors, quickly drove the need for Confederation and Canada becoming de facto responsible for its defence in 1906. Like the Canadian Army at the end of the Cold War, suddenly facing a fundamental questioning of the principles that had governed it for over half a century, the Canadian Militia, now alone, had to learn how to train itself and modernize itself to meet the changing demands of war and the growing overseas commitments of the Canadian government. Canada then faced increasing pressure to commit an expeditionary force for imperial defence during times of emergency as almost happened during the 1880s and 1890s, and which transpired by end of the century during the Boer War.

As the role of the militia evolved, so did its organization, training and capabilities. Obligatory service gave way to the volunteer movement, which combined with the advent of new technology and innovation, created demands for more and more training, which were often unsatisfied. Structure also changed and greater effort went into improving combat capabilities and providing the necessary services to support the army in the field. The culmination of this evolution was the formation of infantry and cavalry brigades, and later a divisional structure that included all the basic elements, though not the equipment, of a modern division.

For political reasons, none of the structure that existed at the end of the nineteenth century was used during the Boer War. Rather than rely on existing units, new ones were raised as part of a special force for the duration of the conflict. This approach would often resurface through two world wars and in mobilization planning until the end of the Cold War. Staff training was also undertaken, beginning in 1903, and after several interruptions, exposed 124 officers to the theoretical aspects of modern warfare between 1908 and 1914.

One must be careful, however, to assess these advancements with care as there were still significant limitations and shortfalls. First, the annual camps varied considerably in the quality of the training, and the exercises, or "schemes" as they were known, organized as a series of "sham battles" for the pleasure of audiences and to boost the morale of the soldiers. Recruiting and retention difficulties often resulted in units being under-strength and rarely exercised above company level. If the small permanent force was rarely allowed opportunity to perfect its own skills, then it was never suitably prepared for its primary role of training the non-permanent militia. Any proficiency gained during military operations or exercises was quickly dissipated as several years might pass before a similar opportunity arose. Nonetheless, a number of innovative exercises were conducted, based upon the lessons of the most recent conflicts and employing new weapons systems, such as aircraft, to drill soldiers on concealment and evasive action. Fiscal limitations did not lessen the imagination of militiamen.

During the 1890s and early 1900s, British officers in Canada attempted to increase the professionalism and structure of what they saw as a Canadian imperial army. However, what was really needed was an end to the political interference and imperial sentiment. This could only be accomplished if an assertive, professional Canadian officer came forward, demanding Canadian control of the militia. For the Canadian Militia to become an army, Canada had to control it. The creation of the Militia Council and a Canadian position of chief of the General Staff in 1904 sought to do just that and the presence of strong characters, such as Sam Hughes, helped make this a reality. Nonetheless, aside from General William Otter's brief stint at chief of the General Staff, British officers continued to occupy that post until 1920.

The militia staff both in Ottawa and in the districts proved adroit at calling up, concentrating, moving, and generally supporting units in the field. This was done repeatedly, and never perfectly, but the ability of these small groups of staff officers to translate, implement, and execute government policy was incredible.

The nineteenth century was noteworthy for the contrasting successes and failures of the Canadian Militia. Military operations, whether they be conducted against an invading army or in support of the government authority cannot rely on amateurism or wishful thinking. Every operation of the nineteenth century demonstrates that individual and collective training, planning, and leadership were necessary ingredients for success, or factors in mitigating other serious problems. Crises can erupt quickly and often there was little time to make up these shortfalls before battle calls. In the end, not only a government, but a nation "that structures its defences to achieve social and political, not military, ends should not be surprised when its forces fail the test of war."[114] Despite all the hurdles, the Canadian Militia demonstrated a modicum of professionalism and proved essential to the development of Canada in the nineteenth century.

NOTES

1. At a masquerade ball and dinner held in Montreal in March 1814, the marquis of Tweeddale hosted 700 people, most of whom paraded through the streets of the city when the party broke up at dawn. See Donald E. Graves, ed., *Merry Hearts Make Light Days: The War of 1812 Journal of Lieutenant John Le Couteur, 104 Foot* (Ottawa: Carleton University Press, 1994), 228.

2. Dr. Dunlop, *Recollections of the American War* (Toronto: Historical Publishing, 1905), 101.

3. Gerald S. Graham, *Sea Power and British North America, 1783–1820* (Cambridge, MA: Harvard University Press, 1941), 14.

4. André Charbonneau, *The Fortifications of Île aux Noix* (Ottawa: Parks Canada, 1994), 56.

5. Greenough, *The Halifax Citadel*, 14.

6. Graham, *Sea Power and British North America, 1783–1820*, 221.

7. The duke's wife was famous for the parties she hosted, most particularly that held in Brussels on the eve of the Waterloo campaign.

8. Richmond to Bathurst, November 10, 1818, Public Record Office (henceforth PRO), Colonial Office (CO), 42/179, 119–123.

9. Greenough, *The Halifax Citadel*, 16, 17.

10. *Ibid.*, 17.

11. Chartrand, *Canadian Military Heritage, Vol. 2, 1755–1871* (Montreal: Art Global, 1995), 140.

12. Desmond Morton, *Ministers and Generals: Politics and the Canadian Militia, 1868–1904* (Toronto: University of Toronto Press, 1970), 4.

13. Yvon Desloges, *The Forts at Point Levy* (Ottawa: Parks Canada, 1991), 17–18.

14. J. Mackay Hitsman, *Safeguarding Canada, 1763–1871* (Toronto: University of Toronto Press, 1968), 185–187. See also Chapters 1 and 2 of this volume.

15. C.P. Stacey, "Britain's Withdrawal from North America, 1864–1871," *Canadian Historical Review*, Vol. 36, No. 3, 1955, 186.

16. Cardwell to Granville, January 25, 1869, in "Returns of the Addresses of the Senate and House of Commons relative to the Withdrawal of the Troops From the Dominion," Ottawa, 1871, 4.

17. These units were 5 Battery, 3 Brigade, Royal Artillery and 60 Rifles.

18. The numbers are based on the total number of officers and men in the authorized establishment of 1879. The figures for 1871 may have been slightly different. See *Regulations and Orders for the Militia, Canada, 1879* (Ottawa, 1879), 216.

19. Stacey, "The Garrison at Fort Wellington: A Military Dispute During the Fenian Troubles," *Canadian Historical Review*, Vol. 35, No. 2, 1933, 173.

20. Christian Rioux, *The Royal Regiment of Artillery in Quebec City, 1759–1871* (Ottawa: Parks Canada, 1982), 38.

21. *Ibid.*, 198. Generally from 1871 to 1906, the British garrison at Halifax included two infantry battalions (reduced in the 1880s to one), six or more batteries of artillery and a company of Royal Engineers that were later joined by a company of submarine mining detachment, RE. There were also elements of other corps that supported these units. See PRO, War Office (WO) 73/17, Returns for Halifax, 1871–1906.

22. C.P. Stacey, "The Withdrawal of the Imperial Garrison from Newfoundland, 1870," *Canadian Historical Review*, Vol. 17, No. 2, 1936, 149, 158.

23. Morton, *Ministers and Generals*, 4–5.

24. *Ibid.*, 5.

25. For a discussion of the termination of this alliance, see Chapter 8 of Robert S. Allen, *His Majesty's Indian Allies: British Defence Policy in the Defence of Canada, 1774–1814* (Toronto: Dundurn, 1992).

26. See "Statutes of the Province of Canada and the Dominion of Canada, an Act Respecting the Militia and Defence of the Dominion of Canada, 31 Vict. Cap, 40, Assented 22 May 1868."

27. S.W. Horrall, *The Pictorial History of the Royal Canadian Mounted Police* (Toronto: McGraw-Hill Ryerson, 1973), 21.

28. Captain Ernest J. Chambers, *The Canadian Militia: A History of the Origin and Development of the Force* (Montreal: L.M. Fresco, n.d.), 61, 63.

29. Owen Arnold Cooke, "Organization and Training in the Central Canadian Militia, 1866–1885," MA Thesis Queen's University, 1974, 9.

30. George F. G. Stanley, *Canada's Soldiers, 1604–1954: The Military History of an Unmilitary People* (Toronto: Macmillan, 1954), 211.

31. *Ibid.*, 212.

32. "Report on the State of the Militia of this Province, Ottawa, 1857," 7.

33. Cooke, "Organization and Training," 10.

34. In this instance, "brigade" denotes an organizational structure incorporating a number of artillery batteries and not a formation of several battalion-sized elements.

35. See, "An Act to Regulate the Militia of This Province, (18 Victoria, Chapter 77), 1855."

36. Each rifle company received the same allocation of ammunition as a regular British battalion, plus another 10 rounds per rifle held by the company commander for use when called out in aid of the Civil Power. See "Report of the State of the Militia of the Province, 1857," 26n.

37. "Report of the State of the Militia, 1857," 5.

38. *Ibid.*, 25–26.

39. "Report of the Militia of New Brunswick for the Year Ending 31st October, 1865," 3.
40. Joseph Plimsoll Edwards, *The Militia of Nova Scotia, 1749–1867*, n.d., 36–37.
41. Morton, *Ministers and Generals*, 7.
42. Major Thomas J. Egan, *History of the Halifax Volunteer Battalion and Their Companies, 1859–1887* (Halifax: A. & W. MacKinlay Publishers, 1888), 33.
43. "Statutes of the Province of Canada and the Dominion of Canada, An Act respecting the Militia and Defence of the Dominion of Canada, 31 Vict. CAP. 40," 427. The act also included provision for naval and marine militia, which again were not formed until much later.
44. Jean Pariseau and Serge Bernier, *French Canadians and Bilingualism in the Canadian Armed Forces, Volume I: 1769–1969: The Fear of a Parallel Army* (Ottawa: Directorate of History and Heritage, 1986), 39–53.
45. Chartrand, *Canadian Military Heritage, Vol. 2*, 142–144. Surprisingly these events are not discussed in any detail in Pariseau and Bernier, *French Canadians and Bilingualism in the Canadian Armed Forces, Volume I*. See previous note.
46. Roger Sarty, "Local Boys and Redcoats: The Relations of the Militia in Nova Scotia and the British Garrison at Halifax, 1860–1906," Master's of Arts Thesis, 1976, 48–49.
47. Cooke, "Organization and Training," 66.
48. "Regulations and Orders, 1879," 2.
49. Morton, *Ministers and Generals*, 50–51.
50. *Ibid.*, 51.
51. *Ibid.*, 101.
52. The final withdrawal of the British Army from Canada was directly linked to the withdrawal of the Royal Navy from Halifax and Esquimalt. Established as a naval base in 1749, Halifax proved an excellent base for mounting and supporting several amphibious operations in several wars. Its importance varied over time and in 1819 the North America and West Indies Squadron was moved permanently to Bermuda, but Halifax continued as its summer station. In 1904, the squadron was eliminated as part of the consolidation of British forces against the growing threat from Europe, eliminating the reason for the army garrison. The naval station at Halifax was finally transferred to the Canadian government in 1907, and three years later the Royal Canadian Navy was formed. Thus impetus to establish both a regular army and the navy came from the withdrawal of British forces.
53. "Halifax: Amended Defence Scheme, March 1890," PRO, Cabinet Records (CAB), 11/28 Part 3, 2.
54. These units were 1 and 2 Divisions of 1 Halifax Artillery and 63 and 66 Battalions, Canadian Militia.
55. "Halifax, Amended Defence Scheme, 1890" 3. "Halifax. Defence Scheme, Revised to January 1901, May 1901," PRO, CAB 11/28, Part 3, 14.
56. Sarty, "Local Boys and Redcoats," 54–55.
57. *Ibid.*, 51, 56, 57.
58. This campaign included successfully convincing the minister of militia, John Patterson, to offer Britain a Canadian battalion to garrison Hong Kong *without* consulting Cabinet. See Guy R. MacLean, "The Canadian Offer of Troops for Hong Kong," *Canadian Historical Review*, Vol. 38, 1958, 275–283.
59. Morton, *Ministers and Generals*, 149–150.
60. Sarty, "Local Boys and Redcoats," 61, 65.
61. Richard A. Preston, *Canada and Imperial Defence: A Study of the Origins of the British Commonwealth's Defence Organization, 1867–1919* (Toronto: University of

Toronto Press, 1967), 233–244. Morton, *Ministers and Generals*, 135, 137–138. Sarty, 65.

62. Morton, *Military History of Canada* (Toronto: McClelland & Stewart, 1992), 73–74; and Carl Benn, *Historic Fort York* (Toronto: Natural Heritage, 1993), 93.

63. This occurred on December 7, 1837. The provincial lieutenant-governor called out 1,200 militia, led by Colonel James Fitzgibbon of Beaver Dam fame, who found the tavern "defended" by 450 rebels. Fitzgibbon's forces attacked the tavern in the early afternoon and within 30 minutes the rebels were outflanked and dispersed, while the tavern was put to the torch. Five government supporters were wounded, one rebel killed and several others wounded, some of whom died later. In a significant move, the lieutenant-governor, Sir Francis Bond Head, chose not to employ two British army officers then in Toronto, as he considered it necessary the rebellion be put down by Canadian and not British troops. See Benn, 96–99.

64. Chartrand, *Canadian Military Heritage, Vol. 2*, 155.

65. Donald E. Graves, *Guns Across the River: The Battle of the Windmill, 1838* (Toronto: Robin Brass Studio, 2001), 157–159.

66. Chartrand, *Canadian Military Heritage, Vol. 2*, 92; and Stanley, *Canada's Soldiers*, 222.

67. Brian H. Reid, "The Battle of Ridgeway, June 2, 1866," in Donald E. Graves, ed., *Fighting for Canada, Seven Battles, 1759–1945* (Toronto: Robin Brass Studios, 2000), 138–139.

68. Sarty, "Local Boys and Redcoats," 11.

69. Captain John A. MacDonald, *Troublous Times in Canada: A History of the Fenian Raids of 1866 and 1870* (The London Stamp Exchange, n.d.), 5.

70. Reid, "The Battle of Ridgeway," 146.

71. *Ibid.*, 171.

72. Cook, "Organization and Training," 34–37.

73. Reid, "The Battle of Ridgeway," 181.

74. Steve Harris, *Canadian Brass: The Making of a Professional Army, 1860–1939* (Toronto: University of Toronto Press, 1988), 15–16.

75. *Ibid.*, 16.

76. Cook, "Organization and Training," 57.

77. Morton, Desmond "Aid to the Civil Power: The Canadian Militia in Support of Social Order, 1867–1914," *Canadian Historical Review*, Vol. 51, No. 4, 1970, 415–417.

78. "An Act Respecting the Militia and Defence of the Dominion of Canada, 31 Vict. Cap, 40, Assented May 22, 1868," paragraph 27.

79. Desmond Morton, "Aid to the Civil Power: The Canadian Militia in Support of Social Order, 1867–1914," 424–425.

80. *Ibid.*, 407.

81. Major J.J.B. Pariseau, *Disorders, Strikes and Disasters: Military Aid to the Civil Power in Canada, 1867–1933* (Ottawa: Directorate of History, 1973), 24, Annex F.

82. The literature tends to recognize the 1870 expedition as the *first*, whereas a number of expeditions, beginning in 1816, were sent to the region. See G.F.G. Stanley, *Toil and Trouble: Military Expeditions to Red River* (Toronto: Dundurn Press, 1989) for a full discussion on this topic.

83. Chartrand, *Canadian Military Heritage, Vol. 2*, 175.

84. In spite of their name, the Royal Canadian Rifles were a British regular regiment drawn from veterans of line regiments. It was formed in 1840 and disbanded when the British garrison withdrew from most of Canada in 1870. See Chartrand, *Canadian Military Heritage, Vol. 2*, 163.

85. *Ibid.*, 203.

86. "Militia General Order 17," Ottawa, May 12, 1870.
87. With advertisements published in newspapers and militia orders, each contingent was a new force raised to replace the older one, similar to today's "roto" system.
88. "Militia General Order 10," Ottawa, May 16, 1873.
89. Stanley, *Toil and Trouble*, 193, 195.
90. Not all units were recruited to full strength. The 1873 Militia List showed the following units spread throughout the province: St. Boniface Troop of Cavalry, formed September 1, 1871 Field Battery, formed October 13, 1871. Nine companies at St. Andrew's, Mapleton, Winnipeg, Poplar Point, Portage la Prairie, Kildonan, St. Boniface, Headingly, and Lower Fort Garry. See "The Militia List of the Dominion of Canada, Corrected to August 1, 1873," 80, 81.
91. Cooke, "Organization and Training," 114.
92. *Ibid.*, 103. See also Desmond Morton, *The Last War Drum: The North-West Campaign of 1885* (Toronto: Hakkert, 1972), 178–180.
93. Preston, *Canada and Imperial Defense* (Toronto: University of Toronto Press, 1967), 260.
94. See Chapter 4 of this book, "The Primacy of National Command: Boer War Lesson Learned"; Carman Miller, *Painting the Map Red: Canada and the South African War, 1899–1902* (Montreal: Canadian War Museum and McGill-Queen's University Press, 1993), 48.
95. "Organization, Equipment and Despatch and Service and the Canadian Contingents During the War in South Africa, 1899–1902, Ottawa, 1901," 4.
96. Preston, *Canada and Imperial Defense*, 273.
97. Miller, *Painting the Map Red*, 294–295.
98. Of the 352 men enrolled in 2 Battalion, Canadian Mounted Rifles, 134 came from the NWMP. See "Organization, Equipment and Despatch," 71, 157–158.
99. "Organization, Equipment and Despatch," 94–95.
100 In 1906 20 infantry brigades were established along with two cavalry brigades. By 1911 this had expanded to 23 infantry brigades and seven cavalry brigades. "General Order, 1906."
101. "General Order 59," April 12, 1911.
102. This overview is provided from the Quarterly Militia Lists of 1906, 1910 and 1911.
103. Doctrinally, infantry brigades were to include four regiments, but in some areas insufficient units were available to achieve this.
104. "Report of the Department of Militia and Defence, Year Ended 1910," 5–6.
105. "Report of the Department of Militia and Defence, Year Ended June 30, 1894," 1.
106. "Report of the Department of Militia and Defence, Year Ending March 31, 1910," 14.
107. R.C. Fetherstonhaugh, *The Royal Canadian Regiment, 1883–1933* (Private Printing: Royal Canadian Regiment, Reprint 1981), 63.
108. "Militia Order 118," June 24, 1899, 2–3.
109. "Militia Order 167," August 23, 1899, 1–2. It should be noted that this Militia Order is essentially the equivalent of a modern Post-Exercise Report.
110. Fetherstonhaugh, *The Royal Canadian Regiment*, 57–60.
111. *Report of the Militia Council for the Dominion of Canada on the Training of the Militia During the Season of 1907*, 11–12.
112. *Interim Report of the Militia Council for the Dominion of Canada for the Fiscal Year Ending March 31, 1908*, 68, paragraph 18.
113. *Interim Report of the Militia Council for the Dominion of Canada on the Training of the Militia During the Season of 1908*, 2, paragraph 16.
114. Reid, "The Battle of Ridgeway," 183.

PART II

Fighting Abroad

CHAPTER 4

The Primacy of National Command:
Boer War Lesson Learned
by Bernd Horn and Ronald G. Haycock

In October 1899, after much debate, Canada joined Britain in a war in South Africa. The Anglo-Boer War, as it became known, lasted an unexpected two and a half years. It turned into a major conflict that consumed hundreds of thousands of British and colonial troops including well over 8,000 Canadian volunteers. For Canada, the experience indelibly influenced the structure and training methodology of the Canadian military, but it had an even greater pivotal effect on military and political thought. In addition, the war highlighted the cleavage in national support for imperialist ventures — a chasm that would divide the country many times over the next several decades. However, it clearly accented a nation coming of age.

The war shattered a long-held myth of British military supremacy and colonial inadequacy in regards to questions of armed force. As such, the perceived impotence and apparent incompetence of the British Army had a dramatic effect on Canada's political leaders and military commanders. Successive defeats and repeated pleas by Britain for more troops destroyed the idolized image of the unconquerable empire. It quickly became apparent that the prophesy of the nationalist Lieutenant-Colonel Sam Hughes, that quintessential Canadian militiaman, Tory Member of Parliament (MP), and official opposition militia critic, was correct when he predicted in 1899 that "British regular soldiers were so incompetent that they would be defeated by the Boers ... If British officers persisted in their outmoded military ways, the old plugs of Boer farmers would surely defeat them."[1]

Moreover, the shortcomings of the British Army in South Africa, particularly the failure to provide adequate accommodation, food, and proper medical attention, were not lost on the soldiers of the Canadian contingents. There were also deaths and casualties among the Canadian ranks and the question soon arose — were these sacrifices done in the best interests of Canada? Indeed, what were the interests of the nation in this conflict, and were they being well-served.

Furthermore, the war turned out to be expensive. And it let loose national passions that could have only Canadian responses. It also further defined the Canadian way of war at the time. In the final analysis, these experiences distilled down to two simple questions: who was in command and who was in control. The answers did not come easily, but come they did. The entire Anglo-Boer war experience led to an astute prediction by a writer of the time who remarked, "an idol was shattered. One future effect of this will probably be to cause Canadians to resist any attempt at too great centralization of the military system of the Empire."[2] Quite simply, Canadians realized that national command and control involved both civil and military imperatives. Military command of Canada's own forces was not only desirable, as an extension of Canadian pride and a mechanism to gain rightful recognition; but it was also consequential to equitable, just, and responsible employment of Canadian soldiers overseas — and that meant political control.

At the onset of the crisis, in 1899, Canada was 32 years old. Its huge landmass made it the world's second largest country, but its population was only about five million, and still largely rural. A regionalist mentality, created by a colonial past and the vastness of the land and its still immature transport systems, was yet very strong. Nevertheless, the railway and infant industrialist policies of successive governments since 1867 had induced small but growing steel and other support industries, especially in household products manufacturing and agriculture machinery. There was a great deal of late nineteenth century optimism in view of Canada's potential to be a modern industrial nation similar to that of the United States. Wilfrid Laurier, the French Canadian Liberal prime minister, elected in 1896, was convinced that the twentieth century would belong to Canada.[3]

Although immigration from Eastern Europe was beginning to change the nation's profile, the Canadian stock was still primarily English or French speaking and concentrated in the two eastern provinces of Ontario and Quebec. Culturally, there was a history of intermittent and occasionally acrimonious relations between two founding races stretching back to the defeat of the French on the Plains of Abraham at Quebec in 1759. Yet the two groups had come together in an uneasy alliance for self-preservation mostly against the Americans. As a sizable but nevertheless minority group, the French Canadians were concerned with preserving their identity in the face of the swiftly increasing power of English Canada. Canada's French minority and English majority consistently debated and bickered about culture, education, religion, and participation in imperialist ventures.[4]

Moreover, the new wave of imperialism progressing steadily through many English-speaking circles increasingly alarmed French Canadians. These seemingly British ideas only added to the pressure felt by the minority. As for Canada's federal politicians, they had to be sensitive to popular opinion in both Ontario and Quebec simply because either province could, and did, make or break governments since their huge representation in the national Parliament rendered the vote of the rest of the country mute. Significantly, it was Quebec that most often delivered its federal seats "en bloc" and prime ministers, then as now, had to be wary of that fact either as a way into power or as a means of losing it.[5]

In external relations, Canada was a dominion of the British Empire, indeed the senior dominion with domestic sovereignty, but short of extra territorial independence and the machinery to exercise it. The Dominion of Canada was reliant on Whitehall for most things, especially foreign relations and external military matters. Militarily, Canada depended on England. With the onset of the Boer War, Canada had a minuscule volunteer permanent force meant primarily as instructors for a larger citizen militia, which numbered approximately 37,000 in 1868.[6] It was organized across the country into army, cavalry, and artillery units theoretically training 16 days a year. But the truth was that it was all in deplorable shape with little training and even poorer equipment. And it was smaller in 1895 than it had been 20 years earlier, with the government spending only $0.44 per capita on defence that year.[7] Most of the senior staff was British officers on loan, including the general officer commanding (GOC) the entire Canadian militia structure. Moreover, it had no modern services and few of the amenities of a modern headquarters staff system. Yet there was an abiding faith that these citizen militiamen were the first line of Canadian defence and they fed on the historical myth that they had saved Canada on many occasions in the past, such as the War of 1812 with the Americans. The one bright spot for defence matters after the election of the new Liberal government of Wilfrid Laurier in 1896, was that Laurier had made Dr. Frederick Borden the new militia minister and he was determined to reform the entire military establishment.[8]

When the relationship between Briton and Boer deteriorated in the spring and summer of 1899, ostensibly over the denial of civic and social rights of the Uitlanders in the Boer republics, the call from London spread through the empire to support the British policy.[9] Whitehall wanted to

Library and Archives Canada C-001867

At the Commonwealth Conference in 1897 the British colonial secretary, Joseph Chamberlain (seated), poses with the colonial prime ministers. Sir Wilfrid Laurier (front row, second from left) stands next to Chamberlain as the senior of the dominions.

show the world that the empire was united, but at that moment it did not place as much value on having colonial troops as it did on obtaining official public endorsement from their governments. "We do not want the men," wrote Joseph Chamberlain, the British colonial secretary, to the Canadian governor general, "the whole point of the offer would be lost unless it was endorsed by the Government of the Colony."[10]

Even though Canada ultimately went to war, it responded in a variety of disparate ways. First, at the government level, Prime Minister Laurier instinctively realized that answering the siren imperial call officially was far too expensive in dollars and Canadian lives, and a threat to Canada's fragile national unity. He concurred with his predecessor, Sir John A. Macdonald, who, during the 1884–85 "Chinese Gordon" affair in the Sudan, refused "to get Gladstone and Company out of the hole they have plunged themselves into by their own imbecillity[*sic*]."[11]

So in 1899, Laurier resisted doing anything. No doubt he hoped that it would all go away. But he did not know then that his British GOC,

General E.T.H. Hutton, had secretly been drafting a plan to send a sub-stantial Canadian contingent to South Africa. With the sub rosa assis-tance of the governor general, the earl of Minto, and Joseph Chamberlain in the British Colonial Office, the GOC made sure that at every military mess dinner and inspection he primed the audience on the possibility of sending Canadian troops. He even hinted to influen-tial militia officers that they might have a role in the force.[12]

There was also a certain amount of subtle encouragement for the vocal Canadian imperialists to speak out in favour of the idea. All of this public pressure finally forced Laurier in July 1899, to accept a much watered-down, even innocuous resolution in the House of Commons decrying the treatment of the Uitlanders. Still the government made no commitment to participate officially or unofficially in any future com-bat. As such, Laurier thought he had things in hand.[13]

By this time, the issue had become public and just as hot as that Canadian summer. It was also very complex and opinions cut right across the full spectrum of Canadian society. It was also riddled with acrimo-nious political and racial partisanship. In the political arena, it was between the Liberals in power and the Conservatives seeking it. In racial debates, it was the Anglo-Saxon stock against mostly French. Perhaps because of lack of information, or not caring, or simply being too busy, a great many Canadians simply did not participate in the war debate at all.[14]

Nonetheless, it is far too simple to use the conventional interpreta-tion that the pro-war element was the singular child of the imperialists; or that the only group opposing war were the French Canadians. On the pro-war side, it was a mélange of English Canadians, especially from Ontario and the English-speaking parts of Quebec. The urban, informed middle class of a liberal and often practical business bent dominated it. The imperial ideas were more readily acceptable in one form or another to these people.

But it was resented by many, particularly vocal militia command-ers and politicians such as Lieutenant-Colonel Sam Hughes, who resented arrogant professional British soldiers, especially the GOC, Sir Edward Hutton, who argued that Canadian militiamen would be use-less to the British Army in any combat. So like many other national-ists, Hughes's mission was to prove them all wrong. There were also those who were just plain nationalists. They wanted to prove Canada could do anything. This, they believed could even lead to more auton-omy; and some felt it would be a good way to escape the shadow and control of Great Britain. Others were convinced that they ought to trade imperial interests in South Africa now for a later British defence in their quarrels with the American.[15]

Some saw the events unfolding in South Africa connected to the process of Canadian history. After all, Canadians had won their own civil liberties through constitutional and occasionally even violent struggle. Parliamentary democracy triumphed; the franchise was extended; some minority rights were protected; in the 1830s and 1840s they had gotten rid of the arch-conservative establishments of the Family Compact and the Chateau Clique in Upper and Lower Canada, respectively. By the late 1870s, they had brought all of this and law and order too as an inevitable and natural process by populating the Canadian West. In 1885 the supposedly chronic discriminatory treatment of the pro-Canadian western settlers by Louis Riel's Métis, and the increasing western migrations of eastern Canadians, culminated in an open act of rebellion. In part driven by public pressure from Ontarians, Ottawa sent a punitive Expeditionary Force of mostly militiamen to what are now the three plains provinces to crush the self-declared Métis Republic. This they accomplished. Moreover, they hanged the rebellion's leader. They then established what they felt was a proper government representing Canadian interests. In 1899, this event was still fresh in the minds of many Canadians. To their way of thinking, there was a similar process taking place in South Africa and the reactionary forces of "Oom Paul" Kruger and company was standing in the way.[16]

Finally, there were those pragmatic Canadians who saw business opportunities coming-out of supporting British ambitions in Boer Republics. War meant demands for Canadian foodstuffs, cloth, hay, horses, transport of all types and much more. Indeed one of the arguments that Laurier's militia minister, Frederick Borden, used in trying to persuade his reluctant prime minister to go to war was exactly that: the economic benefits to Canada. And there were many others who saw these opportunities both during the war and after it.

For those opposed to the war, there were as many reasons why. The largest vocal group was the French Canadians. Their chief spokesperson was a well-educated and articulate young liberal MP and Laurier protege in the province of Quebec, Henri Bourassa. Bourassa would remain in the federal Liberal Party and in Parliament only as long as the prime minister made no commitments. But he grew increasingly strident in his denunciation of the pro-war stand and the "Imperialists," and they "upped the ante" all during the summer and early autumn of 1899.[17]

Unlike many others for and against, French Canadian opposition was unanimous for the simple reason that they had been conditioned for the previous two decades by bitter quarrels over their cultural protection that had dominated French-English relations. Smarting and sensitive because of this, they could see ready similarities in the Boers' case to protect themselves from the voracious British, but were less able to see wrongs done to the Uitlanders. The Québécois appreciated the Boer farmers' struggle to maintain their life style against all the evil English "isms": secular, commercial, urban, material, and industrial. And if that was not enough, there was no perceived Canadian interest at stake in far away Transvaal or the Orange Free State. It was hard — as it always had been for French Canadians — to understand how one could have a loyalty to the British Empire and to Canada at the same time. Defence of Great Britain was one thing, especially since it was the ultimate protector of Canada against the Americans, but Canadian participation in British aggrandizement in colonial ventures was quite another.

Moreover, it could lead to the hated and feared conscription, or an even bigger, more expensive and anglicized Canadian military establishment that already had fewer and fewer places in it for French Canadians.[18]

And if one did not understand any of this, there, were always the economic arguments against such foreign adventurism. Troops cost money, and the limited funds available would be better spent on national development and improving infrastructure in Quebec.

Although the anti-war sentiments of *les canadiens* were heard the loudest, they were not the only ones speaking out. Most historians have downplayed, or ignored the fact, that many in English Canada did not want to have anything to do with South Africa. Some of the reasons were shared with their French Canadian brethren. Perhaps the main one was the inability to see any vital Canadian security or other interest involved — so why then should young Canadians die, their families grieve, and taxpayers bear the burden for something about which they would never be consulted? Canada had by this time significant Irish and German immigrant communities spread through out the country. As one would expect, they did not receive prospect of war enthusiastically, because from their point of view it was nothing more than another example of British subjugation.[19]

Furthermore, many in labour circles interpreted the conflict as little more than the big business machinations of financial swashbucklers such as Cecil Rhodes, who sought only to aggrandize profits and exploit workers. Some felt that with the monumental effort needed for national development, Canada could ill afford to send away its vital personnel. It

"Royal Canadians" in the Orange Free State, February 1900.

would be too disruptive to agriculture and emerging industry alike. Both of these were just coming into their own after a serious 20-year depression had begun to ease.

Then there were the pacifists like the Doukabors and Mennonite communities who simply opposed all war. The national Women's Christian Temperance Union (WCTU) was against not only the evils of drink but also the evils of war. As one can easily see the opinions for or against this war were myriad and diverse.[20]

Therefore, as mentioned earlier, like prime ministers before and after, Wilfrid Laurier tried vigorously to do nothing. That summer, he told the governor general, the earl of Minto, that Canada should not commit to anything because French Canada was opposed to all such British imperial adventures. Besides, he conceded there was not enough money in the treasury to support an expeditionary force, moreover, the Alaska Panhandle boundary dispute with the Americans was heating up again now that the southern neighbour's attention was turning away from its war with Spain.[21]

Unfortunately, for the increasingly beleaguered prime minister, forces were afoot that rapidly reduced his options. One of them was that several members of his Cabinet, like his militia minister, favoured action. In military circles, General Hutton, the British GOC, was quietly working up hopes by letting the militia know that he had a well-organized plan for an expeditionary force and that certain supportive individuals were to be in it.[22] Members of the imperialist press, like the Montreal Star published by the jingoist Hugh Graham, were constantly beating the commitment drum louder and louder. And throughout August and September there were other citizens of reputation who were making separate offers to raise private units to fight for the Uitlanders' freedom and British Justice against the so-called medieval tyrant Kruger.

Then, on October 3, 1899, the *Canadian Military Gazette* (the widely distributed newspaper of the Canadian Militia) published details of Hutton's secret plan adding confidently that the government was likely to send the force.[23] Conveniently and simultaneously, a Colonial Office circular arrived in Canada thanking the Dominion for offering troops — which of course it had not. It too found its way into the public domain. Evidence pointed to Hutton's behind the scenes manipulations. If so, it was a clear challenge to Cabinet authority. Eventually, when enough facts accumulated, the government insisted that the British recall the abrasive GOC. In the meantime, political pressure mounted. To pro-war Canadian nationalists worried about status, news that "little" New Zealand had already offered troops and the Australian colonies were on the verge, was hardly tolerable.[24]

Immediately and publicly Laurier denied that any of these Canadian "facts" were true; then he naïvely left for Chicago. A week later, Briton and Boer were at war, and Canada, still having done nothing concrete, suffered another paroxysm of pro-war agitation. Laurier hurried home, and after two stormy days of Cabinet meetings finally announced on October 14 that Canada would send an official contingent of 1,000 volunteers. Canada was now at war.[25]

Whether the Canadian prime minister then realized it, this decision to participate in a British foreign war had grand implications for the issue of national control. Laurier was acutely aware that somebody would command Canadian troops and that somebody would have to pay the costs. These were the immediate concerns, and, in comparative terms easiest solved. But issues of national command have much larger, longer term, and less obvious aspects. Some would be organizational. They would deal with the nature of the machinery of government, or of professional military development and force structure. Others would affect Canada's defence policy and the relationship with the empire and perhaps with the rest of the world, especially the United States. As well, implications touched on raw nerves of divisive national emotion, Canadian identity, and Canada's role in world events. However, in that October of 1899, the beleaguered Laurier was likely not thinking in such large terms. Yet he and his colleagues soon would be, as the events of the next 30 months quickly unfolded with their many surprises.

Once the government approved sending a force, the immediate issue of national control was, as one might expect, the military one. The ultimate composition and arrangements for the Canadian contingent, however, would prove to be significant. From the beginning, political, and military commanders on both sides of the ocean understood that Canadian troops would be under British command. For Laurier, a redeeming feature of this arrangement may have been that it made the best of a dangerous political situation — at least most of what would happen and the associated costs could be accredited to London and not Ottawa.

Upon accepting the Canadian offer, Joseph Chamberlain quickly cabled the governor general and detailed that the contribution, preferably infantry, should be organized into units of approximately 125 men, with one captain and no more than three subalterns for each unit, adding that the officer commanding the whole force should have a rank no higher than major. The cost of mounting and equipping, as well as transport to South Africa, was to be paid by the Dominion. Once they disembarked they would become imperial troops and pay, rations, clothing, supplies, and ammunition would be provided by the British government.[26]

Quite simply, the intent was for the Canadian contingent, like the other colonial contingents, to be absorbed into British units and formations. That would probably mean that Canadian and other colonial troops would be used for garrison, picket, and rear area security tasks, since British regulars had little faith in the martial prowess of militiamen, and even less of colonials. After all, the British government wanted colonial contingents for political reasons, not for their military application or worth.[27]

British intentions were dashed quickly, however. Nationalist sentiment pushed the idea of a strong unified Canadian contingent. Surprisingly, Governor General Minto pressed Laurier to acknowledge the popular will and push Britain to accept a Canadian contribution worthy of Canada's position in the empire. "You will see from the cable that it is evidently intended that the Canadian troops on arriving in South Africa should be attached to the different units which they represent, and that they should not remain constituted as a Canadian contingent," warned Minto. "I think," he proffered, "it would be better if troops are to be offered at all, that they should be offered as a Canadian contingent to act as such." Days later he penned another note to reinforce his recommendation and added: "It would appear [an all arms Canadian contingent] an offer really worthy of Canada and that would find favour with the Canadian public."[28]

As a result, on October 18, Laurier and his Cabinet approved the establishment and deployment of a regiment of infantry, namely 2nd (Special Service) Battalion, Royal Canadian Regiment (RCR) — 1,000 strong commanded by Lieutenant-Colonel William Otter.[29] With Minto's urging, the British government and the War Office accepted the Canadian offer. They also agreed to the official request to keep the Canadian contingent together as much as possible. However, the commander-in-chief in South Africa cautioned that he "cannot guarantee that the Contingent shall always be kept together during operations." He added, the "General must be free to dispose of the force to the best advantage."[30] In the end, this position was accepted by the Canadian leaders. After all, for as long as could be remembered, British commanders had ensured the security of the empire and everyone realized that they must be allowed to make the requisite decisions in the field to attain victory. Besides, they could be blamed if anything went wrong.

Ironically, after the hard fight to send the first contingent, within the next two weeks the government offered a second contingent, consisting of artillery and mounted infantry on November 1, 1899.[31] It was as if Laurier finally realized the depth (and political danger) of committed war sentiment in English Canada, and among those in his Cabinet such as the militia minister himself. However, the British did not immediately respond to the offer. Two days later, they politely declined. The political criterion of a unified front was already achieved, so they were reluctant to take on the costly burden of more "ineffective" colonial troops.[32] Moreover, the British political and military leadership were confident that the conflict would quickly be terminated. The Boers, after all, were viewed as little more than "the levies of two insignificant Republics whose forces were but loose gatherings of armed farmers."[33]

London's rebuff to Ottawa's quick generosity, if that is what it was, apparently went unnoticed in the Senior Dominion. For many Canadians, the opportunity to serve overseas against the Boers was seen both as an imperial duty, and as a chance for the neophyte Canadian military, specifically its officers and senior non-commissioned officers, to acquire experience. No one, other than a few overly opinionated nationalists, believed that the nation's military contribution would actually be significant. How could it? In the main, the Canadian militia was a simple colonial citizen force. Put next to the professional British Army there was no comparison.

An editorial in the influential *Canadian Military Gazette* asserted, "The Canadian contingent goes to South Africa not so much to fight as to gain experience in modern campaigning."[34] A later editorial added that "it is a proud thing, for it is the removal of the old stigma that Canada, while enjoying all the benefits and protection, was reluctant or indifferent to assume the duties and sacrifices of Empire."[35] Colonel T. Denison, dedicated imperialist, prominent Canadian lawyer, and long-time militia officer who had already given a son to imperial service, opined, "We have been children long enough, let us show the Empire that we have grown to manhood."[36] But nothing was more telling of the unquestioning belief in British arms than the reaction of the volunteer troops. "When the Canadian soldiers from the west arrived here [South Africa]," confided one Canadian subaltern, "they looked at the Soldiers of the Queen with interest and admiration, and no doubt thoughtfully considered whether they would be able to as worthily uphold the flag in the day of trial."[37]

However, the veneration of the "Soldiers of the Queen" suddenly vanished once serious operations started. Moreover, the circumstances that brought this about had a wide-ranging impact. In what remained of that autumn of 1899, the British soldiers and politicians alike were shocked at the fighting prowess of the Boers who on one occasion after another inflicted humiliating and costly defeats on the British Field Force.

These unexpected "drubbings" pointed out that the imperial army was woefully inadequate to meet the challenges of modern warfare. The humiliating dénouement came during the week of December 10–15, 1899, when three separate British formations were decisively beaten at Stormberg, Magersfontein, and Colenso. These fateful seven days were appropriately labelled "Black Week." Empire-wide, imperialists went into a funk and the critics of the South African adventure smugly felt redeemed. To the War Office, the colonial troops like the Canadians suddenly took on an entirely new relevance. Maybe they had skills that could be used. In addition, other military blunders on the battlefield with their excessive British casualties only underscored the defects in British military leadership, organization, and training.[38]

The impact in South Africa was equally frantic. On December 1, a very worried high commissioner in Cape Town, Alfred, Lord Milner confided hurriedly to the British foreign secretary, Joseph Chamberlain. "The list of casualties at Modder River was communicated to me to-day," wrote Milner, "They are terribly heavy. The list has not yet been published here — wisely, as I think."[39] Ten days later during "Black Week," his spirits were even lower. Once again he cabled London then wrote in his diary:

> Fuller details of General Gatacre's fight put, if anything a worse aspect on the matter than the first report. It is evident that the force under him found itself in a complete trap, and was simply routed. The two infantry battalions would have been entirely lost had it not been for the artillery, which seems to have done good service in covering their retreat. We have, however, lost two guns, and, besides a few known to be killed or wounded, there are nearly 700 missing — mostly prisoners, it is to be feared. This is the worst blow we have sustained yet during the war. The impression it has created here is simply deplorable, and this is sure to be the case throughout the Colony.[40]

The next day was no better. Milner's alarming entry had more than a hint of panic:

> December 12th [1899] — The news to-day is again extremely bad. There can be no doubt that General Gatacre's defeat on Sunday was a very severe one, and the effect of a large number of British prisoners being taken through a rebel district of the Colony into the Orange Free State cannot but be most injurious. One consequence is that, as reported by various magistrates, armed men are leaving their homes in various parts of the eastern districts, and going to join the enemy.[41]

Two days later, he acknowledged that there existed a "deep depression in loyal circles in consequence of the three disasters of the past week." He lamented, "General Buller's defeat on the Tugela [River], coming on the top of Stormberg and Magersfontein, has been rather too much for the bravest."[42] By Christmas, he informed Chamberlain "The effects of the reverses at Stormberg, Magersfontein, and Colenso is cumulative." He warned, "Even in the remotest country districts it is now known that the enemy have had great successes. The exultation of the colonial Boers is open — and naturally makes the lives of the loyalist a burden to them." Moreover, he added, "the spirit of rebellion has received an enormous impetus — even in districts hitherto comparatively quiet."[43]

Ironically, this imperial proconsul had masterminded the political situation that ultimately had led to the war. At the time, he thought it would be easy for Britain to overpower the two Boer republics by force of arms. So far it had been just the opposite as the military tool failed. But there was an even more disturbing problem. The Cape Colony was as yet full of what Milner and company, sitting in idyllic surroundings of Cecil Rhodes's estate of Groote Schuur, deemed "loyal" Boers. With all these defeats, the real question was for how long would they remain so? Milner could see his supposed neat little "Cabinet conflict" turning into a general revolt if the heretofore quiet Cape Colony Afrikaners bolted to their Orange Free State and Transvaaler bruder. More immediate was the strategic threat to the current military operations. For instance, if the North West Cape Colony rebelled, the entire British military effort aimed at Bloemfontein, and Pretoria would be put into a giant enfilade position.[44]

The effect elsewhere in the empire was similarly dramatic. "The military situation is without doubt at this moment most grave and critical," reported Winston Churchill, the future prime minister of Britain, who was a correspondent at the onset of the conflict. "We have been at war three weeks," he explained, "[and] the army that was to

A Canadian bivouac outside Bloemfontein in South Africa.

Library and Archives Canada C-3477

have defended Natal, and was indeed expected to repulse the invaders with terrible loss, is blockaded and bombarded in its fortified camp." He added, "at nearly every point along the circle of the frontiers the Boers have advanced and the British retreated. Wherever we have stood we have been surrounded ... All this is mainly the result of being unready ... It is also due to an extraordinary under-estimation of the strength of the Boers."[45]

Not surprisingly, after the shock of "Black Week" the Canadian offer for a second contingent of artillery and mounted infantry, which was now almost two months old, was eagerly accepted.[46] Similar desperate pleas throughout the empire for additional men were quickly perceived by the colonies as "an admission of the weakness of the British Army, unable to beat an armed peasantry."[47] The former adulation was lost. In early December 1899, the *Canadian Military Gazette* asserted, "Much impatience continues to be felt by the public" as a result of the perceived slow progress of the British Army in South Africa.[48] Less than a month later, it confirmed, "It is indeed humiliating to have to record the series of checks to the British arms and the apparent tactical mismanagement." Moreover, it criticized the "apparent contemptuous disregard of the most ordinary and commonplace precautions against surprise" and condemned the "old-time English prejudice against colonials," which it labelled the "bane and curse of nearly every Imperial officer conducting war in the British Colonial Empire."[49]

Quite simply, Canadian confidence in the efficiency of British generals, if not the army in its entirety, was severely undermined. The minister of the militia openly derided the British GOC in Canada by stating, "I ask myself in face of the reverses which the British Army has received, if it is worth the while of Canada to remain part of the Empire."[50] Even the staunchly anti-war proponent, Henri Bourassa, avowed in the House of Commons that he "hoped that Great Britain will recover its prestige that has been injured in South Africa."[51] Clearly, an idol had fallen. In Ottawa it was at this point that appreciation of issues of national command demanded far more foresight. The first issue was the immediate problems of the Canadian volunteers in the field so far away.

In spite the crisis, or perhaps because of it, the Canadian government delivered on its earlier offer. It now promptly dispatched a second contingent comprised of two battalions of mounted infantry and a brigade (three batteries) of artillery. In total, the second contingent numbered approximately 1,289 men.[52] It represented the last official Canadian contribution to the war.

Although other Canadians served, they were not raised as Canadian contingents. Rather they were volunteers to formations created by the British, the South African Constabulary, or privately sponsored units such as Lord Strathcona's Horse.[53] However, the Canadian government did volunteer to garrison the fortress of Halifax with a battalion of Canadian troops (3rd Battalion, RCR), approximately 1,000 men, for the duration of the war so its British garrison could be deployed to South Africa.[54]

But service with the British Army did not assist in rejuvenating the fallen icon. If the popular Canadian characterization of the British Army and its generals had been thus far impugned, it now took a mortal blow. Canadian volunteers, dependent on the British for leadership and management of their basic needs, were woefully disappointed. And they were quick to share their displeasure. As historian Carman Miller notes, this war, unlike the next one at the same stage, was a conflict in which the early volunteers were mostly Canadian. He goes on to say, most of them easily turned into a collection of unofficial war correspondents for the people back home who were anxious to hear first hand.[55] This flood of personal observations from South Africa, as well as the stories passed by returning veterans, depicted Canadian troops suffering for long periods due to inadequate food, accommodation, clothing, and medical care. During the advance on Bloemfontein, Sergeant Hart-McHarg revealed that despite the hard marching, they had been on reduced rations for almost a month. He recounted, "We were hungry all the time." The trek became a feat of endurance. During one four-day period, they lost 796 mules and 3,500 oxen.[56]

Equally frustrating were their uniforms. They could not be replaced, but were in tatters by mid-campaign. "Most of the men," explained veteran A.S. McCormick, "were in rags."[57] It was not abnormal for shoes to lack soles, pants to lack knees or backsides, while shirts lacked sleeves and buttons. Moreover, the cold nights on the veldt became intolerable, particularly when it rained, as it often did during the campaign. With inadequate clothing, a single thin substandard blanket, and no tents — the exhausted soldiers found themselves cold, wet, and unable to sleep properly.[58]

But no issue drew more criticism or censure than the medical care provided the sick and wounded. A Canadian officer, a medical doctor in civilian life, who visited a military hospital, was "ashamed of the professional standards."[59] Reports by journalists and soldiers soon revealed the scope of the problem. A lack of adequate accommodation, bedding, and blankets, as well as a dearth of qualified caring staff to look after the soldiers — keep them clean, sanitary, and free of flies and vermin — who were too weak do so themselves, transformed a serious problem into a tragedy. And, if matters were not bad enough, men were treated according to rank rather than illness or wound.[60] In the end, the Canadians could not help but feel that the British Army placed a low priority on looking after its men, particularly colonials.

Although the harsh terrain and nature of the campaign were at fault for some of the problems, others stemmed from the cultural and institutional biases of Britain's army. The fact that British regular units received their tents and replacement clothing sooner than the colonials, may not be surprising, but it left a lingering resentment with the Canadians.[61] Most important, the fact that the British Army was so incapable of providing for the Canadian's basic needs added to the loss of reverence for the British military and its generals. It also fuelled the growing realization that Canada would have to look after its own sons and daughters if it wished to ensure their well-being and fair treatment when deployed overseas. In the end, such concerns were questions of national command and control.

Despite the hardships of the campaign and the apparent ineptitude of the British military, the two Canadian contingents acquitted themselves well. The First Contingent after an initial two-month period of training and garrison duty, joined Field Marshal Lord Roberts's field force for the march against Bloemfontein, the capital of Orange Free State. As such, on the night of February 26, 1900, the Canadians were in the front lines and participated in a night assault on General Cronje's laager at Paardeburg, which had held out for almost 10 days. Although the attack itself failed because of the heavy fire of the Boers, and confusion caused by questionable orders yelled in the darkness, two RCR companies on the flank, not aware of the general retreat that had taken place elsewhere, remained and proceeded to dig-in close to the enemy trenches. As the darkness melted away and dawn appeared, the two companies of Royal Canadians, less than 100 yards from the Boer position, prompted Cronje to surrender. In reality the Boer commander had already made the decision to give up. The extended siege had depleted their supply of food and water and the families that accompanied the Boer combatants began to suffer. Exacerbating this dire situation was the continuous British artillery bombardment with high explosives that destroyed their livestock and wagons and forced all to stay hidden in holes dug into the ground.

Notwithstanding their courage, a degree of good luck had provided the Canadians with an enviable situation — they seemed to be the key element in Britain's first and most important victory of the war.[62] In fact,

Paardeburg marked the turning point of the conflict. On March 13, the Canadians, as part of Roberts's field force entered Bloemfontein and on June 5, 1900, they occupied Pretoria, the capital of Transvaal.

The Second Contingent did not have the good fortune to share in such an epic battle; however, the occupation of the capitals of the two republics did not end the war, so they did get to see action. Because of their late arrival into theatre, the Second Contingent was employed with British columns protecting the British lines of communications, as well as trying to run down the small Boer forces that had now taken up a bitter struggle of guerrilla warfare plunging the conflict into a desperate and merciless war of attrition. This mobile, unconventional type of war seemed suited to the Canadians — who were adept at marksmanship, horsemanship, and wide-open spaces. Not surprisingly, once again, they performed extremely well.

Overall, the Canadians earned a remarkable reputation. Accolades from British commanders and press were profuse. Adjectives such as "dashing," "fighting like devils," "gallant," and "courageous" were lavishly doled out.[63] London's *Daily Telegraph* asserted, "The Canadians had nothing to fear from even such keen and competent critics as our German friends. It would be hard to find again in Europe a fighting unit equal to the battalion [Canadians] that attracted the attention of the German Attachés."[64] Lord Roberts himself telegraphed Lord Minto to say, "I have much pleasure in bringing to your Excellency's notice the

Typical Canadian "rough-riders."

Library and Archives Canada C-17611

good work done by the First and Second Battalions Canadian Mounted Rifles, who have been repeatedly conspicuous for their gallant conduct and soldierlike instincts."[65] Similarly, Major-General Sir Horace Smith-Dorrien in regards to the RCR declared, "There are no finer or more gallant troops in all the world."[66] In addition, in regards to the Royal Canadian Dragoons (RCD), the Canadian Mounted Rifles (CMR), and the left section of "D" Battery, Royal Canadian Artillery, he unabashedly stated: "that he would choose no other mounted troops in the world before them if he had his choice."[67]

The performance of the Canadians, and all colonials in fact, in South Africa created at the time a re-examination of the age-old prejudice against colonial military competence. The pendulum now seemed to swing to the other far extreme. The *Canadian Military Gazette* noted that the war "has brought home to Englishmen the value of colonial troops."[68]

The influential *Army and Navy Gazette* in Britain commented on the effectiveness of "a few really skilled riflemen of good physique, like the colonials."[69] In fact, it went so far as to say, "The rough-riders of our colonies are the only men who can meet the Boer on equal terms and beat him."[70] Based on his observations in South Africa as a journalist, Winston Churchill "judged a militia army not very much less competent than a standing army."[71] He went on tell an audience, "nor was it soothing to their pride [cavalry] to find squadrons of Colonial Horse and South Africa Corps, raised at 10 days' notice, considered as good as, and often better than, the finest and most zealous regiments."[72]

Field Marshal Lord Wolseley believed that the colonials would have stood up against European regulars. "The colonial contingents," he believed, "would have fought anybody." But he quickly added, "I would not extend that same expression of opinion to the very large bodies of men we sent out from here [England]."[73] The commissioners from the Elgin Commission of Enquiry, established to examine the conduct of the war, themselves described the colonies as "half soldiers by their upbringing."[74] In the same vein, "Canadians," proclaimed the *Army and Navy Gazette*, "are largely offspring of old military stock of two famous fighting nations, the British and French, consequently their qualities for soldiering cannot be doubted."[75]

The Canadians themselves began to realize that they easily matched the courage and effectiveness of those that they had formerly so highly esteemed. In fact, familiarity bred contempt. Lieutenant Morrison observed, "And it must be said that Canada's soldiers compare favorably with the 'reg-lars.'" What they lacked in drill, they more than made up for in "physique" and "in spirit and dash and a certain air of self-reliant readiness to hold their own."[76] Others echoed those same sentiments. "The Imperial soldier is not taught to think," criticized Stanley Brown, a journalist. "The Canadians were different," he continued, " and therein lay the secret of their success, when they had to, on almost a moment's notice take the field and compete with some of the best regiments in the British army." Brown concluded, "that is where the soldier who could think and did think, and who could rely, to a small extent at least, on his own resources, was able to take his place along with the British man of the line, and not only equal but surpass in nearly every way the average Tommy."[77]

What was not lost on the Canadian veterans was that their performance was equal to if not at times superior to that of British regulars. "We have seen the First Contingent," wrote one journalist, "side by side with the bravest and the best of the Imperial regiments, taking with them the hardships met with on campaign."[78] A veteran revealed, "you could feel your head swelling as the truth gradually dawned on you that the term *colonial*, instead of being the designation of a people 'a little lower than the angels,' was in future to be synonymous in the military Valhalla with that of Mars himself."[79]

The success of the Canadian troops and the international respect they apparently garnered soon triggered a nationalist outpouring of pride in Canadian military prowess. After Paardeburg, Lord Roberts told survivors, that they "had done noble work, and were as good a lot of men as were in the British Army." Roberts went on to say, "Canadian now stands for bravery, dash, and courage."[80]

Even the reluctant prime minister, Wilfrid Laurier, was not immune from exploiting Canadian success in the field and beating the martial drum. "Is there a man whose bosom did not swell with pride, the pride of pure patriotism, the pride of consciousness," thundered Laurier in the House of Commons, "that day [Paardeburg] the fact had been revealed to the world that a new power had arisen in the West."[81] It all made for good listening in English Canada. Of course, politically Laurier could hardly do otherwise. Nonetheless, this was a dimension of national command he no doubt enjoyed even if he got it by default.

Another Member of Parliament had an increasingly popular Social Darwinist view of the conflict. Victory in the war was at hand and the first battle victory had been Canadian: "The fruits of the war," he gloated to his fellow MPs, "are commendable and are of a character to make us realise that the war was not a misfortune, but was on the contrary, something that led to the development of our power, and to the breaking down of the rebellion against that power."[82]

No one can argue that likely preconditions to national command are the pride of accomplishment and nationalism itself. The Anglo-Boer conflict gave those to Canada. But with them came an inflated and dangerous belief in the capability of the citizen soldier and the structure of the Canadian military force. The myth of the "natural soldier" and the belief that "much soldier blood runs in the veins of Canadians" got a great boost when peace came in 1902.[83] A commentary in the *Canadian Military Gazette* that year reflected a popular sentiment of the time. "We proceed," it explained, "on the idea that the soldier, especially the Canadian soldier, is born, and that no making is necessary."[84]

That was the message Sam Hughes, a Tory MP and official opposition militia critic, had believed for years, and his service in the war only helped confirm it. In 1899 and part of 1900, he had soldiered in North Cape Colony with some very incompetent senior British soldiers and some very good Canadian ones. His very public criticism of bad British leadership in both South African newspapers and in Canada while on active duty had got him sent home by an irate Field Marshal Sir Fred Roberts. Once back, his nationalism bristled. Although he would not be in a position to exercise national command in this war, as militia minister he would be in the next; and he did not hesitate to do so. In the meantime, South Africa was to him more than a just a military proving ground — it was also one of citizens' political command. As for his ideas on what type of force structure there should be, the Boer War had demonstrated that, as he said, "long conflict and standing armies had given way to mobile, well-trained, and outfitted citizen-soldiers who could shoot straight and withstand hardship."[85]

For his part, the minister of militia, Frederick Borden, was increasingly sensitive to who commanded what. The conflict was very personal for him, as his only son, Harold, had been killed in South Africa in July 1900. Very likely, questions regarding the relevance of sacrifice, recognition, competence, care, notification, and national interest swirled in Borden's mind, as they did in the minds of many other Canadians similarly affected by death in far away battle. Casualties always raise issues of national responsibility. But whatever relationship he personally made, in public it was clear that the militia minister wanted to build a modern citizen militia force.

The concomitant Alaska Boundary dispute allowed him to connect the Boer War experience to national defence policy. For one, he had supported the British policy (and Canada's participation) in South Africa because he believed, like many others, that Canada could count on the British to reciprocate in the Dominion's quarrel with the Americans over the Alaskan Boundary dispute. But they did not. Anger and disappointment spread across the Dominion. It seemed that Canada could count neither on British competence to care for Canadians in South Africa, nor its statesmen to look after Canadian territorial interests in North America.

When Washington appeared to be threatening with the "big stick," Fred Borden, in a not so subtle reference to the Americans proclaimed, "The lesson that has been taught in the recent wars is that the defence of the country is comparatively much more easy now than it was supposed to be in past times, and that if you have a really formidable body of men who are somewhat used to discipline and understand the use of arms it is an enormous undertaking for a nation of 40 or 50 million people to enter a country of one-tenth or one-fifth of that population and wage a successful war of subjugation."[86] Borden's trust in the citizen soldier was such that he proclaimed, "Let the permanent force understand that their office is to teach, we have no standing army and do not need to have one."[87]

Undeniably, the participation in South Africa advanced a nationalistic martial sentiment within the country, particularly among its military and political leaders. The war gave Canadians a new sense of their place as a nation.[88] Whether Laurier wished to acknowledge it or not, Canada had set a precedent for overseas military expeditionary assistance to

Photographer: W.F. Athawes, Library and Archives Canada PA-113042

Members of 2 Canadian Mounted Rifles in their bivouac at Newcastle, Natal, in February-March 1902.

Britain. "We are taking a step today on the threshold of a new century," prophesied Reverend F.G. Scott before the embarkation of the First Contingent, "from which there can be no recession and which will one day give to Canada a voice in the councils of the British Empire."[89]

His prognostication was not far off. Canada got a voice in the next war, but by 1918 the price would be high, and that in turn helped make the case for more comprehensive national command and control.

The Boer War also solidified the requirement for Canadian control of its military forces when assigned to the British Army. This was imperative because Canada was due recognition as a sovereign nation, and its soldiers needed to be properly cared for.

In addition, the war led to dramatic advancements in the nation's military. Since coming to office in 1896, Borden was convinced that he must improve the militia. Before the war, political patronage, inertia, and public apathy made the task very difficult — but the conflict and the new sense of martial prowess gave him the opportunity to do it. Despite the reputation earned by Canadians, the course of the war had highlighted serious problems with supply and services, munitions availability, command and control, civil military relations, and Canada's military autonomy. Borden was committed to a broad three-part policy of producing a Canadian citizen army, distancing it from British control by making it as self-sufficient as money would permit, and cooperative with but not integrated into imperial defence.

Borden realized that the Boer War experience indicated that mobilizing and then sustaining a war effort required a modern staff system. By 1904 he revised the Militia Act, landmark legislation that established a Militia Council (modelled on the British Army Council) and the provision for a Canadian to be head of the militia.[90] His reforms ensured that the duly elected and appointed minister of the militia was clearly in control and that military officers, even the GOC, were merely advisers. As a result, episodes such as the Hutton affair, where a British GOC would try to manipulate Canadian policy, would become near impossible. However, the reforms did provide the organizational basis for those same staff officers to form the skeleton of a modern general staff system.

The Militia Act included a myriad of other reforms, as well. Militia strength was increased to 100,000, pay was improved, Canadian troops took over the garrisons at Halifax and Esquimalt, and an inspector general was appointed for the Cadet movement. Borden also added an array of modern services to the staff system. By 1905, he had consolidated 11 military districts into only five, each with its local staff and services, making command, control, and supply more efficient, especially in the case of a future mobilization. Military education was also extended. The Royal Military College was reformed and its curriculum made more relevant to modern military demands, and schools of instruction for promotion were established and officers were forced to pass through them.[91]

Supply was also revamped. First, the minister took it out of civilian hands where it had been since 1868, as a patronage plum, and gave it military ownership and competence. When the only, and very small, government cartridge factory in Quebec City had been found wanting under war's demand, plans were laid to upgrade it. It was now to be called the Dominion Arsenal and was intended to be the centre of excellence for munitions manufacturing skill in any future conflict.

Modern rifles had also been in short supply for Canadian soldiers. Requests to the War Office had always netted silence or cast-offs. In the dying days of hostilities, Borden decided to have rifles made in Canada.[92] The nation would now have its own small arms supply of a uniquely "Canadian" pattern and the new citizen army would have lots of rifles with which to develop the shooting skills that the war had so clearly proved were necessary.[93] And so began the troubled odyssey of the ill-fated Ross rifle in Canada.

The Canadian sense of independence coupled with the militia reforms that grew from the war also resulted in resistance to Britain's attempts to raise an Army Reserve of an Imperial Force that would automatically embroil Canada in Britain's conflicts with little to no influence or input into the decision making process. The prime minister and his minister of militia, consistently rebuffed any efforts at establishing an "Imperial Force" for overseas commitments.[94]

In part, the bankruptcy of British military leadership at the start of the conflict made Canada, and the other colonies, loathe to commit colonial military forces irrevocably to imperial command and control in time of war to serve British policy. Any other position was particularly untenable in Canada where support of imperial ventures had always proven to be fraught with divisiveness. Although Canada continued to submit annual defence plans and agreed to standardize training and organization on British models, belief in autonomy and control of its own forces was irreversible. That lesson of the Boer War had got through to many.

One could even argue that in later years the message of national command and control was planted firmly enough to be central to the creation of Canada's naval forces. When the great naval debates arose after 1906, the hard-won Laurier solution four years later was to create by an act of the

Canadian Parliament a separate Canadian Navy. This was done to mitigate the cultural antagonisms of French and English Canada unleashed by the issue. It was also done to avoid the loss of national command of Canadian units paid for by Canada's tax dollars, which would have happened if the force were raised directly for the Royal Navy. While it could be put at the British Admiralty's disposal, Canadians would decide.

This naval issue also illustrates why national command and control are important socio-political factors, just as participation in the Boer War participation had been a decade earlier. Put simply, without the application of both civil and military national command concepts, the cultural serenity of the nation was at a much higher risk. Granted, Canadians were (and are) not always successful in maintaining serenity, especially in the area of French and English Canadian relations; but the chances are always better if national self interests reflect the needs of both groups. In terms of Canada's extra territorial interests, the Boer War first tested these ideas.

By the end of the Boer War, in May 1902, 8,372 Canadians had served in South Africa — 224 lost their lives and another 252 were wounded.[95] Without question, their participation and achievements awakened a nationalistic pride and awareness in Canadians. It represented the nation's first global military effort. Canada learned many lessons that were incorporated into a wide sweeping and deeply influential Militia Reform in 1904. Equally important, the dispatch of distinct Canadian contingents, under Canadian commanding officers, answerable both to their British commanders and to the Canadian government, set an important precedent. The nation rejected the concept of scattering small units throughout the British field force. Rather, it insisted on a national contingent that would be employed as a unified body. From now on, Canadian soldiers fighting on behalf of the empire would do so as distinct and independent Canadian formations responsible before all else to their sovereign government. Never again would Canada blindly subordinate its sons and daughters to the absolute control of the "mother," nor would they automatically assume that the interests of the senior ally were always the same as those of Canada. Even though some Canadians could not see it, the Boer War had identified a right path for many things. Civil and Military national command and control was the route on which Canada would never look back.

NOTES

1. Ronald G. Haycock, *Sam Hughes* (Waterloo, ON: Wilfrid Laurier University Press, 1986), 70.
2. Sanford Evans, *The Canadian Contingents* (Toronto: Publishers' Syndicate Ltd., 1901), 319–320.
3. J. Murray Beck, *The Pendulum of Power: Canada's Federal Elections* (Scarborough, ON: Prentice -Hall, 1968), 97.
4. Contention revolved around such platforms as the right of the French to have separate education to protect language and religion, and to maintain at least a majority in the province of Quebec against the growing anglicization of the rest of the country. The relationship was made even more difficult in the decade before the South African War by merging Protestant extremism with traditional Catholic conservatism. For a discussion of these issues, see P.B. Waite, *Canada, 1874–1896: Arduous Destiny* (Toronto: McClelland & Stewart, 1971), especially Chapters 10 to 15.
5. H. Blair Neatby, "Laurier and Imperialism" in Ramsay Cook, et al.,eds., *Imperial Relations in the Age of Laurier* (Toronto: University of Toronto Press, 1969), 1–9.
6. Desmond Morton, *Ministers and Generals: Politics and the Canadian Militia, 1868–1904* (Toronto: University of Toronto Press, 1970), 201, appendix A, table 1.
7. *Ibid.*, 203, table 5, "Federal Government Expenditures on the Canadian Militia, 1869–1904.
8. Carman Miller, "Sir Frederick William Borden and Military Reform, 1896–1911," in *Canadian Historical Review*, Vol. 50, No. 3 (September 1969), 265–284.
9. See Thomas Pakenham, Lord Longford, *The Boer War* (New York: Random House, 1979), Chapters 5 to 9, which discusses the British motives and the Byzantine negotiations between Briton and Boer in the immediate pre-bellum period. For the Canadian events, the two best works are Carman Miller, *Painting the Map Red: Canada and the South African War 1899–1902* (Ottawa: Canadian War Museum, 1993), 3–15; and Brian A. Reid, *Our Little Army in the Field. The Canadians in South Africa* (St. Catharines, ON: Vanwell, 1996), 9–13.
10. Joseph Schull, *Laurier: The First Canadian* (Toronto: Macmillan of Canada, 1965), 381.
11. C.P. Stacey, *Canada and the Age of Conflict: A History of Canadian External Policies*, Vol. 1, 1867–1921 (Toronto: Macmillan, 1977), 44.
12. J.L. Granatstein, *Canada's Army* (Toronto: University of Toronto Press, 2002), 42–44; Richard A. Preston, *Canada and Imperial Defense* (Toronto: University of Toronto Press, 1967), 233–259; Stephen J. Harris, *Canadian Brass. The Making of a Professional Army 1860–1939* (Toronto: University of Toronto Press, 1988), 63–67; and Norman Penlington, "General Hutton and the Problem of Military Imperialism in Canada, 1898–1900," *Canadian Historical Review*, Vol. 24, 1943, 156–171.
13. Haycock, *Sam Hughes*, 68–70.
14. R.C. Brown and Ramsay Cook, *Canada, 1896–1914: A Nation Transformed* (Toronto: McClelland & Stewart, 1974), 38–44.
15. See Miller, *Painting the Map Red*, Chapter 2, "The Anatomy of Canadian Opinion," for a detailed analysis of this complicated debate.
16. Desmond Morton, *The Last War Drum: The North-West Campaign of 1885* (Toronto: Hakkert, 1972), introduction and Chapters 2, 4, and 8; Bob Beal and Rod MacLeod, *Prairie Fire: The 1885 North-West Rebellion* (Toronto: McClelland & Stewart, 1994), Chapters 2, 9, and 16–18 give a good analysis of the events and motives of Canadians of all stripes during this earlier and "first" national military

adventure. For the best analysis of what drove Canadians 14 years later, read Miller, *Painting the Map Red*, 3–14 and 16–64.

17. G.F.G. Stanley, *Canada's Soldiers: The Military History of an Unmilitary People* (Toronto: Macmillan, 1960), 277–282 and 287–289; and Haycock, *Sam Hughes*, 67–82.

18. C.P. Stacey, *Canada and the Age of Conflict*, Vol. 1, 57–68; Gwynne Dyer and Tina Viljoen, *The Defence of Canada* (Toronto: McClelland & Stewart, 1990), 157–163; Miller, *Painting the Map Red*, 31–50; and Evans, 8–19.

19. Carl Berger, *The Sense of Power: Studies in the Ideas of Canadian Imperialism 1867–1914* (Toronto: University of Toronto Press, 1970), 131–147, and 235–36; and Brown and Cook, 38–44.

20. Miller, *Painting the Map Red*, 16–30.

21. Norman Pennlington, *The Alaska Boundary Dispute: A Critical Re-Appraisal* (Toronto: McGraw-Hill Ryerson, 1972), 48–65.

22. Desmond Morton, *The Canadian General, Sir William Otter* (Toronto: A.M. Hakkert Ltd., 1974), 160–164. See also endnote 6.

23. "Canadian Troops for Transvaal," *Canadian Military Gazette*, Vol. 14, No. 19, October 3, 1899, 11.

24. Stacey, *Canada and the Age of Conflict*, Vol. 1, 57–70; Desmond Morton, *A Military History of Canada* (Toronto: McClelland & Stewart, 1992), 113–115. On the role of the Australians and New Zealanders in this conflict, see Peter Dennis and Jeffrey Grey, eds., *The Boer War: Army, Nation and Empire* (Canberra: Army Historical Unit, 2000). This is a compendium of articles on various aspects of the war including the long-term effects on Australia of the experience. There are remarkable similarities with their "Canadian cousins."

25. The anti-war side lost because they were too diffuse. Unlike the pro-war faction, they had neither the power nor the ideas that could converge into a homogeneous effort. Happenstance also worked against them. As they say about revolutions, there was 20 percent for and 20 percent against and 60 percent who did not care or could go one way or the other. In the end, enough of them went to the pro-war side. Moreover, Laurier realized that once riled an alienated English Canada could be more deadly for political careers than French Canada.

26. Canada, *Official Report of the Debates of the House of Commons of the Dominion of Canada* [henceforth *Debates*], Vol. 61, March 24, 1902, 1685; "The South African War, 1899–1902: Considerations Leading Up to Decision to Provide a Contingent," Library and Archives Canada [henceforth LAC], RG 24, Vol. 1850, File G.A.Q. 13–39 (7–13), 263; "Canada's Field Force for the Transvaal," *Canadian Military Gazette*, Vol. 14, No. 20, October 17, 1899, 11; and Stacey, *Canada and the Age of Conflict*, Vol. 1, 59.

27. Preston, 261; Dyer and Viljoen, 160–161.

28. Stacey, *Canada and the Age of Conflict*, Vol. 1, 60–66; Evans, 54, and 73; and Preston, 262. The definitive work on Minto as Canada's governor general is Carman Miller, *The Canadian Career of the Fourth Earl of Minto: The Education of a Viceroy* (Waterloo, ON: Wilfrid Laurier University Press, 1980).

29. Stacey, *Canada and the Age of Conflict*, Vol. 1, 67. The all arms concept was rejected by the Cabinet and they decided only to send infantry — the artillery and Mounted troops envisaged in the "all arms brigade" were not to be deployed. The battalion was raised from volunteers, although it did draw a significant number of officers and men from the Active Militia. Its name, linked to the permanent force Canadian infantry regiment was a further indication of the nationalist sentiment that surrounded the contingent. Furthermore, Carman Miller argues that the ponderous

title given to the contingent was carefully chosen to underline the fact that the contingent was not a levy of British army recruits but rather men with a temporary appointment in the Canadian permanent militia. Miller, *Painting the Map Red*, 51.

30. "The South African War, 1899–1902. Considerations Leading Up to Decision to Provide a Contingent," 264–265; and Stacey, *Canada and the Age of Conflict*, Vol. 1 pp.65–68. For a good description of the enthusiasm that Canadian regular soldiers had to join the fray both to get experience and have adventure at the same time, read Brigadier-General Septimus J.A. Denison's *Memoirs* (Toronto: Best Publishing, 1927). He was the younger brother of Colonel G.T. Denison cited in fn 28. and a "Royal" (RCR).

31. "The South African War, 1899–1902. Considerations Leading Up to Decision to Provide a Contingent," 266; Reid, 32; and Stacey, *Canada and the Age of Conflict*, Vol. 1, 69.

32. See Canada, *Department of Militia and Defence of the Dominion of Canada, Report for the Year Ended 30th June, 1893* (Ottawa: Queen's Printer, 1894), 1; Preston, 206, 209, 229, and 232; "The Special Service Contingent," *Canadian Military Gazette*, November 21, 1899, 9; W. Hart-McHarg, *From Quebec to Pretoria with the Royal Canadian Regiment* (Toronto: William Briggs, 1902), 105; and Morton, *The Canadian*, 164.

33. The British Army and Modern Conceptions of War," *Royal United Services Institute (RUSI)*, Vol. 60, No. 40, September 1911, 1181. See also Sanford Evans, *The Canadian Contingents* (Toronto: The Publishers' Syndicate Ltd., 1901), 36. Lord Dundonald so doubted the capability of his opponents that he actually queried an officer of the locally raised scouts, on the eve of battle, if "the Boers would [actually] fight when they saw Her Majesty's troops...." Gordon McKenzie, *Delayed Action: Being Something of the Life and Times of the Late Brigadier General, Sir Duncan McKenzie, KCMG, CB, DSO, VD, Legion d'Honneur* (Private Printing, no date), 163.

34. "Comment," *The Military Gazette*, November 7, 1900, 1.

35. "The Second Contingent," *The Military Gazette*, January 2, 1900, 9.

36. Quoted in Dyer and Viljoen, 159.

37. Lieutenant E.W.B. Morrison, *With the Guns in South Africa* (Hamilton: Spectator Printing Company, 1901), 20.

38. For a detailed account of the British military failure see Bernd Horn, "Lost Opportunity: The Boer War Experience and Its Influence on British and Canadian Military Thought," in Bernd Horn, ed., *Forging a Nation: Perspectives on the Canadian Military Experience* (St. Catharines, ON: Vanwell, 2002), 81–106. In brief, the British problems had many causes: a traditional, conservative, arguably anti-intellectual officer corps that placed greater emphasis on courage and dash than on tactical acumen and the study of modern war; the failure to understand the advances in technology and their impact on combat; overconfidence bred from a litany of wars against poorly armed tribesmen; an over all absence of initiative and innovative thought at all levels; and the failure to practise the most rudimentary fieldcraft skills such as using camouflage, seeking cover, and conducting detailed reconnaissance before an attack. See also: "Military Criticism," *Army and Navy Gazette*, Vol. 61, No. 2105, May 26, 1900, 503 and "Some Lessons of the War," No. 2106, 532; "The War Summary," (Toronto) *Globe*, December 27, 1899, Vol. 55, No. 15,555, 1.

39. David Throup, ed., *British Documents on Foreign Affairs: Reports and Papers from the Foreign Office Confidential Print. Part I, Series G, Africa, 1885–1914. Vol. 8 Anglo-Boer War I: From Eve of War to Capture of Johannesburg, 1899–1900* (Bethesda, MD: University of Publications of America, 1995), 229.

40. *Ibid.*, 235.

41. *Ibid.*, 235.

42. *Ibid.*, 236.

43. *Ibid.*, 239.

44. See Pakenham's, *The Boer War*, especially Chapters 8 and 9, "Preparing for a Small War" and "The Ultimatum." A classic study of this conflict is Rayne Kruger's *Goodbye Dolly Gray* (London: Cassell, 1961).

45. Winston S. Churchill, *The Boer War — London to Ladysmith via Pretoria, Ian Hamilton's March* (London: Leo Cooper, 1989), 31–32.

46. Miller, *Painting the Map Red*, 154.

47. *Ibid.*, 414.

48. "The Progress of War," *Canadian Military Gazette*, December 5, 1899, 9.

49. "The Reverses in South Africa," *Canadian Military Gazette*, January 2, 1900, 10.

50. See Harris, 68; Preston, 253; Pennlington, 166; and Norman Hillmer and J.L. Granatstein, *Empire to Umpire: Canada and the World to the 1990s* (Toronto: Copp Clark Longman, 1994), 24. When the prevailing GOC intimated that Lieutenant-Colonel Sam Hughes would be incapable of serving along side British regulars, Hughes retorted, "Why, could I not retreat or surrender quick enough to the Boers?" Harris, 87. Another anecdotal story revealed the mood. A dignitary visited a school and spoke to the children about the war and asked, "Why were not the British successful at first?" The prompt reply was "because the Canadians had not arrived." Evans, 323.

51. *Debates*, Vol. 55, May 22, 1901, 5886.

52. Miller, *Painting the Map Red*, 155–165; Reid, 41; "The Second Contingent," *The Military Gazette*, January 2, 1900, 9; and "Considerations Leading Up to Decision to Provide a Contingent," 266–268. The two mounted infantry battalions were called 1 and 2 Canadian Mounted Rifles (CMR). The former was renamed the Royal Canadian Dragoons in August 1900, while 2 CMR, largely based on the North-West Mounted Police, was renamed 1 CMR. Unlike the first contingent, the second contingent was actually a coalition of three smaller units that were given different tasks and that were attached to various different British formations. The guns were especially dispersed. "It was expected when the Royal Canadian Artillery came to South Africa that it would be taken through the war as a brigade division," noted a serving subaltern, "but Col. Drury has never had his three batteries together since they landed, and the organisation is now hopelessly broken up." Morrison, 118.

53. Miller, *Painting the Map Red*, 414–423; Reid, 159–171; and "Considerations Leading Up to Decision to Provide a Contingent," 268–269. In the case of the South African Constabulary, the Canadian government acted as the agent of the War Office in raising men. See also *Debates*, Vol. 54, March 12, 1901, 1303–1308.

54. R.C. Fetherstonhaugh, *The Royal Canadian Regiment* (Private Printing: Royal Canadian Regiment, Reprint 1981), 157–175; Reid, 40; and "Considerations Leading Up to Decision to Provide a Contingent," 267.

55. Miller, *Painting the Map Red*, xiii.

56. Hart-McHarg, 147; and Reid, 69. See also Fetherstonhaugh, 121; "South-African Letter," *Canadian Military Gazette*, April 3, 1900, 7; Page, 14; and Miller, 119.

57. Quoted in Morton, *The Canadian*, 203.

58. Morton, *The Canadian*, 203; and Miller, *Painting the Map Red*, 84 and 119.

59. Reid, 70.

60. Hart-McHarg, 156–158; Morton, *The Canadian*, 210–212; Fetherstonhaugh, 122; and Miller, *Painting the Map Red*, 83 and 120–121. The outcry in England and

Canada as a result of the reports eventually led to a Royal Commission to investigate the matter. Overall the problems encountered were attributed to the harsh environment and exigencies of the campaign.

61. *Debates*, June 6, 1900, 6790; Miller, 119; and "Considerations Leading Up to Decision to Provide a Contingent," 272. The issue was brought before Parliament by a MP as a result of an article in the *Military Gazette* that stated: "Evidence is forthcoming, however, which goes to prove that the question of the comfort and good health, and even the lives, of our troops in South Africa has been sacrificed to consideration which we can only say call for strict investigation."

62. See Morton, *The Canadian*, 169–199; Fetherstonhaugh, 111–117; Granatstein, *Canada's Army*, 40–43; "General Cronje's Surrender," (Toronto) *Globe*, February 27, 1900, 1; J. C. Hopkins and Murat Halstead, *South Africa and the Boer-British War* (Brantford, ON: The Bradley-Garretson Company, 1900), 424–429; and Miller, *Painting the Map Red*, 102–112. Lieutenant-Colonel Otter himself confessed that the victory "was not quite as satisfactory and complete as we had hoped for." He was aware that, in the words of renowned Canadian military historian Desmond Morton, "only pure accident left the two companies on the right in position, able to appear victorious as dawn broke." Morton, *The Canadian*, 201.

63. For example, see *Debates*, February 22, 1900, 813, and February 26, 1900, 1039, and July 7, 1900, 9486; (Toronto) *Globe*, "Toronto's Soldiers in Battle," January 3, 1900, February 1 and February 27, 1900, 1; Hart-McHarg, 117 and 133; and Hopkins and Halstead, 427 and 429.

64. Quoted in Morton, *The Canadian*, 234.

65. Evans, 205.

66. Quoted in "Considerations Leading Up to Decision to Provide a Contingent," 275. Sir Redvers Buller stated of Lord Strathcona's Horse that he "had never been served by a nobler, braver or more serviceable body of men." *Ibid.* The British Official History of the war describes Lord Strathcona's Horse as "a body of Canadian rough-riders unsurpassed for daring and endurance in the field." Quoted in C.P. Stacey, "Canada and the South African War, Part III," *Canadian Army Journal*, Vol. 4, No. 4, September 1950, 42.

67. Morrison, 284–285.

68. "Comments," *Canadian Military Gazette*, January 2, 1900, 6. Later that month the paper commented, "The whole trend of feeling in Britain with regard to the value of colonial soldiers is rapidly changing, and not only in Britain but at the seat of war." *Ibid.*, January 16, 1900, 4.

69. Editor, "Some Lessons of the War," *Army and Navy Gazette*, Vol. 61, No. 2106, 532.

70. "Army Notes," *Army and Navy Gazette*, Vol. 61, No. 2088, January 27, 1900, 79.

71. Tuvia Ben-Moshe, *Churchill Strategy and History* (Boulder, CO: Lynee Rienner Publications, 1992), 10.

72. Winston S. Churchill, "Some Impressions of the War in South Africa," *RUSI*, Vol. 45, No. 281, July 1901, 843.

73. Quoted in Preston, 266.

74. *Ibid.*, 267.

75. "The Royal Canadians," *Army and Navy Gazette*, Vol. 61, No. 2098, April 7, 1900, 343.

76. Morrison, 20. See also "South African Letter," *Canadian Military Gazette*, February 20, 1900, 7.

77. Stanley McKeown Brown, *With the Royal Canadians* (Toronto: The Publishers' Syndicate, 1900), 136–137. The journalist also revealed, "A British general after viewing the work of the Canadians in attack at Paardeburg said: 'Those men can go

into battle without a leader they have intelligence and resourcefulness enough to lead themselves.'" *Ibid.*, 138.

78. *Ibid.*, 291. "That the Canadians have made such a name for themselves in this war is distinctly due to their quality and not to their numbers." *Ibid.*, 214.

79. Morrison, 293.

80. John Marteinson, *We Stand on Guard* (Toronto: Ovale, 1992), 63; and Miller, 109.

81. Quoted in Robert Page, *The Boer War and Canadian Imperialism* (Ottawa: Canadian Historical Association, 1987), 14; and C.P. Stacey, "Canada and the South African War, Part IV," *Canadian Army Journal*, Vol. 4, No. 5, October 1950, 10.

82. *Debates*, June 7, 1900, 6910–6911. See also Morton, *A Military History of Canada*, 117.

83. Evans, 6.

84. "The Rifle," *Canadian Military Gazette*, October 7, 1902, 9.

85. On Sam Hughes's views coming out of the conflict, see Haycock, *Sam Hughes*, 83–96 and 99. He went on to state in Parliament, "All authorities on constitutional law and government agree that one of the greatest dangers to permanent stability of any nation is the maintenance of a large standing army." *Debates*, April 21, 1902, 3156.

86. *Debates*, July 11, 1905, 9180.

87. Quoted in Harris, 32.

88. Perhaps the most important result of this war was what it did for promoting a sense of Canadian identity. The war was the first truly national effort in a foreign enterprise. Canadians now had a common experience that lasted well beyond the war; it did not matter if one was from Rossland, British Columbia or from Lunenberg, Nova Scotia. All the contingents were made up primarily of Canadian-born volunteers. Furthermore, the battle at Paardeberg was hailed as a Canadian victory. In the national psyche, it was only overshadowed as a triumph of arms by the far bloodier Canadian battle of Vimy Ridge in 1917. On the home front, the experience of the soldiers was translated in the same way. For two and a half years the Canadian public devoured a virtual flood of daily newspaper reports and soldiers' letters to local newspapers. Even many of those who had originally opposed the war, once it got going quietly joined in. And clearly, as more contingents were raised, there was seldom a problem getting volunteers anxious to go. The war was seen as a national effort. For instance, a variety of national volunteer support agencies like the Canadian Patriotic Fund were quickly established to aid soldiers and their families. On the local front, citizens enthusiastically contributed to drives to send comfort amenities like tobacco, socks and food to their "boys" As they came home, it was usually to some sort of parade occasion. Even the government offered free land in the Canadian West to returned soldiers.

89. Fetherstonhaugh, 89. See also Morton, *A Military History of Canada*, 118.

90. Robert Brown and Ramsay Cook, *Canada 1896–1921: A Nation Transformed* (Toronto: McClelland & Stewart, 1974), 167; and *Debates*, July 11, 1904, 6367. In response to the queries in Parliament, in regards to the soundness of these changes, Sir Frederick Borden bristled and retorted, "The question is rather: Has Canada assumed such a prominent position by her growth, by the heroic acts of her officers at home and in the South African War, as to entitle her to appoint one of her own sons to the command of her militia? Has she not assumed a position when at least there should be removed from the militia of this country the reflection that we cannot rear a man competent to take command of our own forces?" *Debates*, March 22, 1904, 289. See also *Debates*, May 1, 1899, 2343–2345, and 2355; Debates, April 10, 1900, 3482; and *Debates*, March 1, 1900, 2751.

91. For Militia reform, see Horn, "Lost Opportunity," 94–97; Morton, *A Military History of Canada*, 120–122; "The New Militia Bill," *Canadian Military Gazette*, July

26, 1904; Miller, 438; and Harris, 62–82.

92. Borden accepted the offer of Scottish rifle manufacturer Sir Charles Ross, to build a factory in Quebec City. Ross would produce a state-of-the-art rifle of straight pull design. Significantly, Ross was another Boer War veteran who had seen the inefficiency of the "Long Tom" Lee Enfield compared to the modern high velocity Boer Mauser. By the summer of 1902, a government contract with very generous financial incentives and a free factory site conveniently in the prime minister's home riding near Quebec City was signed and factory construction started. Ultimately, this Canadian rifle met an ignominious end during the First World War because of political interference and some minor technical flaws. Nevertheless, the policy idea was sound and the new industrial capability it brought to Canada, and to Quebec laid the basis for private munitions manufacturing. See R.G. Haycock, "Early Canadian Weapons Acquisition: 'That Damned Ross Rifle,'" *Canadian Defence Quarterly*, Vol. 14, No. 3 (Winter 1984–85), 48–59.

93. Commentary in the *Canadian Military Gazette* remarked that "We trust that the day is not far distant when every city, town, yes and village, too, in the Dominion will have at least one range within easy reach." It also attacked the British government for its reticence in financing suitable facilities for rifle shooting in the United Kingdom. It questioned, "Why are auxiliary forces kept up, if their efficiency is not regarded as of the first moment? Certainly they cannot be deemed efficient if skill with the rifle is absent." (October 7, 1902, 9). The difference in support was due in large part to the difference in the priority put on the citizen force by the British and Canadian governments. The Rifle Clubs in Canada, due to the belief in the "born citizen soldier," were given a substantial boost and by 1902, a total of 95 Clubs, representing 5,060 members, were in operation. In addition, 719 rifles and over 1.5 million cartridges were issued. Canada, Department of the Militia and Defence. *Report of the Department of Militia and Defence, 1902*, 2 and 32. See also: Canada, Department of Militia and Defence. *Report of the Department of Militia and Defence, 1901, 28; Report of the Department of Militia and Defence, 1903*, 5–6; "The Rifle Clubs," *Canadian Military Gazette*, May 7, 1901, 9; *Report of the Department of Militia and Defence, 1903*, 6; Col J. Peters, "Teach the Boys to Shoot," *The United Service Magazine*, Vol. 28, 1903–104, 599; and *Debates*, July 11, 1905, 9196. Reverend C.G. Gull, ("Military Training in Secondary Schools," *RUSI*, Vol. 45, No. 276, February 1901, 115–120), argued that "The object in view [marksmanship training] is not to make soldiers, but to give all boys a military training of such a character as to enable them to take their place in the ranks in after years with but short preparation." A similar view stated: "With a knowledge of drill and the use of arms diffused among the youth of the country, England would in a time of danger, without conscription, have an entire male population ready to take their place with the regular army on active duty. "The Value of Cadet Corps," *Canadian Military Gazette*, February 3, 1903, 6. See also "Military Cadet Organization," *Canadian Military Gazette*, February 9, 1904, 8).

94. See *Colonial Conferences Relating to Defence*. This document covers the conferences of 1887, 1897, 1902 and 1907.

95. Granatstein, *Canada's Army*, 45. The number serving includes the Halifax garrison and the volunteers for the South African Constabulary. Of those who died, 89 were killed in action and 135 died from disease. See also "Considerations Leading Up to Decision to Provide a Contingent," 270; Page, 15. As a comparison, New Zealand contributed 6,000 troops and Australia dispatched 16,500 to the conflict in South Africa. *Ibid.*, 15.

CHAPTER 5

Canadian Military Effectiveness in the First World War
by Andrew B. Godefroy

After beginning the twentieth century with expeditionary forces fighting in South Africa, Canada spent an additional four and a half years as a major combatant with Allied forces in the First World War. This conflict, described at the time as simply "the Great War" or more naïvely as, "the war to end all wars", witnessed the largest deployment of Canadian soldiers, sailors, and airmen into combat in the country's history. In total, 619,636 men and women served in uniform overseas. At its end, 59,544 Canadian soldiers lay dead, mostly in France and Belgium, while another 154,361 men and women returned home wounded and forever scarred.

The First World War changed Canada in every way. As Canadian military historian C.P. Stacey once wrote: "Politically, economically, and socially it was a different place when the war was over. In some respects, the First War was more important to Canadians than the Second, simply because it was the first."[1] At home, the Dominion matured as it faced internal political and cultural challenges, while overseas, its armed forces melded into one of the most professional and successful allied formations in the European theatre of war. After breaking its teeth at Ypres, Mont Sorrel, and the Somme during the first two years of conflict, the Canadian Expeditionary Force (CEF) brought a series of watershed victories to the allies at Vimy Ridge, Hill 70, and Passchendaele in 1917. Again in the fall of 1918, Canadian units were at the forefront of the last push against Germany's Western Front armies, winning successive set-piece battles at Arras, Amiens, Canal du Nord, and Cambrai. On the last day of the war, Canadian soldiers led the way into Mons, the town where the war began. Everywhere it seemed General Sir Arthur Currie's four Canadian divisions brought success. In fact, the title CEF was then, and remains, synonymous with Canada's greatest military achievements.

How did Canada achieve such effectiveness during the First World War? Politically nascent in foreign and military affairs in 1914, the country did not enter the conflict of its own accord but was automatically at war because Britain was at war. Ottawa also largely deferred strategic and operational matters to Britain for resolution, and let the decision to employ the CEF on the Western Front reside within an imperial chain of command. Canada's soldiers were organized and trained on a British system, used a mix of Canadian and British technology, and fought (at first) using British formulated doctrine and tactics. Finally, with its first overseas contingent formed primarily of British ex-patriots and with many more to follow throughout the war, was there ever any difference or separation of strategic agenda or operational style between dominion and empire? Indeed there was, but it took the catalyst of four and a half years of fighting and dying on the Western Front for Canada to win the right to define its own future. For better, or in some cases for worse, the country's political effectiveness and military success in the Great War reshaped the nature of the relationship between Canada and its British mentor.

Effectiveness

A group of historians once noted that the study of conflict often reveals "how intractable, complex, and resistant to analysis and calculation are the problems roused by war."[2] Perhaps nothing is truer than when assessing the political and military effectiveness of a nation at war, and by doing so, attempting to explain why an empire or country (or in this case a dominion) succeeded so well at some points while it failed so miserably at others.

Though political and military effectiveness largely remain ill-defined concepts even in modern-day analyses of state and interstate conflict, this chapter assesses the Canadian experience in the First World War drawing upon the concepts of military effectiveness similar to those employed previously by other military historians including Allan R. Millet, Williamson Murray, and Kenneth H. Watman.[3] According to these scholars, strategic effectiveness was the process of employing national armed forces to secure by force national goals as defined by political leadership, while political effectiveness addressed the effort to obtain national resources, such as financial support, a sufficient military-industrial base, and a sufficient quantity and quality of human resources, for military activity. As for military effectiveness, this was more broadly defined as the process by which armed forces converted resources into fighting power. In essence Millet, Murray, and Watman argued that, "a fully effective military is one that derives maximum combat power from the resources politically and physically available."[4]

As was the case for its allies, Canada's Great War political and military experience was a mural of mixed success and failure. Yet unlike its allies, Canada has undertaken few analyses that examine the experience in terms of political or military effectiveness.[5] Perhaps this is because since its conclusion the Great War has never been synonymous with the concept of political or military effectiveness. On the contrary, as historian Paul Kennedy once noted, it has offered an abundance of evidence for a plethora of studies on political and military incompetence.[6] Certainly, Canada's military historians have categorically summed up their nation's Great War experience as some form of a march to Armageddon. Nonetheless, we need to know how effective the country was in wartime, and what lessons emerged to shape Canada's post-war political and military existence.

Although there is a consensus among most Canadian historians of the First World War that the Dominion far exceeded expectations in the pursuit of an allied victory, they remain reluctant to suggest that Canada was politically effective in its pursuit of that victory. This view stems from four main issues: first, Canada did not enter the war of its own accord but was automatically at war when Britain declared war against Germany; second, as a dominion Canada largely deferred to Britain on political strategic issues and had little control over the general direction of the allied war effort; third, the war caused serious internal political strife; (for example, support for war, conscription, et cetera), and last, Canada's significant military contribution earned Ottawa very little political influence at the Peace Conference in Versailles or in subsequent allied or international relations in the 1920s.

Even as a self-governing dominion of the British Empire, Canada was not politically independent of all British foreign policy and decision-making. Although the Dominion had a greater degree of flexibility in deciding its own fate than some of Britain's other colonies, it was integrated into the overall imperial defence scheme and was therefore expected to support the empire when it went to war.

More important perhaps, Canada wanted to join the war as much as Britain needed her to do so. Despite the country's polite rejections towards most requests for armed forces to support British campaigns in the late nineteenth century, neither the government in Ottawa nor the majority of its population intended to avoid the call to arms in 1914.

Therefore, Canada's automatic inclusion in Britain's response to Germany should not be perceived as a slight against the country's political effectiveness or independence, but a validation of it. As historian Ian Miller demonstrated in his detailed study of Toronto during the First World War, Canadians were anxious to join the fight; the fact that their political options were limited given the general initial public reaction to war seems moot.[7]

Canada did choose to defer most matters of overall strategy to the War Office in London; however, based on its South African experience it did take an active role in the administrative control of its own military forces. Soon after the outbreak of hostilities, Ottawa arranged for the establishment of an overseas administrative office in London. The Ministry for Overseas Military Forces of Canada (OMFC) was responsible for overseeing all activities associated with the Canadian Expeditionary Force and remained in operation through 1919. Far from relinquishing control of Canada's army to British generals, Ottawa was engaged as much as possible in providing for the country's soldiers throughout the war.[8]

There is no question that recruitment for overseas military service in Canada during the First World War led to considerable domestic political strife, especially with respect to Quebec's participation in the war and its reaction to the federal government's invocation of conscription in 1917. Recent scholarship has demonstrated, however, that previous generalizations about public reactions to recruitment, initially, and later to conscription, have been somewhat misleading. Miller's examination of wartime Toronto, for example, paints a dramatically opposite impression of the war's impact on the lives of Canadians at home. While acknowledging the current body of work that deals with the analysis of the memory and meaning of the First World War in Canada, Miller quickly departs from this school of thought explaining that "comparatively little attention has been devoted to the impact of the war on the lives of citizens as it was happening."[9]

In doing this, Miller takes issue with prior analyses by historians such as Jeffrey Keshen, author of *Propaganda and Censorship During Canada's Great War* (1996) who suggested that Canadians at home were largely uninformed and manipulated participants, by contending that the home front was well educated in the realities of the war and yet still, "people were willing to fight for God, King, and Country." Statistics show that this was obviously the case. In personnel alone, Canada's contribution to the war effort far exceeded rational expectations, and despite daily casualty lists that often covered whole pages of local newspapers Canadians of all backgrounds continued to either volunteer or later on, submit to conscription. Between 1914 and 1919 Canada contributed over half a million uniformed men and women to the allied armies, of which nearly 30 percent, essentially nearly one in three, were either killed or wounded. Whatever domestic political turmoil the war created, one must question as Miller did whether it truly overshadowed the country's desire to fight and win.

Finally, much emphasis has been placed on Ottawa's lack of a role in the peace process following the armistice in November 1918. Historians lamented afterwards that Ottawa's influence in post-war international politics was nowhere near commensurate with the sacrifices the country made to the war effort. There is some substantiation to this argument. War service had decimated Canada's small population, and the Canadian Corps had been instrumental in the defeat of the German Armies on the Western Front. Still, even after victories at battles such as Second Ypres, Mont Sorrel, Vimy Ridge, and Canal du Nord had irreversibly affected the national consciousness of the Dominion, politically Britain still spoke internationally for Canada, and would continue to do for another decade. Canada's sacrifice was also England's sacrifice, regardless of what English and French Canadians thought.

Military Effectiveness

Unlike Canadian wartime politics, military historians have little difficulty shining a positive light on the effectiveness of the CEF on the Western Front.[10] From what is often described as rather amateurish[11] and disorganized beginnings, Canada mustered four 18,000 man infantry divisions and supporting artillery, engineer, medical, and logistics units to build the Canadian Corps, arguably one of the most combat-effective formations in all the allied armies of the First World War.[12] Canadian troops fought their first engagements in early 1915, and after cutting its teeth in several subsequent actions in Flanders and France during the next two years, the Canadian Corps captured a string of operational successes in 1917 and 1918 that were central to the achievement of overall victory.[13]

Canada's central role in this military victory has not gone unnoticed. Contrary to the perceptions of some and the writings of others, the CEF enjoys a reasonably well-studied past.[14] However, the majority of published works focus only on the operational history of Canada's largest battles, histories of single units (most often infantry battalions), or the memoirs of private soldiers. Many other critical areas of study such as institutional organization and evolution, training and education, professional development, and leadership and command have received much less attention, resulting in many generalizations about the military effectiveness of the Canadian Corps that have yet to be disqualified or fully proven.

The seed of the success of the Canadian Corps was planted much earlier than most have previously indicated. Canada's army began preparing for the First World War, though unknowingly, immediately after the Boer War.[15] In 1903 a period of modernization and reform began largely as a result of politics and the need for improved defence within the Dominion, but also because of the successful integration of many valuable operational lessons learned by Canadian soldiers who had just fought a new type of war in South Africa. As an adversary the Boers were unlike any of the other opponents that the British had previously faced in South Africa. They were not a body of ill-armed and outgunned Natives, rather these European immigrants knew the veldt, were comfortable in the saddle, and were deadly with the rifle at long range. By combining technology and firepower with guerrilla tactics they had painfully exposed the obsolescence of traditional Victorian era British doctrine, and they killed many British soldiers who failed to recognize their influence on the nature of the war.

Improved Boer armaments in well-trained hands had seriously eroded the effectiveness of traditional British closed formation fighting and massed, unsupported infantry assaults. Although parade square drill was useful for moving large formations between battlefields, once engaged, such manoeuvres became useless if not dangerous. Canadians learned quickly that fieldcraft and battle drills superseded parade ground ceremony, and formations were reorganized to take advantage of smaller unit tactics, patrolling, and skirmishing. Canadian artillery tactics and employment also changed. Instead of parking guns wheel to wheel as in the past, artillery was spread out to avoid being vulnerable to punishing Boer rifle fire.[16] Even the artillery systems were re-examined, as the need for more rapid fire support challenged traditional designs that previously could not dampen recoil or support sustained accurate firing.

As early as 1905, Canadian infantry training officially abandoned parade square drills in favour of offensive action based on fire and manoeuvre. The army's newly published training guide stated: "constant practice in a stereotyped formation inevitably leads to want of elasticity, accustoms all ranks to work by rule rather than by exercise of their wits, and cramps both initiative and intelligence."[17] Still, Canadian doctrine and tactics continued to be heavily influenced by the British, and the British Army had reached its own conclusions about offence supported by machine guns and artillery. Despite some reservations, it was less concerned that the effectiveness of its fire and manoeuvre tactics would be seriously challenged. As a result less consideration was given to what should be done should offensive action fail, or how the British Army might operate, if put on the defensive or under siege-like conditions.[18]

Fire and manoeuvre based on offensive action continued to influence Canadian infantry, cavalry, and artillery doctrine and tactics up until the outbreak of war. Whatever its later deficiency in the face of battle, one cannot criticize the Canadian Army for adopting such ideas. British influence aside, given the technology then available, and the experiences of South Africa, the adoption of such principles was a logical if not entirely satisfactory evolution of the Canadian way of warfare.

The Canadian Army continued to improve both individual and collective training in the years leading up to the outbreak of war. Despite consistent funding shortages and a chronic lack of readily available equipment, units continued to train with what they had, some more successfully and seriously than others did.

Between 1904 and 1914, military school standards were slowly improved and specific skills germane to war fighting such as gunnery and musketry were strongly encouraged. Canadian artillery and rifle teams competed regularly in imperial competitions, and contrary to earlier assessments of their skills performed admirably and frequently won these contests.[19]

Although seldom recognized in the literature, these dedicated "amateurs' formed an important core within the first Canadian contingent. Unquestionably there was considerable disorganization and chaos during the initial mobilization, equipping, and training of 1 Canadian Division, but this did not diminish the reality that many of those at Valcartier already had considerable peacetime individual and unit training. As well, many had at least once annually participated in brigade-level collective training at one of the many summer concentrations. Although the sheer size of the first contingent (30,000 plus soldiers) was administratively a nightmare, it was not entirely strange to those who had the unenviable task of preparing it for war.[20]

The state of preparedness of the Canadian Army to mobilize for war in 1914, or the lack of it, is often put forward as a reason for the general

Library and Archives Canada C-2468

Lieutenant-General Sir Sam Hughes watching the departure of the Canadian Expeditionary Force, Quebec City, 1914.

lack of military effectiveness of the CEF during the early years of the war. Canada had formalized its plans for mobilization in the event of war before 1914 but these carefully detailed instructions were quickly dismissed when the actual declaration of war arrived on the desk of the energetic and egocentric minister of militia and defence, Sam Hughes. Caring little for the formalities of force development and employment as conceived by the chief of the General Staff, Colonel William Otter, Hughes sent instructions directly to various unit commanding officers ordering them to report along with their men at Camp Valcartier as quickly as possible. As a result, units from all across Canada arrived at Camp Valcartier ill-equipped and not entirely prepared for what might happen next. Still, within a matter of weeks the contingent, for better or for worse, was aboard ship and on its way overseas. Canadian soldiers began arriving in England on October 14, 1914, only 10 weeks after war was declared.[21]

Given the circumstances one is left to wonder what exactly was so militarily ineffective about delivering 30,000 troops to reinforce England within such a short period. Unquestionably, Canadian mobilization was poorly executed and logistical travesties abounded in the transportation of Canadian troops overseas. However, one might simply juxtapose Canada's mobilization experience against that of England, France, or even Germany. Within such a context, Canada's mobilization and deployment was arguably no worse than any of the others actors preparing for warfare on the Western Front.

Command and Control

The issue of who would form the senior leadership and command of the CEF was hotly contested. At the highest level, the Conservative Party minister of militia and defence, Sam Hughes, considered himself to be the best choice to lead the first contingent of Canadian civilian-soldiers. Not surprisingly, both the British War Office in London and the British commander-in-chief, Lord Kitchener, quickly disagreed. Despite repeated attempts to be placed at the top of the chain of Canadian operational command, Sam Hughes finally conceded the point, if only temporarily, and grudgingly accepted that another would be nominated for the post.

Many felt that another Canadian, Major-General François-Louis Lessard, was the most suitable candidate. The 53-year-old experienced, respected, and bilingual Lessard had commanded the Royal Canadian Dragoons in action in South Africa, and received considerable praise for his efforts at Leliefontein where three of his dragoons were awarded the Victoria Cross. Hughes, however, would have none of it, and rejected any notion of Lessard receiving overall command of the first Canadian contingent.[22] In the end, command of Canadian forces went to a British officer as the War Office had suggested. The man selected for the task was Major-General E.A.H. Alderson.

A career officer with considerable operational experience, Alderson had been previously exposed to Canadian troops during his time in South Africa during the Boer War. He was comfortable with the assignment of commanding 1 Canadian Division, but soon found that other aspects of the position invited only headaches and frustration. Though often praised by the Canadian soldiers whom he led early in the war, Alderson regularly found himself caught between Canadian politicians and British General Headquarters who were often at odds with each other over countless issues concerning the administration and employment of Canadian troops. Despite the fact that Sam Hughes willingly conceded to his government in the House of Commons that "We have nothing whatever to say as to the destination of the troops once they cross the water"[23] he routinely badgered and criticized Alderson's decision-making with respect to the training and preparation of the 1 Canadian Division for combat. Obviously frustrated that he had been passed over for command, Hughes set out to make Alderson's life miserable wherever possible and continued to defame his character even after the Canadian Corps had proven itself in combat.

In the end Hughes's cantankerous oratory was somewhat successful against Alderson, though it did not lead to the eventual replacement of the British officer with himself or one of his political friends as he undoubtedly hoped. In May 1916 another British officer, Lieutenant-General Sir Julian Byng, replaced Alderson. Byng retained command of the Canadian Corps until after the victory at Vimy Ridge in 1917, when he turned over the appointment to Arthur Currie, a Canadian militia officer who had previously commanded 2 Canadian Infantry Brigade and then 1 Canadian Division. In the interim Hughes had been sacked. Canadian Prime Minister Robert Borden could no longer accommodate his minister's antics and intrusions into the administration of the war and had him removed. Hughes's military career was over.

Departing from the political issues surrounding the highest levels of command in the Canadian Corps, the story of other senior leadership is much less well known. Though critical to any assessment of the military effectiveness of the Canadian Corps, individual and collective biographies of the senior military leadership (from divisional command down to battalion or battery command) are noticeable only by their absence. Despite countless publications that attest to the superiority and effectiveness of Canadian troops, few historians have supported such arguments with anything beyond anecdotal evidence. Sadly, surprisingly little is known about the 126 wartime Canadian generals who commanded troops both at home, in England, and in combat in Belgium and France.[24] Instead, assessments of Canadian military organization and administration are too few in number, while operational and tactical effectiveness are too often characterized not by the senior officers who planned and executed these battles, but by the recollections of corporals and privates. Although at the very heart of combat, men in the lower ranks often knew little if anything of the many factors and constraints affecting the operational and tactical decision-cycle of the battlefield commanders.[25]

Only the most senior commander of the Canadian Corps, Sir Arthur Currie, has merited more than a single academic examination of his life.[26] Of the remaining 125 Canadian wartime generals, less than six have received any serious biographical attention. Given that so little is known about the men who shaped it, an observer feels compelled to reconsider the completeness of current assessments of Canadian operational and tactical effectiveness on the Western Front.

Slightly down the chain of command of the CEF the situation improves little. The infantry battalion, consisting of approximately 1,000 men and commanded by a lieutenant-colonel, was the primary unit employed in action in France and Flanders.[27] Yet, nearly a century after, 260 of these battalions were recruited in Canada for possible combat on the Western Front, there has appeared but a single comprehensive biography of one of the infantry battalion commanders who led one of the 48 fighting battalions.[28] The lucky subject was George Pearkes, undoubtedly chosen for study because he was a recipient of the Victoria Cross at Passchendaele. He served as a major-general during the Second World War and as minister of national defence in the mid-1950s.[29]

In fact, it remains evident that far less is known about the machinations of leadership and command of Canada's First World War army than might be otherwise perceived, let alone how such skills were tested and proven on the battlefield. For example, more recent scholarship on the CEF officer corps has revealed a very different culture than previously suggested. As historian Patrick Brennan noted:

> Once the nature of trench warfare became clear, and the Canadian Corps began the process of institutionalizing and universalizing learning, it would appear that Byng and Currie settled on a pattern of identifying junior combat officers who were proven leaders and fighters with an aptitude for organization, morale-building and training. These men were then given the demanding and dangerous role of commanding infantry battalions. Once in command, they stuck at it until, in some cases, they were found wanting, or as happened far more often, they couldn't [physically or mentally] go on, Byng or Currie found something more important for them to do, or the war ended. It seems that the great majority of the amateur warriors had become capable professionals. Their contribution to the successes achieved by the Canadian Corps has too long been understated.[30]

Given the increasingly complex nature of the battlefield especially during the last two years of the war and the constant physical and mental demands it placed on Canadian commanders to continually serve up one operational victory after another, the Canadian Corps was undoubtedly well served by those who led it. Yet the persistent lack of knowledge and awareness about the CEF officer corps as an institution or how these men commanded their forces in the field has let numerous popular assumptions become ingrained as historical fact over the last several decades, myths that can neither be validated nor challenged until greater attention is paid to this field of biographical study.

Organization and Early Execution

The Canadian Expeditionary Force arrived in England in a piecemeal fashion. After the initial influx of units that became 1 Canadian Division, Canada organized and transported individual infantry battalions, artillery batteries, engineer, medical, and support units over to England as quickly as they were recruited. Most of these units were broken up and reorganized once they reached England, but the CEF eventually fielded a Canadian Corps with four divisions. Each division contained three brigades, each with four infantry battalions plus supporting artillery, engineers, and other units.

The true validation of the military effectiveness of the Canadian Corps was its ability to successfully convert its resources into fighting power. Despite initial British chauvinism towards Canadian units arriving at Salisbury training grounds in October 1914, 1 Canadian Division prepared itself for combat as best it could. Some, but not all, ineffectual officers were weeded out, and the men were toughened up to meet the challenges of warfare that lay ahead. Still, the Canadian "colonials" could not escape all criticism. J.F.C. Fuller, then a young officer serving in the British Expeditionary Force, remarked that the Canadian troops would perform well if only all their officers were shot.[31] Such degradation, however, was simply cultural prejudice and largely unfounded. After approximately 12 weeks of training in England, 1 Canadian Division was considered ready for deployment and sent to France.[32]

The division had only a brief period to familiarize itself with the Western Front before it saw action. The formation was assigned to the British front lines at the Ypres Salient in March 1915, already a scene of some the most deadly engagements of the war. There, soldiers quickly learned how to live and fight in a modern war zone. Daily routines were carried out amongst constant shelling, sniper's bullets, and the ever-increasing number of corpses. The consequences for making careless mistakes were quickly realized and usually fatal. Still, the men accepted their condition with some stoicism and tried to focus on staying alive long enough to fight.

In the early hours of April 22, 1915, the German Army attacked French positions on the Canadian left flank at Ypres. Employing a new and deadly weapon — gas. The German attack quickly caved in the French defensive line as terrified soldiers abandoned their positions before choking to death. Their rout left a huge gap in the allied line through which the Germans poured more troops. The Canadian defenders suddenly found themselves horribly outflanked and facing a new and unknown threat.

Although not flawless, the successful Canadian defence at what later became known as the Second Battle of Ypres was undoubtedly the result of training. Whatever its deficiencies in leadership and command, logistics, or support, the First Canadian Division confronted overwhelming enemy forces on their front and immediate flank employing unknown weapons and effectively stopped them. Though the Germans obviously failed to fully realize and exploit the damage they had inflicted against the French line, all accounts of the battle reveal how near disastrous the engagement might have been for the allies had the Canadian troops not fought the Germans to a standstill. Canada's first blood at Ypres was costly, with the First Canadian division suffering 5,975 casualties between April 22 and May 3, but it ended most if not all British chauvinism towards the fighting ability of the Canadian soldier.

Subsequent battles around Ypres throughout the summer and fall of 1915 were less successful as allied doctrine and tactics failed to realize any victories of substance. Canadian commanders were frustrated by the lack of natural terrain cover and their inability to manoeuvre as machine guns and obstacles stopped them from effectively taking and holding ground. Much of the area of Belgium and Flanders where the Canadian Corps fought consisted of no more than low ridges, rolling hills, or wide expanses of flat open terrain. The many wooded areas were rapidly reduced to nothing more than a collection of burnt stumps by constant shelling. Soldiers were forced to dig themselves down into the ground to survive.

Within a short while the whole Western Front consisted of a series of interconnected trenches, protected by row after row of barbed wire entanglements covered by machine gun emplacements and pre-registered artillery fire. In between the opposing armies lay an often narrow strip of cratered and desolately abandoned terrain that was commonly referred to as "no man's land" due to the perception that it was impossible for anyone to survive beyond his own trench lines for long.

Most trenches across the Western Front were based on a similar concepts or patterns, but German trench systems were often much more solid and complex than the British and Canadian lines. Unlike the Western allies, who saw their trench lines as a temporary cover while preparing for the next advance, the German Army expected that their western lines of defence might become home for some time while they focused on winning the Eastern Front. As a result, German trenches were often better constructed, dryer, and had semi-permanency in mind. They often contained several interesting features such as solid concrete bunkers, fortified sniping posts, and protected forward ammunition dumps. Allied lines, by contrast, often consisted of nothing more than semi-connected communication trenches with intermittent firing parapets and limited cover.

Facing complex German fortifications and defence in depth, the Canadian Corps sought to modify its doctrine and tactics to overcome these new obstacles. Improvements to the straightforward tactic of fire and manoeuvre were needed and alternatives were sought. Organizations right down to the section were modified, reorganized, and provided with new training, equipment, and weapons. New ideas were tested first on a smaller scale, often in the form of a trench raid.

The trench raid was by no means a Canadian invention, but as historian Daniel G. Dancocks once wrote: "If [Canadians] had not initiated this form of warfare, they elevated it to an art form."[33] Trench raiding had originated as part of the British Expeditionary Force policy to maintain the offensive, keeping the allied soldiers from falling into the monotony of trench warfare, while constantly harassing and demoralizing the enemy. One of the first recorded trench raids was carried out by British Indian troops, the Gerwhal Rifles of the Lahore Division, of which two battalions harassed the German lines on the night of November 9, 1914.[34] In February 1915, the Princess Patricia's Canadian Light Infantry (PPCLI) raided the German lines opposite their own and thus undertook the first operation of what would later become a trademark of the Canadian Corps.

Carried out against the German lines between May 1915 and March 1918, these attacks gave the Canadian Corps the base of knowledge it needed to win in the unique environment that was the Western Front. The trench raid, noted historian Bill Rawling, "was the laboratory" by which the Canadians developed a successful battlefield doctrine.[35] The raids helped develop tactics for not only surviving the routine of trench warfare, but also for overcoming the barren waste in between the trenches that was so often an obstacle in the attack. New Canadian military doctrine tactics were widely circulated throughout the entire BEF and French Army commands for review and discussion, and were later disseminated among their own soldiers when the Canadian Corps had shown success after success in its small-scale operations.[36] By late 1917 the set-piece attack that worked so well in trench raids was ready for application in larger-scale operations.

Operational Doctrine and Tactics

Since the summer of 1915 the successful execution of large scale battles posed considerable difficulty to Canadian senior commanders. The battles of the summer clearly showed that although Canadian soldiers were well trained and led, they were neither doctrinally nor technologically ready for the new kind of war that was thrust upon them. Carefully planned attacks rapidly fell apart as unit leaders were killed and their battalions decimated by enemy artillery and machine gun fire. As well, the coordination of thousands of troops on the battlefield proved a daunting task; communications were generally poor and local commanders had to rely on land lines that were easily cut by shrapnel or runners that might not survive their trip from one position to the next. Negligence in staffing

Library and Archives Canada PA-2084

Canadian Pioneers carrying trench mats during the Battle of Passchendaele in Belgium in 1917. In the background wounded men and prisoners are being brought back to friendly lines.

was not the problem; plans were carefully and thoughtfully constructed and more often than not adequate logistics were made available. It was doctrine and tactics that needed to improve.

Technological innovation was also a necessity. The Canadians had to improvise gas masks at the Second Battle of Ypres and their Canadian designed Ross rifles proved horribly inadequate and prone to jamming after sustained use. The Colt machine gun issued to Canadian troops was cumbersome and slow. Furthermore, the soldiers lacked other types of personal weapons; they did not even have grenades. The one item of equipment that had performed exceeding well at Ypres, however, was the 18-pounder artillery piece. Combined with innovative gunners, it served the Canadian Corps throughout the remainder of the war and up to the beginning of the next war.

Like the British, the CEF learned early on that they could not fight major battles solely with infantry. Although Canadian infantry battalions were able to fight largely independently of each other in a defensive battle at Second Ypres, they could not continue to do so while on the attack. Advances in new technology, especially in communications and artillery, meant that German defenders could more easily coordinate their own protection against an assault, and this forced Canadian tacticians to include these elements within their own plans, as well, or suffer accordingly. This meant learning to coordinate the various elements of the infantry division and its supporting units when out of physical sight of them and teaching them how to fight together as larger formations rather than as single units. The adoption of these methods within the CEF improved chances for success on the battlefield in 1915 and in some cases actually did work, though the infantry continued to suffer high casualties especially in the leading waves.

Both the British Expeditionary Force (BEF) and the CEF adopted a new practice in 1916 of dividing attacking waves into several different functions. The forward platoons, for example, might form the assaulting function, and bypass small pockets of resistance to quickly and decisively capture an objective. Follow-on platoons might be designated support platoons and carrying platoons, bringing forward additional firepower and immediate re-supply to ensure that captured objectives could be held. Other platoons might be employed for mopping up the bypassed pockets of resistance, capturing prisoners, and ensuring that wounded were safely returned to the rear. This tactic was consistent, noted historian Paddy Griffith, "with the BEF's 1916 doctrine of an aggressive front line push forward wherever possible, and rearward lines to mop up and consolidate."[37] But it had even more important ramifications. By giving much more flexible objectives to sub-unit commanders rather than rigidly detailed orders, senior leaders could allow the man on the ground to interpret his immediate situation as he saw fit to reach his objective successfully, rather than demanding that he follow some prescribed, and potentially disastrous, scheme.

Canadian offensive doctrine continued its evolution throughout 1916. After an April attack in bad weather at St. Eloi that was poorly planned and commanded,[38] the Canadian Corps proved remarkably capable of achieving success during the summer months on the Somme. Employing aerial reconnaissance and providing adequate time for the artillery to register their guns at Mont Sorrel, for example, the Canadians were able to turn around the devastating German attack launched against them a few days before and restore the original lines.

Though Canadian doctrine and tactics continued to improve throughout 1916 many challenges remained unsolved. The infantry were generally better equipped than they had been the year before. The Ross rifle had been replaced by the British-issue Lee Enfield .303 calibre rifle and the colt machine gun with Vickers and Lewis machine guns. Standard grenades made their appearance and gradually replaced bombs improvised out of ration tins stuffed with glass and nails. Stokes mortars were issued to directly support the infantry, as well. Finally, soft caps remained but soldiers were also issued with steel helmets to protect them from shrapnel, flying debris, and, to some small extent, inclement weather. Proper gas masks were issued, as well.

The addition of new weaponry to the arsenals of the assaulting infantry increased their chances of successfully traversing no man's land. A single Lewis gun added the equivalent of an entire platoon's worth of Lee Enfield firepower, while the Stokes mortar gave the infantry immediate indirect fire support. Battalions also had increasing access to a number of specialists such as engineers, signallers, and artillery forward observation officers who helped direct artillery barrages. It was not a perfect solution by any means but these changes reflected the ongoing technical and tactical evolution within the CEF throughout the war.

Still, evolution had not yet guaranteed continuous success on the battlefield and despite improvements to personal equipment, other technologies were still lacking. Reliable communications seemed to be an insurmountable problem at the Somme, and artillery was still struggling to adequately support advancing infantry across no man's land.

Canadian gunners began experimenting with the creeping barrage concept, previously employed with success by 18 British Division on July 1, 1916, as well as counter battery fire, but it would still be several months before these techniques were perfected.

Though the CEF was considerably more lethal by 1916–1917, so too was the war in which it was engaged. The brutal fighting in the Somme campaign had cost the Canadian Corps 24,029 casualties, nearly a quarter of the original strength of the corps. Doctrine and tactics were better but waves of men were still being killed trying to take their objectives. Further technical and tactical innovation was required. As historian Bill Rawling noted, "The Canadians at the Somme learned that they had not yet learned enough."[39] Commanders at all levels assessed their performance and passed lessons learned up the chain of command. These comments received further consideration and were incorporated with appropriate changes into doctrine and the subsequent training. By this point in the war the Canadian Corps had developed a reasonably robust system for ensuring that lessons were not just captured but learned, and the corps as a whole was improved before its next battle.

Library and Archives Canada PA-2121

(Left to right) Prince Arthur of Connaught, Lieutenant-General Arthur Currie, Major-General David Watson, and Brigadier-General Victor Odlum observe "practice attacks" in 1917.

In 1917, the Canadian Corps began solidifying the strategy and tactics that would carry it to final victory the following year. Though certainly bloodied after the Somme it remained intact and combat effective thanks in large part to the nature of its organization. The Canadian Corps was physically larger than any other BEF corps having four full-strength infantry divisions. It was also a very homogenous organization, its infantry and supporting arms having consistently trained and fought together over the last three years. This allowed doctrinal development and technical innovation to become standardized and more easily incorporated into plans and training. The same could not be said for other British formations, which were routinely shuffled and reorganized and therefore lost their ability to fully develop critical coordination routines and combat skills among their sub-units.[40]

The months leading up to the successful Canadian attack against Vimy Ridge witnessed the final experimentation for what later was described operationally by Canadian commanders as the "set-piece" attack.[41] A series of raids were carried out against the German lines validating various tactics and techniques that were later successfully employed on a larger scale, but on at least one occasion poor planning and execution reminded 4 Canadian Infantry Division of the terrible cost for carelessness in preparing for battle.[42]

Despite such losses, Canadian commanders continued their assessment of German tactics. As one Canadian general observed in his reports, the Germans characteristically would launch a counter-attack against any position it lost within 24 hours, and if required, send a fresh division against the position within three days.[43] Such attacks would begin with heavy shelling of the captured front line, followed by infantry attacks supported by more artillery. To counter this, infantry were trained to aggressively defend their gains, and to move their new lines of defence out of the captured trench line and farther towards the enemy. This way when the counter-attack's barrage began, German shells landed in empty trenches instead of killing Canadian troops. Combined with other tactics, the Canadian Corps had found a means for dealing with German counter-attack based defensive doctrine.

Recently validated Canadian doctrine and tactics ultimately led to the capture of most of Vimy Ridge in a single day during the 1917 Arras offensive.[44] It was one of the few highlights of the British 1917 Arras campaign and a crowning moment for the Canadian Corps. Most important, it was a shining validation of the CEF's ceaseless commitment to tactical and technical evolution.

Once the commanders in the Canadian Corps were confident that they had the means to successfully defeat the tactics of their German opponents they applied them aggressively in all future engagements. At the same time, however, they also continued their analysis of German trends and learned to take advantage of their tactical predictability. The German army would habitually counter-attack a lost objective immediately, therefore the new commander of the Canadian Corps, General Arthur Currie, seized on this routine to inflict heavier casualties.[45] He chose more limited objectives for the infantry on the attack and adequately equipped and supported them to aggressively hold onto captured positions, and pushed his artillery father forward to catch German counter-attacks out in the open. When ordered to capture Lens in August 1917, Currie instead requested permission to assault and capture the highpoint overlooking the town identified as Hill 70. He predicted that the Germans would consider the Canadian possession of the tactical vantage point so intolerable that they would immediately attempt to retake it. He launched his set-piece attack against Hill 70 on August 15, 1917, and occupied the high ground without serious difficulty.

Currie's assessment of the likely German reaction proved correct, yet instead of having to fight a brutal close combat in the built up area of Lens, he held the vital ground over the target and had a commanding view deep into the German lines. For the next few days, Currie used accurate and aggressive artillery and machine gun fire to cripple the German counter-attack force in its assembly area, while the infantry chewed up no fewer than 21 counter-attacks against their positions. Over the course of the battle the Canadian Corps suffered approximately 5,600 casualties, while German losses were estimated at close to 20,000. Currie noted, "Our gunners, machine-gunners, and infantry never had such targets."[46]

By the end of the year the set-piece attack had proven itself. Even the morass of mud at and confusion at Passchendaele could not deny the Canadian doctrine from succeeding, and General Currie noted in his assessments back to British General Headquarters (GHQ) that key factors in the planning and execution of Canadian operational doctrine had allowed his corps to prevail.[47] In particular, he emphasized the critical importance of being allowed to adequately prepare for the battle; artillery and logistics were allowed to ensure that they could properly support the battle and assault troops were given time to train and were brought into the line days ahead of their attacks to familiarize troops with the ground. The Canadian Corps also emphasized liaison and intelligence work in the planning phase, and this attention to detail ultimately saved lives.

Department of National Defence RE-19664-4

A Canadian pilot in his Sopwith fighter prepares to take off on patrol.

Finally, lessons learned in earlier engagements were applied with continued success at Passchendaele. Having learnt to pace the advance of artillery barrages Canadian soldiers could maximize its cover and protection, often reaching otherwise impregnable German strong points across terrible ground with fewer casualties. Also, by subduing German artillery with Canadian counter-battery fire and using direct artillery support to isolate German pillboxes, bunkers, and machine gun nests, Canadian troops were able to unhinge the web of German defence in depth at Passchendaele one strand at a time.[48]

Few changes were made to Canadian operational doctrine in 1918. The Canadian Corps had by then evolved into, as one Canadian historian described it, the "Shock Army of the British Empire."[49] Its doctrine was tested and proven leaving only some tactical modifications as the nature of fighting on the Western Front returned to more open-style manoeuvre warfare. The infantry was taught further self-reliance and the capabilities and efficiency of supporting units was refined. Recognizing the possibility that the Canadian Corps might be engaged in open style warfare (as opposed to closed fighting between static trench line systems) these tweaks were critical to continued success.

All the learning by trial and error was put to the final test in the last 100 days of the war. The Canadian Corps was engaged in a number of successive actions starting with the Battle of Amiens on August 8 and ending on the day of armistice with attacks at Valenciennes and towards Mons. Again Canadian doctrine and tactics ensured victory, but the cost in lives remained high. The fighting at Amiens alone had cost the Canadian Corps 13,808 casualties in nearly a week of fighting, while the

Library and Archives Canada PA-002253

The Allied conception of the tank was to assist the infantry in breaking into the enemy trench system. The Allies, however, failed to realize the tank's full potential.

following engagements at Bourlon Wood and Canal du Nord caused a further 13,500 casualties. In fact, the Canadian Corps suffered its greatest casualties not at the beginning of the war but at the end, when leading the spearhead to victory.

Conclusion

After the end of the South African War, the Canadian Army slowly matured its modest reservoir of resources and experience to ensure that a small but solid foundation would exist when the next war came. Still, in the period between the Boer War and the start of the First World War it was often a wanton child, lacking many resources with which to train and only limited experience from which to draw on for technical and tactical innovation. As with other Western armies during this period, it was often forced to simply make do with whatever was already at hand. Despite the modest existence of Canada's forces, however, one cannot dismiss the fact that tactical and technological innovation was taking place between 1903 and 1914, or that it had some influence on the origins of the Canadian Expeditionary Force. Canadian historians have often previously dismissed the pre-war evolution of Canada's army when examining the First World War.[50] Yet even existing analysis suggests that the CEF was a far more professional force in 1914 than it has previously been given credit for.

In war, the CEF was militarily effective. After the 1915 summer campaign, it worked ceaselessly to convert all of its available political and physical resources into fighting power. Opportunities to learn were exploited at every level from the corps commander down to the private soldier, and the continued effort paid dividends in successful engagements. Doctrine was not only formed but also tested both in small level engagements and if successful, then in larger scale battles. After each engagement, lessons were not only captured but analyzed and disseminated back out to the corps to be learned. Doctrine and tactics that did not work or cost too many lives was dismissed and new and different options were tried. By combining these efforts with technical innovation and competent senior leadership in theatre, the Canadian Corps was able to evolve its own style of warfare on the Western Front that other allied armies would envy and later emulate. True to the definition of military effectiveness, the Canadian Corps remains to the present day one of the finest combat formations ever fielded by Canada.

NOTES

1. C.P. Stacey, "The Second World War As a National Experience," in S. Aster, ed., *The Second World War As a National Experience* (Ottawa: Canadian Committee for the History of the Second World War, 1981), 17.

2. A. Millet and W. Murray, eds., *Military Effectiveness Volume 1: The First World War* (Boston: Mershon Center on International Security and Foreign Relations, 1988), preface.

3. *Ibid.*, Chapter 1. The Millet and Murray study focused mainly on the European powers, with the United States being the only non-European nation examined. This chapter seeks to expand on this initial work.

4. *Ibid.*, 2.

5. The single best examination of Canada's Great War overseas political and military administration remains Desmond Morton, *A Peculiar Kind of Politics: Canada's Overseas Ministry in the First World War* (Toronto: University of Toronto Press, 1982).

6. P. Kennedy, "Military Effectiveness in the First World War," in A. Millet and W. Murray, eds., *Military Effectiveness Volume 1*, 329.

7. I.H.M. Miller, *Our Glory and Our Grief: Torontonians and the Great War* (Toronto: University of Toronto Press, 2002).

8. For details of the OMFC see Canada. *Report of the Ministry, Overseas Military Forces of Canada* (London: OMFC, 1919); and D. Morton, *A Peculiar Kind of*

Politics: Canada's Overseas Ministry in the First World War (Toronto: University of Toronto Press, 1982).

9. Miller, *Our Glory and Our Grief*, 14.

10. Accounts of the successful nature of the CEF may be found in B. Rawling, *Surviving Trench Warfare: Technology and the Canadian Corps* (Toronto: University of Toronto Press, 1992); W.F. Stewart, *Attack Doctrine in the Canadian Corps, 1916–1918* (Fredericton, NB: University of New Brunswick: unpublished MA Thesis, 1980); Ian Brown, "Not Glamourous, But Effective: The Canadian Corps and the Set-piece Attack, 1917–1918," *Journal of Military History* (July 1994); and Shane Schreiber, *Shock Army of the British Empire: The Canadian Corps in the Last 100 Days of the Great War* (Westport, CT: Praeger, 1997).

11. There is a trend within Canadian military history to constantly depreciate the status, quality, or value of Canadian military organizations. For example, while British history often refers to forces recruited after the start of the war as the "New Army," Canadian historians employ terms such as *amateur, disorganized, disorderly,* et cetera. Chaos was prevalent in all allied forces that were entirely unaccustomed to mobilizing and caring for such large numbers of troops, and as such the situation within Canada's army should not be perceived a shamefully unique but typically normal within the context of the period.

12. Recent scholarship in Britain is demonstrating that while the CEF was undoubtedly one of the allied armies' most effective and forward thinking combat formations, its activities and record were by no means unique as is often suggested by Canadian military historians.

13. In particular, considerable attention is given to the role of the Canadian Corps during the last hundred days of the war. See Colonel G.W.L. Nicholson, *Official History of the Canadian Army in the First World War: Canadian Expeditionary Force, 1914–1919* (Ottawa: Queen's Printer, 1964); and Schreiber, *Shock Army of the British Empire*.

14. A comprehensive bibliography of works on the history of the Canada's military may be found in O.A. Cooke, *The Canadian Military Experience 1867–1995: A Bibliography.* (Ottawa: Directorate of History and Heritage, 3rd ed., 1997).

15. Bill Rawling has very briefly examined the interwar learning process between 1902 and 1914 in *Surviving Trench Warfare: Technology and the Canadian Corps, 1914–1918.* (Toronto: University of Toronto Press, 1992), 9–15.

16. *Ibid.,* 9–10.

17. Directorate of History and Heritage (DHH), file 83/358, *Infantry Training, 1905,* 123. Cited in Rawling, *Surviving Trench Warfare,* 11.

18. *Ibid.,* 14–15.

19. Rawling suggests that the British high command assumed in 1910 that the Canadian Army was adequately prepared for war provided "the next war was similar to the one they had fought in South Africa". See Rawling, *Surviving Trench Warfare,* 14. Perhaps so from a logistical point of view, but the adoption of modern artillery doctrine and the continuous honing of practical skills to competition winning levels also suggests that they could (and subsequently did) perform well in a modern war against an industrialized European foe.

20. Even the army of today cannot necessarily boast more frequent opportunities to train collectively prior to operations, and neither is it so quick to dismiss the value of peace time training for what it is. Just as militia soldiers went to Salisbury Plain to prepare for deployment to France and Flanders in 1914, so to do modern day reservists report to Petawawa, Valcartier, or Gagetown for training before going overseas. Such was the way things were then and such is the way things are today.

21. Nicholson, *Official History of the Canadian Army in the First World War*, 29.
22. The event is well covered in J. Macfarlane, "The Right Stuff? Evaluating the Performance of Lieutenant-Colonel F.L. Lessard in South Africa and His Failure to Receive a Senior Command Position with the CEF in 1914," *Canadian Military History*, Vol. 8, No. 3 (Summer 1999), 48–58.
23. Report to the House of Commons, August 21, 1914. See Morton, *A Peculiar Kind of Politics*, 5; and D. Morton, "Exerting Control: The Development of Canadian Authority over the Canadian Expeditionary Force, 1914–1919," in Keith Neilson and Ronald Haycock, eds., *The Cold War and Defense* (New York: Praeger, 1990).
24. Senior leadership of the Canadian Corps is examined briefly in A.J.M. Hyatt, "Canadian Generals of the First World War and the Popular View of Military Leadership," *Social History/Histoire Sociale*, Vol. 12, 24 (November 1979), 418–30. For more recent scholarship beginning to address this deficiency, see P.H. Brennan, "A Still Untold Story of the Canadian Corps: Byng's and Currie's Commanders," *Canadian Military History*, Vol. 11, No. 2 (Spring 2002).
25. This situation was ameliorated later on during the war. After 1916, Canadian senior commanders often conducted operational and tactical briefings of upcoming operations down to the company and platoon commander level, and senior non-commissioned members were at times issues with maps and were told what the tactical objectives were should their officers become casualties (and they often did).
26. Biographies of Currie include Daniel Dancocks, *Sir Arthur Currie: A Biography* (New York: Methuen, 1985); A.M.J. Hyatt, *General Sir Arthur Currie: A Military Biography* (Toronto: University of Toronto Press, 1987); and Hugh M. Urquhart, *Arthur Currie* (Toronto: J.M. Dent & Sons, 1950).
27. CEF battalions were recruited at home to a strength of approximately 1,000 men. Most of these battalions were broken up in England to provide reinforcements for units already fighting in France and Belgium. Still, units engaged in fighting on the Western Front were almost never at full strength because of constant casualties both in and out of direct action against the enemy.
28. For some recent insight on CEF battalions see P.H. Brennan, "Amateur Warriors: Infantry Battalion Commanders in the Canadian Expeditionary Force," (unpublished paper).
29. For Pearkes's biography see R. Roy, *For Most Conspicuous Bravery* (Vancouver: University of British Columbia Press, 1977).
30. Brennan, "Amateur Warriors," 26.
31. A.J. Trythall, *Boney Fuller: The Intellectual General, 1878–1966* (London: Cassell, 1971), 34.
32. Acknowledging that the British needed to reinforce their position on the Western Front and replace losses suffered the previous year, the Canadian contingent was still able to prepare itself for battle in a remarkably short period. Today, Canadian units scheduled for deployment might train for as long as six months before being sent overseas for a tour of only six months. In 1914 there was no guarantee where or for how long Canadian soldiers might be expected to fight.
33. Daniel G. Dancocks, *Spearhead to Victory: Canada and the Great War* (Edmonton, AB: Hurtig, 1987), 21.
34. Rawling. *Surviving Trench Warfare*, 47.
35. *Ibid.*, 47.
36. Dancocks, *Spearhead to Victory*, 22.
37. P. Griffith, P. *Battle Tactics of the Western Front: The British Army's Art of Attack, 1916–1918* (New Haven, CT: Yale University Press, 1994), 57.

38. D. Campbell, "A Leap in the Dark: Intelligence and Command During the Battle of St. Eloi," Unpublished paper, University of Calgary.

39. Rawling, *Surviving Trench Warfare*, 86.

40. Historian Denis Winter argued that both strength and homogeneity were critical factors contributing to the combat effectiveness of the Canadian and Australian corps. See D. Winter, *Haig's Command: A Reassessment* (London: 1991), 148. Both Ian Brown and Shane Schreiber concurred with this assessment in their more recent works. See Brown, "Not Glamorous but Effective," and Schreiber, *Shock Army of the British Empire*.

41. *Ibid.*, Brown and Schreiber.

42. On March 1, 1917, 4 Canadian Infantry Division executed a large scale raid against the German lines employing two full infantry battalions, 54 and 75. Gas was employed to support the attack but the winds shifted and much of it was blown back towards the advancing raiders. Poor communication and a general lack of coordination resulted in total failure and very high casualties.

43. "Attack 1917," Brigadier-General Victor Odlum Papers, Library and Archives Canada (LAC), MG 30 E300, Vol. 23.

44. The Canadian Corps launched its attack against Vimy Ridge on Easter Sunday, April 9, 1917. By April 14 the entire ridge was in Canadian hands, ending three years of failed allied attempts to take it. More important, the victory outshone all other aspects of the 1917 Arras offensive and later became for Canadians the moment at which the country psychologically separated from Britain.

45. Lieutenant-General Sir Arthur Currie, a Canadian, was appointed to command of the Canadian Corps on July 7, 1917. He had previously commanded 1 Canadian Division in the attack on Vimy Ridge.

46. Arthur Currie Diary, August 15, 1917, LAC, MG30 E100, Vol. 43, file 94, Currie Papers. Also cited in Brown, "Not Glamorous but Effective," 427.

47. For a history of Canadians at the battle of Passchendaele (Third Ypres) see Daniel Dancocks, *Legacy of Valour: The Canadians at Passchendaele* (Edmonton, AB: Hurtig Publishers, 1986).

48. The German adoption of defence in depth tactics is examined in Millet and Murray, *Military Effectiveness Volume 1: The First World War*; see also T. Lupfer, *The Dynamics of Doctrine: The Changes in German Tactical Doctrine During the First World War* (Kansas: Fort Leavenworth, 1981).

49. See Schreiber, *Shock Army of the British Empire*.

50. The most notable exceptions being Harris, *Canadian Brass*, Rawling, *Surviving Trench Warfare*, and K. Eyre, "Staff and Command in the Canadian Corps," unpublished paper, Duke University MA, 1967.

CHAPTER 6

A Canadian Way of War: 1919 to 1939
by Stephen J. Harris

On November 11, 1918, forward elements of the Canadian Corps entered the Belgian city of Mons, symbolically closing the circle for the military forces of the British Empire on the Western Front in the First World War. For it had been at Mons, on August 24, 1914, that the British Expeditionary Force (BEF) had begun its retreat to what eventually became the trench lines of France and Flanders and the bloody battles associated with them: Somme, Ypres, Arras, and Passchendaele.

That the citizen-soldiers of this corps — a homogenous Canadian field army more than four divisions strong — would secure the reputation as the shock troops of the British Empire had been unimaginable when the BEF's "Old Contemptibles" had turned and marched south from Mons four years before. Although quick to heed the call to arms, in August 1914 Canada had no standing army to speak of: the first contingent of volunteers for the Canadian Expeditionary Force (CEF) then gathering at Valcartier was woefully inexperienced, under-equipped, and under-trained, and it was led by officers who were in positions of authority more because of whom, than what, they knew. Indeed, although J.F.C. Fuller saw potential in the men when the CEF began to arrive in England later that autumn — they were healthy and strong compared to the average Englishman or Scot — he had only contempt for their leaders: "the officers," he said, should be "all shot."[1]

Four years later, however, and under a largely home-grown command and staff, the Canadians began the last 100 days of the war with their startling August 8 success at Amiens and then proceeded to best the better part of 47 German divisions in the complex conditions of near-open warfare in the three months that followed. Already masters of the set-piece and bite-and-hold battle, they proved adept at flanking attacks off the line of march, and they had learned how to exploit. Moreover, they did it their way — although their doctrine and organization were

British-based, the debt was not absolute and the model was not slavishly adhered to. Details of the differences have been dealt with elsewhere;[2]
however, it is clear that by the end of the First World War the idea there
was something approaching a distinctive Canadian way of war was widely accepted. Quite simply, guided by the twin notions that men were
more valuable than shells, and that men could be trusted to know what
they were about to do, General Sir Arthur Currie, his staff, and those
leading his divisions, brigades, and battalions, had the critical mass, the
shared collective tactical experience, and the conscious self-confidence
and will to do things the way they wanted and, in doing so, to do them
better than most.

Photographer: W.I. Castle, Library and Archives Canada PA-832

*Canadians returning from the trenches during the Battle of the Somme in France
in November 1916.*

Itself more professional and adaptive than when the war began, in
early 1919 the British Army called for a post-bellum conference to discuss,
sometimes in infinite detail, the lessons learned that were likely to last,
which should, therefore, shape the future organization and equipment of
all the armies of the empire.[3] Canadian officers participated as full partners
in the process, and they gladly preached the wisdom of adopting the
Canadian engineer organization, the science of counter-battery fire, the
role of motor-machine gun brigades in the attack and defence, the doctrinal distinctiveness of the machine gun corps, and the flexibility inherent in
the way Canadian sections and platoons remained fighting entities even

after their officers had been killed. Canadian machine gun organization was "a year ahead of all other armies," Lieutenant-Colonel J. Sutherland Brown told the adjutant general, and the British knew it.[4] "The MG [machine gun] service must be regarded as a separate service with tactics of its own," a 1 Army doctrinal statement dated April 30, 1918, had observed, mirroring Canadian practice "In all respects, it is intermediate between the Infantry and the Artillery, its tactics being radically different from the former."[5] Indeed, as Lieutenant-Colonel T.V. Anderson found a year later, the British Army Staff College still looked upon the organization and operational methods of the Canadian Corps as a "shining beacon"[6] for all the armies of the empire. It had set standards worth emulating.

Initially, indeed, it seemed that the post-bellum conference would propose a divisional organization reflecting everything the Canadians had developed or maintained: the square brigade of four battalions; three brigades of artillery; engineers organized as a brigade; machine guns battalions not under command of brigade commanders; and the motor-machine gun brigade as corps troops.[7] The corps organization of the British Army would only accept Canadian practice where practicable, because British corps would continue to be less homogenous with fewer permanent structures than Currie's command. There was, however, a "but." The organization that Currie and the senior Canadian officer at the conference, Brigadier-General J.H. MacBrien, favoured so readily had been adduced from the experience of the Western Front and a large continental war against the main armies of a major power. With Germany defeated, France broken, and Russia in disarray, the most likely roles for the British Army lay outside Europe, in small colonial wars and imperial policing; and for these, the structure of the Canadian Corps and a Canadian division were simply too heavy and too centralized. In particular, the machine gun organization seemed ill-suited for the kind of semi-independent sub-unit missions common in imperial policing; it was also difficult to reconcile with the Cardwell system upon which the British Army was built — linked battalions of the same regiment, one serving at home, the other abroad. Accordingly, the Canadian machine gun battalion would have to go, to be replaced by a more decentralized battery structure that would see smaller machine gun detachments under infantry command.[8] Similarly, the division itself would be made less complex (and smaller) to suit the needs of small wars. Although this meant a reduction in the overall engineer complement, one Canadian innovation would be retained — the combined engineer/pioneer component.[9]

Some things — how armoured cars and tanks would be incorporated, whether the horse would remain, either in the cavalry or as the main hauler of transport — were left for later, pending mechanical and technological advances. But by and large, the basic shape of the future British Army had been decided upon by the end of 1919 and, in the War Office at least, there was an expectation that the dominions would follow suit. "It is necessary," the War Office explained, "to provide as far as possible a machinery whereby in future all Imperial force may be trained to fight in a war, as one homogenous whole and not as unconnected parts hastily thrown together in a time of crisis."[10] If imperial politics had dictated that the British Army need not plan for a second continental war in Europe, there was no reason for a dominion army to organize itself for such an eventuality. As good and workable as the Canadian model had been against the Germans, in other words, it was excess to requirements for small wars in Africa and Asia.

In its physical form, that model melted away soon after the end of the war. Although some units of the Canadian Corps crossed into Germany in December 1918 and others moved deep into Belgium, they did not remain long. By the end of 1919 practically all the brigades, battalions, and batteries had moved through the staging areas of France and Flanders to transit camps in Britain and thence onto the ships that would bring them home. Raised only for the duration of the conflict, the CEF was struck off strength, unit by unit, as the men were dismissed, "turned right, and broke off" to find their individual ways in the peacetime world of North America.

The critical mass was gone, at least temporarily, until decisions were taken as to what shape the post-war Canadian army should take — and how large it would be. (Equipment, for the moment, was not an issue: five divisions worth of surplus kit, excepting tanks, the full complement of trucks, and the heaviest artillery, were to be shipped to Canada in the next year or two.) But the pride and self-confidence did not immediately disappear. When, in October 1920, the head of the Army Historical Section wondered whether he should accept an invitation to analyze American lessons learned, Major-General J.H. MacBrien replied acidly: "We have not very much to learn from the United States with regard to the recent World War.... The experience of the United States troops in the war was so limited that they really left off where we began."[11]

Arthur Currie came home to considerably less than a hero's welcome, but his stature could not be denied: he was offered, and accepted, the senior appointment at army headquarters, and made it a priority to use this authority to ensure that the talent of the last 100 days of the corps was not lost. The pre-war regulars had to go — at least those who had not seen service at the front — if the mediocrity of the old permanent force was to disappear and a new generation of officers with experience of real soldiering was to have a chance to inculcate the army with their ethos of professionalism and competence.[12] Moreover, that army was to be a large one, or so it seemed. Proposals already put forward by the wartime chief of staff (CGS), Willoughby Gwatkin, as well as by MacBrien and Major-General W.D. Otter, all agreed that post-war military organization should include provisions for compulsory military service, a regular component of 30,000 (about two divisions) and a part-time militia which, in about a decade, would amount to some 15 divisions of trained soldiers.[13] That would be ample to make the Americans think twice about attacking Canada should their relations with Britain deteriorate, and would provide the foundation for a Canadian Expeditionary Force of seven divisions in the event of another world war — a contribution Currie believed fitting given the Dominion's population base.[14] It was also, in Currie's view, an army large enough to provide the CEF officers he hoped to entice to stay in uniform with the prospects of a rewarding military career.

In a narrow way, the logic was impeccable, and had Currie's vision come to pass there was at least a chance that the post-war regular army

General Sir Arthur Currie (left) with Field Marshal Sir Douglas Haig in February 1918.

could have built on the knowledge and experience of the Canadian Corps. Many of its best officers would have remained in uniform, and inspired by its credibility there was every reason to believe that they would continue to think critically and innovatively. Others would be in the militia which, over time because of conscription, would strengthen the army's overall critical mass. And together, these would sustain Canadian military self-confidence. That is a presumption of course, not specifically articulated in any staff paper, but nonetheless inherent in Currie's aspiration that the post-war army would provide an opportunity for "real soldiering" in its broadest context.

And, in the beginning at least, it seemed that the logic might also be compelling. The proposals for post-war conscription put forward by Willoughby Gwatkin were actually well-received by militia minister S.C. Mewburn, one of the Liberals who had joined Borden's Union government, and they were still under consideration when Currie became inspector-general.[15] The support, however, was not to last. As in Britain, politicians rightfully had the power and responsibility to determine how much of Canada's Great War legacy would survive. Conscription had divided the country badly during the war, it was not part of Canada's military heritage, and there was no obvious enemy within reach to warrant both a fundamental change in military policy and the considerable expense it would entail. Compulsory service was rejected even before Mackenzie King's Liberals came to power,[16] and so, too, was Currie's scheme to retire pre-war regulars: "I am afraid that we are not going to get into the Permanent Force as many [CEF veterans] as I had hoped," he told a friend in January 1920. "Reorganization has taken so long that many chaps got tired of waiting ... and it seems harder to get rid of some officers of the Permanent Staff and Permanent Corps."[17] Indeed, six months later the situation was, if anything, even worse: old-style "political pull" had left so much "dead wood" in place that he feared the regular force would never be able to win the respect of militiamen who now knew "what a thoroughly trained officer is."[18] What was worse was that just a month before, in June 1920, he was told that the regular establishment he had asked for — some 30,000 all ranks — would be cut to 10,000 and manning would be limited to half that number, just 15 percent of his recommendation.[19] Not only would many of the old officers be keeping their jobs, in other words, but there would be fewer vacancies for those Canadian Corps veterans who might still be interested in them. Critical mass had disappeared in the regular army, taking broad collective experience with it.

Major-General Sir William Otter.

That left the part-time militia as the likely repository for the knowledge and experience gained by the Canadian Corps, but here, too, there was to be disappointment. Although veterans of the CEF had argued strenuously that the post-war army should be built around the numbered battalions of the Canadian Corps — those who had won glory at the front — instead it was the named regiments of the pre-war militia, with whom most veterans had no association whatsoever, that survived; and this was likely one reason why (it was felt) so few returned men considered continuing their service in uniform after the war, even on a part-time basis. The same was true of the officers. By 1924, the list of generals and lieutenant-colonels who had commanded at the front during the last 100 days and now had no ties to the army was long indeed, despite a generous provision in the post-war establishment for reserve lists permitting the maintenance of informal ties.[20]

It was a few, then, both regular and reserve, who would have to maintain the wartime legacy of the many. Among them, some of Currie's favourites commanded military districts and militia brigades — D.M. Ormond, J.H. Elmsley, H.C. Thacker, W.B.M. King, H.D.B. Ketchen, D.R. McCuaig, A. Ross, Victor Odlum, J.F.L. Embury, and J.B. Rogers. But the main players in the reorganization of the post-war army were in Ottawa: Currie himself (who would soon retire), J.H. MacBrien, Andrew McNaughton, and James Sutherland Brown. Of these, it was the latter two who, more than anyone else, would determine the nature of the Canadian way of war over the next two decades of peace. McNaughton was unarguably the senior — he would become deputy chief of staff when MacBrien replaced Currie, and CGS a year after MacBrien resigned — but for the moment Brown held the critical staff appointment of Director of Military Operations and Plans (DMO & P).

As an empire man, Brown should have easily accepted the logic of the Imperial Post-Bellum Conference and the inference that, as part of one imperial army, the Canadian Militia should pattern itself on the British model in every detail. And, indeed, in 1919 he had agreed that although what the British were doing with their machine gun corps was neither as good as Canadian Corps practice nor particularly useful for aid of the civil power obligations, it was nevertheless right to follow the British lead to maintain uniformity.[21] As Canada's DMO & P, however, Brown had also to concern himself with Canadian, as well as imperial, security, and in that respect he saw his job as producing an army that could hold its own, for a few days or weeks, against Canada's only contiguous continental neighbour, the United States. The structure to do that — some 15 infantry and cavalry divisions — existed (at least on paper) in the permanent force and militia establishment, and in Defence Scheme No. 1. Brown produced a plan which he believed would allow the Dominion to buy time in a war with the Americans until British and Indian Army reinforcements landed on the U.S. Atlantic and Pacific coasts.

The details of the scheme are incidental to this study. But the intent provided a theoretical alternative to the army organization Brown had accepted following the post-bellum conference. Although it was never his dogmatic purpose, the possibility of Canada's having to go it alone against the Americans, even if only for a limited time, opened up the prospect of a "national" army rather than a mere appendage to the armed forces of the empire — a national army organized and equipped primarily for the defence of Canada. And that possibility, remote as it may have been, also opened a gap between Brown and his onetime friend, McNaughton.

The split first appeared in 1923, when the quartermaster general (QMG), E.C. Ashton, observed that the five divisions worth of equipment brought back from Europe was no longer enough for the 15 division militia establishment designed to fight the Americans, nor modern enough for a major war.[22] McNaughton agreed that the army was "short" of equipment, but saw no reason for real concern, and no need to fill its stocks with additional surplus kit that would likely be obsolete in the next war. Furthermore, 15 divisions were too much. Canada would meet all its requirements, he told MacBrien, if it obtained full mobilization equipment for one division, one cavalry brigade, and one artillery brigade, using British "small war" establishments as the benchmark.[23] Clearly, he had overseas commitments in mind as Canada's principal military obligation.

Brown was appalled. Although fully prepared to help Britain in the defence of its imperial possessions, he argued that a country must first provide for its own defence, and in that vein he did not believe that "the military authorities should accept responsibility for anything less than the full mobilization equipment (as far as compatible with perishability and obsolescence) for the authorised forces of the Dominion — the 15 divisions of 'The Canadian Militia, active and reserve.'" If Cabinet could not accept the requirement, the responsibility should be the Cabinet's. "The soldier," he asserted, "is always made the goat in war, both for his own mistakes (wars are won by those who make the least mistakes) and for the mistakes of others. I think it is our duty to place the responsibility, which is not ours, on the proper authorities and then, if unhappily, war takes place we should do our best with whatever instruments are available, but we cannot then be responsible for improper organization or for the lack of military equipment or the munitions of war." Canada, Brown added, "cannot be thought lightly of by any foreign power."[24]

Library and Archives Canada PA-132648

Lieutenant-General Andrew G.L. McNaughton.

Sensing that the DMO & P had scored at least one goal, McNaughton explained that he had advocated adopting British war establishments for a small war only because the British Army had not yet worked out how it would organize for a major war; but he did not alter his view that Canada needed only one division fully equipped.[25] Brown, meanwhile, continued to argue that the mere size of the U.S. Army, and "the Americans" palpable interest in the Arctic archipelago, indicated that they were still looking north, seeking to complete their manifest destiny."[26] And that called for larger-scale preparation.

As professional head of the army, it was for MacBrien to choose between the two options he had been given, but although he would never direct Brown to cease work on Defence Scheme No. 1 — and the North American priorities it entertained — he realized that for practical purposes the Liberal government of Mackenzie King was unlikely to support the contingency of a North American war and expenditures required to provide the 15 divisions of more modern stores underlying Brown's arguments. He therefore chose to do what he felt was possible: McNaughton's one division plan.[27] But even that proved impossible when, later in the year, the government ordered the department of national defence to keep its estimates as low as possible — and certainly not to exceed the fund voted in 1924–1925. As the QMG explained, that meant that there could be no new capital spending — simply maintenance of the current force and its rapidly depleting stocks of ammunition and usable equipment.[28]

MacBrien had been right about the government's position, and Brown had been terribly naïve — holding out the possibility of war with the United States was not the most persuasive argument for rearmament. In fact, however, the CGS had not yet abandoned all hope of someday equipping at least the 11 infantry divisions, but like McNaughton he increasingly saw the army's responsibility as preparing a one-division expeditionary force for service overseas in an imperial war.[29] And, indeed, that became the focus of the staff's mobilization and procurement planning early in 1927. With the proviso that documents refer to a field force rather than an expeditionary force to downplay the fact that the emphasis was on an overseas commitment, the new policy received approval from the minister. Sutherland Brown still argued his case, but with H.C. Thacker and then McNaughton who replaced MacBrien as head of the army. Clearly, the die was cast.

There is no getting around the fact that Brown was more suspicious of the United States than almost any other Canadian, because of what he saw as its sense of manifest destiny — he believed the Americans were a direct threat to Canada because they wanted Canadian territory — and because he was certain that American and British interests overseas would one day collide; leaving Canada as the natural battleground in the clash of empires. McNaughton also mistrusted what he saw as American desire for hegemony, but he trusted the British government to defuse any quarrels before they led to war. More than anyone else, however, Brown believed that Canada could, if prepared, protect its sovereignty by fighting, buying time until imperial reinforcements arrived. That was why procuring mobilization stores for so many divisions was so crucial to him: a war with the United States would permit no gradual rearmament, while the militia would have to be more than rudimentarily trained. In particular it had to be ready for quick decisive movement, using all motorized and mechanized means at its disposal, initially to seize the vital points inside the United States that he had identified, and then to conduct a staged and controlled fighting withdrawal as the Americans brought their much larger forces to bear.

Finding his optimism preposterous, given the disparity in strength between the American and Canadian armies, few agreed with Brown at the time. Indeed it was this more than anything else that turned McNaughton so decisively against his former friend. Yet, as bizarre, outlandish, or impractical Brown's insistence on building an army to fight the Americans was (and is) seen, Defence Scheme No. 1 and the militia organization on which it was supposed to depend contained an implicit requirement for the general and district staffs to work out concrete military solutions to concrete military problems in the context of stand-alone Canadian military operations in a North American setting. Indeed he called on them to be innovative in their thinking, employing "flying columns" of motorized infantry, mobile machine gun battalions, truck-drawn artillery, and cavalry to advance quickly on multiple but coordinated axes before undertaking a controlled — and equally coordinated — withdrawal. There were no trench lines in his thinking, and the objectives he set out were places of genuine strategic or operational significance, not merely convenient geographical features. There were rivers to cross, urban areas to avoid, and speed and exploitation of success were the driving criteria.[30]

The broad outlines of the scheme were communicated to the military district staffs even though it had not been submitted for political approval, and one can see in the district files the initial work it called for — route reconnaissance; intelligence-gathering on the roads, bridges, and defiles that would be encountered, and attempts to identify nodal points. But when it became clear that political support was lacking — which meant money, men, and materiel — the district staffs became increasingly uneasy with Brown's call for an offensive strategy, and active work on the plan in these headquarters more or less came to a halt. The scenario had simply become too surreal to warrant serious consideration, at least to most.

There were nevertheless a few — a very few from the documentary evidence that has survived — who saw the emphasis on overseas operations and commitments as debilitating to Canadian military thinking. What else to make of the *Canadian Defence Quarterly* editorial of October 1931 declaring that

> We have not the means to experiment ... and it is only by experiment that practical difficulties can be recognised....
> It is incumbent upon us, therefore, to adapt a "wait and see" policy and apply the results of British experiments to our own particular requirements.[31]

The most thoughtful of these critics was a young militia lieutenant from Montreal, W.W. Goforth (he would rise to full colonel and hold the appointment of director of staff duties at Army Headquarters by the end of the Second World War) who won the *Canadian Defence Quarterly* prize essay for 1932. Although he accepted that the chances of war with the United States (or any other power on North American soil) were remote, he argued that preparing only to fight another war in Europe was "narrow-sighted," particularly if that entailed slavishly following British doctrine and organization and procuring British equipment simply because it was British. Should a home defence become necessary (defence of Canadian neutrality in the event of a U.S.-Japanese war would have been included in that), he observed, the "close" conditions of Europe were no guide to a successful defence of Canada's wide open spaces in the west. Rather, the Russians would provide a better model. In the east, meanwhile, closely wooded country and bridges not strong enough to bear the weight of tanks suggested that the latter were not the ideal armoured fighting vehicle for Canada. Furthermore, while the British Army did not prepare for winter warfare as such, climate suggested that it should have a high priority in Canadian military training. Was it not "reasonable," Goforth asked, that reorganization in Canada "should be subjected more to indigenous experiment [to find a Canadian doctrine] than to follow kaleidoscopic changes of Imperial models ... in the paper stage?" By all means test British tanks and become familiar with them so that Canada would not be completely unprepared to help the British in a major war, but the militia should focus on those things appropriate to home defence — motor guerrilla swarms and cold weather operations. And done well, he added, the knowledge gained thereby might one day usefully supplement British organization and doctrine.[32]

Another militia officer, Lieutenant-Colonel H.F.G. Letson, commanding the Canadian Officers' Training Corps (COTC) at University of British Columbia and who would be adjutant-general from 1942 to 1944, shared Goforth's concerns. Canada's increasing political independence, he argued, opened up the possibility of "independent dispute with nations that may not have any impact on the rest of the British Commonwealth, and that meant the militia should concentrate on Canada defence requirements — motorized guerrillas and light infantry."[33] Two regular force majors, G.B. Soward and J.C. Murchie, agreed with Goforth, but the only evidence of their concurrence came in private letters to Sutherland Brown, in which they decried recent proposals for militia reorganization because they "slavishly follow organiza-

The warrior chief with his political master: William Lyon Mackenzie King and Lieutenant-General Andrew McNaughton.

tions that have been based upon requirements for warfare outside this continent. Our own needs should come first."[34]

Neither Goforth, Letson, Soward, Murchie, nor Sutherland Brown were "separatists" when it came to Canada's relation to Britain and the empire, and their call for indigenous experimentation and thinking — and venturing into things not practised by the British (winter warfare in particular) — was not meant to supplant the notion of imperial uniformity. But the essence of their arguments, and Goforth's article in particular, were held out by Loring Christie, J.W. Pickersgill, and A.R.M. Lower as solid and compelling evidence that the Canadian Army's close relationship with (and dependence on) British military thinking and planning were contrary to the national interest. To Christie, the overseas hypothesis which lay at the heart of imperial cooperation blocked the chance to "stimulate native inventive genius" and "must always completely discourage original thinking in the most important fields of our defence problem."[35] For his part Pickersgill, one of the prime minister's closest advisers, argued that the principle of imperial uniformity meant that there was no "critical analysis" of defence issues in Canada and no independent thought about what was best for the Canadian militia.[36] Convinced that the Japanese were the main threat to Canada (because of their souring relationship with the United States), historian Arthur Lower argued that it was "utterly foolish ... traditionalism" that caused the Canadian Army to rely on British supply for Canadian defence. "We should change over to American equipment," he concluded, and seek closer military ties with the U.S. armed forces.[37]

That was the rub, of course. Calls for greater Canadian military independence by Canadian officers reinforced the arguments made by politicians, academics, and those close to politicians who challenged the imperial tie. And since most Canadian officers were imperialists (given the usage of the day) who feared what Liberal politicians were up to, they were reluctant to do anything that would strengthen the latter's view. As early as 1923, for example, Colonel J.P. Landry, commanding Military District No. 5, criticized Defence Scheme No. 1 because it had been drafted in Canada. "The main defence scheme," he complained, "should actually be prepared and considered by the Imperial Defence Council [sic] as the war in great part will be fought by imperial troops and all that is required of us is to draw up plans for the preliminary operations so as to buy time."[38]

Rejecting as it did Canadian paramountcy in Canadian home defence, Landry's position was extreme, but those who have read the *Canadian Defence Quarterly* between the wars will recognize the underlying viewpoint. Brown himself would tell the CGS in 1926 that the Canadian Militia, himself included, would generally be "content to leave our [foreign] affairs to the trained personnel furnished by Great Britain at International conferences," that "we need, really, a truly Imperial army," and that, except where climate suggested otherwise, the British War Office and Imperial General Staff should do the "major design work" for all the armies of the empire.[39]

That was the view that prevailed, publicly and privately, within the army. As Maurice Pope recalled, "Our army was indeed British through and through with only minor differences imposed on us by purely local conditions.... All our manuals were British and so was our tactical training. Practically all our equipment had been obtained in the United Kingdom ... [and] to qualify for higher rank our permanent force officers were required to sit for examinations set and marked by the War Office."[40] The best Canadian officers did their utmost to absorb the changes taking place within the British Army, and the keenest of them all — Ken Stuart, Guy Simonds, and E.L.M. Burns — understood enough to debate the role of armour and the structure of divisions with as much sophistication as any of their British counterparts. But they understood from afar — and knew that their commentary was also from afar, and that if war came, they would fight according to the doctrine and organization laid down in London.[41]

In short, given the politics of the time, both domestic and external, the contingency underlying Defence Scheme No. 1 was completely unrealistic as the basis of Canadian security policy. Canadian officers, consequently, were never forced to devise Canadian solutions to Canadian military problems, and most seem not to have given such concerns any second thought. The priority was ensuring that the Canadian Army would be ready to take the field with a British expeditionary force. Indeed, at times independent thought was seen as a direct threat to the more important problem of ensuring empire uniformity. The critical mass of 1918 was gone by 1939; the first-hand experience had rusted away in 20 lean years of peace; and the self-confidence to be different (yet still interoperable) that had marked the Canadian Corps had evaporated.[42] Although McNaughton (and others) were determined that any Canadian expeditionary force helping the British be recognized as a national army under national command,[43] there was no distinct Canadian way of war in 1939 because so far as the army was concerned, there was no need for one. By and large, only those wary of imperial commitments thought otherwise. Yet, on a larger level, the debate, political attitudes and subsequent decisions were in consonance with the philosophical and pragmatic national approach to the existence of, and use of the military and military force.

NOTES

1. See Stephen J. Harris, *Canadian Brass: The Making of a Professional Army, 1860–1939* (Toronto: University of Toronto Press, 1988), 98.

2. See Shane B. Schreiber, *Shock Army of the British Empire: The Canadian Corps in the Last 100 Days of the Great War* (New York: Praeger, 1997); Bill Rawling, *Surviving Trench Warfare: Technology and the Canadian Corps, 1914–1918* (Toronto: University of Toronto Press, 1992), Andrew Godefroy's article in this book, and Jack English, "Lessons from the Great War," *Canadian Military Journal* (Summer 2003), 55–62.

3. War Office to Overseas Military Forces of Canada, n.d., file C71.33, Library and Archives of Canada (hereafter LAC), RG 9IIIB1, Vol. 2702.

4. Brown to Adjutant-General, May 12, 1919, HQ640-1-18, Vol. 1, LAC, RG 24, Vol. 6534.

5. Copy in Canadian Corps GS notes, G126/3-6, file 165, LAC, Currie Papers, Vol. 37.

6. Anderson to James Sutherland Brown, August 20, 1920, Box 2, Folder 19, Sutherland Brown Papers, Queen's University.

7. See file 0-5-3, LAC, RG 24, Vol. 967, for Canadian comments, and particularly Currie to 2 Army, January 14, 1919, in which he noted "as we have" in the margin beside each of these items.

8. Brown to Adjutant-General, May 12, 1919, HQ 640-1-18, file Vol. 1, LAC, RG 24, Vol. 6534.

9. MacBrien, "Notes on the Organisation of the Army," n.d., and MacBrien, 3rd Report, March 3, 1919, HCQ 2953, LAC, RG 24, microfilm reel C-5059.

10. War Office memo to Committee of Imperial Defence, Secret, E-2 (CID Paper 134-C), February 1921, Canadian Copy in Library and Archives Canada, Records of the Governor General, file 33391: "Wars, Attachments, and Interchanges," LAC, RG 7 G21, Vol. 610.

11. CGS to DHS, October 4, 1930, file 650–52–4, LAC, RG 24, Vol. 57.

12. Currie to MacBrien, March 15, 1920, file 34, LAC, Currie Papers, Vol. 11; Currie to MacBrien, April 12, 1920, LAC, MacBrien Papers, Vol. 1; MacBrien to Currie, May 21,

1920, LAC, MacBrien Papers, Vol. 3; file E-17-33, LAC, RG 9 III, Vol. 2777; file HCC 1-1-89, LAC, RG 24, microfilm reel C-5046; Currie to Farmer, January 5, 1920, file 34, LAC, Currie Papers, Vol. 34; and, in general, file 76, LAC, Currie Papers, Vol. 39.

13. See, in particular, MacBrien's memorandum, "The Future Military Force of Canada," HQ 420-18-52, part 1, LAC, RG 24, Vol. 6522.

14. See MacBrien to Deputy Minister, Overseas Military Forces of Canada, May 14, 1919, July 14, 1919, and to Minister, Overseas Military Forces of Canada, August 27, 1919, file T-7, LAC, Kemp Papers, Vol. 146; MacBrien to Currie, October 6, 1919, LAC, MacBrien Papers, Vol. 1; and MacBrien, "Interim Memorandum on the Future Organization and Distribution of the Military Forces of the Empire," October 1919, file HQC, 3149, LAC, RG 24, microfilm reel C-5061.

15. Gwatkin to Deputy Minister, November 20, 1918, and Mewburn minute, file HQ 420-18-152, part 1, LAC, RG 24, Vol. 6522.

16. Mewburn to Kemp, August 6, 1919, file E-9, LAC, Kemp Papers, Vol. 141. See more generally J.L. Granatstein and J.M. Hitsman, *Broken Promises: A History of Conscription in Canada* (Toronto: Oxford University Press, 1977), chapter 4; and James Eayrs, *In Defence of Canada, Vol. 1: From the Great War to the Great Depression* (Toronto: University of Toronto Press, 1964), chapter 1.

17. Currie to Farmer, January 5, 1920, file 34, LAC, Currie Papers, Vol. 11.

18. Currie to Radcliffe, July 6, 1920, "Correspondence P-R," LAC, Currie Papers, Vol. 5.

19. Mewburn to Kemp, August 6, 1919, file E-9, LAC, Kemp Papers, Vol. 141. See more generally Granatstein and Hitsman, *Broken Promises*, chapter 4; and Eayrs, *From the Great War to the Great Depression*, chapter 1.

20. Among the names no longer found were Burstall, Loomis, Watson, Smart, Griesbach, Tuxford, J.A. Clark, Draper, Hilliam, Kirkcaldy, Swift, Pearson, McLeod, Nelles, Crawford, Raddall, Peck, Millen, Desrosiers, Ritchie, Day, Brown, McIntyre, Doughty, Spender, Gardner, Cameron, Davies, Dawson, Keegan, Carey, McFarlane, Andros, Macdonald, Paterson, J.S. Stewaert, Piercey, Ross, Ogilvie, Lindsay, Malcolm, Hayter, and Hore-Ruthven.

21. Brown to Adjutant-General, May 12, 1919, HQ 640-1-18, LAC, RG 24, Vol. 6534.

22. QMG to Militia Council, August 27, 1923, LAC, RG 24, Vol. 2679.

23. DCGS to Chief of Staff, September 21, 1923, *ibid.*

24. Brown to Chief of Staff, December 29, 1923, *ibid.*

25. See DCGS to Director of Supply and Transport, May 21, 1924, *ibid.*

26. Brown to Chief of Staff, January 22, 1924, *ibid.*, for example.

27. Chief of Staff to DCGS, July 2, 1924, *ibid.*

28. QMG to MND, October 29, 1924, *ibid.*

29. DCGS to QMG, October 5, 1926, *ibid.*

30. See the outline of the scheme, April 12, 1921, HQS 3496, LAC, RG 24, Vol. 2925.

31. See "Editorial", *Canadian Defence Quarterly*, Vol. 9, No. 1 (October 1931), 5–6.

32. Lieutenant W.W. Goforth, "The Influence of Mechanization and Motorization on the Organization and Training of the Non-Permanent Active Militia," *Canadian Defence Quarterly*, Vol. 10, No. 4 (July 1933), 431–451.

33. Lieutenant-Colonel H.F.G. Letson, "The Influence of Mechanization and Motorization on the Organization and Training of the Non-Permanent Active Militia," *Canadian Defence Quarterly*, Vol. 11, No. 4 (October 1933), 431–451.

34. Soward to Sutherland Brown, October 1932, and Murchie to Sutherland Brown, November 30, 1932, James Sutherland Brown Papers, Queen's University, Douglas Library, Vol. 8, Box 190.

35. Christie memo, February 26, 1930, folder 8, LAC, Loring Christie Papers, Vol. 27.

36. Pickersgill memorandum, "Principle of Uniformity of Equipment," December 5, 1938, *ibid.*

37. A.R.M. Lower, "The Defence of the West Coast," *Canadian Defence Quarterly*, Vol. 16, No. 1 (October 1938).

38. Landry to DMO, December 24, 1923, HQS 3496, Vol. 2, LAC, RG 24, Vol. 2925.

39. Brown to MacBrien, May 29 and September 21, 1926, HQS 5046, LAC, RG 24, Vol. 2681.

40. Maurice Pope, *Soldiers and Politicians: the Memoirs of Lt.-Gen. Maurice A. Pope* (Toronto: University of Toronto Press, 1962), 54.

41. In his article "A Division That Can Attack," Lieutenant-Colonel E.L.M. Burns took pains to emphasize: "the British regular division is the prototype of all the divisions of all the forces of the Empire," *Canadian Defence Quarterly*, Vol. 15, No. 3 (April 1938), 283, while in "The Attack," Captain G.G. Simonds assumed as a matter of course the use of British doctrine and training pamphlet, *Canadian Defence Quarterly*, Vol. 16, No. 4 (July 1939).

42. At the Defence Council meeting of April 17, 1936, it was pointed out that militia units were losing those officers who had served in the First World War. See file HQC1-1-89, FD17.

43. That was the whole point of the Visiting Forces (1933) Act. See also McNaughton's Imperial Defence College Papers, LAC, McNaughton Papers, Vols. 104–107.

CHAPTER 7

When Harry Met Monty: Canadian National Politics and the Crerar-Montgomery Relationship
by Douglas Delaney

"Monty" did not think much of "Harry" as a soldier, but it had not always been that way. There was a time when Field Marshal the Viscount Montgomery of Alamein regarded General Harry Crerar with fondness and favour. In 1942, following the arduous training exercise "TIGER," Montgomery, as commander of the Southeastern Army in England, piled praise on Crerar for his performance as commander of 1 Canadian Corps. He generously stated:

> I would like to congratulate you on your handling of the Canadian Corps in the TIGER Exercise. You did splendidly. As you know, I always say what I mean and generally in no uncertain voice! And when I say you did well, I mean it.... I hope we shall have some good battles together on the other side.[1]

But 24 years after the end of the Second World War, Montgomery reflected that his Canadian wartime subordinate had been "unfit" to command the First Canadian Army in the field.[2]

So what went wrong? How did Montgomery's opinion of Crerar degenerate from "splendid" to "unfit to command an army in the field"? As might be expected, there were several reasons. Training for wars was different from fighting them and the added stresses were difficult and wore away much goodwill. The two men also had markedly different command styles — Montgomery being decisive and resolute, Crerar being more tenuous and fastidious. And Crerar's mediocre operational performance in Northwest Europe did not help either.[3] All these things undermined the rapport between the senior Canadian combatant officer overseas and his operational superior, and all of them exerted a stronger influence at one time or other. But there was one irritant that continually piqued the relationship and made other matters worse — Canadian national politics and Crerar's insistence on playing them.

Crerar was a masterful bureaucratic operator whose nationalism had been stoked during his service as an artillery staff officer in Sir Arthur Currie's Canadian Corps (1917–1918). To him Canadian autonomy and the right of the senior Canadian officer overseas to be consulted on the employment of all Canadian troops, including those temporarily assigned to other formations, mattered. To Montgomery, a career infantry soldier who was wounded at Ypres in 1915, such considerations were an annoyance, and possibly dangerous. There was bound to be tension.

Field Marshal Bernard "Monty" Montgomery (left) visiting General H.D.G. "Harry" Crerar at First Canadian Army Tactical Headquarters on February 9, 1945.

Montgomery would have preferred the freedom to treat Dominion formations as he would have done any other British brigade, division or corps. Unfortunately, neither the Canadian government, nor the most senior Canadian officers saw it that way. In the government of William Lyon Mackenzie King, clipping the colonial apron strings, however slowly and timidly it may have been done, was a key foreign policy objective.[4] It had been for some time. During the Chanak Crisis of 1922, King's government had ignored Britain's call for help in its showdown with the Turks. Then, within two years of the Balfour Declaration of

1926, and Britain's recognition of equal status for the dominions, Canada had established its own legations in Washington and Tokyo. These were steps on the road to autonomy to be sure, but they were baby steps. Even after Britain acknowledged full Canadian autonomy in the Statute of Westminster of 1931, adolescent Canada was not particularly anxious to wander all that far from the imperial mother.

However, World War II forced Canada to grow up fast. As a start, the possibility of a British collapse following the fall of France in the summer of 1940 led King to seek a joint continental defence arrangement with the United States. In August 1940, he and President Franklin Delano Roosevelt signed the Ogdensburg Agreement, establishing the Permanent Joint Board on Defence. More important, in the face of the Second World War, part of independent nationhood entailed making a substantial military commitment to the war against Hitler. Canada did that. Most of its contribution of a million men and women served in Canadian formations, ships and squadrons, but those organizations were usually placed under some higher command, almost always British. Still, in spite of those higher command arrangements, Canadians consistently insisted on having the final say on all senior military appointments and Crerar held the line on this, though not nearly as fanatically as his predecessor as commander of 1 Canadian Corps and the First Canadian Army, General A.G.L. McNaughton.[5] Montgomery, on the other hand, thought ability should be the lone criteria for command and had little time for officers who concerned themselves with national nit-picking when men's lives were at stake. He had little time for those he considered "political" soldiers, in the British Army or any other.

By the time Crerar had succeeded McNaughton, he had heard enough about Montgomery to grasp fully his disdain for "political" soldiers, so he muted his concern for Canadian national issues when he joined the Southeastern Army as acting commander of 1 Canadian Corps in December 1941.[6] McNaughton's consistent obstinacy concerning the employment of Canadian troops had rubbed British commanders the wrong way, something that Crerar was determined to avoid. Whereas McNaughton had maintained an almost uncompromising "hands-off" policy concerning British input on the employment of Canadian formations and senior command appointments in 1 Canadian Corps, Crerar made clear his willingness to be more flexible. This was a good start as far as Anglo-Canadian relations were concerned. After meeting with Crerar on January 7, 1942, the chief of the Imperial General Staff (CIGS), General Sir Alan Brooke, penned an advisory letter to Montgomery outlining the difficulty of dealing with Canadians and their national politics, as well as the changed atmosphere with Crerar at the helm of the corps:

> They [Canadians] are grand soldiers, that I fully real-
> ized after spending one-and-a-half years with them in
> the last war. But they are very touchy and childlike in
> many ways. You will therefore have to watch your step
> with them far more than you would with British
> troops. I had Crerar to lunch, and he is delighted with
> all your help, and all set to play to the utmost.[7]

That he was. First, Crerar was not nearly as dogmatic as McNaughton, who insisted that the Canadian Corps, and later, the army, had to be used as a cohesive formation, preferably in the decisive battles to defeat Hitler's Germany. Crerar held the same convictions concerning Canadian autonomy. However, he also believed that the necessity of bat-tle experience outweighed the desire to commit Canadian army units and formations *only* as a cohesive whole. Participation in selected com-bat missions, he believed, would give the Canadians a cadre of battle-experienced officers and non-commissioned officers to lead them in the great campaigns to come. Crerar also knew that fighting was key to establishing Canadian credibility in the coalition, so he discreetly made clear his willingness to employ Canadian formations separately. Thus, he pushed for a Canadian role in the raid on Dieppe and for 1 Canadian Division's participation in the invasion of Sicily.[8] He also readily accept-ed Montgomery's input concerning appointments and training in the Canadian Corps:

> A few weeks in Acting Command of the Corps con-
> vinced me that a good many shifts in Unit and B[riga]de
> Commanders were necessary if the command element
> was to be brought up to an adequately high standard. I
> discussed this with General Montgomery, pointing out
> at [the] same time that in the absence of LtGen
> McNaughton ... my hands were tied. The C[ommander]
> in C[hief] then suggested that he would like to visit each
> of the Canadian formations, in turn, and that he would
> give me his personal views on their efficiency, and that
> of their units and commanders, as such might assist me
> in my own conclusions. This proposal, I accepted.[9]

Accepting a proposal that McNaughton would have rejected out of hand, ostensibly on the grounds that it would strengthen Crerar's hand in making changes to senior appointments during McNaughton's absence, conveyed Crerar's message that he wanted to mitigate the influence of national politics and "play to the utmost." That appealed to Montgomery.

So too did Crerar's willingness to agree with just about all of Montgomery's observations. After visiting every formation in the Canadian Corps down to battalion level, Montgomery submitted his "very confidential" thoughts on commanders to Crerar. Some were extremely negative — "This is the most ignorant C[ommanding] O[fficer] I have met in my service in the Army"; others were positive — "first class ... will be a Div[ision] Com[man]d[er] before the war is over."[10] But, overall, the comments did not reflect well on the leadership of the Canadian Corps. In Montgomery's opinion, too many officers and staffs did not know their jobs and too many Warrant Officers and non-commissioned officers (NCOs) were "too old for service in a fighting battalion." Crerar thanked the army commander for his observations, adding: "In the great majority these [comments] serve to confirm opinions which I have already formed in the course of the weeks I have now been in command of the Canadian Corps.... It has long been my firm conviction that a unit is as good as its commanding officer."[11]

Crerar wanted Montgomery to know that he was astute enough to tell a good battalion commander from a bad one, but he also felt compelled to point out that, as acting commander, he could not immediately take action on key command appointments. That would have to await the return of McNaughton to the corps. In the meantime, Crerar tried to give the impression that he was a "real soldier" who saw things in the manner of Montgomery, but that he was somewhat hamstrung by the non-operational unpleasantries of Canadian national politics.

In the honeymoon of their relationship, Crerar also eagerly agreed with Montgomery's observations on how the Canadians were preparing for war. In the course of his visits, the army commander picked up on serious problems with Canadian training methodology and regimen. "There is a great lack of training ability in the C.Os.," complained Montgomery, "A great deal of time has been spent in teaching people how to make war and how to fight; little time seems to have been spent in teaching officers *how to train troops*."[12] As such, officers and NCOs received little training as tactical decision-makers, brigade and battalion headquarters seldom practised how to monitor or control battles, and too many unimaginative exercises bored too many troops to tears. In what was a painfully repetitive pattern, Crerar agreed, while letting his military boss know that he was already on top of the issue. He was seldom brief:

> I think your point that the teachers (C.O.'s) have never really been taught how to train is well made. One of the objects I had in mind for reducing, for the time being, the considerable percentage of officers and N.C.O's, who until recently have been absent from their units undergoing courses of every description, was to bring about a situation which would facilitate, and indeed impel, formation, unit, and sub-unit commanders to organize and carry out the training of their own commands. If an officer is not a natural trainer, or has not been taught how to train, the best way of developing whatever abilities are his is to face him with the practical problem. Circumstances then compel him to solve that problem, if he has the solution in him.[13]

One feels for Montgomery, having to wade through such painful prose. Still, Montgomery was genuinely pleased with how readily Crerar took to implementing the many recommendations on training. On reading several of Crerar's training directives, Montgomery heartily sounded his approval. "They are excellent," he praised, "and if all commanders will act on them it will be good." He added, "There is no doubt that the training in the Corps is now beginning to move on sound lines; and there is real enthusiasm, which is a very important point. Under your leadership the Corps will soon be in fine fettle."[14]

In truth, Crerar "parroted" many of Montgomery's directives and training instructions in his own promulgations, all of which he shared with his senior.[15] Whatever reservations Montgomery may have had at this stage, the army commander was content with the fact that his Canadian subordinate had latched on to the "Montgomery Way", and he passed on similar accolades for Crerar's written instructions on formation-level field training exercises, as well as the many memoranda on NCO training and discipline.[16]

By the time the spring and summer field training exercises of 1942 arrived, their relationship was in full bloom. The correspondence grew warmer. In April, while observing numerous brigade and divisional training exercises, at Crerar's invitation, Montgomery switched from addressing his letters, "My Dear Crerar" to "My Dear Harry," and his sign-off took the form of Monty, the more formal "B.L. Montgomery" having been permanently discarded.[17] Not surprisingly, "Dear Monty" made its appearance in Crerar's letters shortly thereafter. The nature of their letters was still different and reflected their personalities — Montgomery's letters were mostly hand-written, curt, and to-the-point; Crerar's tended to be typed, "prosy, and stodgy."[18] Those differences notwithstanding, the correspondence was agreeable. It also helped when Crerar performed well as a corps commander during Exercise "TIGER" (May 19–30, 1942), an arduous field training event that marked the culmination of collective training in Montgomery's Southeastern Army. Monty was happy. "I am very well satisfied with the corps," he revealed, "if we can now put the polish on, there will be no other corps to touch it."[19]

General Harry Crerar in 1943.

The first fissures in the relationship appeared in July 1942 as 2 Canadian Infantry Division was preparing for Operation RUTTER (later JUBILEE), the raid on Dieppe. The operation was to be conducted under the direction of Combined Operations Headquarters (COHQ), a command to which neither Montgomery's Southeastern Army, nor Crerar's 1 Canadian Corps belonged. To Montgomery, the matter was simple. Since 2 Canadian Infantry Division was attached to COHQ for the operation, 2 Canadian Infantry Division should answer only to COHQ. Outside interference — except, perhaps, his own — should be minimized. Crerar thought differently, and insisted on his right to be consulted on the employment of Canadian troops and to monitor the events of the raid from 11 Fighter Group Headquarters. When Montgomery refused on the grounds that "too many chefs could spoil the soup," Crerar threatened to take the issue to "the highest political levels."[20] Montgomery relented, but he was not happy. Commanders hate it when subordinates go over their heads and Montgomery was no exception. More important, the incident was the first real indication that Crerar was as willing as McNaughton had been to play the political card if the situation warranted it. Maybe Crerar was not the mini-Monty he had made himself out to be.

Despite the brief confrontation over Dieppe, they continued to exchange cordial letters even after Montgomery had departed England for the Eighth Army and North Africa in August 1942. Shortly after taking command, Montgomery wrote Crerar, inquiring about the fate of his "friends in 4 and 6 B[riga]des" after the disastrous Dieppe raid. He also asked the Canadian Corps commander to "come and stay with me for a few days."[21]

Crerar was not the only senior commander to receive an invitation. Montgomery made the offer to take on British generals as well, because, as he explained to the CIGS, he was "filled with alarm at the low battle fighting knowledge of our senior commanders in England; the Generals who came out here for my tactical discussions at Tripoli knew really *nothing* about it; they were just full of theory, and would have bad disasters in battle."[22] He feared the same fate for Crerar, who managed only a very brief visit in February 1943.[23] "I don't think he has any idea as to how handle a Corps in battle," conceded Montgomery, "but I am really fond of him and he is very teachable. I fear he won't learn much from Andy [McNaughton]."[24] For his part, Crerar wanted to take advantage of the opportunity to visit but, unfortunately, visits by the minister of national defence and various "other projects" precluded his departure for the North African theatre of operations.[25] For his part Montgomery, whose premium on battle experience increased with every fight he fought, was sympathetic, but disappointed. He wrote:

> I had hoped that you might be able to come and visit me and pick up some practical tips. But it seems not to be. It is a great pity; you could pick up much knowledge that would save Canada many lives when you eventually put your corps into battle. I would love to have your corps fighting under me; if it does I will take care that all is well.[26]

To compensate, Montgomery enclosed "Brief Notes on the Conduct of Battle," a pamphlet that outlined "the tactical doctrine on which we will work, and how we will fight our battles."

But pamphlets and brief visits were no substitute for battle experience, and Crerar knew it. Canadian credibility and his own were at stake. He confided to Montgomery that:

I am increasingly worried at the situation which the Canadian Forces continue to face. From the military point of view, there is a limit to the useful training we can do under the conditions and from which the psychological and political aspects, this continued lack of participation in this battle has dangerous implications.[27]

Lest Montgomery should wonder who was responsible for the state of Canadian inactivity, Crerar hinted: "I keep clear of London and policy discussions concerning the employment of the Canadian Forces, which are Andy's [McNaughton's] responsibility and which he, naturally enough, does not share with me." After their spat over Dieppe, Crerar thought it important to re-emphasize that he was not, at heart, a political general. He continued to share his various instructions and memoranda with Montgomery, pointing out the obvious. "I think you will find," he explained, "a number of views which coincide with your own and which, in a good many instances, were inspired by your own remarks to me."[28]

The truth, of course, was that Crerar played the political game as well as anyone, both inside and outside military circles. He had managed to convince a government obsessed with the spectre of conscription that Canada needed, and could support, an army of five divisions and two independent brigades with voluntary enlistment.[29] He had deftly dodged blame for the catastrophe at Dieppe, despite having lobbied so hard for a Canadian role in the mission. And while he was exchanging pleasantries with Monty in the spring and summer of 1943, he was actively undercutting McNaughton's position as the commander of the First Canadian Army.

Capitalizing on his strong performance as a corps commander on Exercise SPARTAN — and McNaughton's poor showing as an army commander — he dined with Alan Brooke. The CIG's diary entry following the meeting is telling. " I had a long discussion with him," it revealed, "as to which was the best method of having MacNaughton [*sic*] recalled back to Canada to avert his commanding a Canadian Army which he is totally incapable of doing!"[30]

Crerar also spoke to the Canadian High Commissioner in London, Vincent Massey about McNaughton's removal, although he adroitly gave the impression that he was "never disloyal to his chief."[31] Crerar was playing both ends, Canadian and British, and to good effect. Eventually, Brooke broached the issue of replacing McNaughton with the minister of national Defence, J.L. Ralston, and the Canadian chief of the General Staff

(CGS) Lieutenant-General Ken Stuart, who, in turn, relayed British concerns to the prime minister.[32] Within seven months, McNaughton was out and Crerar was in as commander of the First Canadian Army.

McNaughton's poor generalship, his inveterate opposition to any splitting of the Canadian Army, and British anxiety for the fate of that army under his command, conspired to effect his removal in December 1943. Crerar nimbly helped the process along, wherever and whenever he could. He knew full well that he was the most viable Canadian successor, the only alternative being Guy Simonds who was still far too junior. Montgomery had watched Simonds fight 1 Canadian Infantry Division with poise in Sicily, and although he believed the young division commander to be a better prospect for senior command over the long term, Simonds still needed time at division and corps level to hone his skills.[33] Crerar got the nod.

But he did not take command of the army right away. Crerar still required battle experience, something that he had been trying to gain for months. As he wrote to Montgomery in September:

Teacher and pupil: Field Marshal Bernard Montgomery (left) and General Guy Simonds in Sicily in 1943.

> I have several times put it up to Andy [McNaughton]
> that I should have personal experience. I believe I could
> run a good show in battle but I would like to test out
> these beliefs by practical experience. In fairness to those
> I might command in battle, it seems to me an essential
> personal preparation. However, there always seems to
> be some reason why this ambition cannot be fulfilled.[34]

In October, Montgomery had suggested that Crerar take command of 1 Canadian Infantry Division — from the far junior Simonds — and fight it for a while to get a feel for the conduct of battle. Montgomery had made a similar suggestion to a British corps commander, Lieutenant-General Gerald Bucknall, who subsequently complied, taking a reduction in rank to major-general in order gain valuable command experience.[35]

But with the Canadians, things were different. McNaughton had already ordered Crerar to establish 1 Canadian Corps headquarters in Italy and take under his command 1 Canadian Infantry Division and the newly arrived 5 Canadian Armoured Division. Montgomery might have questioned Crerar's commitment to his own professional development, but having the Canadian vacate his post as corps commander for a junior one was just not an option at this stage. The corps was already on its way to Italy, and it definitely would have been awkward for Crerar to take a position formerly held by his junior.

More than that, Crerar was growing to resent Simonds's experience and the favoured relationship the now battle-savvy divisional commander had forged with Montgomery. From Sicily, Montgomery had kept Crerar appraised of 1 Canadian Infantry Division performance. "[Y]our Canadians have done magnificently"[36] he extolled, "Simmonds [*sic*] handles his division well and the 'Q' side is first class."[37]

On top of his strong performance in command of a division in Sicily, Montgomery appreciated Simonds's apparent disregard for national politics and willingness "to play to the utmost." When McNaughton, as the First Canadian Army commander, had insisted on visiting the Canadians during their fighting in Sicily, Simonds had reportedly asked Montgomery — "For God's sake, keep him away."[38] Long a believer that fighting formations should be left alone to concentrate on fighting, Montgomery was only too happy to oblige. However, Brooke, who understood the imperatives of national politics, convinced Montgomery to reverse his decision. Still, Montgomery admired Simonds's battlefield focus. Crerar, who had played the national political card in the Dieppe episode never gained the same currency with Montgomery, despite his best efforts at portraying himself as a soldier's soldier who had reluctantly accepted the political responsibilities of the senior Canadian commander.

Crerar tried to make the most of his three months of corps command in an operational theatre, but breaking into the "Eighth Army Club" was not easy for a newcomer, especially one burdened with the baggage of national politics. Early on, he sent his staff officers to spend time with their Eighth Army counterparts, to find out how things were done and to tweak their operating procedures accordingly.[39] Then, after Montgomery left the Eighth Army to prepare for the invasion of Normandy, Crerar worked under Lieutenant-General Sir Oliver Leese, the new Eighth Army commander. Unfortunately, Crerar's period of active command was not that active, the majority of the time being spent in a defensive posture as the formations of the Eighth Army prepared for the spring offensive. Equally unfortunate, Crerar rubbed Leese the wrong way. Leese, a seasoned if somewhat bland commander who had fought XXX Corps under Montgomery in North Africa and Sicily, had his doubts about the inexperienced Crerar. "He is nice," commented Leese, "but an academic soldier and I doubt if he is a Commander in the field."[40] A week later he wrote: "Harry Crerar ... of course knows nothing of military matters in the field.... I have to teach him for a time." Knowing that Crerar was the commander designate of the First Canadian Army, Leese was a little resentful that his predecessor, Montgomery, had left him with the chore of training the untried Canadian. "[He] refuses to take [Crerar] as Army Commander," complained Leese, "till I've held the baby for a while."[41]

Canadian resistance to independent divisional tasks annoyed Leese too. Given the seriousness of war fighting, the army commander thought that kind of touchiness inappropriate. In August 1944, he hinted at the central difficulty facing any British commander with Canadian formations under command. "The Canadians have once again started off this Boundary Commission game," he grumbled, "They always seem to have such a complex. Their men are magnificent but many of their senior officers are dreadful."[42] Crerar went back to England in March 1944, having commanded his corps in positional defence and instituted a series of dress regulations, but not much more.

This did not help his credibility with Montgomery, whose suspicions of Crerar's political inclinations were growing. Regarding the employment of 3 Canadian Infantry Division and 2 Canadian Armoured Brigade in Second (British) Army for the D-Day invasion, he wrote:

> I have had to be firm with [Lieutenant-General Ken]
> STUART, who is Chief of Staff at the Canadian Military
> H.Q. in London. He wrote a letter to the C.I.G.S about
> CRERAR's right to be consulted in the planning stages;
> I have a feeling that CRERAR put him up to it.
>
> In my reply, I made it quite clear that I could not
> admit that CRERAR had any operational responsibility
> for Canadian troops temporarily in another Army....
>
> There is no doubt that the national political feeling
> is very strong in Canadian senior ranks. My view is that
> what people really want is victories, and they will put
> all national feelings into the background till the war is
> over in order to get victories.
>
> It is victories that win wars and not public opinion.[43]

He was right. Victories are what win wars. They also keep national morale up and sustain the drive to keep fighting. But he was wrong that the Canadians would "put all national feelings into the background till the war is over." Crerar took up the issue with Brooke, who, in turn, had Montgomery give ground on keeping the Canadian army commander in the know in regards to the dealings with Canadian formations in Second (British) Army.[44] In Montgomery's world, the military mission came first; real generals did not concern themselves with other esoteric matters. The CIGS, on the other hand, dealt with coalition and policy issues every day. He knew the dangers of piquing the dominions and he offered Montgomery some advice on how to deal with Crerar:

> I had about one-and-a-half intimate years with the
> Canadians in the last war & know well what their feelings
> are. They will insist that Canadian forces should be com-
> manded by Canadians. I have already had MacNaughton
> [*sic*] kicked out & if we don't watch it we shall be accused
> of throwing out Canadians to try to make room for
> British Commanders. For that reason, I want you to make
> best possible use of Crerar, he must be retained in com-
> mand of the Canadian Army, and must be given his
> Canadians under his command at the earliest possible
> moment. You can keep his army small & give him the less
> important role, and you will have to teach him.[45]

Montgomery reluctantly complied, although he did delay Crerar's entry into battle as long as possible. Shortly after D-Day, Crerar tried to clear the air:

> I shall carry out my responsibilities to you as an Army Com[man]d[er] with loyalty and understanding.... I will "play the game" by your policies, very straightfor-wardly, and you need not fear that I will attempt to twist them behind your back.[46]

By the time of the Normandy Campaign, however, Montgomery's mind was made up — Crerar was a political general whose appointment as army commander rested more on his being the senior Canadian than it did on battlefield experience, or even operational ability.

Nothing that happened in the early days of the Campaign in Northwest Europe changed that opinion. Within a day of his First Canadian Army becoming operational, Crerar had an almighty row with Lieutenant-General John T. Crocker, commander of I (British) Corps, then serving under First Canadian Army command. Crocker objected to some of the army commander's overly detailed direction, arousing the worst of Crerar's insecurities. Immediately, Crerar sought Montgomery's assistance in removing Crocker who he believed was "temperamentally unsuited to be one of my corps com[man]d[er]s" and would likely "never play up."[47] Montgomery stepped in to "restore peace" — neither Crerar, nor Crocker, handled themselves well in the incident — but the incident added to Montgomery's apprehensions about Crerar. "I fear he thinks he is a great soldier," explained Montgomery, "and he was determined to show it the very moment he took over command at 1200 h[ou]rs on 23 July. He made his first mistake at 1205 hrs; and his second after lunch."[48]

Crerar's deliberate manner of doing business did nothing to improve his reputation. After the Seine River crossings, when Crerar's army lagged some 100 miles behind General Sir Miles Dempsey's Second (British) Army, Montgomery complained to Brooke that the Canadian Army's operations had been "badly handled and very slow."[49] Fuel was added to the fire when Crerar missed a conference at 21 Army Group Headquarters to attend a Canadian memorial ceremony at Dieppe. This was an important occasion for 2 Canadian Infantry Division — and for all Canadian servicemen — and Crerar had deliberately made himself scarce to his army group commander. Reacting a

Field Marshal Montgomery (left) with General Crerar at Cleve, Germany, in February 1945.

bit callously, Montgomery fumed and suggested that their "ways must part."[50] Crerar did not take the matter lightly and promised to raise the issue with the Canadian government. Again, Montgomery had little choice but to back off. He knew that the Canadians would support Crerar. But perhaps more important, he knew that Brooke, based on his earlier counsel to be judicious in his dealings with Crerar, would not support the removal of the Canadian, especially when there was no obvious Canadian successor. Three days later, Montgomery apologized.

Of interest is the fact that Crerar performed adequately during the remainder of the campaign and the acrimony in his relationship with Montgomery dissipated somewhat. Crerar missed most of the Scheldt battles because of illness, and Montgomery was only too happy to leave those operations in the hands of the acting army commander, Guy Simonds.

However, in the battles of the Rhineland and Holland, Crerar handled his army well. During Operation VERITABLE (February 8–21, 1945), for example, Crerar slugged the largest force ever commanded by a Canadian — 13 divisions strong — through prepared German defences to clear the west bank of the Rhine River. It was a huge undertaking and the evidence suggests that Montgomery would have preferred if Dempsey had done it, but operational considerations precluded such an undertaking.[51] In any event, Montgomery was satisfied with Crerar's handling of the battle. It also helped that no serious political issues surfaced in the last seven months of the war. Their correspondence resumed its cordial tone, though it never really regained the warmth of their 1942 letters, with the exception of one that Monty wrote in the glow of final victory:

> My Dear Harry,
> I feel that on this day I must write you a note of personal thanks for all that you have done for me since we first served together in this war.
> No commander can ever have had a more loyal subordinate than I have had in you. And under your command the Canadian Army has covered itself with glory in the campaign in western Europe. I want you to know that I am deeply grateful for what you have done. If ever there is anything I can do for you or your magnificent Canadian soldiers, you know you have only to ask.
> Yours always,
> Monty[52]

Montgomery may have been trying to smooth over the ragged relationship, or may have been flushed with the final success of the war against Hitler's Germany. Whatever the reason, the goodwill did not last. It faded as the years and decades passed. In a 1969 letter to one of his wartime aides-de-camp, exasperation was the only sentiment Montgomery had left: "What I suffered from that man!"[53]

It would be wrong to conclude that any single factor soured a relationship that had started so well. Crerar and Montgomery were too different in their personalities, too dissimilar in their command styles, and ultimately too far apart in their abilities for the honeymoon to last.

Montgomery was supremely confident and decisive, while the less-experienced Crerar's confidence in his military abilities left him far less resolute and inclined to seek the approval of superiors. Montgomery sought no one's approval. And, although Crerar can be said to have performed competently in battle, Montgomery was a much more accomplished and able field commander. But even at that, the relationship might not have turned so bad if had not been for the intrusion of Canadian national politics. Crerar knew that that the Canadian refusal to be subsumed in the British chain of command would cause problems. That is why he did his best to downplay such friction in his earliest dealings with Montgomery. But as his military responsibilities grew, first as corps commander then as army commander, so too did his political responsibilities to the Canadian government. He could not stay silent on Canadian political issues for long. This was particularly true in the period leading up to events like D-Day and Dieppe. It is no coincidence that the most tumultuous episodes of their relationship occurred during the preparatory stages for major operations.

The Victors. Seated left to right: Field Marshal Sir Bernard Montgomery, General Dwight Eisenhower, and Lieutenant-General Omar Bradley. Standing left to right: General Harry Crerar, Lieutenant-General W.H. Simpson, and Lieutenant-General Sir Miles Dempsey.

Montgomery believed that undue concern for national issues, especially by commanders he considered novices, only served to "spoil the soup" and placed soldiers in unnecessary danger. A general's first job was to win battles, not please politicians. Unfortunately, Crerar was as political as they come, both in his willingness to comply completely with the Canadian government's policy of asserting its sovereignty and in the management of his own career. This amplified the difficulties between Montgomery and Crerar, ultimately eroding whatever goodwill there had been between them.

NOTES

1. Library and Archives of Canada (LAC), MG 30 E 157, Papers of General H.D.C Crerar (Crerar Papers), Vol. 2, Montgomery to Crerar, 30–5–42.

2. Imperial War Museum (IWM), Papers of Lieutenant-Colonel Trumbull Warren (Trumbull Warren Papers), Montgomery to Warren, January 1, 1969.

3. On Crerar's mediocre performance in Northwest Europe and the uneasy relationship with Montgomery, see Stephen Ashley Hart's excellent chapter in *Montgomery and "Colossal Cracks": The 21st Army Group in Northwest Europe, 1944–1945* (Westport, CT: Praeger, 2000), 155–183.

4. The definitive work on Canadian policy during the Second World War is still J.L. Granatstein, *Canada's War: The Politics of the Mackenzie King Government, 1939–1945* (Toronto: Oxford University Press, 1975). See also B.J.C. McKercher's recent chapter, "The Canadian Way of War, 1939–1945," in Bernd Horn, ed., *Forging a Nation: Perspectives on the Canadian Military Experience* (St. Catharines, ON: Vanwell, 2002), 123–134.

5. For an analysis of how Crerar and McNaughton differed in their dealings with British military authorities, as well as Crerar's role in removing his one-time mentor from command of the First Canadian Army, see Paul D. Dickson, "The Hand the Wields the Dagger: Harry Crerar, First Canadian Army and National Autonomy," *War and Society*, Vol. 13, No. 2, October 1995, 113–141.

6. Crerar was acting commander 1 Canadian Corps during McNaughton's absence on sick leave. The appointment was substantiated in April 1942.

7. IWM, Papers of Field-Marshal the Viscount Montgomery of Alamein (Montgomery Papers) BLM 20/5, Brooke to Montgomery, January 8, 1942.

8. J.L. Granatstein, *The Generals: The Canadian Army's Senior Commanders in the Second World War* (Toronto: Stoddart, 1993), 102.

9. LAC, Crerar Papers, Vol. 2, Notes on Correspondence with C-in-C S.E. Command (no date).

10. *Ibid.*, Notes on Inf[antry] B[riga]des of Canadian Corps.

11. *Ibid.*, Crerar to Montgomery, February 3, 1942.

12. *Ibid.*, Notes on Inf[antry] B[riga]des of Canadian Corps.

13. *Ibid.*, Crerar to Montgomery, February 3, 1942.

14. LAC, Crerar Papers, Vol. 2, Letter Montgomery to Crerar, 10–3–42.

15. For example, Crerar borrowed Montgomery's standing orders from 3 Division. LAC, Crerar Papers, Vol. 2, Crerar to Montgomery February 3, 1942. See also Hart, *Montgomery and Colossal Cracks*, 165.

16. LAC, Crerar Papers, Vol. 2, Crerar to Montgomery February 3, 1942; and Montgomery to Crerar, 16–3–42, Montgomery to Crerar, March 25, 1942.

17. *Ibid.*, Montgomery to Crerar, 16–4–42.

18. Liddell-Hart Centre for Military Archives (LHCMA), Papers of Field Marshal Lord Alanbrooke (Alanbrooke Papers), 14/27, Montgomery to Brooke, December 23, 1943. I am grateful to Jack Granatstein for sharing his research papers from *The Generals*, particularly documents from the Alanbrooke Papers and the Massey Papers.

19. LAC, Crerar Papers, Vol. 2, Montgomery to Crerar, 30–5–42.

20. *Ibid.*, Memo on Conv with BLM, 4 Jul 42,. Quoted in Hart, *Montgomery and Colossal Cracks*, 161.

21. LAC, Crerar Papers, Vol. 7, Montgomery to Crerar, 2–9–42.

22. IWM, Montgomery Papers, BLM 49/19, Montgomery to Brooke, 28–2 –43.

23. C.P. Stacey, *Six Years of War: The Army in Canada, Britain and the Pacific* (Ottawa: Queen's Printer, 1966), 249.
24. IWM, Montgomery Papers, BLM 49/19, Montgomery to Brooke, 28–2 –43.
25. LAC, Crerar Papers, Vol. 7, Crerar to Montgomery, November, 5, 1942
26. *Ibid.*, Montgomery to Crerar, 9–1–43.
27. *Ibid.*, Crerar to Montgomery, April, 8, 1943.
28. *Ibid.*, Crerar to Montgomery, May 27, 1943.
29. Granatstein, *The Generals*, 93–98.
30. Alex Danchev and Daniel Todman, Eds., *War Diaries, 1939–1945: Field Marshal Lord Alanbrooke* (London: Weidenfeld and Nicolson, 2001), 391 (entry for March 31, 1943).
31. LAC, Papers of Vincent Massey Papers, Vol. 311, Diary, May 12, 1943.
32. See Dickson, "The Hand That Wields the Dagger," especially 123–131.
33. *Ibid.*, 129.
34. LAC, Crerar Papers, Vol. 7, Crerar to Montgomery, September 20, 1943.
35. David French, "Invading Europe: The British Army and Its Preparations for the Normandy Campaign, 1942–1944," *Diplomacy and Statecraft*, Vol. 14, No. 2, June 2003, 285.
36. LAC, Crerar Papers, Montgomery to Crerar, 25–8–43.
37. *Ibid.*, Montgomery to Crerar, 23–7–43.
38. Field Marshal the Viscount Montgomery of Alamein, *Memoirs* (London: Collins, 1958), 184.
39. LAC, Crerar Papers, Vol. 7, Crerar to Montgomery, November 5, 1943.
40. IWM, Papers of General Sir Oliver Leese, Box 2, Letters to his Wife, Letter Leese to Lady Leese, January 11, 1944.
41. *Ibid.*, Letter Leese to Lady Leese, January 17, 1944.
42. *Ibid.*, Leese to Lady Leese, August 30, 1944.
43. IWM, Montgomery Papers, BLM 73, May 26, 1944.
44. Granatstein, *The Generals*, 108–110; Hart, *Montgomery and Colossal Cracks*, 161–162.
45. IWM, Montgomery Papers, BLM 1/97, Brooke to Montgomery, July 7, 1944. Quoted in Granatstein, *The Generals*, 109–110.
46. NAC, Crerar Papers, Vol. 7, Crerar to Montgomery, July 4, 44.
47. *Ibid.*, Crerar to Montgomery, July 24, 44.
48. LHCMA, Alanbrooke Papers, 14/1, Montgomery to Brooke, July 26, 1944.
49. *Ibid.* 14/31, Message Montgomery to Brooke, September 4, 1944.
50. NAC, Crerar Papers, Vol. 3, Notes on the Situation Which Developed between C in C 21 Army Group and GOC in C First Cdn Army September 2–3, 1944.
51. Hart, *Montgomery and Colossal Cracks*, 176–8.
52. LAC, Crerar Papers, Vol. 7, Montgomery to Crerar, 8–5–45.
53. IWM, Trumbull Warren Papers, Montgomery to Warren, January 1, 1969.

PART III

Assuring Global Stability

CHAPTER 8

The Road from Innocence:
Canada and the Cold War, 1945 to 1963
by Ronald G. Haycock and Michael Hennessy

Less than a month after the explosions of the atomic bomb had brought a brutally shocking but abrupt end to the Second World War, Canadians were horrified to learn that their wartime ally, the Soviet Union had a well-developed spy ring working out of Canada's capital city aimed at gathering information on Canada, as well as Washington and London. These surprises came in early September when Igor Gouzenko, a cipher clerk in the Soviet embassy in Ottawa walked into the offices of the Ministry of Justice with all the evidence. What it revealed would later stun usually complacent Canadians.[1] It was a loss of innocence, and it pushed the country onto a completely different road than it had ever travelled before.

For decades before, Canadians were "an unmilitary people" sheltered by their colonial past and their particular historical and geographical circumstances. After the post–American Civil War settlements had ended antagonisms with the Americans in the 1870s, there was little real threat to Canada. All the country needed for its protection was a rag-tag part-time militia. When Canada did go to war, it raised volunteer citizen soldiers, and only after the crisis had started.

Such was Canada's military posture in 1914. However, by war's end Canada had sent 620,000 personnel overseas in the Great War. But after 1918, that caustic experience with its approximately 60,000 deaths on the European killing fields confirmed much about getting too heavily involved in a dangerous world, and the country and its politicians took on an uneasy isolationist stance all through the 1920s and 1930s.

Moreover, Canada had always been a very junior partner in a large alliance system. Seldom was it ever asked, or expected, to take part in the great strategic questions. As a former prime minister put it in 1919, it was made safe from "the vortex of European Militarism" by time and distance.[2] In the minds of most citizens, questions of domestic development were far more important than military or strategic ones at home or abroad. For its part, the senior "partner" usually only wanted the young Dominion's human or natural treasures. And so, the Canadian peacetime worldview did not develop much beyond a very basic tactical and technical level. In 1939, when Canada went to war its professional soldiery numbered approximately 5,000, and its navy and air force contributions were even smaller.

The Second World War had many characteristics of the first, though with fewer deaths. For six years there had been a huge and successful military and industrial effort, and it seemed to prove that mostly volunteer citizen soldiers could hold their own. There is no doubt that it was a new industrialized country with a proud fighting record that emerged in following the armistice. By the same token, there were many citizens who simply wanted to get back into a tranquil peacetime civilian life to enjoy the new prosperity, and, to use the words of a popular song of the day, "let the rest of the world go by." But in 1945, the Gouzenko affair abruptly ended that.[3]

For the next 18 years, it was the Cold War that would rivet Canada's attention whether it liked it or not. The issues that sprang from this were varied and not always immediately clear. A select group of Canadians, mostly in federal political circles or associated with the Department of External Affairs, like the future prime minister, Lester B. "Mike" Pearson, had known for some time, even before the Gouzenko affair, that there was no going back to the halcyon days.

The Second World War had given them experience in the international community and they knew that only a proactive stance aimed at keeping the world as peaceful as possible would maintain the hard-won Canadian prosperity and keep the nation safe from the future ravages of war. During the war, politicians had developed what the prime minis-

Lester B. Pearson and his wife, Maryon, inside the Kremlin Wall, Moscow, 1955.

ter called "the functional principle" as a sort of Canadian way of thinking about the country's ability to interact with those alliance partners of much greater power. Put briefly, the principle held two things: first, since Canada had made great contributions to winning the conflict, it should be accorded a post-war role commensurate with its contribution. Second, if it had an expertise in a given area, it ought to be allowed to contribute that quality to the alliance for the common good. Implicit in the concept was that Canada would have something to contribute that the alliance wanted. This meant that a balance between "ends and means" and "commitment and capability" were a key to the functional principle's usefulness.[4] It would remain to been seen if the balance could be kept. Be that as it may, even as the last shots of the conflict were being fired the reluctant Canadian prime minister, W.L. Mackenzie King, fortunately bolstered with enough of his "new men" of the internationalist bent, was in San Francisco determined to use the new United Nations (UN) as a means to establish the peace. Although this agency would remain a prime focus of Canadian internationalism for many years, it was not enough as other forces came to bear.

In the post-war world as it had been for centuries before, Europe held a special place for most Canadians. It was part of their historical posture and political space.[5] Now it had to be rebuilt and defended, especially Western Europe. War should not be allowed to break out there, and if it did, it had to be won.

The British Commonwealth provided new leadership possibilities for Canada as Britain went into its imperial retreat. Meanwhile, the United States replaced Britain as Canada's prime concern in trade and national security issues both at home, and in whatever came out of the ashes of Europe. It was a siren call harder and harder to resist.

Yet the past had taught Canadians that being too close to a "senior partner" could be as risky as not being close enough. Sovereignty had to be preserved, and Canada's new status — the result of its tremendous wartime effort on behalf of the alliance — needed to be recognized.

Complicating all of this was the fact that Canada was in North America, and, though often slow, the Dominion had always subscribed to the continent's security and defence. The American Monroe Doctrine made it hard to escape such a conclusion. In 1938, the American president, Franklin D. Roosevelt (FDR), had made it clear that the United States would "not stand idly by" if Canada was attacked. No doubt it was then reassuring to Canadians, but it also contained the subtle message that if they did not protect their turf, the Americans would do it for them.

And so in the immediate post-war world Canadian policy makers had to balance two competing imperatives: European peace and stability in the face of a rapidly widening east-west estrangement, and the security of North America. The former would demand collective defence, likely within multilateral arrangements;[6] the latter meant bilateral connections with the great power to the south. The Canadian questions were how to apportion their resources and how much was enough. The answers were not easy or simple. As it soon turned out, the Cold War created several events that tested Canada's ability to handle these issues, not the least the creation of the North Atlantic Treaty Organisation (NATO) in 1949, followed over 12 short years by the Korean War in 1950, the permanent commitment of Canadian forces to Europe, the Suez Crisis, the formation of the North American Air Defense Command (NORAD), and the Cuban Missile crisis in 1962. Canada moved along this "road from innocence" with remarkable agility and coherence but not without problems and introspection.

The post-war Canadian Liberal government of Mackenzie King had hoped that the once the big citizen armies were demobilized in 1945, the defence budgets could return to the low levels of the interwar years. Professional forces, it was hoped, could easily return to their usual small size and not cost the taxpayer much. The Reserve Forces (the citizen militia) would remain the first lines of Canadian defence. But by 1946, with Communist aggrandizement extending itself in many spheres, the "Iron Curtain," as British Prime Winston Churchill described it in Fulton, Missouri, had descended on Europe. This meant that Canada, as it had always done in the past, would be looking for allies to guarantee the security it felt it could not pay for. Consequently, getting involved with the Americans and keeping them involved in Europe became a long-term goal in Ottawa. The Truman Doctrine and the Marshall Plan were clear indications that Washington was already convinced that Stalin's policy would not stop at simply building a buffer zone around the Union of Soviet Socialist Republics (U.S.S.R.).

After 1947, events such as the Soviet endorsement of the Maoist victory in China, the Communist takeover in Hungary and Czechoslovakia, and the Soviet pressures against Greece, Turkey, and Finland, coupled with the Berlin blockade marked the true onset of the Cold War.[7] For Canada, the same events only pushed the Canadian government, which shared U.S. concerns and was now headed by the much more internationalist Liberal administration of Louis St. Laurent, to get into the shelter of an alliance that had a military mutual support component to it.

To Ottawa politicians such as Lester Pearson, St. Laurent's new external affairs minister, there was no question of withdrawing from international participation for several reasons. First, ultimately it would mean that Canada would be not only isolated in North America, but in a de facto bilateral relationship whether it wanted it or not with the neighbouring behemoth that was itself involved in Europe. If this was so, there would be no independent Canadian representation in Europe to act in its national interests: economic, military, or otherwise; nor would Ottawa benefit from efforts by other countries to mitigate the lop-sided nature of American power in North America or Europe. Besides, to pick another version of the former path — an independent foreign and defence policy — would involve unimaginable defence spending. It was therefore more practical if not easier — in the words of Denis Smith — to accept the traditional prerequisite foreign and defence policy umbrella of having "the approval and protection of the United Kingdom and the United States."[8]

Library and Archives Canada C-004047

Prime Minister Louis St. Laurent and his external affairs minister, Lester Pearson, pose with British Prime Minister Winston Churchill and his foreign affairs secretary, Anthony Eden, on the Britons' arrival at Rockcliffe Airport in Ottawa in June 1954.

In early 1948,when Clement Attlee, the British Labour prime minister urgently cabled Ottawa that there was an immediate danger of a Soviet attack possibly on Norway, and that a regional Atlantic pact of mutual assistance was the best way to counter it, alarms went off. Admittedly, the Canadian authorities took these urgent warnings on their face value without much consideration to determine if the threat was real.[9] Canada then worked hard at helping to establish that first child of the Cold War, the North Atlantic Treaty in 1949. And so, NATO was born and Canada had been a prime player. The cost of playing was not yet known, but that would soon change.

But for the moment, Canada was fulfilling a role it had often played before — it was an interpreter in the North Atlantic Triangle; this time it was explaining not only the United Kingdom and the United States to each other, but now to the Western Europeans, as well.[10] Moreover, if any one then saw it, Canada seemed poised to exert an influence far larger and more important than its long-term resources might sustain. Certainly, this new Atlantic Alliance would give the smaller powers a greater say in the direction of policies, and possibly in military strategy, than had been afforded them by the Allied Combined Boards in the Second World War.

What was also true was that in the realm of strategic thinking Canada had deferred to the ideas of its two great allies rather than developing its own, and its fate seemed more dependent on maintaining its interests in the NATO alliance than elsewhere. Perhaps that was just hard power reality tempered by the conviction that it could work to soften whatever harshness the big partners tried to impose on the alliance. Such a position could have also given the comfortable illusion that Canada was participating in high-policy decisions. Whatever the case, Canada's high commissioner in the United Kingdom, Norman Robertson, thought that the North Atlantic Treaty was a "providential solution for so many of our problems."[11]

One of the problems was the escalating cost of defence in light of the new Cold War. Canada had hoped that a formal alliance would allow a reduction or stabilization of its defence budget. Compared to the ruined state of most European countries in 1949, Canadian military capability and material resources were good. Yet, for Canada, like the war-ravaged Europeans, the real attraction was that mutual defence pooling meant that everyone might spend less.[12] Furthermore, in Canada, however obsolete, there was lots of munitions and equipment left over from the war. Emptying the Dominion's warehouses into Europe was magnanimous alliance diplomacy, and, happily for the senior officers of the much reduced Canadian Forces, the generosity put pressure on the Canadian government to buy them modern replacements.

The Europeans were willing to take the surplus kit because they simply had very little of their own. What Canada could give the alliance was munitions, raw material, and training. The training was much like the country had offered before in the old British Commonwealth Air Training Plan (BCATP) during the war.[13] The contributions would help the Canadian economy and give further life to the marvellous munitions manufacturing capability Canada had created in the war. This was especially important since the American congress had imposed a "Buy American" policy that kept the Canadians from benefiting from the revival in the U.S. arms market as a result of the Soviet threat. In the end, during the early 1950s, Canada outfitted several Dutch, Belgian, and Italian divisions with old British pattern equipment. Ottawa also initiated a smaller Mutual Aid program for others in Europe. This eventually included newly manufactured munitions.[14] And there were many NATO military personnel trained in Canada.[15]

Other Canadian contributions came not in equipment and training but in defining the NATO organization and planning procedures that helped make it a better relationship for the lesser powers. For instance, Ottawa saw the treaty as more than one of just mutual defence; if ultimately to be in vain, Canada originally hoped to develop the economic and social aspects of a true Atlantic Community. The treaty's Article 2 referred to this and became known as the "Canadian article."[16] But, it was only reluctantly accepted in a much watered-down form by the rest of the signatories. Perhaps its real intent for Canada was to exercise its role as a middle power being able to influence alliance policy by means other than military activities. Fortunately, some of the Canadian initiatives were less idealistic but more productive in these early alliance years.

In Canada's view, initial alliance defence planning and subsequent demands for member contributions laid down by NATO's Defence Committee were found to be unrealistic and dominated too much by British and America ideas and resource scales. Consequently, Canada proposed that the defence contributions be based on what the other members could afford.[17] Canada was also one of the first to suggest a full-time Secretariat. It was the Canadian general and chair of the Combined Chief of Staffs Committee, Charles Foulkes, who early on promoter promoted the idea of a supreme commander for NATO. And he wanted Eisenhower.[18]

On the planning front, Ottawa drew on its wartime experience of joint planning inside a regional alliance (the Canadian–American Permanent

Joint Board on Defence [PJBD] which had operated since the two nations signed the Ogdensburg Agreement on bilateral cooperative defence in 1940) to get a similar process in NATO. Moreover, our diplomats gained recognition for a position that said there was a difference between what members agreed was the common defence plan and the right of any of them to implement its share. These assumptions, along with the new Secretariat, helped guide the first Medium Term Defence Plan circulated by the NATO Defence Committee shortly after the outbreak of the next Cold War crisis — the Korean War.[19]

In late June 1950, when the Canadian Cabinet heard that Communist North Korea had invaded and was in the process of overrunning the American- and UN-sponsored South, they were surprised to say the least. No one had really expected a confrontation in this part of the world so far away from Canadian interests. An even harder reality was the fact that when asked by the United States to help form a UN Force to protect South Korea, the Canadian Armed Forces were unprepared in numbers and equipment. The question was "what was the crisis" — a "red herring" to mask a general Soviet attack on the West's defences in Europe, or a simple North Korean territorial excursion? Immediately obvious, however, was the obligation of Canada to the United Nation's collective security. And that is where Canada started its, at first very small and reluctant, combat role on the Korean Peninsula.[20]

Initially, the Canadian Cabinet was only slowly responsive to the call from the United States for help through the UN. Its initial statement in the early summer of 1950 committed three Royal Canadian Navy (RCN) destroyers, and subsequently some air services. The Americans were chagrined at the small Canadian contribution and were vocal about it. One U.S. spokesman labelled the destroyers as a "token force" only. The indignant Canadian reply was that one could hardly call three destroyers a "token force," to which the American comment was "Okay, — lets call it three tokens."[21]

The criticism stung as much as the situation in Korea deteriorated. Finally, by August the Cabinet announced land forces, but not units of the regular army, rather a Canadian Army Special Force of about 10,000 personnel recruited from civilian volunteers. In fact, because of an economic slump, and because the Second World War had ended just five years earlier, the force was full of battle experienced but very rough citizen soldiers. The plain facts were that the regulars were too few[22] and significant numbers of permanent force non-commissioned officers (NCOs) failed to re-enlist that summer, some because they were obvi-

Three tokens: destroyers of the Royal Canadian Navy serving with the United Nations in Korea in November 1950. Left to right: HMCS Athabaskan, Cayuga, *and* Sioux.

ously reluctant to go to war again. Finally when the Special Force was raised, it trained on American soil and used significant amounts of American equipment.[23]

As the conflict see-sawed back and forth over the next three years and took on the very dangerous possibility of a general or even nuclear war with China, Canadians ultimately contributed over 20,000 troops and suffered 1,557 wounded and dead. Ostensibly they fought on behalf of the United Nations and collective security — as indeed they had. But the ominous reality was that the Americans were in charge of the Korean action. One could even argue that this United Nations experience was, for Canada, more a response to temper its southern neighbour's overly aggressive military policy, than it was motivated by altruistic allegiance to UN collective security.[24] Such a reaction was likely spawned by the revelations in General Douglas MacArthur's adventurism towards the Chinese border in the fall of 1950, and President Harry Truman's comment in late November that the United States was not discounting the use of the "bomb."[25]

And there was more. Canada's External Affairs diplomats seemed more convinced than the military that the Korean action was in fact a diversionary one to mask a general Soviet threat to Europe; in short it was simply an extension of the Cold War in Europe. As for the Ottawa soldiers, in July 1950, the Chiefs of Staff Committee had originally believed that a war precipitated by the Soviet Union out of the Korean situation "was slight." But they quickly warmed to the idea of a diversion as their small forces and their role expanded with the crisis. This suggests that even at this early date the most important aspect of evolving Canadian defence and security policy was the North Atlantic posture, and that Canada was reacting because of the weight and the subsequent acceptance of the policy of the great powers in that alliance.[26]

In any case, because of the thesis that the Korean War was simply a diversion in the Cold War, the Canadian government began a rapid expansion of its defence capabilities at home and in Europe. In mid-1953, by which time the Korean conflict had been negotiated to a belligerent stop in a *status quo ante bellum*, Canadians were well on their way along this route. They promised the NATO alliance both an infantry brigade group and 12 squadrons of the RCAF to form an air division permanently situated in Europe. Components of these were to remain there in ever-decreasing numbers for the next 40 years.

Photographer: Bill Olson, Library and Archives Canada PA-114888

Against the rugged backdrop of the Korean countryside, members of 2 Princess Patricia's Canadian Light Infantry deploy to a new position in March 1951.

At home, defence budgets almost tripled from their 1949 levels of 2.2 percent of the Gross National Product (GNP). In monetary terms, the budgets increased from about $360 million to $1.9 billion in three years.[27] The number of personnel in the regular armed forces grew from 47,000 to 104,000 in the same period. All three services started on massive modern re-equipage. The government even re-established its old wartime munitions ministry with full Cabinet status and the same man, C.D. Howe, took charge.

But this time they called the new portfolio the Department of Defence Production. Its job was to co-ordinate the tremendous Cold War defence procurement production process. Significantly, this was the first time that Canada had ever created a munitions ministry in peacetime. The country actually moved another step closer to the American policy by reaffirming its defence sharing relations with the United States, through the Joint U.S.-Canadian Industrial Mobilization Planning Committee (JIMPC), established in 1949. In the next three years, Canada got nearly $400 million worth of American munitions orders, but, by the same token, managed to spend over twice as much in the United States.[28]

International events between 1949 and the end of the Korean War were defining moments for Canada. First, there was the permanent connection to the defence of Europe. Essentially this represented an acceptance of the Cold War policies of its two great partners, with the Americans being clearly the first among the equals. Yet this deference also meant that Canada was far more active on the world stage than it had ever been before. The Cold War had forced the issue. Second, and very importantly, was the effect on the Canadian military: here the modern professional Canadian Armed Forces were born. For the first time in Canada's history the old volunteer citizen militia was no longer considered the first line of Canadian defence. The new larger number of regular units demanded a continuing and expensive military commitment in peacetime. These formations demanded infrastructure, as well, including professional schools, large permanent training bases, and professional and social services. For example, once there was the commitment to Europe, the defence minister allowed families to accompany Canadian troops to European postings. And so the Canadian military communities in Europe were created. They remained there 40 years, the last one, CFB Lahr in southern Germany, was not closed until the mid-1990s when the Canadians finally left Europe.

Foreign commitments also meant foreign exchanges so that military personnel spent lots of time practising, learning, and even teaching the profession of arms in alliance forces. There was no doubt that this incremental direction was steadily moving towards the "professional-ism" of the United States Forces and of inter-operability with them.

As the 1950s wore on and the Canadian military establishment crept steadily towards a strength of 120,000 personnel, a few doubts started to grow about the Cold War posture. For example, one could argue, as Prime Minister Pierre Trudeau did later, that Canadian foreign policy was being determined more by its military alliance commitments in Europe than by the formulation of any independent thought about Canada's national interests. Furthermore, a few officials in government, especially in External Affairs, wondered if NATO was obsolete. Such voices questioned whether it was the European alliance or Canadian troops in Europe that protected Canada, or was it simply the American nuclear deterrent.[29]

There was also the sky rocketing dollar value of the new armament, itself made more costly by the technology of nuclear weaponry. These costs were in competition with the other great domestic development projects in Canada in the 1950s, namely, the Trans-Canada pipeline to bring Canadian natural gas energy to eastern (and American) markets, and the huge engineering feat that was the construction of the St. Lawrence Seaway. And there were lots of other demands contending for the limited financial resources such as health care, pension plans, baby bonuses and the expansion of post-secondary education.[30]

These Cold War commitments even raised some old cultural and social issues. Finding soldiers for the Korean force had been difficult. Maintaining personnel for the new European units proved also to be no easy task. There were those who advocated that anathema of Canadian military politics — conscription. Canadians never believed in it; even in the two world wars they only accepted compulsion at the last desperate moments of war. It was political suicide to attempt it in peacetime. The result was that recruiting in the Canadian Armed Forces (CAF) remained a difficult task as the new prosperity of the decade after 1945 siphoned personnel into the better paying jobs of a thriving civil economy.

Some units started to reflect parts of Canada where there was chronic unemployment and other social or ethnic difficulties. The Royal Canadian Regiment, for instance, had a very high proportion of Natives and unemployed Newfoundlanders in its battalions. Over a third of the population was French Canadian but they did not share proportionate-ly to their numbers within the culturally stifling and heavy historic anglophilia of our navy or the air force. In the army they were nearly all clustered in the one French Canadian unit, the Royal 22 Regiment.[31]

Another problem raised by the Cold War was that the new professional demands coupled with the high costs and immediacy of the nuclear threat had shoved the Canadian Reserve Forces farther and farther into the shadows. Nuclear conflict meant there was only enough time to go to war with what one had "in being." No longer, it was believed, could there be the usual time to mobilize the traditional Canadian citizen soldier. The consequence was that the relations between the militia and regulars became strained at best, with one often accusing the other of uselessness or arrogance. By the end of the decade, the combat role of the militia had all but ended. Its new job was aid to the civil power and emergency measures. Disillusioned, the enthusiastic part time members quit; they wanted to be soldiers not sand bag fillers. Unfortunately, the militia's social imprint, that traditionally had made the connection between civil and military in society also faded. The Canadian people were becoming separated from their military consciousness; they were indeed becoming more and more an "unmilitary people." The military's constituent political clout waned as the militia shrank. From now on it would be easier for politicians to do with the armed forces "what they will."[32] Nevertheless, as the Cold War of the 1950s ground on the regular Canadian Armed Forces developed a solid reputation for being good, even exceptional soldiers. As it was with Canada's diplomats, they got used to thinking about "punching above their weight."

In the Cold War of that decade, two other important events facilitated Canada's voyage from innocence: the Suez Canal crisis of 1956 and the creation of a North American Air Defense Command (NORAD). Here again the "Road from Innocence" took a new turn. On the surface, the Suez Crisis seemed to have little to do with the Cold War and perhaps at its beginning hardly anything to do with Canada. As we know the immediate crisis started when the United States and Western European powers apparently reneged on a promise to finance Egypt's Aswan Dam. The new, supposed despot of that country, Colonel Abdul Nasser had been tweaking Britain's imperial nose, since King Farouq had been deposed, to get the 70,000 British troops out of the canal area — then he promptly nationalized the mostly British privately owned Suez Canal Company.[33]

With all of this going on, the Soviet Union was quick to exploit the Cold War situation. It provided bargain-priced arms for the Egyptians, and it offered to fund the Aswan Dam without any strings attached. The strategic locus of Western hegemony in the Middle East appeared to be shifting towards the "Communists." With the rebuilding of Europe's and their own economies still on going, Great Britain and France needed the access to the Suez Canal to maintain vital international trade and the sustained flow of oil.

The short of it was an Anglo-French and Israeli scheme to invade the Canal area. This, in a bungled way, they did in the late fall of 1956.[34] The United States was horribly angry with Britain. In Washington, John Foster Dulles had secretly hoped that the Soviets would foolishly finance the Egyptian dam scheme and when it proved unviable would be saddled with huge and continuing costs. But the pre-emptive invasion threatened the U.S. strategy on the Aswan project. It seemed that the North Atlantic alliance was coming apart. Now was Canada's opportunity to play the role of constrainer, explainer, and healer.

Like the United States, Canada was repelled by the precipitous Anglo-French invasion. To Ottawa, it was handing the Soviets just the opportunity they wanted. This time, unlike Korea six years earlier, it was the other "partner," the United Kingdom that had to be constrained for the sake of the alliance. The prime minister fired off a blunt condemnation to his counterpart in London claiming that the Anglo-American alliance was being destroyed by unacceptable British action. NATO was unravelling. This seemingly last sputter of Victorian colonialism, as Louis St. Laurent explained it to Anthony Eden, had alienated most in the United Nations and fractured the British Commonwealth.[35]

For his part Pearson, still minister of external affairs, and many others also saw a direct and harmful link to the revolutionary events simultaneously unfolding in Hungary as that country tried to throw off the Soviet yoke. The Soviet Union's military units, he told a hushed Canadian Cabinet in early November, were now crushing the freedom fighters in Budapest and the "deplorable" British-French action in Egypt was all the more reprehensible because it prevented the free world from taking a united stand ... against this naked [Soviet] aggression."[36]

Britain had to be brought to its senses, but finding it a not-too-humbling a way out for was necessary. Borrowing an idea from a conversation with some American contacts, Pearson formulated the simple plan of offering through the United Nations a UN Emergency Force under Canadian command. He had the whole-hearted support of Washington because it kept the Soviets out and them in without much cost. And so the first truly Canadian Peacekeeping force materialized not only because of good diplomacy, but also because Canada had the military effectives to give substance to its diplomacy. The Cold War had already greatly increased and professionalized its military effectives and it had the strategic lift to get them there. Hence the Suez situation was diffused, and Pearson got the Nobel Peace Prize for his efforts the following year.[37]

The Suez Crisis of 1956 again pointed clearly to the fact that Canadian policy glass was sighted on collective security with a European Cold War focus. Paradoxically its binocular lens also increasingly looked at bilateral North American defence with the United States. Initially, focusing on both priorities was possible because the Americans' primary security commitment was towards Europe. But in the 10 short years of the 1950s, nuclear weapons technology and advanced delivery systems shifted this strategic balance towards bilateral defence in North America. The continental "partner" was so powerful and determined on all levels that Canada was in danger of being subsumed in the arrangement. The Soviets had exploded their first atomic device in 1949; their long-range bombers could reach North American shores the following year, and penetrate well into its interior shortly thereafter. Then there was the appearance of Soviet intercontinental ballistic missiles (ICBMs) at the end of the decade.[38]

Obviously any confrontation between the Soviets and the Americans would take place high in the skies over Canadian territory. The Dulles nuclear weapons policy of "massive retaliation" announced in 1954 made it all the more chilling for Canadians. And for those worried about such things, the Americans had developed this brutal idea without consulting anyone. The multilateral alliance in Europe was being challenged by the reality of defence at home through a bilateral agreement with its southern neighbour whether Canada liked it or not. As Joseph Jockel wrote, there were "no boundaries upstairs"[39] in the military minds of either country. But to some Canadians that was not true in politics.

In 1957, the newly elected and inexperienced Conservative government of John Diefenbaker agreed with Washington to create the NORAD. There has been hardly any single issue of Canadian–American relations as controversial as was this Cold War agreement. For many Canadians, it raised the thorny issues of civil-military relations, the acceptability of having nuclear arms, of Americans failure to consult, of threats to sovereignty, and even of the relationship to NATO. As we know, military cooperation between Canada and the United States had its genesis in the Second World War with the PJBD. Then Ottawa had sniffled that sometimes its great ally took the Dominion for granted. Moreover, there were many American servicemen stationed on Canadian soil and involved in the building of such projects as the Alaska Highway — sometimes so many that one could have thought they were an "army of occupation."[40] With the onset of the Cold War, the PJBD again picked up and became more comprehensive in its bilateral function.[41]

By the time the Soviet bomber threat ended the historic protection of geography, both Canadian and U.S. air forces were easily cooperating in each other's services and over each other's airspace. But there were two separate commands. And, given that warning time was getting ever so short, there was not always quick enough communication to co-ordinate speedy continental defence. With the hugely increased emphasis on air power by the both the Truman and Eisenhower administrations, especially in the form of the Strategic Air Command (SAC), the Royal Canadian Air Force (RCAF) had responded in growth to the point where, in the mid-1950s, it was larger than the Canadian Army and received nearly 50 percent of Canada's defence dollars. This fact alone encouraged inter-service antagonisms and expensive procurement competition. Canada had also embarked on designing and building its own supersonic jet fighter, the much applauded but very costly Avro CF-105 Arrow.

Furthermore, operational continental air-defence cooperation was intense. By 1954, there were three radar lines stretching across Canada, to which the United States had supplied significant portions of the funding and technology. With so much American presence on our territory, Ottawa was concerned about the independence of its command and control, as well as its sovereignty.[42]

Indeed, the continental defence issues generated a momentum in Canada of trying to "keep up with the Joneses" to the south. The chief advocates for this position were in the military in both countries. Making their minds up purely on the basis of operational necessity rather than the larger national security implications, air force leadership decided that an integrated and unified North American air defence command was what was needed. Officers of both countries pushed very hard on their governments to approve. They also organized themselves well along this path at the operational level. In 1951, they attached Canadian liaison officers to the U.S. Army Air Force (USAAF) Air Defense Command in Colorado Springs, Colorado. Three years later they formed an even closer coalescence of a joint planning group there.

And there were "no boundaries upstairs" for what the air forces of both countries were concerned about.[43] The Eisenhower administration was the first to approve of a formal bilateral air defence agency. Then, in 1957, just after the Canadians had changed their government, the Canadian top soldier General Foulkes privately convinced the new prime minister, John Diefenbaker, to sign the NORAD deal. There was no discussion in the Cabinet Defence Committee, nor was there any debate in Parliament before the decision. And it seems that events were orchestrated by the RCAF senior officers towards this end. Foulkes had not briefed his prime minister on the sovereignty or the command and control implications for Canada, which was surely his duty.

As for Diefenbaker, he was a novitiate; he did not ask the correct or relevant questions which indicated that he had very little idea of what he had too easily, almost nonchalantly, agreed to.[44] The short of it was that the enthusiasm that some senior Canadian officers had for cooperative operational efficiency determined Canada's strategic and national security policy.

When the NORAD agreement became public in 1958, it raised many more issues. One was that the prime minister, then under substantial public pressure in Parliament and elsewhere to explain what he had done, again naïvely claimed that NORAD as simply an extension of Canada in NATO. Since the Canadian electorate approved of the latter, surely, he likely thought, they would also accept the former. Added to this were the implications that there would be, as in NATO, multilateral consultation and collective security. That was not the Washington view, North American defence was completely separate from and none of Europe's business. There was also the omnipresent concern of having an American general commit Canadian forces to combat without the approval of the Canadian government as a result of a policy not necessarily of Canadian making or interest. In due course these aggravations were in part solved by "double nuclear keys," having a Canadian as second-in-command at NORAD Command, and "red telephones" in Ottawa and Washington.[45]

Perhaps the most contentious issue coming out of NORAD's creation in 1958 centered on Canadian use of nuclear armaments. The recommended stationing of U.S. troops in charge of these weapons on our soil was also as troubling as it was complicated. Both implied far more than just what sorts of weapons were present. Earlier, when our government had accepted a NATO air role attached to the American command in Europe where nuclear munitions were part of their force arsenal, it meant that Canada too would be a handler of such devices. The Canadian Air's Division's task for instance was stated to be nuclear strike/reconnaissance. In northern Europe, our land battle group got the "tactical" nuclear weapons in the form of the Honest John Rocket. Even the Royal Canadian Navy was operating on the assumption that they would have nuclear depth charges as part of the anti-submarine capability.

In NORAD, it was the same. Such weapons were the core of Washington's massive retaliation strategy delivered by Strategic Air Command. Air defence devices such as the Bomarc missile were also intended to use nuclear warheads against whatever was incoming. Canada was part of that. The Arrow would be built to fire nuclear missiles. Moreover, the Canadian Chiefs of Staff Committee had recognized their use in early 1957.[46]

However, the public debate over these weapons only became contentious in the late 1950s. Some Canadians baulked at the cost, believing that we could not keep it up. Others increasingly felt the utter futility of nuclear war and believed something had to be done to stop the mad race to oblivion. Still others were so worried that the skyrocketing nuclear weapons costs would side-track some of the anticipated social and civilian national development programs intended to raise the Canadian quality of life and keep the country internationally competitive.

There were massive schemes going on like the national health plan, or huge construction projects like the grossly over budget Trans-Canada natural gas pipe line and the St. Lawrence Seaway, and all were vying for a fixed purse of money. Something was going to give way. In early 1959, when the RCAF's Arrow project was suddenly cancelled by the Diefenbaker government, it seemed to be the articulation that Canada was coming to a new place on its "road from innocence" in the Cold War.[47] The story about this Canadian military icon is interesting.

The Avro Arrow had been conceived in the early 1950s as the RCAF's response to the Soviet long-range bomber threat. Canada's air force was confident that our domestic scientific and industrial talents were good enough and that the resulting superior airframe would make an excellent contribution to the defence of North America, as well as Canada. When it finally appeared in prototype in late 1957, this state-of-the-art Canadian fighter may have been the best airplane of its type in the world, but right from the start the cost was enormous.

The RCAF knew this, as did the Liberals, in power until their unexpected defeat in 1957. But they had not let the politically embarrassing knowledge get too far out in public. Some of the air force leadership and people in the Department of Defence Production had hoped to offset the huge costs by selling it to the allies. But none of them were interested, especially the Americans, afflicted as they often are with a mixture of the usual nationalism and a touch of xenophobia. If the United States was going to have a new fighter airplane, Congress was not in the mood to have anything but a home-produced weapon. Besides, the size of U.S. industry, their armed force demands, and the state of their own air weapons research and development, which was hot on Canada's tail with aircraft of a similar high performance quality as the Avro Arrow. And no doubt they also wanted to sell to the allies just like Canada did. Senior partners always seem to prevail in strategic procurement.

In the end, however marvellous, the Arrow was an expensive attempt to keep up to the new high technology demands of the Cold War, at a pace forced by the United States and the Soviet Union. The same day Diefenbaker shut down the Arrow project, the Canadian Company laid-off 14,000 of its employees, many of who subsequently had to leave Canada for places such as NASA to practise their talents. Perhaps the lesson was that if there is any validity in the "functional principle" it is to assess realistically what one can do.[48]

But when Prime Minister Diefenbaker cancelled the Arrow project in early 1959, he was less than forthright with the public about the reasons why. There is no doubt that he feared that his party would be held responsible and that he had been "set-up" by the previous Liberal administration that had generated and begun the expensive fighter scheme. Instead of giving a reasoned explanation for the cancellation, all the prime minister said was that in light of the new Cold War intercontinental missile capabilities, manned fighter interdiction was obsolete. Instead, he declared that air defence missiles like the Bomarc B, a U.S.-developed weapon meant to carry a nuclear warhead, were the answer.

But the problem by now was in the Cabinet. It was split on the issue of nuclear weapons, with Howard Green, the minister of external affairs, the most vocal of the anti-nuclear advocates. And there was a growing sympathy for that point of view among the electorate, reacting against the possibility of a nuclear Armageddon as a result of the arms race in the Cold War. Consequently, the ever-nimble prime minister bought in the American Bomarc scheme, which the air force leadership had already accepted.[49] When reminded that the missiles were intended to carry a nuclear load, he refused to accept the warhead that made them potent, telling Canadians that there were conventional warheads available for the Bomarc instead. But this was simply not true. Then he claimed that the U.S. Strategic Airforce was "our only hope of survival."[50]

The result was that Canada's Bomarc missiles sometimes had bags of sand put up front of them. This brouhaha also exposed the inconsistencies with Canada's position on nuclear weapons in our NATO role in Europe. Evident, too, was the fact that the prime minister did not know much

A conceptual drawing of the Avro Arrow in flight. The state-of-the-art fighter jet was prohibitively expensive based on Canadian needs, and the extremely protective national arms industries of other countries, particularly the United States, made export sales difficult. In the end, the project was scrapped.

about his own nation's strategic interests. Furthermore, his faulty ideas were not corrected or even challenged by military personnel who did not tell him soon enough or with sufficient accuracy what he had a right to know. Diefenbaker of course did not ask the correct questions either, and he was animated by his dislike of Americans and his inherent distrust of his soldiers whom he often felt were conspiring against his government. Until Diefenbaker's Conservatives lost the election in 1963, the nuclear question remained increasingly contentious and unresolved.[51]

By the fall of 1960, Canada was in the middle of a substantial downturn in the economy. This highlighted some of the Cold War problems such as escalating cost. Originally the Canadian NATO theory was that when the Europeans re-established their economies and became able to defend themselves, Canada would begin a withdrawal. That did not happen. This was in part because many Canadians were worried about the increasing dependence on, and integration with, the American economic juggernaut. Quite simply, Canada's ownership of its corporate assets, investment, and culture was steadily being eroded by the United States. Diefenbaker, for one, blamed all of this "creeping republicanism" on the previous 22 years of having Liberal "continentalists" in office. In response, he wanted to redirect at least 15 percent of Canada's trade away from the United States, preferably towards England, but Europe too. That did not happen, however, and the drift towards the United States continued.

And then there was the old Canadian animator that said membership in a multilateral alliance could still offset a unilateral one. As a result, instead of looking at the hard costs of keeping so many forces in Europe, Diefenbaker reaffirmed the Cold War European strategy by deciding to keep them there. In return, he hoped that having a seat at the table would provide access to European markets and political gains.[52] And so, Canada entered the 1960s with both a huge European commitment and a clear North American defence obligation: the two would come together with a vengeance in 1962.

The last event of this portion of Canada's sojourn on the "road from innocence" culminated in one of the most frightening of Cold War confrontations: the Cuban Missile Crisis of October 1962. The actual details of the event are well known. It looked like the world had come to the brink of nuclear holocaust in the showdown between U.S. President John F. Kennedy and the Soviet Union's prime minister, Khrushchev, over attempts to put Russian ICBM installations in Communist Cuba. Put succinctly, the Cold War had spread to the new world.

Meanwhile, in Canada the Diefenbaker government was on its last legs. Problems related to the use of nuclear weapons, lack of consultation regarding issues of North American defence, the effect long-standing military cooperation and integration, and the sense of horror and helplessness in the face of possible nuclear conflagration — these were all present.

And again, when Washington asked Ottawa to support its tough stand against the Soviets, the Cabinet was split and the prime minister prevaricated. The defence minister's pleadings for supportive action went nowhere. He wanted to go to the same high alert as had Washington; he also wanted to activate the existing bilateral arrangements between U.S. and Canadian NORAD forces. But Diefenbaker refused to mobilize Canada's portion, to arm the Bomarcs, or even allow the Americans to fly over Canadian airspace to get their nuclear weapons in position in Alaska.

Finally, after a critical Cabinet meeting in which the prime minister remained obdurate, the frustrated defence minister secretly ordered his service chiefs to have the operators go to the appropriate state of alert. But in the case of the Maritime Command Atlantic, the chief of the naval staff would not let his commander there initiate plans. There was no waiting given the fast and dangerous countdown of events, so on his own authority, Rear Admiral K.L. Dyer mobilized some of Canada's Atlantic ships to replace American naval units on anti-submarine warfare (ASW) duty, thereby freeing them for any war zone. Clearly the admiral, with a mind-set developed through years of practising his profession while integrated with the U.S. Navy, was more concerned about the immediate operational crisis than he was with the niceties of responsible government.[53] In the end, the Soviet Union backed down, but Canada's defence policies — to quote one of the few strategists Canada had at the time — were "in disarray its reputation a little tarnished, but its nuclear virginity intact."[54]

What did the Cuban Missile Crisis reveal? First, to the Americans at least, it showed that while the senior members of the Canadian NORAD Forces were willing and capable professionals anxious to cooperate, Canadian politicians were not. They appeared irresolute and did not want to fulfill their continental defence obligations. Diefenbaker had publicly criticized Kennedy for his lack of consultation even though the president had made personal calls to the prime minister to get him to show alliance solidarity in the coercive strategy.

Although Canada's defence minister may have broken the principle of collective Cabinet responsibility, as the minister in charge, he could legally raise such military alerts under his mandate. There was also a default in civilian control of the military. This was not only because of Diefenbaker, who did not communicate with his military personnel, and who showed, like many others in the Cabinet, that he had little understanding of the workings of the military or of the NORAD agreement and its subsequent obligations.[55]

There certainly was a problem caused by the absence of a central command structure at defence headquarters in Ottawa. After the Second World War, the then defence minister had set up a headquarters organization at the top of which was a chair of the Chiefs of Staff (COS) Committee who in turn sat on the Cabinet Defence Committee. He was not a "central commander" who synthesized all the ideas, needs, and wants of the service chiefs into coherent and enforceable defence policy recommendations for the Cabinet. Nor, was there a flow in the other direction in which the chair of the COS Committee necessarily carried the will of the Cabinet to the three service commanders. If there had been a central commander and staff with the authority to carry out the Cabinet directives, it would have established a clear civilian control. But this weak arrangement had been put in place when the Cold War and NATO began, because it had simply and naïvely been assumed that there was no need for a central control since the individual Canadian services would be put under NATO command after the politicians had had their input.[56] Given all these considerations, blame for the Canadian problems with the Cuban Missile Crisis lay heavier with the politicians than with their senior service personnel.

However, this does not absolve military leaders either. For their part the military were once again driven by the narrow concerns of operations more than anything else. This is one manifestation of what a later commentator claimed was a historical failure of Canada's military to think at the highest strategic and command levels.[57] Moreover, as individual services they were too competitive and did not consult easily. The concept of "jointness" now so highly valued in Canada's senior Command and Staff College was not there. There is little doubt that some military personnel took advantage of the lack of expertise and interest among the politicians to pursue their own agendas. But wherever fault lay, some politicians remained suspicious of the military, and some others began to think that it should be brought under closer civilian control. In all, the Cuban Missile Crisis was but a sign post — albeit a major one — along the road begun at the onset of the Cold War.

The fallout of the missile crisis was immediately political. Diefenbaker's crippled regime staggered into 1963 under the onslaught of the nuclear arms debate: would Canada have nuclear weapons or not? Defence debates are a rarity in Canadian electoral politics. That they were a major concern in this one showed that Canadians were indeed at the parting of the ways in their Cold War experience. As we know, Diefenbaker had denied that the NORAD or the NATO agreements required that Canada have nuclear weapons. Then, in early January 1963 the retiring NATO supreme commander in Europe, the American General Lauris Norstad, stopped off in Ottawa where he told newspaper reporters that Canada had definitely accepted the nuclear role in Europe. He implied that the governments past statements were a lie. He added a non-too-subtle message that Canada was really not pulling its weight if it did less than fulfill its nuclear obligations.

That an American general said such things on Canadian soil stung to say the least. Within a week the Liberal Party leader, who had also opposed the nuclear devices in 1959, made what became known as the "Pearson flip-flop." Having experienced an obvious epiphany, Pearson now accepted the warheads because there was a "commitment that we must honour."[58] Shortly thereafter, Washington waded into the fray by issuing a blunt statement confirming that Norstad's allegations concerning what Diefenbaker had either tried to conceal or had denied were in fact true: Canada had nuclear obligations both in NORAD and NATO.

Three members of Diefenbaker's Cabinet promptly resigned, including the minister and associate minister of national defence. Then in February, the government failed in a vote of confidence. Six weeks later it lost the federal election. Lester Pearson, now a nuclear advocate, had hammered the issue all through the election campaign and he had won. So it was that the Cuban missile crisis was the denouement of the most volatile period in Canadian national security history that started with the election of the Diefenbaker government in 1957. The Cold War and defence controversies of 1962–1963 were the first time that the country had assessed the utility of being on a road that it had been on for the preceding 18 years.

But the fall-out did not stop at mere self-examination of policy. The next five years saw some fundamental changes in defence and foreign policy. One of the most immediate and important was the unification and integration of the Canada's three services into a single force. Perhaps trying to get a better control of its "soldiers," the government also induced a civilianization of the Department of National Defence.

When Pierre Trudeau succeeded Pearson as prime minister at the end of the decade, he was concerned that the Ottawa's European defence commitment was driving Canadian foreign policy. And he vowed to get out of the obligation in the early 1970s. But he found that such a decision might lead Europe to ignore Canada in a variety of scenarios — especially economically. It was important to have a seat at the table and the price seemed to be staying in NATO, even though the force would be much reduced and repositioned. It took another two decades before the Canadians finally left Europe.

While the country would remain in Europe for the next generation of the Cold War, the 1960s also initiated a move towards another form of function: peacekeeping, ostensibly because it was cheaper, humanitarian, and non-nuclear. It was also a role one could do with smaller forces that earned the country lots of international kudos. Consequently, Canadians served all over the world in this capacity. But it seemed contradictory in as much as the country's leaders had not really given up the old pledge to Europe while accepting a new task.

Some historians have even argued that the peacekeeping role was really just the "Cold War by other means" — a continuance of Canada's North Atlantic posture to defend Western interests.[59] Within the new force the duality sparked another sometimes equally divisive debate of whether being peacekeepers meant the armed service was really a professional military body or just a group of international policemen. It also heightened competition for decreasing funds among the "all green" services.

Outside of the military, many voices also openly questioned whether our past NATO defence posture was continuing to dominate foreign policy.[60] Others in the academic community felt that during the early Cold War period, Canada was too weak or disinterested in developing its own strategic policies, and had blindly accepted those of the major players, particularly the United States. At the time, Colin Gray even called the phenomenon "strategic theoretical parasitism." Fortunately, later studies have demonstrated that this was not so.[61]

However, in 1963, the effects of this part of the Cold War story were not yet known. What was known was that the "road from innocence" for Canada had been neither smooth nor straight.

NOTES

1. Canada. Department of External Relations, *Documents on Canada's External Relations, Vol. 11, 1944–1945*, Part 2 (Ottawa: Supply and Services Canada, 1990), doc.1228, "Translation of a Note from the Embassy of the Soviet Union," Ottawa, September 7, 1945; *ibid.*; Doc. No. 1233, Ambassador in Soviet Union to Sec. of State for External affairs, dispatch 368, September 25, 1945, secret. For the entire run of documents on the atomic secrets spying issue and the deteriorating relations of the West and the Soviet Union in 1945, see *ibid.*, docs. 1229 to 1245. Hereafter cited DEA, *Documents*. Canadians would not be told of the spy ring until February 1946.

2. C.P. Stacey, *Canada and the Age of Conflict: A History of Canadian External Policies, 1867–1921, Vol. 1* (Toronto: Macmillan, 1977), 311.

3. For a general survey through a series of articles, see those in Greg Donaghy, ed., *Uncertain Horizons: Canadians and Their World in 1945* (Ottawa: Canadian Committee for the History of the Second World War, 1995).

4. For an analysis of the "functional principle," see the late A. J. Miller's article, "The Functional Principle in Canada's External Relations," in the *International Journal*, Vol. 35, No. 2 (Spring, 1980), and Alex Morrison, "Canada and Peacekeeping: A Time for Re-Analysis," in David Dewitt and David Leyton-Brown, eds., *Canada's International Security Policy* (Toronto: Prentice Hall, 1995), 202–203.

5. Paul Buteaux, "NATO and the Evolution of Canadian Defence and Foreign Policy" in Dewitt and Leyton-Brown , 155–156.

6. H.V. Riekhoff in Dewitt and Leyton-Brown, 227–250, discusses the collective security arguments for Canada from the League of Nations until the Gulf War.

7. For a scholarly interpretation of the origins of the Cold War, see Thomas Paterson and Robert McMahon, eds., *The Origins of the Cold War* (Lexington, MA: Heath and Co., 1991, 3rd ed.). This is a broad compendium of articles on various aspects of the Cold War.

8. Denis Smith, "Canada and Nato: Adjusting the Balance," in Keith Neilson and Ronald Haycock, eds., *The Cold War and Defence* (New York: Praeger, 1990), 174.

9. Secretary of State for Commonwealth Relations to High Commissioner for the United Kingdom, London, March 10, 1948, Top secret, personal and most immediate, in DEA, *Documents*, Vol. 14 , 1948, No. 296. Also see in *ibid*. Prime Minister of Canada to Prime Minister of the United Kingdom, March 11, 1948, top secret. No. 298. King promised Attlee that he would send immediately "one of our officials to Washington just as soon as he is required, to join officials of the United Kingdom and the United States government in the exploratory talks suggested."

10. On this traditional role, see B.J.C. Mckercher and Lawrence Aronsen eds., *The North Atlantic Triangle in a Changing World: Anglo-American-Canadian Relations, 1902–1956* (Toronto: University of Toronto Press, 1996), especially the chapters by Aronsen and Martin Kitchen covering the period 1945 to 1956.

11. Canadian High Commissioner to Secretary of State for External Affairs, April 2, 1948, DEA files 264(s) cited in Smith, "Canada and NATO: Adjusting the Balance," in Neilson and Haycock, 174, fn 8.

12. Desmond Morton, *Canada and War: A Military and Political History* (Toronto: Butterworth's, 1981), 159.

13. DEA *Documents*, "Extracts from Report of the Minister of National Defence," No. 418, "Notes on Defence Meetings November 26 to December 14, 1949 in Europe, the United Kingdom and Ireland," top secret.

14. Jon B. McLin, *Canada's Changing Defence Policy, 1957–1963: The Problems of a Middle Power in an Alliance* (Baltimore: Johns Hopkins University Press, 1967), 18.

15. Desmond Morton, *A Military History of Canada* (Edmonton, AB: Hurtig, 1985), 232–3.

16. John Hilliker and Donald Barry, *Canada's Department of External Affairs, Vol. 2, Coming of Age, 1946–1968* (Montreal: McGill-Queen's University Press, 1995), 76–78. Over the next 40 years, Canada had little success in turning this hope into a reality in NATO. Indeed the creation of the European Union has developed that aspect. It remains to see how separate NATO remains from the EU.

17. DEA, *Documents*, Vol. 16, No. 479, "Extract from Minutes of the Cabinet Defence Committee," Ottawa, April 25, 1950, minute V11, "NATO: Progress of Defence Planning," top secret.

18. James Eayrs, *In Defence of Canada, Vol. 4, Growing Up Allied* (Toronto: University of Toronto Press, 1985), 132–5 and 172–6.

19. Douglas Bland, *The Military Committee of the North Atlantic Alliance: A Study of Structure and Strategy* (NewYork: Praeger, 1990), 113–160.

20. Herbert Fairlie Wood, *Strange Battleground: The Official History of the Canadian Army in Korea* (Ottawa: Queen's Printer, 1966), 4–7.

21. J.L Granatstein and Norman Hillmer, *For Better or For Worse: Canada and the United States to the 1990s* (Toronto: Copp Clark Pitman, 1991), 179.

22. DEA, *Documents*, Vol. 16, Doc. No. 45, " Memorandum from the Under-Secretary of State to the Secretary of State for External Affairs: Korea: the UN Secretary-General's Letter of July 14," Ottawa, July 18, 1950, top secret. Heeney told Pearson that "Korea is but a side show" and that Western Europe is "still the main theatre." He also said that given the need to defend Canada and the NATO agreement, there were no Canadian troops available for Korea. At the time the total regular force was about 47,000.

23. C.G. Rennie, "Mobilization for War: Canadian Army Recruiting and the Korean Conflict," in the *Canadian Defence Quarterly*, Vol. 15, No. 1, 1985, comments on the lack of enthusiasm for NCOs to join. The official history, Lieutenant-Colonel H.F. Wood, *Strange Battleground*, in 1966, and more recently David Bercuson, *Blood on the Hills*, cover the conflict's details.

24. Dennis Stairs, *The Diplomacy of Constraint: Canada, the Korean War and the United States* (Toronto: University of Toronto, 1974) analyzes the role of tempering the elephant and why.

25. DEA, *Documents*, Vol. 16, Doc. No. 174, Secretary of State for External Affairs to Canadian Ambassador in Washington, secret. December 4, 1950, containing the memo "Korea and the Atomic Bomb" (*Ibid.*, Doc No. 175); also see *Ibid.*, Doc. No. 164, "Extracts from Cabinet Conclusions," Ottawa, November 29, 1950, top secret. This Cabinet minute extract notes that on several occasions Canada had expressed concern over the American "reckless action in Korea."

26. All through the 213 diplomatic documents on the Korean conflict published in the DEA for 1950 alone, the continuous themes are a central focus on what the Americans have as policy, a worry that they will overreact, an attempt to mitigate and guide it where possible to avoid war. There are also constant references, especially by the diplomats, to the North Atlantic threat. And so they promoted the need to bolster Western Europe's defences, as well as their own. See DEA, *Documents*, Vol. 16, 1950, Doc. No. 48, "Minutes of a Meeting of the Cabinet Defence Committee," July 19, 1950; *ibid.*, Doc. No. 171, Pearson's "Memorandum on Korea," December 2, 1950, for samples of both the diplomats' conviction and the soldiers initial hesitation about the larger threat. For the entire group of "Korean documents," see Doc. No. 10 to 223. The rest relating to the Korean conflict are found in DEA, Documents, Vols. 17–19.

27. Granatstein and Hillmer, 181.

28. Morton, *Military History of Canada*, 236–9, and Granatstein and Hillmer, 180–1. On the RCAF Air Division see, Major B.C. Frandsen, "A Blunted Sword or Rapier: 1 Canadian Air Division in NATO," an unpublished War Studies MA paper, RMC, Kingston, August 28, 2000.

29. For a good survey of Canada after World War I, see Robert Bothwell, Ian Drummond and John English, *Canada Since 1945: Power, Politics and Provincialism* (Toronto: University of Toronto Press, revised edit. 1989), 421–23.

30. Bothwell, et al., is a good survey of Canadian politics after 1945.

31. J.L. Granatstein and J.M. Hitsman, *Broken Promises: A History of Conscription in Canada* (Toronto: Oxford University Press, 1977), 245–60.

32. J.C. Willett, *A Heritage at Risk: The Canadian Militia As a Social Institution* (Boulder, CO: Westview Press, 1987) covers the fate of the militia in the 1950s and 1960s. Also see Douglas Bland, *The Administration of Defence Policy in Canada: 1947 to 1987* (Kingston, ON: Frye, 1987), 23.

33. For a good survey of the various aspects of Suez, see W.R. Louis and Roger Owen, eds., *Suez 1956: The Crisis and Its Consequence* (Oxford: Clarendon Press, 1989).

34. P.J. Vatikiotis, *The History of Modern Egypt: From Muhammad Ali to Mubarak* (London: Weidenfeld and Nicolson, 4th edition, 1991), 392–406.

35. Martin Kitchen, "From the Korean War to Suez: Anglo-American-Canadian Relations, 1950–1956," in Mckercher and Aronsen, eds., *The North Atlantic Triangle*, 249–252.

36. DEA, *Documents*, Vol. 22, Part 1, "International Situation; Middle East; Hungary; Policy at the United Nations" from "Extracts from Cabinet Conclusions," Ottawa, November 3, 1956, Doc. No. 126. St. Laurent made the same point to Eden two days later in another firm condemnation but this time offering a Canadian Force for Egypt. See *ibid.*, "Prime Minister to Prime Minister of United Kingdom," November 5, 1956, Doc. No. 136.

37. Kitchen, in Mckercher and Aronsen, *The North Atlantic Triangle*, 252.

38. Canada. *Canada's Defence Programme, 1954–1955* (Ottawa: Queen's Printer, 1955), 23 and 55; and Eayrs, *Growing Up Allied*, 275–318. Eayrs's book covers the sky-rocketing defence budgets of the mid-decade. This included large amounts of Mutual Aid to Western Europe.

39. Joseph T. Jockel, *No Boundaries Upstairs: Canada, the United States and the Origins of North American Air Defence, 1945–1958* (Vancouver: University of British Columbia Press, 1987), 91–117.

40. R.D. Cuff and J.L. Granatstein, *Ties That Bind: Canadian-American Relations in Wartime from the Great War to the Cold War* (Toronto: Hakkert, 2nd edit. revised, 1977), 93–112.

41. Joel Sokolsky, "A Seat at the Table: Canada and Its Alliances," in *Armed Forces and Society*, Vol. 16, No. 1 (Fall 1989), 11–35.

42. J.T Jockel, "Military Establishments and the Creation of NORAD," in *American Review of Canadian Studies*, Vol. 12, No. 3 (Fall 1982), 1–16.

43. Jockel, *No Boundaries Upstairs*, 93.

44. The classic analysis of the time is James M. Minifie, *Peacemaker or Powder Monkey* (Toronto: McClelland & Stewart, 1960). Jockel's *No Boundaries Upstairs* is definitive. Also see David Bercuson, "Continental Defence and Arctic Sovereignty, 1945–1950: Solving the Dilemma," in Haycock and Neilson, 153–170, and Ron Purver, "The Arctic in Canadian Security Policy," in Dewitt and Leyton-Brown, 81–110.

45. George Lindsey, "Canada-U.S. Defence Relations in the Cold War," in Joel Sokolsky and Joseph Jockel, eds., *Fifty Years of Canada–United States Defence Co-operation: The Road from Ogdensburg* (Lewiston, NY: Mellon Press, 1992), 66–68.

46. DEA, *Documents*, Vol. 22, Part 1, No. 641, Permanent Representative to North Atlantic Council to Sec. State for External Affairs, March 6, 1957, and *ibid.*, N0.642, "Extracts from the Minutes of the Chiefs of Staff Committee," March 19, 1957.

47. Morton, *Canada at War*, 173–181.

48. Granatstein and Hillmer, *For Better or For Worse*, 198–199.

49. DEA, *Documents*, Vol. 22, Part 1, Doc. No. 462, "Extracts from the Minutes of the Chief of Staff Committee," March 19, 1957, secret.

50. J.M Beck, *The Pendulum of Power: Canada's Federal Elections* (Toronto: Prentice Hall, 1968), 356.

51. On the Diefenbaker administration, see Peter C. Newman, *Renegade in Power* (Toronto: McClelland & Stewart, 1963), and John G. Diefenbaker, *One Canada: The Years of Achievement, 1957 to 1962* (Toronto: Macmillan, 1976).

52. Bothwell, et al., *Canada Since 1945*, Chapters 20 and 21.

53. Peter Haydon, *The 1962 Cuban Missile Crisis: Canadian Involvement Reconsidered* (Toronto: Canadian Institute of Canadian Studies, Canadian Printco Ltd., 1993), 121–147. This is the most definitive treatment of the crisis to date.

54. Robert Spencer quoted in the *Canadian Annual Review of Public Affairs, 1962*, 136, as cited in Bothwell, Drummond and English, *Canada Since 1945*, 233.

55. Haydon, 216–221.

56. *Ibid.*, 206–211.

57. Adrian Preston, "The Profession of Arms in Canada, 1945–1970: Political Authority as a Military Problem," in *World Politics*, Vol. 23, No. 2, January 1971. For a look at a similar problem in officer education in Canada, see R.G. Haycock, "Athena and the Muses: Historical and Contemporary Dimensions of Military Education in Canada," in the *Canadian Military Journal*, Vol. 2, No. 2 (Summer 2001), 5–18.

58. Beck, *Pendulum of Power*, 351–371, covers the 1963 Canadian election campaign in detail.

59. Sean M. Maloney, *Canada and UN Peacekeeping: Cold War by Other Means, 1945–1970* (St. Catharines, ON: Vanwell, 2002).

60. For a good synopsis of the unification effects, see Rod B. Byers, "Peacekeeping and Canadian Defence Policy: Ambivalence and Uncertainty," in Henry Wiseman, ed., *Peacekeeping: Appraisals and Proposals* (New York: Pergamon Press, 1983), 130–160; and W. Harriet Critchley, "Civilianization and the Canadian Military," in *Armed Forces and Society*, Vol. 16, No. 1 (Fall 1989), 117–136.

61. Colin Gray, "The Need for Independent Canadian Strategic Thought," *Canadian Defence Quarterly*, No. 1, 1971, 6–12. Also see his *Canadian Defence Priorities: A Question of Relevance* (Toronto: Clarke Irwin, 1972). Earlier, Adrian Preston had levelled much the same charges in part aiming them at the limited professional development of Canadian officer corps. See Adrian Preston, "The Higher Study of Defence in Canada: A Critical Review," *Journal of Canadian Studies*, Vol. 3, No. 3, 1968, 17–28. Recently, Andrew Richter has seriously challenged this "school of thought" showing clearly with heretofore classified documents that Canadians were developing their own form of strategic thought based on Canadian national interests. See Andrew Richter, *Avoiding Armageddon: Canadian Military Strategy and Nuclear Weapons, 1950–63* (Vancouver: UBC Press, 2002).

CHAPTER 9

Supporting the Pax Americana:
Canada's Military and the Cold War
by Howard G. Coombs with Richard Goette

> *It is from the outside world that the storms threaten.*
> *Two states of unparalleled power face each other in an*
> *uneasy "peace." Two ways of life, which is not too much*
> *to call religions, clash in mutual denunciations. State*
> *and religion in each case coincide. The atomic bomb*
> *hangs over humanity like Damocles' sword. The*
> *Canadian people show no disposition to deviate from*
> *the pattern of their behaviour on previous occasions, so*
> *that if the uneasy peace were to break down into war,*
> *they would be found "at America's side" just as on pre-*
> *vious occasions they were found at Britain's.*
> — A.R.M. Lower[1]

> *The Pax Britannica of the nineteenth century is to*
> *be replaced in the later twentieth century by a Pax*
> *Americana.*
> — Escott Reid[2]

In the 1949 preface to the forth edition of his seminal work *Colony to Nation: A History of Canada*, eminent Canadian historian Arthur Lower concisely and accurately captured the bipolar world of the late modern era and outlined the tensions that were its raison d'être.[3] Although the end of the Second World War heralded the conclusion of a global struggle against fascism, it also marked the end of an uneasy wartime alliance between another two ideologies, Communism and democracy. The period was also characterized by the recognition that the American Republic and the alliance of Western states had supplanted England and the empire in the new world order. Consequently, it seemed reasonable to most that Canada's relationship to the ascendant United States would be marked by a shifting of allegiances and a severance of the last ties that bound the nation to Britain.

However, given Canada's struggle for recognition of its wartime contribution, most believed that its association with the United States and other major nations would reflect its status as a recognizable nation state in the post-war global community, not co-equal but a country with a degree of influence. Lester Pearson, then at External Affairs, expressed these sentiments in May 1944, noting that Canada's status among the "Big Four," the United States, Britain, the Soviet Union, and China, was vital enough to be required for the prosecution of the conflict but not sufficiently powerful to be considered of equal status.[4] Pearson believed that Canada fell into the category of an "in-between state," a country with power and responsibility but unable to control or direct the war.

This sentiment arose from concern that the great powers were not providing acknowledgment of Canadian efforts towards winning the war by permitting participation in the decision-making bodies of the wartime alliance.[5] Initial attempts to be included were rebuffed on the grounds that if an exception were made for Canada, other smaller allies would wish to participate. Inclusiveness would make the process of policy and strategy formation too complex and time consuming. Views such as those advocated by Pearson eventually resulted in the formulation and recognition of the "functional" principle of representation. Functionalism advocated that in areas where smaller nations had expertise or interests they should be considered in the same light as major powers.[6] In other words, relevance permitted representation in wartime councils. This was an enduring lesson to Canadian statesmen and senior military commanders.

In 1945, Ottawa embraced the term *middle power* to describe Canada's status. Pearson suggested that "our strength and resources as a middle power" should permit Canada to partake of the "special rights and privileges" in influencing international affairs that the larger nations had abrogated unto themselves. This philosophy was first used in an effort to ensure that the leaders of the victorious allies did not dominate the proposed United Nations. Canada sought greater recognition for smaller countries in the post-war world and advocated that middle powers had a role to play in the maintenance of international peace.[7]

However, by the cessation of hostilities it was evident Canada's acceptance as a middle power lay in its ability to establish relevancy on the international stage by participating in constructive international action through multilateral organizations. The entanglement of alliances, particularly the North Atlantic Treaty Organisation (NATO) and North American Air Defense Command (NORAD),[8] and to a lesser extent the United Nations (UN), as well as the necessity of constructing saliency within these alliances de facto determined how Canada would use its military. Although the broad strokes of immediate post-war foreign policy did chart an initial course, early in the Cold War emphasis moved from multilateral to bilateral arrangements for defence. In the absence of coherent and durable political guidance during succeeding decades the use of the Canadian military as an instrument of national power became fragmented and disjointed.[9] By default, the unifying factor in Canadian defence activities became support of a *Pax Americana*. The employment of Canadian military forces from 1946 until 1991 shows the impact of this bilateral approach to defence in Canada.

Governments throughout recorded history have used the military to further the aims of their respective nation states.[10] By the early nineteenth century, the military theorist Carl von Clausewitz formalized Western views of this association: "war is not merely an act of policy but a true political instrument, a continuation of political intercourse, carried on by

Library and Archives Canada C-023273

Whether Canada could capitalize on its wartime contribution and middle-power status was yet to be seen in the post-war period. Left to right: British Prime Minister Clement Attlee, U.S. President Harry Truman, and William Lyon Mackenzie King at the final meeting of the Atomic Bomb Conference in Washington, D.C., in November 1945.

other means."[11] Clausewitz proposed that the nature of war was determined by interplay between government, the people, and the military. Key to this relationship is the link between national policy and the use of military forces. The latter is subsumed by the exigencies of the former. Clausewitz strove for broad explanatory concepts of war and viewed the connection between policy and the violence of war as modified by various gradients of strategy and tactics.[12]

In the twentieth century this linkage developed as a hierarchical arrangement that included Military Strategy, Operations, and Tactics. This sequencing permitted an orderly and methodical transformation of strategic objectives to attainable and measurable tactical goals. Heads of state and their principal advisers normally formulate strategy. It is the level of policy at which a country or a group of countries chooses national or alliance security objectives. Grand strategy concerns the goals of an alliance while national strategy refers to those of an individual nation. Military strategy is the application of the military power of a nation through force or threat of force to achieve the goals of grand or national strategy. Operations involve the creation and implementation of military campaigns to achieve strategic ends. Tactics are the detailed techniques and procedures that military units and formations use to achieve victory in battles and engagements. This hierarchical arrangement is the practical expression of the military as "an instrument of policy."[13]

Interestingly, Canada had and has no formal systemic process such as that contained within the American National Security Act of 1947. This American legislation ensures there is a methodical linking of security objectives to national policy and that those aims are eventually transformed into actions that support policy goals. It also ensures there are mandated periodic reviews and assessments of the effectiveness of United States National Security Strategy. This body of legislation was designed to capitalize on the lessons of political-military coordination learned during the Second World War and makes certain that the authority for policy making is vested in the civilian departments of government, particularly the State Department.[14] At the same time, Canada maintained a Cabinet Defence Committee[15] and now and again initiated defence reviews to provide oversight over the Canadian military. This seemingly ad hoc process did not result in an encompassing methodical approach to formulating lasting and durable defence plans that were in keeping with foreign policy. Instead it seems as if Canada has evolved an informal approach to the employment of military forces that is determined by other factors.

During the initial decades of the Cold War, the heads of the Royal Canadian Navy (RCN), the Canadian Army and the Royal Canadian Air Force (RCAF) formed the Canadian Chiefs of Staff Committee, and provided all military advice regarding defence policy to the minister of national defence and the Cabinet Defence Committee. The chair of the Chiefs of Staff Committee acted in the capacity of the government representative to NATO and NORAD and had immense influence in Canada's relationship with its allies. In the absence of a centralized and coordinated strategic policy mechanism, Major-General W.H.S. Macklin, the adjutant-general of the army, said the chair "became the real arbitrator on defence policy tendered to government," with the ability to prompt desired defence and consequently foreign policy. Conversely the authority of the Defence Council dwindled to matters of administration, budgets, staffing, and logistics.[16] One could argue that in the light of these circumstances the "tacticization" of strategy come to pass, or more simply put, "the tail was wagging the dog."

In an address at the University of Toronto in 1947, Louis St. Laurent, then secretary of state for external affairs, provided what could be considered the groundwork of Canadian policy during the Cold War. St. Laurent's speech placed Canada firmly in the camp of the Western allies and outlined how saliency would be achieved. First, he proposed that Canadian foreign policy would exist as a unifying influence within the country and it could do this best by reflecting the values and ideals of Canadian society, as "The role of this country in world affairs will prosper only as we maintain this principle, for a disunited Canada will be a powerless one." Second, he said Canada should support political liberty, thus "a threat to the liberty of Western Europe, where our political ideas were nurtured, was a threat to our way of life." Third, he argued Canadian foreign policy should support the rule of law and suggested that a lesson could be learned from "the hideous example of the fascist states of the evil that befalls a nation when the government sets itself above the law." This was an allusion and warning to the Soviet Union. Fourth, he continued, foreign policy should be based on "some conception of human values." These values emphasize rights of the individual and should not be determined by considerations of material wealth. St. Laurent expressed the sentiment that Canada should "protect and nurture" these standards of behaviour. Last, arising from the desire to enact policy that was in keeping with the previous principle, he said Canada had an imperative to take on external responsibilities because the "security for this country lies in the development of a structure of international organizations." Unlike the devastated countries of Europe, Canada was intact and should act in concert with a number of like-minded countries, a list from which the Soviet Union was glaringly absent.

The speech stressed the value of numerous alliances and relationships; it attempted to steer clear of encouraging French Canadian criticisms of too close a relationship with Great Britain. Canada would avoid regionalism but acknowledged that there was a close connection with the United States, however, "The relationship between a great and powerful neighbour and its smaller neighbour is at best far from simple." St. Laurent also stressed proportionality in that Canada was "a secondary power" and would cooperate in "constructive international action" but could and would not advocate activities that only larger countries could bear. "There is little point in a country of our stature recommending international action," he explained, "if those who must carry the major burden of whatever action is taken are not in sympathy."[17] Quite simply, Canada would act internationally in concert with allies and partners. This public articulation of policy was the prelude to Canadian military involvement with NATO and NORAD. In conjunction with the principle of achieving relevancy or saliency and an absence of a systemic connection between the formulation and implementation of grand strategy and Canadian military strategy, it created the conditions for an incoherent and disjointed approach to the planning and conduct of military operations that has come to characterize the "Canadian Way of War" during the Cold War.

At the end of the Second World War, the Canadian military consisted of the third largest navy, fourth largest air force, and one of the larger armies. It was a formidable organization.[18] Although the government appeared to rush to reduce its forces in 1945, within five years it seemingly reversed its position and assumed commitments abroad in the form of collective defence. The government committed 25,000 servicemen and 11 RCAF squadrons for the occupation of post-war Germany. A booming economy prompted most Canadians to clamour for demobilization and a return to normalcy. Domestic pressure and collective action by overseas servicemen caused Canada to bring back its occupation troops in the spring of 1946.

Not surprisingly, the plans of the three services for future force structures met with an unenthusiastic response from the government. The navy requested 20,000 personnel to create a proposed task force with two aircraft carriers and four cruisers. The army proposed force levels of 55,788 regulars and 155,396 reserves and a "training force" of 48,500, who would be drafted into compulsory service. The RCAF recommended 30,000 on active service, 15,000 in auxiliary squadrons, and 50,000 in the reserve. These propositions were sharply reduced by the government of Prime Minister Mackenzie King. The RCN proposal was condensed by half, the Army was permitted 25,000 regulars, the RCAF was allowed 16,000, and any ideas of conscription to maintain military staffing levels were flatly rejected.[19]

Regardless of these seemingly sharp cuts, prominent Canadian military historian Colonel C.P. Stacey wrote retrospectively in 1952 that much had changed from the post-war situation of 1919. "A people who traditionally had been very unwilling to do much in the way of military preparation in time of peace," he asserted, "had clearly learned a great deal from the hard experience of two World Wars."[20] The establishments of 1946 did not remain fixed but began to rise again in 1947–1948 in the face of international tension, to meet the demands of alliances, until a high of 100,000 in three services was reached in 1952.[21] These numbers were predicated on commitments to NATO and continental defence.

Although the formation of the UN in 1945 had been met with high expectations the effectiveness of the international body was soon in doubt. In September 1946 Louis St. Laurent characterized the UN as "impotent" and not a venue through which Canada could make an appropriate contribution.[22] The United Nations was viewed as ineffective as long as the Soviets had veto in the Security Council. Sir Brian Urquhart, who was present during the creation of the UN, and was later the under-secretary-general for special political affairs, stated:

> The Charter had been based on the concept of an extension of the wartime alliance into peacetime. The "United" in United Nations came from the Atlantic Charter of 1941 and referred to nations united in war, not in peace. The permanent members of the Security Council with the power of veto were the leaders of a victorious wartime alliance, and the Charter assumed, with a stunning lack of political realism, that they would stay united in supervising, and if necessary, enforcing, world peace.[23]

External Affairs officials believed Western nation states should provide a united front but not attempt to make changes to the Charter that would cause the Soviets to withdraw from the UN and isolate themselves.[24] In Canadian eyes the Cold War threatened middle power states and the UN provided a venue for dialogue regarding potential causes of friction so outright conflict between major powers could be avoided.[25]

The difficulties in achieving consensus in the UN Security Council led to a reassessment of alternative forms of collective security. This re-examination was in part prompted by the issuance of the "Truman Doctrine" in March 1947. This policy committed the United States to provide assistance to any country attempting to maintain their sovereignty and self-governance when menaced by totalitarian aggression.[26] This American policy reflected notions of containment advocated by George Kennan, an analyst with the State Department. "Containment" was a concept designed to discourage the Soviet Union from expansionist aspirations. Kennan believed that "The main element of any United States policy towards the Soviet Union must be that of a long-term, patient, but firm and vigilant containment of Russian expansionist tendencies."[27]

This political philosophy was also supported by Canada.[28] To achieve the desired effect Escott Reid, a high-ranking official in External Affairs, believed that an overwhelming preponderance of force, as opposed to a passive approach was the most appropriate solution. This force was to be a combination of military, economic, and public diplomacy, and increased through participation in alliances.[29]

Containment assisted in the creation of an Atlantic community led by the United States, whose policies, by reason of geographical association, were accepted by Canada. Soviet — American antagonism became the pivotal feature of post-war international relations. Informal discussions commenced between American, British, and Canadian officials in the fall of 1947, regarding a mutual security assistance agreement.[30]

The February 1948 Soviet takeover of Czechoslovakia and the Berlin blockade later that year prompted the United States, Britain, and Canada to engage in further consultation and provided impetus to the signing of a military mutual assistance treaty on April 4, 1949. The original signatories were Belgium, Canada, Denmark, France, Iceland, Italy, Luxembourg, the Netherlands, Norway, Portugal, Britain, and the United States. NATO was the natural outgrowth of this military mutual assistance treaty. As a result of the onset of the Korean War, in June 1950, the NATO signatories decided to form a combined military force under command of General Dwight D. Eisenhower, as the first Supreme Allied Commander in Europe (SACEUR) and by 1951 Canadians were once again deployed to Europe.[31]

The Canadian military experienced no difficulty accepting American guidance, as agreements formed during the Second World War had already supplanted longstanding relationships between the military forces of

Canada and Britain.[32] The military and economic weakness of its traditional ally in 1940 had forced Canada to seek support from the United States. In matters of mutual defence the Ogdensburg Agreement of August 17, 1940, resulted in the creation of a Permanent Joint Board on Defence (PJBD) and marked the first formal indication that Canada had moved from the British sphere of influence to that of the United States.

The Hyde Park Declaration signed in April 1941 strengthened Canada's military-industrial reliance on the United States. It was an accord for the United States to purchase more raw materials and aluminum from Canada, an increase of approximately $200 to $300 million. Additionally, Canada would export to the United States the components and natural resources required to produce munitions for the United Kingdom and the Americans would charge these transactions to the British Lend-Lease account. Because Canada had previously agreed to underwrite this British debt, the Hyde Park agreement reduced this deficit greatly.[33]

The Permanent Joint Board on Defence continued after the Second World War and a subsidiary group, the Military Cooperation Committee (MCC), began integrating continental defences in 1946. The MCC also encouraged standardization of arms and equipment between both militaries. From 1948 to 1950 Canadian politicians lobbied to increase reciprocal defence procurement arrangements and a Joint Industrial Mobilization Planning Committee was established in April 1948.[34] An indication of the growing acceptance of American support in matters of defence was the PJBD initiated bilateral agreement on February 12, 1947, to commit to American equipment, weapons, and modes of operation.[35] All together, these agreements had made Canada and its military comfortable with looking to the United States for guidance and assistance in matters of mutual defence.[36] In conjunction with the environment of the Cold War and a desire to establish and act within alliances, NATO became a natural extension of these previously brokered agreements.[37] Nonetheless the dangers of such an arrangement soon became apparent, as with an absence of formulated national security strategy participation in NATO became foreign policy.[38]

Soon after the formation of NATO, the Korean War commenced. While not directly involving NATO, the United States viewed the initiation of hostilities by North Korea as an expansion of Communism and immediately ordered American forces to the support of South Korea. The United States called upon the other members of the UN Security Council to assist. By early July the Security Council had passed resolutions that offered help to South Korea and empowered the United States as force commander.

Through this process it was clearly apparent that the piecemeal and uncoordinated manner in which Canada entered the conflict was evidence of the absence of a coherent policy making apparatus. Politicians focused on the Soviet threat had little inkling as to appropriate Canadian involvement in the Korea.[39] Consequently, without overarching vision linked to vital national interests, military commitments were incremental reflecting our notions of saliency and the expectations of our allies, particularly the Americans.[40] That month a pattern that was to become increasingly familiar over the next decades commenced with the despatch of three destroyers.[41] The commitment of the RCN provided an immediate military response designed to appease demands for Canadian reaction and give the government a period of grace in which to formulate a decision as to Canada's role.[42]

Soon after the departure of the Canadian vessels the secretary-general of the United Nations, Trygve Lie, formally requested more combat forces from Canada, particularly ground forces. Almost simultaneously a similar American request was received. These requests provoked an embarrassing situation, as the Canadian government neither had troops to send nor was prepared to make a decision on sending some. At the same time the secretary-general's appeal had been released to the press and needed an answer.[43] In response the government announced the deployment of a RCAF transport squadron. All the same, debate continued regarding the contribution of army units with public protest and international pressure finally prompting authorization for the creation of the Canadian Army Special Force with the intent that it would serve as Canada's expeditionary force in Korea. In a note dated September 25, 1950, the service of this formation of brigade size was formally offered to the secretary-general of the United Nations.[44] A pragmatic comment on the debate as to the creation of this expeditionary force was offered by Reid, who opined, "it was a pity we did not act sooner and send fewer men. My motto in this sort of thing is "Get there fastest, with the fewest." We would have got more credit with the United States for sending a battalion almost immediately than sending a big brigade group after a considerable delay."[45]

The St. Laurent Cabinet continued to demonstrate solidarity with the Americans throughout the war, notably in January 1951 when it backed a resolution condemning China as an aggressor with its entry into the Korean War. Canada supported the United States to maintain "allied unity" and keep the United States involved with the machinery of UN decision-making. Later Pearson was quoted as saying, "If

Washington 'went it alone,' where would Ottawa go?"[46] It was necessary to remain relevant.[47]

Months earlier, in May 1951, Canada had deployed into the theatre of war the Special Service Force, designated as 25 Canadian Infantry Brigade Group, under command of Brigadier J.M. Rockingham, a former brigade commander from the Second World War. This brigade became part of 1 Commonwealth Division and took part in operations to eliminate the salient at the Imjin River in September and October of 1951. From October 1951 until the armistice July 1953 the war became static, characterized by defensive actions and offensive patrolling. Unlike the Second World War, ground forces were replaced by fresh troops over time. The principle of rotation for those serving in Korea was that no one would serve longer than one year. By war's end over 22,000 Canadians had served under UN command in Korea and Japan.[48]

The strategic implications of having Canadians serve under unified[49] UN command were highlighted in May 1952 by the employment of elements of the Canadian Army Special Force to quell prisoner of war riots on the island of Koje-Do, without the approval of the Canadian government.[50] Unlike the First and Second World Wars, Canada did not establish the primacy of national command in the employment of its forces. The process by which Canada's forces were committed to the Korean conflict was circumspect and demonstrated a singular lack of political vision, serving instead to provide the means to act with alliances, such as the UN and NATO and maintain saliency. The Canadian Forces Act, passed on September 8, 1950, permitted the government to use military forces to answer the needs of collective security. Through an Order-in-Council, the formal offer of Canadian troops was made to the United Nations secretary-general on September 25.[51] Subsequently, the commander-in-chief of UN forces felt that there was no need to consult governments of contributing nations regarding the usage of assigned military forces. Without military strategic objectives linked to national policy, the Canadian commanders in Korea had no reluctance in accepting an assignment with "political implications."[52]

This lack of clearly formed grand or national strategy was mirrored by waning public interest. In *A War of Patrols: Canadian Army Operations in Korea*, Canadian historian William Johnston suggests, "Canada's involvement in the Korean War was simply the nation's contribution to an international standoff that one only read about in the newspaper."[53] Once military forces were committed, there was little involvement from

Canadian society as a whole and this sense of disinterest permeated the remainder of the conflict. The resources of the nation were not mobilized in support of the military effort and the armed forces of Canada were able to sustain themselves by voluntary recruitment. Because the vital interests of the country vis-à-vis the Korean conflict were not identified by policy but instead mirrored a desire for saliency, the process by which the government committed the Canadian military to the conflict set an enduring pattern of prolonged and indecisive force deployments. This method permitted a government with ill-defined policy goals time to delineate national interests and

Photographer: Paul E. Tomelin, Library and Archives Canada PA-184640

Brigadier John M. Rockingham, commander of 25 Canadian Infantry Brigade Group, points out positions of interest to Lieutenant-General Guy Simonds, the visiting chief of the Canadian General Staff, in January 1952.

formulate an appropriate response. Symptomatic of these actions at the political level were correspondingly disjointed occurrences at the operational and tactical levels of military operations indicating the lack of a clear link between national strategy objectives and military employment.

The end of the Korean War marked a transition in American public sentiment that supported large conventional forces and mandatory military service to nuclear deterrence. Canada was implicated by geography in any potential nuclear exchange between the Soviet Union and the United States.[54] The Canadian relationship with the United States became defined by the bipolar world of the Cold War and the threat of nuclear annihilation. And, Canada expanded defence accordingly. The military went from 40,000 personnel to 120,000 in a few years.[55] NATO was part of Canada's self image in the 1950s — a staunch ally.

Participation in NATO became a means to an end and by the mid-1950s diplomatic efforts were conducted in a cooperative atmosphere stemming from the alliance that impacted greatly on the style and content of Canadian diplomacy. Relations with the United States after 1952 were dominated by defence issues.[56] Also, NATO became the source of most of Canada's military and political intelligence.[57] The provision of this intelligence solely to the Canadian military through American sources marginalized other departments. In 1955, Prime Minister St. Laurent and Pearson, now secretary of state, asked the minister of national defence, Ralph Campney, to facilitate interdepartmental planning and coordination of information between External Affairs and National Defence. The chair of the Chiefs of Staff, General Charles Foulkes, ignored these requests, as he believed that the provision of intelligence would cease if "eggheads" from External Affairs were permitted to partake of the collegial assistance of the Pentagon.[58] Incredibly, this lack of Canadian political involvement in matters of defence did not provoke concern from the military. Almost two decades later Air Marshal M.M. Hendrick, former Air Officer Commanding RCAF Air Defence Command asserted, "It was not our business to worry about politics [policy]; we left that to our Minister, and to our civilian heads."[59]

In the meanwhile, individual services charted their own courses. By the late 1940s, early 1950s, Canada's maritime forces were again faced with the possibility of providing convoy escort to shipping in support of overseas forces. The Soviet military threat was large in comparison to the NATO forces, and alliance war strategy relied heavily on their ability to bring supplies and reinforcements overseas. However, by this time, the Soviets had built up a large fleet of submarines to interdict NATO supply lines in the event of war. As a result, the main role for the RCN and the Maritime Patrol squadrons of the RCAF during the Cold War was a continuation of a similar role to that of the Second World War — cooperating with Allied forces in Anti-Submarine Warfare (ASW) and the protection of trade. In so doing, Canada's maritime forces continued to maintain saliency within alliance and developed strong ties to the United States Navy (USN) and their methods of operation.[60]

The task of the NATO land forces was to impose an effective delay with forward deployed formations to permit NATO time to deploy reinforcements to the theatre of operations to defeat Soviet aggression. The Canadian 27 Brigade, later 1 Canadian Infantry Brigade Group (CIBG), was responsible, as a member of I (British) Corps, to impose this delay in an assigned sector to the Rhine and then defend in place.[61] Overtly Canada was still focused on maintaining interoperability with the British Army but there were indications in the *Canadian Army Journal* from the late 1950s onward that this outlook started to shift, as the preponderance of articles started to migrate from a prevalence of British sources to a greater number of items of American origin. This trend continued in the succeeding years until the majority of *Canadian Army Journal* articles in the 1960s were reproduced from United States military journals.[62] This shift of focus to American sources was reflected in the creation of army doctrine[63] that was an uneasy mixture of American and British sources.

In the midst of doctrinal confusion NATO operational plans for forward defence shaped military methods and strategy, by forcing the formulation of defensive plans based on holding terrain regardless of losses, until reinforcements could arrive. As a result of these influences, the focal point of the Canadian Army became NATO forward defence. There was little political direction to encourage introspective examination of this focus and without overarching defence and foreign policy these operational plans became defence and foreign policy. Prime Minister Pierre Elliott Trudeau spoke to the Alberta Liberal Association in April 1969 and suggested:

> In the situation we had reached NATO had in reality determined all of our defence policy ... And our defence policy had determined all of our foreign policy ... we had no foreign policy of any importance except that which flowed from NATO. And this is a false perspective ... to have a military alliance determine your foreign policy. It should be your foreign policy which determines your military policy.[64]

But the reliance and linkage to Americans was not just rooted to NATO. By the late 1940s, the general population of Canada and the United States had concerns regarding the possibility of strategic attack against North America. Formerly it had been believed that distance from any threat provided protection, or as Canadian Senator Raul Danduard noted during 1927, "We are a fireproof house, far removed from flammable materials." Unfortunately, Senator Danduard's "fireproof house" was no longer fireproof. As the air threat from the Soviet Union continued to grow, the United States desired Canada to continue the close relationship established with its southern neighbour in the defence of the continent and the MCC updated wartime security plans, primarily the Basic Defence Plan, in 1946.[65]

One last check: a Royal Canadian Corps Signals platoon commander checks the wireless set of a signaller preparing for a night patrol. Note the darkened clothing and soft shoes.

Although these updated defence plans received the endorsement of American and Canadian Chiefs of Staff and the United States government, when it came before the Canadian government for approval there was stiff resistance from some politicians, led by the Department of External Affairs and supported by Prime Minister Mackenzie King. Their main concern had to do with concern over American intrusion on Canadian sovereignty.[66]

The Americans quickly reassured their Canadian counterparts, and after much consternation, the Canadian government eventually approved the Basic Security Plan. This plan formed the basis upon which Canadian and American military services planned arrangements for bilateral continental defence measures, becoming, in the words of historian Peter Haydon, an "umbrella for a series of interrelated military agreements for defending the continent and its ocean frontiers."[67] However, the certain provisions in the plan also gave Canadian and American military leaders considerable influence over future continental defence. According to Haydon, the plan "established a framework for operational coordination and cooperation that gave both Canadian and American commanders considerable autonomy without political intervention."[68] Nonetheless, although it was the chairs of the Canadian and American Chiefs of Staff Committees who had the authority to approve revisions to the plan, it was the actual Chiefs of Staff Committee, with appropriate civilian officials (e.g., External, Finance, et cetera) who would be responsible for recommending the degree sequence, and rate of implementation of the agreed plan, with such implementation programs being submitted from time to time (annually) for government decision.[69]

Still, the differences of opinion surrounding the Basic Security Plan were demonstrative of Canadian defence planning in the absence of coherent national strategy. It led military planners to produce a solution that would meet defence needs, and due to a lack of strategy, it became de facto policy.

Essentially, while Canadian and American military officers were amicable towards a more intimate relationship between their services, Canadian diplomats practised increased caution in their approach, as they were suspicious of American intentions and wary about implications for Canadian sovereignty. As a consequence of these differences, military officers from Canada and the United States often undertook informal discussions with each other in an effort to avoid the involvement of the diplomats and the political baggage that came along with them. As one shall see, nowhere was this more evident than in the discussions on the formation of a bilateral air defence command.

During the Second World War, United States Army Air Corps doctrine had emphasized the concept of "forward air defence," an offensive form of defence that used aircraft to seek out and destroy enemy offensive forces.[70] Following the war, this doctrine was transformed into a general forward strategy for continental defence. Smarting from the surprise aerial attack on the United States Pacific Fleet at Pearl Harbor only five years previous, and not wanting to have to "again rush forth into a conflict and ill prepared," the United States Joint Chiefs of Staff developed a forward strategy that would keep "potential enemies" at a "maximum distance."[71] As a consequence, continental defence, from an American perspective, was to be based on what was essentially an offensive strategy.

At the time these ideas were gaining widespread acceptance there was no one from the RCAF charged with constructing Canadian strategic bombing or continental defence theories that might counter American views on continental defence.[72] Nonetheless, some RCAF opposition to American continental defence ideas did exist. In a November 1946 meeting of the Canadian Cabinet Defence Committee, the chief of the air staff, Air Marshal Robert Leckie, informed his colleagues that he disagreed with the United States' view on the threat to the continent from the Soviets, saying that the Americans overestimated the Soviet bomber threat.[73] Nonetheless, Leckie's disagreement with the Americans was not based on United States strategic bombing theories. It was simply a criticism of the American opinions on the degree of the Soviet bomber threat. As a result, when the Soviets strategic bomber force began to grow in numbers, and especially after the Soviets developed their own atomic bomb in 1949, the

RCAF, under a new chief of the air staff, Air Marshal W.A. Curtis, were willing to grasp the American "forward defence" theory and strategy for continental defence.[74]

This is in keeping with writing by Canadian historian Sean Maloney who suggests that Canada has been involved with Forward Security types of operations outside North America since 1898. The purpose of this activity is to ensure that "violent international activity is kept as far away from North America as possible and that Canadian interests overseas are protected." Maloney proposes that Cold War Forward Security operations were directed towards Communist governments who threatened to impose their ideology on others.[75]

These ideas of Forward Security were reinforced by the Soviet Union's explosion of a thermonuclear device in 1953. Whereas before the United States had felt that North American critical points could survive atomic bomb attacks (which would only destroy structures in a one-mile radius), it did not feel that they could survive thermonuclear bombs (10-mile or more radius). As a consequence, the main American strategic policy went from believing that the United States could win a war with atomic weapons to one based on deterring the Soviets from attacking. Since deterrence required credibility,[76] and credibility in this case required the ability to learn about an enemy attack quickly in order to launch a swift Strategic Air Command (SAC) counter-attack, an air defence system, especially aircraft detection, was necessary. As Joseph Jockel notes, "to that credibility Canada contributed its territory for warning lines, its airspace for fighters to verify an attack, and its own forces to participate in those operations."[77]

One of the most important sections of the Basic Security Plan — and indeed one of the most controversial — was entitled the "Air Interceptor Air Warning Plan." The initial provisions of this plan consisted of closely integrated radar systems in the Canadian North. The first to be completed was the Pine Tree Line in 1954. Consisting of more than 30 radar stations, it spread from Vancouver Island to the coast of Newfoundland and was staffed jointly by Canada and the United States.[78] Next to be built were the Mid-Canada and Distant Early Warning (DEW) lines, which spread farther north. On December 1, 1948, the RCAF formed No. 1 Air Defence Group, which later became Air Defence Command, and by 1955 this organization consisted of 19 fighter/interceptor squadrons.[79]

Nevertheless, to maximize the potential defensive value of the radar chains and aircraft, the United States felt that it was crucial to establish a single bilateral command organization embracing all the air defence resources in Canada and the United States. Although hesitant at first, the Canadian government eventually gave approval to the RCAF to begin discussion about such an organization with the United States Air Force (USAF).

In 1954, the RCAF and the USAF established a bilateral planning group in Colorado Springs to study air defence and to see how the two air services could tackle the problem jointly. Since the end of the Second World War, the RCAF had begun to evolve from a service with the rich British cultural traditions and practices of the Royal Air Force (RAF) to one with close cultural and operational ties to the USAF. It was therefore not surprising that the members of this RCAF-USAF joint planning group found much common ground in their explorations of bilateral air defence. In fact, Joseph Jockel has stressed that the RCAF and the USAF

> together constituted the driving force behind the incremental integration of the two national air defence efforts into a single operating system. They initiated all of the proposals from cross-border tactical cooperation and shepherded them all through the process of obtaining approval from the national political authorities.[80]

The result of these endeavours came to fruition on August 1, 1957, when the Canadian defence minister and the American secretary of defense announced the creation of a new bilateral air defence organization, NORAD.[81]

NORAD achieved the integration of operational control of the Canadian and U.S. armed forces that were tasked with the responsibility for air defence in North America. It consisted of RCAF Air Defence Command, the United States Army Air Defense Command, the USAF Air Defense Command, USN forces engaged in air defence, and the USAF Alaska Defense Command. The commander-in-chief (CinC) of NORAD, who was an American four-star general, had operational control over these organizations, called "component commands."[82] An RCAF air marshal served as the deputy CinC of NORAD, exercising operational control of NORAD forces in the absence of the USAF general. NORAD was tasked with defending Canada, the continental United States and Alaska from attack, and its headquarters was (and still is) in Colorado Springs, Colorado.[83]

Officials of A.V. Roe Canada hand over the first CF-100 Canuck all-weather twin-jet interceptor to the Royal Canadian Air Force in October 1951 in Malton, Ontario. The Right Honourable C.D. Howe stands at the podium.

Library and Archives Canada C-85161

While discussions on the establishment of NORAD were still in progress, Canadian politicians became particularly concerned about the American defensive stance that was based on an offensive strategy. Because of the low priority of air defence in the doctrinal thinking of the USAF, the principle task of continental air defence became one of providing an alert/warning for the nuclear bomb-armed SAC. This became an issue in Ottawa because it led to concern over the degree to which Canada had command and control over SAC.[84]

In the end, NORAD did not give Canada any leverage over SAC. Critics argued that this had a direct impact on how and when Canada would go to war — that the Americans could essentially "pull the trigger" and launch a pre-emptive SAC strike before the prime minister was consulted. Historian Desmond Morton explains that Prime Minister John G. Diefenbaker

> had approved a tightly centralized defence system. At Colorado Springs, the NORAD commander (or his Canadian deputy) could order Canadian and American forces into action. Air warfare technology

283

hardly allowed for prolonged reflection but only when he faced Liberal critics in Parliament did Diefenbaker realize the full implications. If politicians such as Robert Borden and Mackenzie King had struggled for Canada's right to control its destiny, Diefenbaker had unwittingly signed away his country's control of when it would declare war.[85]

Most famous of the criticisms was that of General Foulkes, who proclaimed that the RCAF had in fact become "indentured labourer of SAC."[86] From one who valued ties with the Pentagon over that of other branches of his own government, it is a curious statement that perhaps indicates the degree of integration between the RCAF and U.S. Army Air Force (USAAF) produced by NORAD.

The main issue at hand had do with the fact that Diefenbaker unilaterally approved the creation of NORAD himself without first consulting his government colleagues in a Cabinet Defence Committee (that he still had not yet formed after he defeated the Liberals in the 1957 election), or the Department of External Affairs. Diefenbaker had only recently formed the first Conservative government in Ottawa in over 20 years. As such, he suspected that both External Affairs and the Canadian military were still loyal to the former Liberal regime and were therefore not to be trusted.[87] Essentially, Diefenbaker had rejected any educated consultation on the air defence command situation and in the absence of coherent policy had made the decision on his own.[88]

The launching by the Soviet Union of the satellite *Sputnik* in 1957 marked a significant change in continental defence responsibilities for North American armed forces. The main threat to the continent was no longer from the piloted bomber, but instead shifted towards the intercontinental ballistic missile (ICBM). As a result, the importance of interceptor aircraft declined as the focus went to defending against missile attack. However, defence against a missile attack was very difficult,[89] and the main way to counter the threat was through deterrence. As a result, NORAD's ability to detect an enemy attack gave credibility to the American forces, largely SAC, whose role it was to launch counterstrikes on the enemy. With the decline of the piloted bomber and the rise of the ballistic missile, the Canadian government made the conscious, and controversial, decision in 1959 to scrap its increasingly costly Avro CF-105 Arrow interceptor program, and instead put more emphasis into the deterrence strategy.[90]

Nonetheless, whereas the development of intercontinental ballistic missiles saw a decrease in the importance of the interceptor arm of the RCAF to continental defence, it increased reliance on Canada's maritime forces.

This phenomenon had to do with the Soviet Union's development of missile-firing submarines in the late 1950s. At first, these vessels were not as advanced as the American submarines armed with the Polaris missile that could launch from beneath the surface. Instead, the Soviet submarines had to be on the surface in order launch their weapons. This issue, along with the fact that the missiles that the Soviet Navy vessels carried were limited to ranges of 300 to 600 miles, necessitated that Soviet submarines had to surface close to the North American coast to fire their weapons.[91] As a consequence, besides their traditional Anti-Submarine and trade defence role, the RCN and the RCAF's Maritime Air Command took on the added role of locating any missile-carrying Soviet submarines that approached the North American seaboard.[92] Canada's maritime forces therefore reasserted themselves as an important element in the defence of the continent.

The bilateral continental defence provisions that Canada and the United States formulated in the 1940s and 1950s were eventually acted on during the Cuban Missile Crisis. Indeed, the event also demonstrated the failure of the Canadian government to understand the organization of the Canadian military and its bilateral defence responsibilities. Essentially, while Prime Minister Diefenbaker wavered in his responsibility to put the Canadian armed forces on alert, the military leadership "sought to honour alliance obligations and to defend their country at a moment of great peril."[93] The prime minister was angered that NORAD and the rest of Canada's continental defence forces were put on alert without his approval, but what Diefenbaker did not understand was that the NORAD agreement and especially the Canada and United States (CANUS) agreements in the Basic Security Plan did not require further political approval because they permitted the "necessary delegation of authority to enable military commanders to schedule the employment of forces under their control so they could carry out assigned tasks in defence of the continent."[94] Clearly, the Cuban Missile Crisis proved that the Canadian government — or at least its Tory prime minister — did not have as good an understanding of the *Pax Americana* continental defence arrangements as its military forces did.

Following the crisis, Soviet-American tensions eased a little as the Cold War entered into a period of détente. As the three armed services of Canada were pulled apart and unified together, the continental defence relationship between Canada and the United States did not skip a beat. Nonetheless, when the Cold War began to heat up again in the late 1970s following the Soviet invasion of Afghanistan and the election of the more right-leaning President Ronald Reagan, Canada faced a new "threat" to its sovereignty — the cruise missile.

During the 1970s, the Soviets began targeting their new SS-20 missiles on the major cities of Western Europe. In response, the United States began development of the cruise missile as another means of deterrence. Because the terrain in the Canadian north was similar to the terrain in the Soviet Union over which these missiles would have to fly, the United States put pressure on Canada to test cruise missiles over Canadian soil.[95] The Trudeau government was happy to facilitate the Americans in this regard, feeling that it would be a more inexpensive way to make a Canadian contribution to NATO and NORAD. What the prime minister did not anticipate, however, was the degree of public protest and concern that these tests would bring. Nonetheless, as Morton explained, "on the whole the Liberal government ignored the protesters" and the tests went on.[96]

When Brian Mulroney became prime minister in the mid to late 1980s, NORAD remained essentially "status quo." In fact, the government even decided — "with substantial American help" — to rebuild some of the northern radar lines as a new North Warning System.[97] As a consequence, Canadian and American personnel continued to maintain the American deterrent together by watching their radar scopes and reading their sensors for any Soviet activity. However, by the late 1980s the enemy had its own domestic problems, and a crumbling wall in Germany and Red Army tanks in St. Peter's Square had helped usher in a new era of Canadian-American bilateral continental defence.

However, Canadian relevancy was not achieved solely through participation in NATO or continental defence. Participation in UN missions also confirmed Canada's position as a country maintaining saliency within the affiliated block of Western states, while furthering the bilateral interests of NATO and NORAD. The missions permitted Canada to be a committed member of the Western alliance and "an international arbiter with sufficient freedom to act decisively in the cause of peace."[98] In a 1965 report on peacekeeping then Lieutenant J.L. Granatstein explained:

> Canadian isolationism is dead, and its resurrection seems most unlikely. The shrinking of the world has given new responsibilities to every nation, but few are willing to pick

up the burden. If peace is maintained and a nuclear holocaust averted, the credit may well go to those nations that
took steps to prevent wars. Canadians can take justifiable
pride in the role they have played.[99]

Despite Granatstein's thoughts, initial Canadian reception to peacekeeping was at first best described as reserved, as a letter at the time
from the secretary of state to the minister of defence reveals:

There was little enthusiasm in meeting this request [con-
tribute to the Military Observer Group for India and
Pakistan December 1948]. The matter was referred to the
Cabinet by Hon. Brooke Claxton [minister of national
defence], and in his words the Cabinet was "allergic" to
the proposal, wondering why Canada had been asked and
who else had accepted ... The decision whether or not
Canada should participate was left up to the prime minister and the S.S.E.A. [secretary of state for external
affairs] ... There can be no doubt that Mr. Pearson carried
the day. He even offered to have External Affairs pay the
costs for two of the four officers requested.[100]

Canada's formalized military contributions to the UN commenced
in 1949 and since then Canada has contributed to almost all missions.
Regardless of initial hesitancy in committing to peacekeeping, it was
soon embraced as a means of maintaining Canada's status as a middle
power with strong bilateral ties to the United States. The airlift during
the 1960 Congo operation was not possible without American support.
Additionally, the United States provided financial aid and very public
political support throughout that operation. Canadian involvement in
Cyprus was not altruistic. It had acted as a member of NATO to prevent
conflict between two other alliance members. As an anti-Communist,
Western nation, Canada was chosen in 1954 to serve on the International
Commission of Supervision and Control (ICSC) until 1972.[101] The three
nations of the ICSC represented all interests; Poland the East, Canada the
West and India as the neutral arbitrator. Although peacekeeping seems to
have little direct connection with Canadian–United States defence activities, there was sometimes considerable pressure to undertake certain
missions such as service on the International Commission of Control
and Supervision (ICCS, the commission that followed the ICSC) after

Cold War games: a CF-18 exits a hard shelter in Europe during a military exercise.

the 1973 Vietnam Peace Agreement.[102] There can be little doubt that participation in peacekeeping provided a degree of Forward Security within the context of the alliances of the Western *Pax Americana*.

In the absence of strong overarching security policy the desire to achieve saliency within existing alliances permitted the Canadian military to become focused on their own particular and unconnected geostrategic commitments. All three services developed close affiliations with corresponding American military forces. While the RCN embraced the doctrine and procedures of the U.S. Navy (USN),[103] the Canadian Army identified with NATO and European defence, and the RCAF with USAAF. The turmoil of unification and defence restructure led to further fragmentation. Transnational links between the United States and Canada were strengthened through professional association, similar worldviews, and difficulties communicating with their respective political leaders. Both American and Canadian militaries viewed with impatience the international diplomatic intrigues of the Cold War and saw their potential opponent as someone to be destroyed with the weapons under their control. By the early 1960s, the three Canadian services viewed military strategy through the prism of their support to the *Pax Americana* and the form that took through NATO, NORAD, and the UN. Without coherent and enduring national and grand strategy to provide focus to military efforts Canadian defence policy became even more fragmented and diffuse, confirming and continuing a Cold War legacy of operations conducted in neither a logical nor orderly manner.[104]

A number of trends can be discerned within this bilateral and disjointed approach to defence in Canada during the latter half of the twentieth century. First, national policy is at times predicated by alliances and the desire to achieve saliency; the linking of strategic ends, operational ways and tactical ends is not always a smooth progression but can be at times a disjointed series of discrete measures. Second, as evidenced by the Korean War, the employment of NATO forces in Europe, and the formation of NORAD, Canada commits tactical forces as a result of the imperatives of alliance and sometimes has little input into how these tactical forces will be employed. Third, military force is not always deployed in a coherent or decisive manner derived from necessity; it can be determined by the needs of political authorities. In an absence of coherent and enduring security policy, force deployments can be prolonged and incremental to create time and formulate an appropriate national response to demands of alliance partners. Fourth, because the vital interests of the country are not normally at risk the military forces of Canada sustain themselves by voluntary recruitment and thus make a limited impression on the nation as a whole. Without the involvement of Canadian society, the level of concern regarding the employment of the military is very low. Fifth, peacekeeping, like participation in NATO and NORAD, can be taken as a form of Forward Security, and its unspoken objectives reflect a matter-of-fact view of the world not normally attributed to Canada. Last and not least, the tension between the military officers who support bilateral arrangements with the United States and Canadian politicians indicates that not only is there a manner of war determined by the lack of a rational and structured national security strategy, but also a conflict between how the military and the government views defence policy.[105] Together these trends form a comprehensive dialogue that becomes the Canadian way of war during the Cold War.

NOTES

1. Arthur R.M. Lower, *Colony to Nation: A History of Canada* (Toronto: T.H. Best Printing, 4th ed., 1951), xiii–iv.
2. Top Secret Draft Memorandum by Escott Reid, Head, Second Political Division, External Affairs, *The United States and Soviet Union: A Study of the Possibility of War and Some Implications for Canadian Policy* (Ottawa, August 30, 1947), contained in Norman Hillmer and Donald Page, eds., *Documents on Canadian External Relations, Vol. 13, 1947* (Ottawa: Canada Communication Group, 1993), 380–81.

3. Military sociologists Charles Moskos, John Williams, and David Segal propose three developmental periods during the twentieth century that have impacted on Western militaries. First, the Modern era (1900–1945) demonstrates the role of the citizen soldier and levee en masse. Second, the Late Modern phase (1945–1990) encapsulates the continuation of mass armies combined with the continuing professionalization of their officer corps in the context of the Cold War. Last, the Postmodern age (since 1990) illustrates the diminishment of the separation between military and society in the post–Cold War era. Charles C. Mosko, "Toward a Postmodern Military: The United States as a Paradigm," in *The Postmodern Military: Armed Forces After the Cold War*, eds., Charles C. Moskos, John Allen Williams, and David R. Segal (Oxford: Oxford University Press, 2000), 15.

4. The activities that enable a nation to exert power are normally diplomatic, informational, military and economic in nature.

5. For a discussion of the intricacies of alliance between Britain and the United States during the Second World War refer to Christopher Thorne, *Allies of a Kind: The United States, Britain, and the War Against Japan, 1941–1945* (Oxford: Oxford University Press 1978; paperback edition, 1979).

6. Kim Richard Nossal, *The Politics of Canadian Foreign Policy* (Scarborough, ON: Prentice Hall Canada, 1985), 10–11.

7. Quoted in *Ibid.*, 11.

8. In 1981, the "A" in NORAD changed from "Air" to "Aerospace" in recognition of the growing importance of space to continental defence.

9. Defence analyst Douglas Bland argues that one can discern these trends in the employment of the Canadian Forces during the post-modern era. Douglas Bland, "War in the Balkans Canadian Style," *Policy Options* (October 1999), 18–21.

10. Among the first documented instances of the connection between policy and war are in events documented by the historian Thucydides during the Peloponnesian War (434–404 B.C.). In *History of the Peloponnesian War,* Thucydides wrote that a representative of Athens explained to the Melians the necessity of the Athenians destroying Melos, their city state, to ensure the security of Athens: "No; for your hostility cannot so much hurt us as your friendship will be an argument to our subjects of our weakness, and your enmity of our power ... so that besides extending our empire we should gain in security by your subjection ..." Thucydides, *History of the Peloponnesian War*, available from *http://www.mtholyoke.edu/acad/ intrel/melian.htm*, Internet; accessed April 12, 2004, Book 5, Chapter 27.

11. Carl Von Clausewitz, *On War*, ed. and trans., Michael Howard and Peter Paret, (Princeton: Princeton University Press, 1976, paperback edition, 1989), 87.

12. John English, "The Operational Art: Developments in the Theories of War," in *The Operational Art: Developments in the Theories of War*, eds., B.J.C McKercher and Michael A. Hennessy (Westport, CT: Praeger, 1996), 7–8.

13. Clausewitz, 88.

14. Amos A. Jordan, William J. Taylor, Jr., and Michael J. Mazaar, *American National Security*, 5th ed., with a foreword by Sam Nunn (Baltimore: John Hopkins University Press, 1999), 172–176.

15. The Cabinet Defence Committee was formed on August 3, 1945, to decide on defence issues pertaining to the employment of the three services. Douglas Bland provides an excellent overview discussing the evolution of the Defence Policy apparatus in *The Administration of Defence Policy in Canada 1947–1985* (Kingston, ON: Ronald P. Frye & Company, 1987), 147–186.

16. Quoted in Adrian Preston, "The Profession of Arms in Postwar Canada, 1945–1970: Political Authority as a Military Problem," *World Politics*, Vol. 23, No. 2 (January 1971), 200–201.

17. Robert Bothwell, *The Big Chill: Canada and the Cold War*, Contemporary Affairs, No. 1 (Concord, ON: Irwin Publishing, 1998), 20–22; and Louis St. Laurent, "The Foundations of Canadian Policy in World Affairs," Duncan and John Gray Memorial Lecture, presented at the University of Toronto, Toronto, January 13, 1947.

18. Desmond Morton, *A Military History of Canada from Champlain to Kosovo* (Toronto: McClelland & Stewart, 4th ed., 1999), 225.

19. *Ibid.*, 227.

20. Colonel C.P Stacy, "The Development of the Canadian Army: Part IV: The Modern Army, 1919–1952," *Canadian Army Journal*, Vol. 6, No. 4 (September 1952), *Information Warehouse (LLIW/DDLR)*, Version 6.0 [CD-ROM], Canadian Forces Army Lessons Learned Centre, April 1998.

21. George F.G. Stanley, *Canada's Soldiers 1604–1954: The Military History of an Unmilitary People* (Toronto: Macmillan of Canada, 1954), 360.

22. Quoted in Bothwell, 14.

23. Quoted in John Hillen, "Peace(keeping) in Our Time: The UN as a Professional Military Manager," *Parameters*, Vol. 26, No. 3 (Autumn 1996), 19.

24. Escott Reid, Head, Second Political Division, "United States and Soviet Union: A Study of the Possibility of War and Some Implications for Canadian Policy," Top Secret Draft Memorandum, Ottawa, August 30, 1947, Hillmer and Page, 380–381.

25. John Hilliker and Donald Barry, *Canada's Department of External Affairs: Volume 2 Coming of Age, 1946–1968*, Canadian Public Administration Series (Montreal: McGill-Queen's University Press, 1995), 29–30.

26. *Ibid.*, 33–34.

27. George Kennan, "The Sources of Soviet Conduct," *Foreign Affairs*, Vol. 25, No. 4 (July 1947), 575.

28. Escott Read cites prominent American Sovietologist George Kennan and his ideas advocating concepts of containment as the most appropriate manner of dealing with Soviet expansionist tendencies, as well as the role of the United States as a leader in Western efforts to contain the Soviet Union. Escott Reid, Head, Second Political Division, "United States and Soviet Union: A Study of the Possibility of War and Some Implications for Canadian Policy," Top Secret Draft Memorandum, Ottawa, August 30, 1947, in Hillmer and Page, 377–379.

29. Escott Reid, Head, Second Political Division, "Developments in the United Nations during the Next Year," Secret Memorandum to the High Commissioner in the United Kingdom, October 29, 1947, *Ibid.*, 683.

30. Hilliker and Barry, 33.

31. About 10,000 were based in West Germany and France. In the early years Canada's NATO commitment was an infantry brigade group of 6,670, an air division of 12 squadrons (up to 300 aircraft), approximately 40 warships, and reinforcements in time of war. Dean L. Oliver, "Canada and NATO," *Dispatches*, Issue 9 [paper on-line]; available from *http://www.warmueseum.ca/cwm/disp/dis009_e.html*; Internet; accessed February 22, 2001.

32. Before the Second World War some have argued that continentalism already over-shadowed the traditional ties to empire. Liberal Member of Parliament S.W. Jacobs at a speech on immigration policy during July 1927 said that in matters of inter-national policy: "We [Canada] follow blindly what you [the United States] do. We ape your laws and customs. Our government makes the mistake of thinking what

is good for 110,000,000 people is good for 9,000,000. You take snuff in Washington today and we do the sneezing tomorrow. You are suffering from high blood pressure and we are suffering from anaemia, but our government thinks we ought to be given the same medicine." "Declares Ottawa Apes Washington," Extract from the (Montreal) *Gazette*, July 9, 1927, Sutherland Brown Papers, Queen's University Archives, Box 9, File 216.

33. J.L. Granatstein, *How Britain's Weakness Forced Canada into the Arms of the United States: The 1988 Goodman Lectures* (Toronto: University of Toronto Press, 1989), 26–28; and 36–38.

34. Aaron Plamondon, "Casting Off the Imperial Yoke: The Transition of Canadian Defence Procurement Within the North Atlantic Triangle, 1907–1953" (MA Thesis, Royal Military College, 2001), 145–47; and 157–58.

35. Morton, 230.

36. "The old age of imperial defence was over: in 1948 a satisfied Foulkes returned from London to announce its death: the British he reported, 'are taking a much broader and more realistic view of defence matters.' The imperial capital was Washington." *Ibid.*, 229.

37. Escott Reid suggested that such a defence cooperation agreement would facilitate the continuance of present defensive arrangements with the United States. Escott Reid, Head, Second Political Division, Letter to Hume Wrong, Ambassador in the United States, Ottawa, October 27, 1947, Hillmer and Page, 680.

38. It has been proposed that to have a convergence of defence and foreign policy in small to middle states, clear and consistent direction is required from government. If this does not transpire foreign policy may become predicated on defence. However, even when policy makers attempt to align foreign and defence policy a mismatch of resources may cause military divergence in order to maintain what they view as freedom of action. This seems to have reflected the Canadian experience of the NATO years. D. Stairs, "The Military as an Instrument of Canadian Foreign Policy," in *The Canadian Military: A Profile*, ed., Hector J. Massey, 86–118 (Toronto: Copp Clark Publishing, 1972), 88–90; and, the alliance was originally viewed as more than merely a defensive arrangement between member states, in that it should: "encourage cooperative efforts between any or all of them to promote the general welfare through collaboration in the cultural, economic and social fields." Washington to Ottawa, December 24, 1948, telegram WA-3237, Department of External Affairs file 283(s) Quote from page 77. Hilliker and Barry, 76–77.

39. Denis Stairs, *The Diplomacy of Constraint: Canada, the Korean War, and the United States* (Toronto: University of Toronto Press, 1974), 62–63; and, Lester B. Pearson, November 11, 1950: "The main front is Western Europe and we must resist efforts by the Soviet Union to get us committed to a theatre of secondary importance." Quoted in James Eayrs, *In Defence of Canada, Vol. 4, Growing Up Allied* (Toronto: University of Toronto Press, 1980), 209.

40. Canada, National Defence, Directorate of History and Heritage (DHH), "Report No. 62: Canadian Participation in the Korean War, Part I: 22 Jun 50–31 Mar 52," *Army Headquarters Reports* (May 21, 1953), 14.

41. Due to efforts to serve with its American counterpart the RCN "by the time of the Korean War, was perhaps the only navy in the world capable of working effectively and easily alongside the USN." Marc Milner, *Canada's Navy: The First Century* (Toronto: University of Toronto Press, 1999), 169.

42. Thor Thorginsson and E.C. Russell, *Canadian Naval Operations in Korean Waters*

1950–1955 (Ottawa: Department of National Defence Naval Historical Section, Canadian Forces Headquarters, 1965), 3; and Denis Stairs, *The Diplomacy of Constraint*, 71.

43. The public American request to commit Canadian ground forces put the government in a difficult position because it created expectations — both international and domestic — that Canada would send soldiers. Stairs, *The Diplomacy of Constraint*, 71.

44. Canada, "Report No. 62," 15–16, and, 31.

45. Quoted in Stairs, *The Diplomacy of Constraint*, 86–87.

46. Quote from page 81. Hilliker and Barry, 80–81.

47. Both St. Laurent and Pearson viewed Korea as a test of collective security. Morton, 234.

48. Stanley, 374–75.

49. On July 7, 1950, the UN Security Council passed a resolution, which called on all contributing members to place their forces under a unified UN command and asked the United States to choose its commanding general. Effectively the conflict in Korea was to be directed by the Americans. Brent Byron Watson, *Far Eastern Tour: The Canadian Infantry in Korea: 1950–1953* (Montreal: McGill-Queen's University Press, 2002), 6.

50. Koje-Do is located off the south coast of Korea, in the vicinity of Pusan. By the end of 1951 there were about 130,000 Koreans and 20,000 Chinese in confinement at the encampment. Resistance to the American military authorities had commenced in February 1952 and climaxed in May when the prisoners seized the camp commandant. "B" Company, 1st Battalion, Royal Canadian Regiment, was sent there soon after that incident. Lieutenant-Colonel Herbert Fairlie Wood, *Strange Battleground: The Operations in Korea and Their Effects on the Defence Policy of Canada* (Ottawa: Queen's Printer, 1966), 191–92.

51. Prime Minister St. Laurent indicated to the House that the passage of the CFA would permit the government to act in Cabinet to deploy Canadian troops to Korea to restore the peace. Because no opposition to the new Act manifested itself the Cabinet felt empowered to authorize the use of the Special Force in Korea. Canada, "Report No. 62," 30–31.

52. Lieutenant-General Simonds, chief of staff of the Canadian Army, viewed the order as acceptable from a military standpoint but had reluctance regarding the "political implications." Government officials, including Pearson, mirrored this concern. However, Canadian commanders in Korea had no similar reservations. In a lack of clear military-political direction actions will sometimes occur in the field that may create policy rather than vice versa. Quote from page 194. Wood, 192–96.

53. William Johnston, *A War of Patrols: Canadian Army Operations in Korea* (Vancouver: University of British Columbia Press, 2003), 373.

54. Morton, 239.

55. Bothwell, 39–41.

56. Hilliker and Barry, 107.

57. Stairs, "The Military as an Instrument of Canadian Foreign Policy," 112–113.

58. Quoted in George Ignatieff, "NATO, Nuclear Weapons and Canada's Interests," *International Perspectives* (November/December 1978), 7.

59. Quoted in Peter C. Kasurak, "Civilization and the Military Ethos: Civil-Military Relations in Canada," *Canadian Public Administration*, Vol. 25, No. 1 (Spring 1982), 117.

60. Refer to Sean M. Maloney. *Securing Command of the Sea: NATO Naval Planning, 1948–1954* (Annapolis, MD: Naval Institute Press, 1995).

61. Sean M. Maloney, *War Without Battles: Canada's NATO Brigade in Germany 1951–1993*, with a foreword by General Sir John Hackett (Whitby, ON: McGraw-Hill Ryerson, 1997), 491–492.

62. Canada, National Defence, *Canadian Army Journal* (1947–1965) [CD-ROM], Canadian Forces Army Lessons Learned Centre, *Information Warehouse (LLIW/DDLR)*, version 6.0 (April 1998).

63. The term *doctrine* at its most basic level is used to represent the common understanding that is generated by standardized methods of practice. Doctrine is a distillation of history, theory, and accepted techniques. It is not prescriptive but can be likened to a sheet of music that all players may read and interpret, using their own instrumental method. It should be a reflection of the way a country desires to employ military forces. The danger of adopting other nations' doctrines is that a discontinuity between written doctrine and practice will occur resulting in "doctrinal dissonance." In other words, operations are carried out in a manner commensurate with our military culture, not our published doctrine. "There may or may not be nationally determined ways in warfare, but specific military organizations certainly have specific organizational cultures, in much the sense that business theory describes corporate cultures." Paul Johnston, "Doctrine Is Not Enough: The Effect of Doctrine on the Behavior of Armies," *Parameters*, Vol. 30, No. 3 (Autumn 2000), 34.

64. Quoted in J.L. Granatstein, *Who Killed the Canadian Military?* (Toronto: HarperCollins Canada, 2004), 116–117.

65. The original wartime Joint Canadian–United States Basic Defence Plan No. 2 (Short Title ABC-22), July 28, 1941, reproduced in Paul Bridle, ed., *Documents on Relations Between Canada and Newfoundland, Volume I: 1935–1949* (Ottawa: Information Canada, 1974), 894–99; and, the updated plan is reproduced in James Eayrs, *In Defence of Canada*, Vol. 3, *Peacemaking and Deterrence* (Toronto: University of Toronto Press, 1972), 381–88. This new plan did not differ very much from ABC-22 in regards to its command and control provisions. Echoing the 1941 plan almost word-for-word, the new Basic Defence Plan's section on command and control provisions reiterated cooperation as the basis of the Canadian-American relationship and echoed the provision that unified commands would be established only when it was "determined to be appropriate."

66. Eayrs, *Peacemaking and Deterrence*, 338–344.

67. These Canada-U.S., or CANUS, agreements consisted of a series of service-to-service agreements (i.e., a variety of agreements over time) for the coordination of routine military activities. Peter T. Haydon, *The 1962 Cuban Missile Crisis: Canadian Involvement Reconsidered* (Toronto: Canadian Institute of Strategic Studies, 1993), 69.

68. *Ibid.*

69. *Ibid.*; and Canada, National Defence, DHH 87/47, Colonel R.L. Raymont, *The Evolution of the Structure of the Department of National Defence 1945–1968, Report of the Task Force on Review of Unification of the Canadian Armed Forces* (November 30, 1979), Appendix A, "The Organization of Higher Control and Coordination in the Formulation of Defence Policy, 1945–1964," 10.

70. Wesley Frank Craven and James Lea Cate, eds., *The Army Air Forces in World War II, Volume 1: Plans and Early Operations, January 1939–August 1942* (Chicago: University of Chicago Press, 1948), 521–522; Kenneth Schaffel, *The Emerging Shield: The Air Force and the Evolution of Continental Air Defense, 1945–1960* (Washington, DC: Office of Air Force History, United States Air Force, 1991), 3–4; and, Phillip S. Meilinger, "The Historiography of Airpower: Theory and Doctrine," *Journal of Military History*, Vol. 64, No. 2 (April 2000), 476.

71. The statement indicated that accomplishing this goal would require "forces and installations disposed in an outer perimeter of bases from which to reconnoitre and survey possible enemy actions, to intercept his attacking forces and missiles, to deny him use of such bases, and to launch counterattacks which can alone reach a decision satisfactory to us." United States, Department of Defense (DoD), Joint Chiefs of Staff document 1518, October 9, 1945, "Strategic Concept and Plan for the Employment of United States Armed Forces," Files of the Joint Chiefs of Staff, United States National Archives, Washington, as quoted in Joseph T Jockel, *No Boundaries Upstairs: Canada, the United States and the Origins of North American Air Defence, 1945–1958*, with a foreword by Joel J. Sokolsky and Joseph T. Jockel (Vancouver: University of British Columbia Press, 1987), 6.

72. This statement can be explained by the fact that no historian has yet undertaken a study of this issue. Indeed, this void in RCAF historiography is part of a general problem that has plagued Canadian air forces throughout its history: a lack of critical intellectual thought on air power and air forces.

73. According to Eayrs, Leckie "related that he was dissatisfied both with the financial implications and with the strategic assumptions of current American thinking on this subject. He noted that the intelligence upon which the joint appreciation was based had been supplied largely from American sources, allowing the implication to stand that the intelligence was on this account not altogether reliable. The view in Washington was that, in any future war, an aggressor would attempt to destroy the war potential of the North American continent before embarking upon expansion elsewhere. He did not himself share that view. His own notion was that any attack upon North America would likely be a feint, no more, not warranting the establishment of an elaborate defence scheme such as the Americans were proposing, with all its inroads upon Canadian territory and possibly upon Canadian resources. He thought it better to press for much more modest proposals." Eayrs, *Peacemaking and Deterrence*, 341.

74. Refer to Jockel, *No Boundaries Upstairs*.

75. Sean M. Maloney, "The Canadian Tao of Conflict," in Bernd Horn, ed., *Forging a Nation: Perspectives on the Canadian Military Experience* (St. Catharines, ON: Vanwell, 2002), 275–76.

76. R.J. Overy, "Air Power and the Origins of Deterrence Theory Before 1939," *Journal of Strategic Studies*, Vol. 15, No. 1 (March 1992), 73–101.

77. Jockel, 122–123.

78. Eayrs, *Peacemaking and Deterrence*, 358.

79. The elevation of No. 1 Air Defence Group to Air Defence Command occurred on June 1, 1951. Samuel Kostenuk and John Griffin, *RCAF Squadron Histories and Aircraft, 1924–1968* (Toronto: A.M. Hakkert Ltd., 1977), 145.

80. Jockel, 123.

81. The initial agreement between the two countries was in 1957, although the command was not put into effect until 1958. Canada. National Defence. DHH 88/175, *Agreement Between the Government of Canada and the Government of the United States of America Concerning the Organization and Operation of the North American Air Defense Command (NORAD), Signed at Washington May 12, 1958*, Treaty Series 1958 No. 9.

82. D. J Goodspeed, ed., *The Armed Forces of Canada, 1867–1967: A Century of Achievement* (Ottawa: Canadian Forces Headquarters, 1967), 226; Don Nicks, et al., *A History of the Air Defence of Canada, 1948–1997* (Ottawa: 71 Film Canada, Inc., 1997), 13; and, Kostenuk and Griffin, 145.

83. The NORAD commander-in-chief and, in his absence, the deputy commander-in-chief, were directly responsible to the Joint Chiefs of Staff in the United States and

the Canadian Chiefs of Staff Committee, and through them, to their respective governments. Nicks, 13; Goodspeed, 226; and, Kostenuk and Griffin, 145–46.

84. Especially important was the fact that SAC aircraft were armed with nuclear weapons. For the issue of Canada, the United States, and nuclear weapons see the two seminal works by John Clearwater, *Canadian Nuclear Weapons: The Untold Story of Canada's Cold War Arsenal* (Toronto: Dundurn Press, 1998) and *U.S. Nuclear Weapons in Canada* (Toronto: Dundurn Press, 1999).

85. Morton, 242.

86. Quoted in Jockel, 122.

87. Refer to Jockel, Eayrs, *Peacemaking and Deterrence*, and Haydon.

88. Granatstein, *Who Killed the Canadian Military?* 46–47.

89. Indeed, the issue has not disappeared. It has resurfaced a number of times, most notably the United States' recent efforts to secure a National Missile Defence program.

90. Instead of the Arrow, Canada purchased the American-built CF-101 Voodoo interceptors (five squadrons) and BOMARC B surface-to-air missiles (two squadrons), and "agreed to accept the nuclear weapons needed to make those aircraft and missiles effective." Nonetheless, a formal agreement on the transfer of the tactical nuclear weapons was not yet in place when the Cuban Missile Crisis unfolded in the autumn of 1962. Haydon, 73; and, Clearwater, Chapters 2 and 6.

91. Haydon, 79.

92. Canada, Department of National Defence, *Statements on Defence Policy and Its Implementation* (Ottawa: Queen's Printer, 1960). Quoted in Haydon, 101–102.

93. Joel J. Sokolsky and Joseph T. Jockel, "Foreword" to *Ibid.*, xii.

94. Haydon, 70.

95. Morton, 262–65; and, Bothwell, 96–97.

96. *Ibid.*, 265.

97. *Ibid.*, 266–67.

98. Norman Hillmer, "Peacemakers, Blessed and Otherwise," *Canadian Defence Quarterly*, Vol. 19, No. 1 (Summer 1989), 57.

99. Lieutenant J.L. Granatstein, *Report No. 4 Directorate of History Canadian Forces Headquarters: Canada and Peace-keeping Operation* (Ottawa: Department of National Defence, October 22, 1965), 25.

100. Letter from Secretary of State of External Affairs to the Minister of National Defence, January 18, 1948. Quoted in *Ibid.*, 9.

101. James Eayrs argues that Canada committed to mutually exclusive roles in Indochina by the acceptance of the ICSC mission. One role was that of supervisor of the Geneva Accords while the other was as protector of American interests in the region. *In Defence of Canada*, Vol. 5, *Indochina: Roots of Complicity* (Toronto: University of Toronto Press, 1983).

102. Hillmer, "Peacemakers, Blessed and Otherwise," 55–57.

103. Milner, 168–69.

104. John A. English, *Lament for an Army: The Decline of Military Professionalism*, Contemporary Affairs Number 3 (Concord, ON: Irwin Publishing, 1998), 52–4; and, Preston, 201–02 and 209.

105. Bland, "War in the Balkans Canadian Style," 21.

CHAPTER 10

In the Service of Forward Security: Peacekeeping, Stabilization, and the Canadian Way of War
by Sean Maloney

> *The danger that totalitarian despots may take passionate gambles with new power is therefore always with us.*
> — Lester B. Pearson, *Democracy in World Politics*

Peacekeeping or "peace-keeping," as it was called during the first half of the Cold War, is generally perceived to be a non-violent enterprise conducted in pursuit of vague, lofty, utopian goals of the likes found on bumper stickers exhorting us to "Think Globally and Act Locally." Indeed, substantial Canadian mythology has surrounded the origins of peacekeeping, particularly its United Nation (UN) variety.

This concept of Canadian peacekeeping has been deployed by utopian internationalist factions inside the Canadian government and their academic and cultural support structures in several ways: as a means to affirm the UN as a prototype world government at every turn with Canada in a subordinate role; as a means of distancing Canada from its closest neighbour and trading partner, the United States, and to bamboozle the Canadian people into reducing the size of the Canadian Armed Forces and its ability to conduct offensive action.

The realities of Canadian peacekeeping lie elsewhere and cannot be detached from their Cold War origins. As well, Canada has found herself engaged in many operations since the collapse of Soviet Communism that have been erroneously labelled "peacekeeping" but are in fact something different. These "stabilization" operations, like the "peace-keeping" operations of the Cold War, serve to carry out a hundred-year-old Canadian strategic tradition called Forward Security: we project Canadian power (diplomatic, economic, and military) overseas to keep problems that will affect the security of the Canadian state and its people (political, economic, and military) contained and as far away from North America as possible. Forward Security is usually (but

not always) carried out under the umbrella of another Canadian strategic tradition: Alliance and Coalition operations. Canada will work within alliances and coalitions and contribute salient and effective military
forces to generate operational and, hopefully, strategic influence.[1]
Canadian peace-keeping, peacekeeping, and stabilization operations
have, since the late 1940s, functioned within this schema.

"Peace-Keeping": The Early Years 1945 to 1955

The establishment of the United Nations as a formal world organization
at the end of World War II was a catalyst for many who thought that the
new body could somehow prevent another global war. Indeed, with the
employment of atomic bombs against Japan in 1945, with their
immense and immediate destructive power, there was a great impetus
among the Western intelligentsia for a singular body that could police
the world. These sentiments were dashed, however, when the realities of
Soviet power were laid bare. In Canada this took a particularly nasty
turn with the Igor Gouzenko affair that publicly exposed extensive infiltration of Canada by Soviet agents. At the same time, talks were underway in the UN by member states to develop a multi-national world
army. Canada's Department of External Affairs queried Lieutenant-
General Charles Foulkes, who was at the time the chief of the General
Staff (CGS) in Ottawa, as to the plan's military viability. Foulkes turned
this problem over to his staff. In 1948, the Joint Planning Committee
concluded that such a world army was not feasible and that:

> A more moderate requirement to make available to
> the United Nations a small force to deal with a series
> of disputes of a minor nature which have arisen since
> the end of the war of 1939–45: Indonesia, Palestine,
> and Kashmir. In each of the above cases all of the ele-
> ments which might lead to general conflict exist and
> the presence of a small accredited United Nations
> Force in these theatres would, by the moral force of
> its presence, exert an affect out of all proportion to
> actual numbers.[2]

At the same time, Canada was preparing to become a charter member in the new North Atlantic Treaty Organisation (NATO) which,

Canadian national security policymakers believed, was a more realistic response to the burgeoning Soviet threat.

The nature of the Cold War bears some explanation. The Cold War was a unique conflict that is generally book-ended by the dates 1946 and 1991. In essence, however, it was the sequel to a similar conflict that started in 1918 and was only interrupted by the Second World War. The seizure of Russia by the Bolsheviks during the First World War led to the consolidation of an extremely brutal totalitarian regime, one which eclipses the brutality of Nazi Germany (if that is possible!) if one merely measures the millions of people exterminated by it.

Under Joseph Stalin, the Soviet Union conducted covert efforts to undermine and subvert the Western democracies from within. These methods operated in the political realm and were designed to shift allegiances using a bodyguard of lies, violence, and hatred. At the end of World War II, the Soviet Union was an engorged military power: it set about using the existing subversive apparatus in concert with bullying diplomatic and economic behaviour, backed up with the threat of military intervention. The ideological component, Communism, was exported globally and supported covertly.

The creation of NATO linked North America and Western Europe and acted as a declaration that the Western democracies would not succumb to Soviet intimidation. The deployment of military forces to Western Europe by Canada and the United States and the extension of a rapidly growing nuclear umbrella over the defined NATO Area (North America, the Atlantic Ocean, and NATO members in Europe) checked the Soviet advance.

At the same time, however, several European countries were struggling to deal with their colonies in Africa, the Middle East, and Asia. The colonial structures as they existed after the war were critical in Europe's economic recovery, but at the same time, it was a contradiction to retain any form of yoke that could be compared to Nazi (and now Soviet) occupation. The British were the first to recognize this and, by the late 1940s, were withdrawing from Palestine and India.

However, these withdrawals had the potential to create power vacuums, which could be exploited by nefarious elements. If not already directly controlled by Moscow, these elements could be over time, or they could be influenced to interfere with NATO-member interests outside of the defined NATO Area.

Simultaneously, one factor critical to containing Soviet ambitions was the growing American nuclear stockpile. The only means to deliver it was by aircraft and these aircraft had to have bases close to the Soviet Union to reach their targets. American-British-Canadian (ABC) war plans — which pre-dated NATO but were operative in that organization's early years — had earmarked the Palestine-Suez area and the newly formed Pakistan as sites for bases in the event a Third World War broke out. Instability in those regions affected these plans and had spill-over effects in other critical areas, particularly the Persian Gulf with its increasingly important oil reserves.[3]

War did, in fact, break out between the Israelis and the Arab states and Pakistan and India experienced a period of massive ethnic violence. It is not without coincidence that the decision to employ UN military observers to monitor UN-brokered ceasefires in Palestine and the Kashmir was linked to larger strategic issues and the interests of the ABC powers and ultimately NATO. These missions were called the United Nations Military Observer Group in India-Pakistan (UNMOGI-IP) and the United Nations Truce Supervision Organization (UNTSO) both formed in 1948.[4]

UNMOGIIP and UNTSO were multinational observer groups that consisted of military officers working in concert with the senior UN representative trying to solve the regional dispute using diplomatic means. They were unarmed, patrolled "temporary" armistice lines established by the belligerent states and confirmed by the mediating UN representatives. They reported on changes to the local situation that might affect the diplomatic efforts. This was called, at the time, "peace-keeping." Canada contributed military personnel to UNMOGIIP from its inception, but did not deploy with UNTSO until 1954. Of note, the first Canadian killed on a UN peacekeeping operation was Brigadier H. H. Angle, who died in a 1950 plane crash in India while serving with UNMOGIIP.

The concept of operations for these nascent "peace-keeping" missions was firmly established by the early 1950s. The Canadians in UNMOGIIP (who were, incidentally, mostly reserve personnel with World War II experience called up for this duty) and their counterparts in UNTSO, led by Major-General E.L.M. "Tommy" Burns, broke new ground in how to defuse delicate local situations that might be employed as excuses by the belligerents for larger military actions. UNTSO's operations were particularly precarious, so much so that Burns recommended in 1955 that the UN deploy an armed multinational military force to prevent the situation in and around Israel from exploding into war.[5]

Meanwhile, in Asia, France's attempt to hold on to its colonies in Indochina failed at Dien Bien Phu. Asia was in a state of turmoil every-

Major-General E.L.M. "Tommy" Burns led the Canadian United Nations Truce Supervision Organization effort and later commanded the United Nations Emergency Force in 1956.

where, with Communism on the march: Korea, Taiwan, China, Malaya, and Indonesia were all hot spots. The Western powers correctly identified Western Europe as the priority and Asia as a secondary Cold War theatre of operations. There would be no repeat of the Korean experience in the former Indochina. A non-UN peace-keeping operation, the International Commission for Supervision and Control (ICSC), was established. Canada was the West's representative; Poland represented the Communist bloc, while India represented the "non-aligned" states. Canada's contribution of 150 military observers to ICSC dwarfed the contributions to UNMOGIIP (6) and UNTSO (17). The mission acted as a large information-gathering (and incidentally, intelligence gathering) exercise that was used in various diplomatic forums to counter Communist influence when possible. Indeed, ICSC was Canada's main effort in peace-keeping until the events of 1956.[6]

In real terms, however, Canada's peace-keeping efforts at this time must be put into perspective. Canada's overseas military deployments during this period included 12,000 personnel serving in France and West Germany with the fighter squadrons of 1 Air Division (RCAF) and the army's annually rotating brigade group (1 CIBG, 2 CIBG, and then 4 CIBG), plus the 3,000 (though decreasing from 1953 to 1955) from 25 Canadian Infantry Brigade Group that served in the Republic of Korea.[7]

The Golden Years of Canadian Peacekeeping: 1956 to 1967

By the mid-1950s, Canada was a power in ways it had not been at any time in the past. Canadian designed and built jet aircraft patrolled the skies in North America and Western Europe; the Royal Canadian Navy (RCN), sailing Canadian designed and built ships, regularly deployed all around the globe and even participated in "gunboat diplomacy" in certain cases. The Canadian Army had also been expanded and was by now permanently stationed in West Germany. Strategic airlift capacity was being dramatically expanded. Canada was a participant in global nuclear strategy discussions with the United States and the United Kingdom and was contemplating nuclear weapons acquisition, such was the degree of access that no other NATO nation had. Canada was also recognized as a fighting power: World War II was by no means the distant memory it would become in the 1990s and the Korean War was still in progress. These factors were the true basis of Canada's worldwide prestige. They constituted the foundation for Canada's involvement in subsequent UN peace-keeping operations.

At the same time, Canada's participation in 1954–55 strategy discussions with its closest allies, discussions prompted by the development of massively destructive thermonuclear weapons, produced a re-assessment of how Canada planned to use its considerable military power. In the global fight to contain and deter Communist aggression, Western Europe was locked in a relatively stable deterrent state: NATO offset the Warsaw Pact's crushing conventional military superiority with a combination of conventional and nuclear weapons. North America was in the process of improving continental defence air and naval forces. Asia was a patchwork quilt held together by American deterrent forces, British and Australian counterinsurgency operations, peace-keeping in the former Indochina, and an American-led UN fighting force in Korea.

Canadian national security policy makers concluded, however, that the Soviets and their allies would flow around the strong points and into the Middle East and Africa. They would use a combination of subversion, foreign aid, and indoctrination and they would exploit local difficulties, using them as an excuse for intervention whenever possible. They might even create opportunities for intervention. These situations might lead to superpower confrontation in the Third World, which in turn might escalate into the use of nuclear weapons with the inevitable result of North America getting hit.[8]

In no time at all, a prima facie example of such a crisis broke out. Soviet-supported Egyptian pan-Arabist, Gemal Abdul Nasser, nationalized the Suez Canal, a vital sea link between Europe and Asia. Israel invaded Egypt as part of a plan to permit Anglo-French forces to retake control of the Canal Zone. The Soviet Union threatened to use nuclear weapons against London and Paris, which would have activated Article 5 of the North Atlantic Treaty in any case and drawn Canada in.

Numerous options were discussed, one of which involved using Canadian NATO troops from West Germany flown in by American aircraft. These troops would be interposed between the Anglo-French landing force and the Egyptians: the landing force would leave and the Canadians would withdraw. Then another idea was presented whereby a similar force would have to be interposed between the Israelis and the Egyptians in the Sinai.

Major-General E.L.M. Burns was at this time leading the UNTSO peace-keeping operation in the region and as we will recall had already suggested an armed peace-keeping force to keep the peace in and around Israel. He had extensive personal contacts with the Egyptians and Israelis and had a reputation for impartiality. He was the natural choice to organize and lead any force that would conduct these operations. Diplomatic efforts, some of which involved Canada's secretary of state for external affairs, Lester B. Pearson, produced agreement in the UN forum.

A multinational UN peace-keeping force, called the United Nations Emergency Force (UNEF) led by Burns would deploy to interpose itself between the landing force, the Israelis, and the Egyptian forces. The landing force would withdraw, and the Israelis would return to their pre-war borders. UNEF, which included a Canadian reconnaissance squadron, light aircraft, and service support troops, was a lightly armed patrol organization that would remain in place for the next 10 years. Nuclear war was averted.[9]

Nasser, however, received more and more aid from the Soviets. He then infiltrated Lebanon and started to interfere with the delicate and complex ethnic matrix of that country. When a Baathist coup took place in Iraq and assassination plans against the king in Jordan were uncovered, it appeared as though the Pan-Arab leader was going to move on Lebanon next. The United States intervened in Lebanon, and the British in Jordan, with the invitations of the host governments. Nuclear forces were alerted to signal the Soviets to keep well away, which they did. A UN observer force with a significant number of Canadian officers replaced the intervention forces to monitor the borders and confirm that Lebanon was free of Nasserite infiltration.

Two years later, the collapse of Belgian colonialism left a massive power vacuum in the Congo. Geographically, the Congo dominated sub-Saharan Africa. It was resource rich and possessed substantial infrastructure necessary for the protection of sea lines of communication on the west coast of Africa. Communist subversion played on tribal divisions in the new Congolese leadership and Soviet "technicians" started to infiltrate the country. Western European forces could not be used because of the colonial past. American forces were preparing to intervene if necessary, but discussions in NATO led to the concept of asking the UN to deploy a multinational force to fill the power vacuum and prevent the Soviet proxies from taking over. This force, called Organisation Nations Unies au Congo (ONUC), deployed in 1960. Canada handled command and control functions (signals, staff officers, transport aircraft). Unlike UNEF, UNTSO, or UNMOGIP, the ONUC mission did not interpose UN forces between the forces of organized nation states in agreed-to armistice lines. Indeed, UN forces were used to impose order in a non-linear fashion and were not lightly armed. ONUC used Indian Canberra bombers, Swedish close support aircraft, and Irish armoured cars. Operations were conducted on behalf of the central government against tribal factions which were supported by Communist states. The UN forces even worked with Central Intelligence Agency (CIA) contract close support aircraft on some operations.[10]

ONUC marked a shift in Canadian thinking. The Congo mission resembled counterinsurgency more than "peace-keeping" of the unarmed observation variety or of the interpositional "peacekeeping" of UNEF. The terminology as to what constituted peacekeeping was blurred: the hyphen was removed about this time and all three types of missions — what we would today call "peace observation," "interpositionary peace-keeping" and "counterinsurgency"- were referred to as "peacekeeping." Indeed, the distinction between what ONUC was doing and contemporary Canadian thinking on armed intervention in the Third World did not exist. Canadian strategic thinking, based on the 1954 idea and reinforced by Suez and the Congo, was that armed intervention in crises to stamp out "brushfires" before they became conflagrations or nuclear conflicts dominated service and ministerial thinking on the matter of "peacekeeping." In every case, the UN missions had been used by Canada and its NATO allies to further alliance security in one way or another in the fight to stave off Communist domination. It was not impartial "One Worldism" by any means.[11]

This was all starkly demonstrated by the Cyprus crisis of 1964. Adroit British diplomacy conducted in the wake of decolonization of the eastern Mediterranean island permitted the use of several Sovereign Base Areas by British nuclear forces, intelligence gathering platforms (such as the U-2 aircraft), and conventional rapid reaction forces, all of which played a role in maintaining stability in the region. Constitutional issues involving minority representation by the minority Turkish population escalated into violence, some of which was fed by Soviet agitators and agents.

When the Greek Cypriot ethnic majority cracked down, Turkey threatened to invade. Greece threatened to go to war with Turkey. The prospect of two NATO nations fighting over Cyprus made for an unbelievable situation, one that was ripe for Soviet exploitation. Diplomatic discussions conducted in NATO confines produced a plan for a NATO peacekeeping force to be deployed to the island. This was vetoed by the Greek Cypriots. The back-up plan was a UN force dominated by NATO members. Canada committed an infantry battalion, an armoured reconnaissance squadron, and a brigade headquarters. United Nations Forces in Cyprus (UNFICYP) was unlike the previous missions, including ONUC. The mission did not police a boundary (like UNMOGIIP, UNTSO or UNEF) and did not conduct offensive counterinsurgency action like ONUC. UNFICYP did police a boundary in the city of Nicosia, but most of its activities involved presence patrolling and rapid reaction to small hot spots to douse them before widespread ethnic violence could erupt all over the island. If that happened, Turkey would invade and a larger war could erupt. UNFICYP effectively kept the lid on until 1974.[12]

Canada was involved in a number of smaller UN missions, as well. Two float planes were deployed with United Nations Temporary Executive Authority in New Guinea (UNTEA) in West Iriyan, while RCAF light transport aircraft from UNEF were sent to serve with United Nations Yemen Observation Mission (UNYOM) in Yemen. UNTEA had a relationship to NATO politics, while UNYOM was a complete failure at reigning in Nasser's violent pan-Arab political ambitions. The scale of Canadian effort in any given UN peacekeeping should be an indicator of the relative importance of that mission to Canada at this time.

By 1967 however, the sun was setting on the utility of the UN as a tool to contain Communist influence. There were several reasons for this. Decolonization was nearly over. This increased the number of Third World non-aligned states in the UN, altering the character of the organization and its willingness to be used by the West. Belligerent factions had by this time learned how to use the UN presence for their purposes both on the ground and in the UN forums. The presence and activities of the UN forces were subject to propagandistic scrutiny that the UN was unable to address effectively. Indeed, the ONUC mission was withdrawn in 1964 and replaced with direct American military aid. UNEF was forced to withdraw in 1967 before the critical Six Day War which altered the character of the Middle East forever. UNFICYP was in perennial danger of losing control of the situation in Cyprus, while the belligerents in the Kashmir virtually ignored UNMOGIIP. The ICSC mission in Vietnam, even though it was a non-UN observation mission, had also declined in credibility after evidence of massive Communist involvement in Laos, Cambodia, and South Vietnam made a mockery of the 1954 Geneva agreement.

Another factor was domestic political change in Canada. The Liberal government of Pierre Trudeau government was initially loath to consider international (and particularly UN) deployments and was in the process of reducing Canada's NATO forces in Europe. This isolationist stance was in part generated by the need to confront the problem of Quebec separatism but was also a product of a skewed and unrealistic outlook on Canada's role in international affairs brought to the table by Trudeau's new advisers. Indeed, Trudeau's unwillingness to contemplate Canadian involvement in a possible solution to the genocidal Biafra conflict should undermine any notions that Canada was and is the "White Knight" of international affairs. Plans for the deployment of a Canadian infantry battalion in a Commonwealth peacekeeping force were rebuffed.[13]

Welcome to Club Med: 1970 to 1988

The Trudeau government inherited the Canadian commitment to UNFICYP in Cyprus (one infantry battalion), and handfuls of military observers posted to UNTSO and UNMOGIIP. World events took directions that pulled Canada along, something different from the preceding 20 years where Canada was actively involved. Canada still had interests, despite the "touchy-feely" language of the new defence and foreign policy documents or the inclinations of those producing them.[14]

The first such event that confronted the Trudeau government was Vietnam. Canada had been part of the containment effort with ICSC. Now that the United States was preparing to withdraw major combat units and accelerate "Vietnamization," there was some belief that the Paris talks would succeed and a re-vitalized (again, non-UN) ICSC, to be called the International Commission for Control and Supervision (ICCS) would be established to monitor the peace in 1973. ICCS had no real Canadian Forward Security function in the way that most Canadian peacekeeping missions had in the 1950s and 1960s. Indeed, ICCS was more related to Canadian-American relationship issues. It ensured that a close U.S. ally could provide pro-American input into the ICCS "process" to counter the Communist Polish influence on the Commission, and at the same time gather intelligence. ICCS was ineffectual and winnowed away after the collapse of Saigon in 1975. Like its predecessor, the ICCS was a Cold War exercise as opposed to impartial peacekeeping.[15]

The crisis generated by the surprise Egyptian and Syrian attack on Israel in October 1973 was potentially worse than the situation encountered by Canada in the Suez affair of 1956. In 1973 there was a real possibility that Israel might succumb to numerically superior conventional forces and would unleash its nuclear arsenal. As the situation developed, and Israel gained the upper hand by crossing the Suez Canal and cutting off the entire Egyptian Third Army, the possibility of Soviet intervention lurched into view. An American nuclear "flourish" designed to discourage Soviet intervention raised the stakes even higher. Diplomatic efforts succeeded in ratcheting the tension down this time without Canada taking a prominent role.[16] Nor did Canada take the lead establishing the second United Nations Emergency Force (UNEF II). It was led by a Finnish general. UNEF II was an interpositionary peacekeeping operation similar to UNEF, but unlike UNEF or UNFICYP, Canada did not contribute combat troops. Instead, Canada sent a contingent of 1,100 personnel consisting of logistics, signals, and light aircraft.[17]

Courtesy Canadian Armed Forces Museum

On the Green Line in Nicosia, Cyprus, in 1974 a Canadian peacekeeper reaches a local agreement with a Turkish officer.

The reasons for the Canadian commitment, however, were different from previous missions in the region. In the case of UNEF II, the impetus for a Canadian contribution appears to have come not as an expression of Forward Security, but from the UN secretary-general and the needs generated within UN diplomatic circles to balance out the Polish (i.e., Communist bloc) contribution to the force with a Western Group power. The Department of National Defence (DND) was even reluctant to earmark forces for UNEF II. The defence cuts imposed by the Trudeau government strained the system too much.[18]

The diplomatic work established to disengage Egyptian and Israeli forces in the Sinai generated similar activity between the Syrians and Israelis on the Golan Heights. As such, another UN interpositionary peacekeeping force, the United Nations Disengagement Observer Force (UNDOF), was created. Again, the Trudeau government was approached to contribute. But in lieu of sending troops from Canada, a logistics increment from the Canadian UNEF II contribution was tasked to support UNDOF while other nations provided combat troops. UNDOF was initially viewed in Ottawa as part and parcel of UNEF II.[19]

Canadian military participation in UNEF II and UNDOF was essential to the effective operation of both missions. The larger issues of regional security in the Middle East and their relationship to superpower confrontation were understood by Canadian policymakers, but in contrast to the proactive Canadian measures taken over Suez in 1956 and, especially, Cyprus in 1964, the Trudeau government appears to have been a reluctant, or at the least, a second or third row player even though both missions ultimately contributed to Canada's Forward Security.

The situation in Cyprus exploded in July 1974, within six months of the establishment of UNEF II and UNDOF. The Canadian UNFICYP contingent, unlike the UNEF II/UNDOF deployment, consisted of combat troops. A military coup against the Cypriot government conducted by Greek Cypriot extremists provoked a full-blown invasion by Turkey. Greece, itself in political turmoil, stayed out but fighting erupted all over the island. The situation was as dire as it was during the 1964 crisis: Cyprus was critical for NATO's continued presence in the eastern Mediterranean in the face of expanded Soviet influence in the region.

When Turkey invaded, elements from the Canadian Airborne Regiment were in the process of rotating onto the island and wound up caught between both sides. The Trudeau government was forced to decide — should the contingent come out or should it be reinforced? In this case, Canadian policymakers concluded that it was in Canada's direct interests that UNFICYP not fail in the face of this assault.[20] Once reinforced, the Canadian contingent created a protected zone at Nicosia airport and held the existing Green Line in the city. This bought time for UN and NATO diplomacy to kick in. Refugees flowed in both directions: Greeks went south, Turks went north. UNFICYP transitioned from its original area concept to an interpositionary peacekeeping force such as UNEF II and UNDOF. In this case, Canadian combat troops were the backbone of the force.[21]

Within a year of the 1974 war in Cyprus, Lebanon collapsed into anarchy. The diverse ethnic matrix, aggravated by the presence of the Palestinian Liberation Organization (PLO) in the south, vast amounts of Arab money from the newly petrol rich Gulf states, and interference from Syria, all caused the situation to explode. In 1976 a Syrian intervention produced some temporary stability, but they were by no means the impartial peacekeeping force they portrayed themselves to be. Violence continued as the UN attempted to broker a peace while Israel entered southern Lebanon to guarantee its security from the PLO, which was taking advantage of the anarchy. In the end, a UN force was established in 1978 by the diplomatic efforts of the UN secretary-general, again with no prominent Canadian diplomatic contribution.[22]

The Canadian military assessment of the planned United Nations Interim Force in Lebanon (UNIFIL) enunciated by the chief of the Defence Staff (CDS) was that it would become "the first major failure in UN peacekeeping"[23] and that Canada should stay out. These views were overridden by those in External Affairs who argued for the first, and not the last time, that Canada had to participate because Canada had participated in "every major international peacekeeping effort." This of course was not a real argument, but complementary language argued that "a Canadian decision not to respond positively to the UN secretary-general's request would not be consistent with our responsibilities in the international field."[24] Nowhere was there any analysis present to Cabinet outlining specific Canadian interests or the relationship of Lebanon to them. In due course, the Trudeau government deployed a signals unit to briefly serve with UNIFIL in 1978.

By the end of the decade, Canada's track record in peacekeeping was mixed. The reasons for Canadian participation in ICCS and UNIFIL were dubious in some respects. UNFICYP was critical to NATO security and the continued maintenance of peace between Israel and its Arab neighbours was even more important given the potential for superpower clashes in support of their client states. The

Trudeau government leaves the impression of being dragged into each operation and DND was not particularly interested in the missions if they were not supported properly in terms of equipment or finances. One is left with the feeling that the heady days of the 1950s and 1960s were long past.

By the 1980s, UNEF II was disbanded and replaced with a non-UN interpositonary peacekeeping operation called the Multinational Force Observers (MFO). This organization was mandated by the Camp David talks that established peace between Israel and Egypt. There was no equivalent agreement between Syria and Israel, so UNDOF remained in place. Canada shifted some of its UNEF II contingent to UNDOF and took over a logistic function with that force. The UNEF II contingent came home. In the mid-1980s Canada contributed a tactical helicopter squadron and staff officers to the MFO. The exact motives for doing so are obscure. It is likely that an argument similar to that made for UNIFIL was employed — it was peacekeeping, therefore, Canada had to be involved.[25] Canada maintained a combat arms unit with UNFICYP, but the Canadian UNMOGIIP observers came home. A smaller UNTSO contingent remained in Jerusalem. Canada also sent a signals regiment to support the United Nations Iran-Iraq Military Observer Group for six months in 1988 when Iraq and Iran concluded their eight-year war. Canadian military observers served until 1991 with the mission.[26]

Throughout the 1970 to 1988 period, Canada's primary overseas military commitment remained the 6,000-strong air and ground force committed to NATO's Central Region in West Germany. As before, without armed forces trained, equipped, and prepared for high-intensity war against the Warsaw Pact, Canada would have been unable to carry out its peacekeeping operations with the same level of proficiency that it did. For the armed forces, and for that matter, the Canadian public, "peacekeeping" by the late 1980s was interpositionary in nature and was related to a diplomatic agreement between recognized nation-states brokered by the UN. The Cold War was an overriding factor since these crises could involve superpower confrontation that sometimes had the potential for nuclear weapons use. The distinction between combat troops, service support troops, and observers did not exist in the public mind: all wore blue helmets and their vehicles flew UN flags. Peacekeeping was something Canada "just did" on a routine basis.

Photographer: Bernd Horn

Time stands still — by 1984 little had changed on the Green Line in Cyprus. Here a 1st Battalion, Royal Canadian Regiment patrol is briefed prior to its departure.

A World Turned Upside Down: Into the 1990s

The Cold War system that existed from 1945 transitioned to a new era gradually between 1989 and 1991. In essence, this period inaugurated a Communist decolonization period on par with the French and British experiences of the 1950s and 1960s. In the first phase, Soviet backing to its proxies in Africa and Central America dwindled, and in the case of Afghanistan, Soviet intervention forces were withdrawn. Other Communist regimes disengaged pending clarification of their position in the new world order. Diplomatic efforts, some facilitated or other-wise supported by the UN disengagement forces and observers, eased the transition with varying degrees of success. By 1995, most of these operations were complete.

Canada generally sent small numbers of military observers and in some cases, composite support units, for limited periods. The UN Observer Group in Central America — Nicaragua (ONUCA), the UN Observer Mission in El Salvador (ONUSAL), and MINGUA (Guatemala), respectively handled disengagement in Central America from 1989 to 1997. In Namibia, the United Nations Transition Assistance Group (UNTAG) observed the South African withdrawal during 1989 — it included a

Canadian logistics unit.[27] A corresponding UN operation in Angola, the UN Angola Verification Mission (UNAVEM), disengaged UNITA rebels from the Cuban-backed government forces. However, there was no Canadian contribution. Another mission in Africa, ONUMOZ in Mozambique had Canadian observers from 1993 to 1994.[28] The United Nations Transition Authority in Cambodia (UNTAC) conducted disengagement operations between various factions. A Canadian logistics unit, engineers, and military observers operated there from 1992 to 1993.[29] In all cases, these were post–Cold War clean up operations: Canadian participation was generally driven by UN requests as opposed to Forward Security reasons. There was no larger threat to peace on par with, say, Suez in 1956 or Cyprus in 1964.

The situation in the Persian Gulf in 1990, however, was different. Saddam Hussein's Iraq, a national-socialist totalitarian state, launched an invasion of a peaceful neighbour and occupied it. This move into Kuwait threatened the security of the Middle East and the economic stability of a newly globalizing world economy. Once Iraq started to bombard Israel with ballistic missiles, the possibility of Israeli nuclear weapons use existed.

Many commentators in Canada believed that the collapse of Communism now marked a new era whereby the UN could "live up" to its potential "unfettered" by the Cold War. They also felt that the UN would achieve a new level of legitimacy. Initially, the response to Iraqi aggression bore this out. The UN legitimized an American-led war that resulted in the expulsion of Iraqi forces from Kuwait. The UN then established the UN Iraq Kuwait Observation Mission (UNIKOM), to create a buffer zone between Kuwait and Iraq. UNIKOM had the appearance of a UN peacekeeping force (it had a UN mandate, it wore blue helmets, it policed a buffer zone) but it was established under Article 7 not Article 6 and served as a "trip-wire" force to alert Kuwait in case Iraq initiated further hostilities.

Canada participated with token forces in the war. Plans to deploy ground troops to fight, however, were not implemented. One reason given was that this would "compromise" Canada's allegedly "impartial" peacekeeping reputation. Canada did, however, send combat engineers from 1991 to 1992 to serve with UNIKOM. Ultimately, the UN was unable to compel the Iraqi regime to comply with the peace terms and was unwilling to legitimize further American-led action against Iraq. It was, in retrospect, the first major post–Cold War UN failure.[30]

Canada participated in a number of other military activities related to the situation in the Persian Gulf. These included a contribution to naval forces prosecuting sanctions enforcement; the provision of military personnel to the UNSCOM disarmament organization, and the deployment of a field ambulance to serve with Operation PROVIDE COMFORT, the American-led humanitarian mission in Kurdish areas in Turkey. All contributed to Forward Security in that they placed pressure on the Hussein regime to cease its aggressive activity.[31] None of these activities were, however, peacekeeping operations. Public discourse, unfortunately, tended to label any Canadian military activity overseas, including the use of two CF-18 squadrons against Iraq, as "peacekeeping."

This state of affairs was further confused by the plethora of Canadian military operations conducted in the Balkans. The Communist withdrawal from empire around the globe was played out in miniature in Yugoslavia. This Communist state was held together with an iron hand, but this gauntlet rusted after its ruler, Josip Tito, died in 1980. Yugoslavia started to fragment in 1991 when Slovenia won the fight against the Yugoslav National Army (JNA) in a 10-day war. Surprisingly, the Conference for Security and Cooperation in Europe (CSCE) was asked to monitor the withdrawal of JNA forces from the newly sovereign state. The CSCE then "sub-contracted" the European Community to form a monitor mission (then called the ECMM). The belligerent parties insisted that either Canada or the United States join the mission to keep it honest. As a result, Canadian military observers joined the ECMM.[32]

Next was Croatia, who fought to withdraw from the Yugoslav federation — a war that proved to be the most destructive in Europe since World War II. The instability generated by the collapse of Yugoslavia had the potential to spread throughout Eastern Europe, now free of Soviet domination and teeming with agitated ethnic groups and fungible borders that could change at quickly. The Western European Union was unable to agree on how to contain this problem; NATO was not structured to do so. In 1992 the Croatians and the Belgrade government were convinced to permit a UN force into Croatia to establish four protected areas that contained the Serbian minority. As such, the United Nations Protection Force (UNPROFOR) was established to monitor four separate buffer zones and to monitor the disarmament of the Serbian minority. Canada was in the lead, deploying a mechanized infantry battalion from its Europe-based NATO forces. Unlike Cold War peacekeeping missions, the Canadian UNPROFOR force was capable of fighting to protect the integrity of the safe areas.[33]

While this force was deploying, Bosnia-Herzegovina collapsed into three-way ethnic fighting. A UN mandate established what amounted to an extension of UNPROFOR to provide armed protection to international humanitarian aid operations in Bosnia while the fighting raged. This was done against the backdrop of severe media criticism that was directed at the West for "not doing enough" to stop the fighting. UNPROFOR II eventually included a Canadian mechanized infantry battalion later replaced with a light armoured regiment, while a logistics battalion was deployed to support both UNPROFOR I and II.[34] In addition, a company group from the Canadian contingent assigned to UNPROFOR II was temporarily deployed as part of the United Nations Preventive Deployment (UNPREDEP) to Macedonia when it looked as if like there would be a spillover of ethnic violence in that part of the collapsing Yugoslavia.

Courtesy CFB Petawawa Museum

A 2nd Battalion, Royal Canadian Regiment patrol keeps watch near Bijela, Croatia, in November 1992. In February 1993, this Canadian battalion became the first unit, as part of Canada's contribution to the United Nations Protection Force, to deploy into Bosnia-Herzegovina as a long-standing commitment.

UNPROFOR I, II, and UNPREDEP presented Canadians with a confusing situation. Both missions had Canadians wearing blue helmets and riding in vehicles painted white with "UN" painted on them. In Croatia, Canadians monitored a demilitarized buffer zone. On the surface, it looked like UNFICYP in its post-1974 configuration, the dominant public perception of Canadian UN peacekeeping for the past 20 years. Was the armed delivery of humanitarian aid, however, "peacekeeping"? Was the deployment of TOW missile anti-tank vehicles intended to intimidate belligerents actually "peacekeeping"? Was the use of Canadian snipers to kill belligerents "peacekeeping"?

The situation was further confused when the UN authorized NATO to conduct air strikes in support of UNPROFOR II's activities. Then the UN authorized NATO to conduct an economic blockade of the Milosevic regime. Canada committed ships to Operation SHARP GUARD in the same way it committed ships to conduct the blockade against Iraq. A Canadian Hercules conducted humanitarian relief flights into Sarajevo. So, was Canada in fact involved in "peacekeeping" in the Balkans? It was clear that the terminology needed updating, but the media and the politicians continued to refer to Balkans operations as "peacekeeping." Whatever it was called, it all amounted to Forward Security for Canada, as it was not in Canada's best interests to see rampant instability in newly freed Europe, nor was it in Canada's best interests to permit aggression by totalitarian leaders in the Balkans.

Then there was Somalia. A Soviet client state abandoned to its own devices, it collapsed into tribal anarchy at the end of the Cold War. Unfortunately, its collapse was caught on television, which generated public pressure for the West to "do something" in the same way the media pushed for intervention in Bosnia. The Canadian government succumbed to this pressure and joined the American-led component of the UN-mandated armed humanitarian relief operation with a battle group, armoured car squadron, and tactical helicopter squadron. The Canadian component of the Unified Task Force (UNITAF) secured an aid delivery zone and disarmed local militias. But, was this "peacekeeping"?[35]

In 1994, ethnic violence in Rwanda overwhelmed UNAMIR, a UN force mandated and structured to monitor a peace agreement, assist the transitional government, conduct mine clearance, and maintain a weapons-free zone. UNAMIR had significant numbers of Canadians in command and control positions (like ONUC) and was led by a Canadian, but had no Canadian combat troops. The international community, including Canada, were unwilling to reinforce UNAMIR with combat troops. After the genocide, however, several armed humanitarian assistance missions were conducted to clean up the corpses and establish some semblance of order. This included a Canadian field ambulance, combat engineers, an airlift element, and a security element, all called "peacekeepers" by the media and the politicians.[36]

The Balkans, Somalia, and Rwanda starkly demonstrated that the era of Cold War peacekeeping was over. The missions also highlighted the confusion and blurring of how and why Canadian military force was to be used. These missions were non-linear; they employed combat units, and they confronted forces that were not controlled by nation-states and were not subject to traditional diplomacy.

The world was a different one in other ways, as well. These conflicts were not linked to superpower escalation, so the relative importance of a Canadian deployment could not be measured against that standard. Suez, Cyprus, the Congo — these were measurable threats to Canadian interests. Now, only the instability in the Balkans and the Persian Gulf necessitated Forward Security. Somalia and Rwanda had no relation to Forward Security and were driven by media-enhanced or even media-generated emotional factors as opposed to rational policy reasons.

Indeed, the mantra that Canada "always" participated in UN peace-keeping missions was employed time and again to justify continued overseas deployments. The exception was the planned United Nations Observer Mission in Liberia (UNOMIL) in 1993. Canadian policy officers in DND noted that "there are no compelling foreign policy reasons that would justify Canadian participation. Non-participation would, of course, affect our "perfect" record of participation in all UN missions. Our record, however, is probably unsustainable (and largely unimportant) in any event."[37]

From Peacekeeping to Stabilization

The hopes of many Canadian utopian internationalists that the UN would be the primary guarantor of security were dashed by the end of 1995. The UN as an institution failed to come to grips with the aggressive behaviour of the Hussein regime in Iraq; failed in its humanitarian intervention in Somalia; failed to respond effectively to the genocide in Rwanda; had its troops overrun in Croatia, and had its troops humiliated in Bosnia. Trying to adapt Cold War-era peacekeeping to this new world order was a complete institutional failure.

Indeed, the Canadian peacekeeping mythology that was being used to justify continued global Canadian UN operations was being stretched to its limits. Every humanitarian aid operation, no matter how limited in resources or duration (sometimes a single C-130 Hercules aircraft was employed for a week or two) was somehow "peacekeeping." Canada had conducted disaster assistance using its military aircraft since the 1960s, but these were always ad hoc, one-off affairs done with little fan-fare.[38] Maritime interception operations designed to coerce reticent regimes were now "peacekeeping" operations.[39] Election monitoring with volunteer civilians was "peacekeeping." The deployment of civilian police was "peacekeeping." Mine awareness training conducted by Canadian combat engineers for less than a year in Afghanistan used Canadian soldiers; therefore it was "peacekeeping."

The imprecise and opportunistic use of the term *peacekeeping* by a variety of interests, including academics, media commentators, emer-gent non-governmental organizations, and elements within the Canadian government, was indicative of their own fuzzy thinking and their complete (perhaps wilful) lack of comprehension of Canadian his-tory. As we have seen, Canadian Cold War peacekeeping was designed to stave off Communist influence in the Third World and stamp out brushfires before they could escalate into superpower confrontation. It was an extension of NATO strategy. Those missions were not designed to solve long-term political and ethnic problems in the mission areas. They were designed to freeze conflicts in place.

In the 1990s the West was confronted with a withdrawal from empire that generated widespread instability. The pattern of activity in the early to mid-1990s — systematically recognized at the time or not — was a series of independent operations, mostly UN-led, designed to stabilize unstable regions all over the world. The initial intent was sim-ilar to Cold War peacekeeping in that the introduction of peacekeeping troops was supposed to stabilize the immediate situation pending diplo-matic and political resolution of the crisis. However, in many cases there was no legitimate or recognized nation-state to negotiate with. The forces were dealing with armed factions, well-organized and armed, but factions nonetheless. In many cases, the armed factions outgunned the peacekeeping forces that were in turn restricted in their employment of military force (self-defence only). At the same time, large numbers of people working for organizations seeking to improve the quality of life in these conflict regions on par with the West piled into these areas and mutated legitimate immediate humanitarian assistance into dubious nation-building exercises. What was the role of the peacekeeping force in nation building? Was the UN responsible for nation building? Why, exactly, was Canada involved?

The Canadian government of the day led by Jean Chrétien was a prime exponent of this sort of muddled thinking, which employed terms like *human security* and *soft power*. In 1996, the proponents of these concepts were hoisted on their own petard when a combination of political and personal ambition, as well as a good dose of white liberal guilt on Canada's part and outright manipulation by politically astute and media-aware belligerents sucked Canada into leading an abortive and unnecessary armed humanitarian assistance mission in the Great Lakes region of Africa.[40]

The peacekeeping-stabilization missions of the early to mid-1990s served as prototypes for a new pattern of operations. The transitional model from this period to the stabilization operations period consisted of the operations conducted in and around Haiti. Coercive measures against the Cedras regime implemented by the Clinton administration included "soft entry" for humanitarian aid and a naval blockade (both operations involved Canadian forces). These measures failed, so an invasion was launched by American forces in 1994. This invasion had UN concurrence. After American forces stabilized the island, UN peacekeeping/nation building forces arrived and gradually replaced the invasion force. Canada contributed an infantry battalion and a helicopter squadron to the UN effort (that went by various names which changed annually: UNMIH, UNTMIH, and UNSMIH) from 1995 to 1996.[41] From a Canadian strategic perspective, operations in Haiti served many purposes, most of them related to the domestic political situation in Quebec. It also assisted the Americans who were in a jam over the handling of refugee flows from Haiti. Stabilizing Haiti was Forward Security, but the stakes were low compared with other Canadian operations.

The UN was discredited in many ways by 1995. It was clear to a number of nations in the West that other mechanisms had to be found to stabilize regions of the world that affected Western interests. In the Balkans, UNPROFOR I was overrun and UNPROFOR II was disbanded. A NATO-led operation moved into Bosnia. Called the Implementation Force (IFOR), it was structured to coerce the belligerent factions into compliance with the peace arrangements. IFOR had tanks, self-propelled artillery, special operations forces, electronic warfare units, psychological operations units, and could call upon close air support in an unfettered fashion. IFOR's rules of engagement permitted pre-emptive offensive action. IFOR (that was replaced a year later with a smaller but still potent Stabilization Force or SFOR) was the antithesis of the more anemic UN peacekeeping operations conducted in the region previously. Canada contributed a mechanized battalion, a reconnaissance (recce) squadron, and a brigade headquarters to IFOR. Canadian SFOR rotations, which were conducted from 1996 to 2004, usually included a mechanized battalion, a recce squadron, plus a tactical helicopter squadron after 2000.

The time when Canada could cobble together a command element with a few support units and military observers to provide stiffening to a group of Third World and Scandinavian contingents and consider that a significant contribution to a multinational mission was by now long past. Traditional peacekeeping was, by the mid-1990s, for all intents and purposes, dead. Stabilization operations were the order of the day. And they were not peacekeeping. Stabilization operations lay somewhere between peacekeeping and counterinsurgency on the spectrum of conflict. And in rapid succession, Western powers were more likely to intervene with stabilization forces to handle deteriorating situations rather than use the more lethargic UN mechanisms. For example, France conducted Operation TURQUOISE in Rwanda in 1994, while Italy led Operation ALBA into Albania in 1997. Australia and New Zealand went into Bougainville in 1994 and 1997. The British intervened in Sierra Leone in 2000 and the French in Cote d'Ivoire in 2003. Australian-led INTERFET deployed into East Timor in 2000 (that was then followed up by the UN-led UNTAET mission).[42]

The willingness of the Western powers, particularly the ABCA (America-Britain-Canada-Australia) powers, to take the lead in intervention and stabilization around the world was most starkly demonstrated by the Kosovo crisis in 1998–99. Indeed, the Kosovo crisis was in itself a new model for the role of stabilization forces in the global stabilization campaigns. Regional instability generated by the totalitarian Milosevic regime, including the deliberate targeting of an ethnic minority, prompted the introduction of an observation mission and robust diplomacy. Unlike previous situations in the Balkans, the assumption was made that diplomacy would probably fail. The observation mission, the Kosovo Verification Mission (that had a significant Canadian contribution), was withdrawn when there was non-compliance by the Milosevic regime. An air war was launched and preparations were made for a ground campaign to compel Belgrade to quit Kosovo.[43] Canada contributed CF-18s to the air campaign and air and ground recce squadrons to the Kosovo Force (KFOR).

In time, the Milosevic regime was compelled to permit the entry of KFOR into Kosovo, where it set out conducting IFOR-like operations to stabilize the province. Canada then added a mechanized battle group, which included tanks, to KFOR. As a complete force, KFOR could fight across the spectrum of conflict to deter meddling by Belgrade and at the same time could handle security tasks designed to transition from stabilization to nation-building. This was not peacekeeping.

After Kosovo, a three-phase pattern of conflict emerged:

- Phase I is a pre-war manoeuvring stage in which general hostilities have not yet broken out and in which conventional forces have not been employed in combat.
- Phase II is a combat phase in which conventional and unconventional forces are openly employed against enemy conventional and unconventional forces.
- Phase III is a stabilization phase: conventional combat operations have been completed and the coalition forces are employed to stabilize the occupied area.

This pattern held true for operations in Afghanistan and Iraq. In the case of Afghanistan, phase I was rather quick, whereas with Iraq, phase I lasted from 1991 until the invasion in March 2003. Canada has participated with salient and effective military forces in all three phases in Kosovo, and persists with participation in Afghanistan as the international community continues its effort to stabilize that country. It is likely that this is the pattern for the immediate future. And it is not peacekeeping.

Despite all of this, the Chrétien government continued to send Canadian soldiers to serve with UN missions all over Africa. A number of signals personnel were deployed to the Central African Republic in 1998 (MINURCA), while military observers went to Sierra Leone in 1999 (UNAMSIL) and the Congo in 2000 (MONUC). A mechanized infantry company was deployed to Ethiopia and Eritrea in 2000–01 (UNMEE).[44] Like the deployment of an infantry company to serve briefly with INTERFET in 1999–2000, the UNMEE deployment is an example of Canadian tokenism. These missions are very small and/or of short duration. They are in no way comparable in prestige, influence, impact, or size to past missions like UNEF, UNFICYP, or ONUC. Unlike operations in Kosovo and Afghanistan, these Africa missions serve no Forward Security purpose. They appear to be throwbacks to a more nostalgic age of Canadian UN peacekeeping.

The unwillingness of the Chrétien government and factions within it to let go of the peacekeeping myth was still strong late in 2003. The International Security Assistance Force (ISAF), small-scale NATO-led stabilization mission in Kabul, Afghanistan, was labelled "UN peacekeeping" by dissembling PMO spin doctors until a more aware Canadian press

Photographer: Master-Corporal Brian Walsh, Department of National Defence

A Canadian Forces C-130 Hercules aircraft prepares to touch down in Bunia, Democratic Republic of Congo, in June 2003. The aircraft was part of Operation Caravan, Canada's contribution to the French-led coalition to protect civilians from factional fighting in the country.

forced them to admit that it was not peacekeeping and it was not a UN mission. This reflexive requirement to label all Canadian overseas military activity may well continue for some time.

Conclusion

In the end, Canada's peacekeeping odyssey is a case study in the use of military forces for national security purposes, not an exercise in touting Canada's commitment to something as vague as "world peace." In most cases, objectives important to Canada were met by the deployment of peacekeeping and stabilization forces in the pursuit of Forward Security — containing violence and instability overseas and then stabilizing those regions that threaten Canadian interests. Canada has never solely relied on peacekeeping, UN or otherwise, to carry out this function. In general terms, Canadian peacekeeping and stabilization operations were adjuncts to larger alliance and coalition strategies designed to achieve the same thing for Western powers faced with totalitarian threats or instability that would affect their interests.

NOTES

1. These themes are explored in Sean M. Maloney, "The Canadian Tao of Conflict" in Bernd Horn, ed., *Forging a Nation: Perspectives on the Canadian Military Experience* (St. Catharines, ON: Vanwell, 2002), 271–286.
2. Directorate of History and Heritage [hereafter DHH] file 193.009 (D 53) (2 Sep 48) "United Nations Military Staff Committee."
3. The issues dealing with the development of and Canadian participation in UN peacekeeping and its links to NATO planning is covered fully in Sean M. Maloney, *Canada and UN Peacekeeping: Cold War by Other Means 1945–1970* (St. Catharines, ON: Vanwell, 2002).
4. *Ibid.*
5. *Ibid.*, see Chapter 3.
6. *Ibid.* See also Victor Levant, *Quiet Complicity: Canadian Involvement in the Vietnam War* (Toronto: Between the Lines Press, 1986) for details of ICSC activity.
7. These numbers are drawn from a 2001 study conducted by the author for DND's Directorate of Operational Research entitled "Canadian Forces Operations 1945–2000."
8. Maloney, *Canada and UN Peacekeeping*, Chapter 3.
9. *Ibid.*, Chapter 5.
10. Sean M. Maloney, "Mad Jimmy Dextraze: The Tightrope of UN Command in the Congo," in Bernd Horn and Steven Harris, eds., *Warrior Chiefs: Perspectives on Senior Canadian Military Leadership* (Toronto: Dundurn Press, 2001).
11. Maloney, *Canada and UN Peacekeeping*, Chapter 8.
12. *Ibid.*, Chapters 10 and 11.
13. Access to Information (ATI) to PCO, (19 Jul 68) "Cabinet Committee on External Policy and Defence: Minutes."
14. I refer specifically to language like "ensure a harmonious natural environment" as a "policy theme" or establishing as a national aim "that all Canadians will see in the life they have and the contribution they make to humanity something worthwhile in preserving in identity and purpose." See Canada, *Defence in the 70s* (Ottawa: Department of National Defence, 1971).
15. J.L. Granatstein and Robert Bothwell, *Pirouette: Pierre Trudeau and Canadian Foreign Policy* (Toronto: University of Toronto Press, 1990), 52–60; Victor Levant, *Quiet Complicity*, Chapters 14 and 15.
16. See Victor Israelyan, *Inside the Kremlin During the Yom Kippur War* (University Park, PA: University of Pennsylvania Press, 1995).
17. Bill Aikman, "UNEF 2," *Sentinel* 1978/5, 4–8.
18. ATI PCO (3 Apr 74) Memorandum to Cabinet, "Middle East-Canadian Participation in the United Nations Emergency Force."
19. ATI PCO (25 Nov 74) Memorandum to Cabinet, "Middle East-Canadian Participation in the United Nations Emergency Force."
20. ATI PCO (20 Jun 77) Memorandum to Cabinet, "Peacekeeping Review."
21. Fred Gaffen, *In the Eye of the Storm: A History of Canadian Peacekeeping* (Ottawa: Deneau and Wayne, 1987), 97–105.
22. David C. Gordon, *Lebanon: The Fragmented Nation* (London: Croom Helm, 1980), Chapter 7.
23. ATI PCO (20 Mar 78) letter CDS to MND, "Canadian Forces Participation in UNIFIL."

24. ATI PCO (20 Mar 78) memorandum for the prime minister, "United Nations Interim Force in Lebanon."
25. M.R. Dabros, "The Multinational Force and Observers: A New Experience in Peacekeeping for Canada," *Canadian Defence Quarterly* (Autumn 1986), 32–35.
26. ATI DND, (28 Nov 88) A/DGMPO to DCDS "Operation VAGABOND Lessons Learned"; Brian Smith, "United Nations Iran-Iraq Military Observation Group," in William Durch, *The Evolution of UN Peacekeeping: Case Studies and Comparative Analysis* (New York: St. Martin's Press, 1993), 236–257.
27. ATI DND (15 Mar 89) "Peacekeeping Support: Namibia."
28. J-3 (Aug 94) Mission Fact Sheet: United Nations Operations in Mozambique ONUMOZ-Op CONSONANCE."
29. ATI DND (n/d) "UN Peace Process in Cambodia: Canadian Forces Contribution."
30. Sean M. Maloney, *War with Iraq: Canada's Strategy in the Persian Gulf 1990–2002* (Kingston, ON: QCIR Martello Paper No. 24, 2002).
31. *Ibid.*
32. Sean M. Maloney, *Operation BOLSTER: Canada and the European Communty Monitor Mission 1991–1994* (Toronto: CISS, 1997).
33. Sean M. Maloney and John Llambias, *Chances for Peace: Canadian Soldiers in the Balkans, 1992–1995* (St. Catharines, ON: Vanwell, 2002).
34. *Ibid.*
35. Charles S. Oliviero, "Operation DELIVERANCE: International Success or Domestic Failure?" *Canadian Military Journal* (Summer 2001), 51–58; Ron Pupetz, *Canadian Joint Forces in Somalia: In the Line of Duty* (Ottawa: Department of National Defence, 1994).
36. For the details, see Romeo Dallaire, *Shake Hands with the Devil* (Toronto: Random House Canada, 2003).
37. ATI DND (25 Aug 93) memo DG Pol Ops to Assoc ADM (Pol and Comm) "United Nations Observer Mission in Liberia (UNOMIL)."
38. See Sean M. Maloney, "ORD Project Report PR 2002/01: Canadian Forces Operations 1970–2000." Department of National Defence Operational Research Division, March 2002.
39. See, for example, Michael Pugh, ed., *Maritime Security and Peacekeeping: A Framework for United Nations Operations* (Manchester: Manchester University Press, 1994).
40. Michael A. Hennessy, "Operation ASSURANCE: Planning a Multi-National Force for Rwanda-Zaire," *Canadian Military Journal*, Vol. 2, No. 1 (Spring 2001), 11–20.
41. (19 Nov 96) DND backgrounder, "United Nations Support Mission in Haiti"; ATI DND (n/d) "UNMIH II-Possible Future Canadian Contributions," "NDHQ Initial Staff Check: CF Capability to Provide Resources to UNMIH II."
42. Sean M. Maloney, "Evolving International Security Regimes: Implications for Canadian National Security Policy Implementation for the Next Decade." Paper presented to the CISS Fall Seminar, Toronto, December 2003.
43. Ivo Daalder and Michael O'Hanlon, *Winning Ugly: NATO's War to Save Kosovo* (Washington, DC: Brookings Institution, 2001).
44. See Sean M. Maloney, "ORD Project Report PR 2002/01: Canadian Forces Operations 1970–2000." Department of National Defence Operational Research Division, March 2002.

PART IV

Brave New World: After the Fall of the Wall

CHAPTER 11

The Intangible Defence:
Canada's Militarization and Weaponization of Space
by Andrew B. Godefroy

The military application of new technologies such as radar, rockets, jet aircraft, and the atomic bomb during the Second World War made it clear that the next war would look nothing like the last.[1] The science that had successfully contributed to the defeat of Nazi Germany also drove the early Cold War agendas of both the United States and the Soviet Union, as the two post-war belligerents wasted little time organizing their resources for the technological challenges involved in preparing for a possible Third World War.[2] Situated between the two superpowers, Canada's continued alignment with the United States after the Second World War opened it up to the same spectre of Soviet strategic attack that threatened its American ally.[3] At the same time, this alignment created an opportunity for Canada to share new advances in science and technology including that associated with missiles, rocketry, and space flight. Combined with its own defence research efforts, Canada developed a series of missile and space initiatives critical to the strategic defence of the country, while contributing considerable resources to American-led programs. Though politically sensitive and at times militarily intangible, Canada's role in the militarization and weaponization of space over the last 40 years continuously reflected the national interests of a country often required to leverage policy and international cooperation in lieu of financial resources or physical assets.

The Militarization and Weaponization of Space

Like the first great naval powers contemplated the globe hundreds of years ago, so the first atomic powers contemplated space. There were many questions and concerns about this new ocean. "Their existing legal and political conceptions do not cover it, and their experience provides them only with analogies," noted political scientist Hedley Bull in his 1961 work *The Control of the Arms Race*. He added, "They can have little notion of the problems to which it will give rise, or of the political, strategic, and economic importance it will have for them."[4] The transfer of military capability and power into space gave rise to a new terminology of which the terms *militarization* and *weaponization* are germane to this study.

The militarization of space refers to the use of spacecraft and satellites for military purposes. For example, Global Positioning System (GPS) satellites, while aiding civilian navigation, are also used to accurately direct precision-guided munitions (PGM) to their targets. Imagery satellites can photograph, with detail, changes to the Earth's environment, but they can also carry out strategic reconnaissance of foreign targets in support of intelligence gathering. Some satellites may even have exclusive military uses. For example, the Defense Support Program (DSP) satellites were specifically designed for the detection and early warning of missile launches.

The weaponization of space refers to the actual deployment of weapons into or through space, such as missile defence programs, orbital bombardment systems, space-based lasers, anti-satellite weapons, and space military vehicles.

Contrary to popular suggestion, Canada does not have a long history of opposing the militarization and weaponization of space. In addition to avoiding participation in United Nations (UN) initiatives to promote a space sanctuary during the Pearsonian era, Canada vigorously investigated and pursued defence roles that contributed to active missile defence, space control, and the potential deployment of space-based weapons. Canada regularly lent its support and expertise to similar American space initiatives, many of which similarly contributed to the overall transformation of space into a potential battleground. It was only towards the end of the 1960s when Canada, largely influenced by financial and technological change, withdrew from such overt military programs, and yet another decade passed before the Canadian government officially promoted political initiatives that encouraged the non-weaponization of space.[5] Still, Canada otherwise continued its exploitation of space for military purposes throughout the 1980s and 1990s, and continues to do so today. It should surprise no one that Canada has always viewed the military use of space as critical to the protection of its sovereignty.

Canada's Cold War Space Agenda: 1945 to 1967

Canadian interest in the exploitation of space began before the Second World War, when government and defence provided limited sponsorship to university studies in both rocketry and the nature of the upper atmosphere.[6] In 1947 the newly created Defence Research Board (DRB) was given the responsibility of coordinating all research activities between the Canadian armed services and the civilian community, including all activities related to space research and development. Canada's National Research Council (NRC) absolved itself of involvement in further space science research projects except astrophysics and astronomical sciences, placing the remainder of Canada's early post-war space activity under military organization, direction, and supervision.[7]

Missile and space technology became a central component in both Eastern and Western strategic defence arsenals. In the early Cold War period, North American air defence was weak and radar coverage was limited.[8] There were too many unprotected approaches over the North Pole, and the Soviets were menacingly investigating ways to strike North America from the south.[9] Both American and Canadian strategic studies completed during the 1950s concluded that a substantial reduction in North American vulnerability to a surprise Soviet attack would result from the acquisition of accurate and timely intelligence on Soviet strategic and military activities.[10] An American proposal tabled by President Dwight D. Eisenhower in 1955 for an "open skies" treaty allowing both countries to equally monitor the other from the air was rejected by the Soviets, forcing the United States to commit to a program of high-altitude surveillance missions along the Chinese and Soviet Bloc borders and even deep into Soviet territory.[11] Aside from being technologically risky, such missions were in constant danger of discovery and vulnerable to attack. Despite the risk, the United States pursued this course of action, but had to cease its overflights of the Soviet Union after one of its pilots, flying a highly advanced U-2 reconnaissance plane, was embarrassingly shot down and captured.[12] Another means of providing timely strategic surveillance of the Soviet Union was then needed, and it was most likely to come from something launched into outer space.[13]

Early Canadian missile and space science projects flourished throughout the 1950s. Besides the dozens of university research ventures, the DRB sponsored the design and construction of an indigenous launch vehicle system later known as "Black Brant." In 1956, the Canadian Army in cooperation with the United States Department of Defense (DoD), established a launch facility at Churchill, Manitoba where the Black Brant and several American-built rockets and missiles were tested in cold weather. In early 1957, the DRB initiated discussions with the United States for Canadian participation in U.S. ballistic missile defence and a potential future satellite project. When the Soviet Union shocked the world in October with the launch of *Sputnik*, the first man-made object in space, Canada's own space and missile defence program was already underway.

In December 1958, the DRB prepared a study titled, "A Paper in Support of Space Science and Space Technology — Summary of Points Affecting Canada's Future Position," for the Committee of the Privy Council on Scientific and Industrial Research.[14] The newly elected Conservative government headed by Prime Minister John Diefenbaker had been both impressed and concerned by the launch of *Sputnik* during the previous year, and was interested in the possibility of expanding Canada's role in space exploration to meet and potentially surpass Soviet capabilities. At the time the majority of Canada's space-related research programs were focused solely on defence against Soviet ballistic missile threats, rather than space exploration in general. The paper recounted the natural advantage of Canada's geography in contributing towards the evolution of space science and highlighted the obvious advantages that space assets could provide to Canadian defence. To this effect the report advocated the establishment of a national space policy, and an organization to administer and control Canada's growing space program. Though the focus was obviously directed at expanding the military space capability of Canada, the paper marked the first request to Cabinet to formulate an official space policy for the country. The government, however, was content to maintain the status quo for the time being, and no official space policy was tabled.

While the DRB continued as the prime advocate within DND for rocketry and space science research, the Royal Canadian Air Force (RCAF) initiated a military applications space agenda that at first complemented and later competed directly with the agenda of the DRB.[15] Possibly due either to its increasing roles within the newly created North American Air Defense (NORAD) Command, or its growing involvement with ballistic missile re-entry research, the RCAF was the first to adopt missile and space technologies as part of its mandate. At the time, the Navy was largely preoccupied with fleet digitization and automation and the army was immersed in addressing its own combat development for the nuclear battlefield.[16] Thus, given its strategic roles and responsibilities, it was logical for the RCAF to want more direct involvement in

Canada's fledgling military space program, just as the air forces of its allies were becoming responsible for their defence space programs.[17]

The RCAF pursued several advanced missile and space concepts during the 1960s, though it should be noted that these ambitions were often closely linked to American defence space efforts in that they primarily addressed the collective defence of North America against possible Soviet attack. This is not to suggest, however, that Canada simply provided irrelevant additions to a largely American program. Rather, the RCAF excelled in certain niches and on many occasions acted as not only the subject matter expert and primary research and developer, but also at times as the sole provider of a capability.

As such, Canada's smaller physical and financial contributions to the bilateral militarization and weaponization of space in the 1960s should not be taken out of context. There was no reluctance on the part of Canada to militarize or weaponize space; in fact the record suggests that if further resources had been available a higher profile effort may have resulted.[18] Instead, it was by conscious decision, based on national security, fiscal realities, and strategic interests that Canada chose to combine with American-led defence space initiatives rather than attempt to run a parallel space program on its own.

RCAF space activities officially began in 1959. On April 3, the RCAF chief of operational requirements (COR) presented a study on the military potential of space to the Air Council at Air Force Headquarters (AFHQ).[19] The briefer emphasized three main points. First, he suggested that the intercontinental ballistic missile (ICBM) was unlikely to be replaced by a space-based missile carrier as the primary form of deterrence against the Soviet Union unless a high level defence was developed against ballistic missiles.[20] Second, there appeared to be little need for military forces in space. Third, he declared that it was likely that satellites would prove useful for a myriad of defence functions ranging from intelligence gathering to weather prediction.

The presentation, apart from being a remarkably accurate prediction, sparked considerable interest and discussion within the Air Council prompting it to put in motion a plan to explore the potential application of military space programs within the Canadian Forces. Furthermore, seeing the council as the obvious lead agent for such programs, recommendations were made to immediately investigate options for increasing the base of space knowledge within all ranks of the air force. As such, direction was given to senior air force commanders to explore the feasibility of establishing educational programs specifically designed to equip RCAF personnel with a good level of knowledge of developments and problems in the field of space technology. In addition, orders were given to undertake a study of the possibilities for integration of select RCAF members into American missile and space programs at all levels. Furthermore, it was directed that these educational programs also include indoctrination in the field of nuclear warfare, since analysts believed that both ICBMs and spacecraft would mount these lethal warheads. Finally, these space and nuclear warfare briefings were to be delivered to all air force officers of the rank of Group Captain and above.[21]

Plans for the space indoctrination of the RCAF were executed quickly. AFHQ developed a Space Indoctrination Course (SIC) within weeks of the April 1959 Air Council meeting. The new course consisted of a series of classes covering the physics of the solar system, characteristics of rockets, ballistic missiles, and space vehicles, the potential uses of space vehicles, and a review of Canadian work to date in the various fields covered by the SIC.

In 1960 the SIC was delivered to select personnel at AFHQ, Air Material Command (AMC), Air Defence Command (ADC), Training Command, and 1 Air Division. Although the commands gave the course only to headquarters' personnel, at 1 Air Division it was presented to all wings and included presentations to both officers and non-commissioned officers.[22]

Concurrent with the introduction of the SIC, the air force COR and the Director of Systems Evaluation (DSE), K.J. Radford, collaborated to organize a study program to evaluate the potential use that several American space initiatives may have for future RCAF operations. Collectively known as the Advanced Technology Evaluation Program (ATEP), the series of reports provided the basis for determining future requirements and the extent of participation in applications of advanced technology by the RCAF, and it increased the general level of understanding of the impact of these changes.[23]

Initial studies completed in 1960–61 under the ATEP identified four main areas of participation for the RCAF in the rapidly evolving American space program. These were: (a) space surveillance; (b) ballistic-missile defence, in particular the MIDAS (missile-detection alarm system) early-warning program; (c) satellite communications systems, and (d) navigation satellites. Additionally, there was an interest expressed in the American "man in space program" and a desire to potentially integrate one or two Canadian officers into these programs, although the RCAF readily admitted that it was unlikely to prove of great value to its plans at the time.[24]

Within each of these four areas of interest Canada had already engaged in some degree of activity. Since the late 1950s, the RCAF had actively participated in a series of classified projects designed to collect research on ballistic-missile re-entry physics, some of which would prove directly useful to the MIDAS program.[25] In the area of space surveillance Canada had also advanced. In fact, the recently installed Baker-Nunn satellite-tracking camera station at Cold Lake was proving to be of critical value to early American collection of Soviet satellite intelligence.

Likewise, senior Canadian security and intelligence officials were made privy to the large amounts of data obtained from highly classified American imagery satellite programs, adding to Canada's knowledge of the potential in this area.[26] Although neither the RCAF nor other Canadian agencies had made dedicated advances in the field of satellite navigation, the Defence Research Telecommunications Establishment (DRTE) was heavily involved at the time with preparations for the launch of Canada's first experimental satellite, *Alouette 1*.

While the SIC was underway in 1960, the RCAF initiated further plans to integrate members into the evolving American missile and space architecture. Discussions through its air member in Washington,

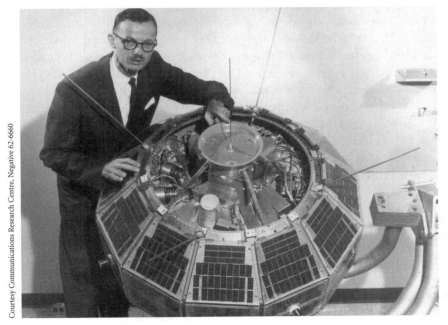

Dr. J.H. Chapman poses with a back-up Alouette/S-27 *satellite, October 18, 1962. The top solar panels are removed to show the internal electronics.*

Courtesy Communications Research Centre, Negative 62-6660

D.C., with each of the American armed services verified the potential opportunity for integrating select RCAF personnel into various U.S. missile and space programs. At first progress was slow, as the United States was heavily engaged in many programs and was not sure if the addition of foreign officers would help or hinder American efforts in space. However, it was later reported that General Curtis Lemay, the United States Air Force (USAF) chief of staff, took a personal interest in the Canadian offer. Of particular interest was the participation of RCAF officers with science and engineering backgrounds. As a direct result, a number of potential postings were identified before the end of the year. By December 1960, negotiations were in motion for the integration of Canadian officers into selected American programs.[27]

In 1961 the RCAF selected its first 12 officers with technical backgrounds to be inserted into a wide variety of American space programs ranging from launch systems to manned space flight, under what defence documentation called the Space Indoctrination Program (SIP).[28] Officers in the SIP were normally assigned for a period of three to four years, though on the odd occasion the tour of duty may have been shorter.

Most, if not all, RCAF officers fell under the command of the USAF Headquarters Space Systems Division (SSD) in Los Angeles, California, though members worked at various facilities throughout the United States.[29] SSD was tasked with the planning, programming, procurement, development, and management of dozens of space projects and systems, and acted as a primary center for capabilities and future systems research including weapons systems concepts and development.

Another critical element of space technology development was imagery. In the West, the catalyst for designing and launching an Earth satellite was based on the critical requirement for advanced strategic surveillance and reconnaissance of the Soviet Union. The United States devoted considerable resources to this endeavour, committing to a highly classified satellite reconnaissance program early on in the space race. Later known publicly as *Corona*, the project was made operational before 1960 and ultimately included 145 satellites that photographed nearly 487 million square nautical miles of foreign territory.[30] At the time a strategic asset of utmost secrecy, few foreigners, among them a handful of very senior Canadian security and government officials, ever knew of *Corona's* imagery products let alone the assets that collected them.[31]

Still, surveillance and reconnaissance was not restricted solely to looking down at Earth. As the Russian satellite population continued to grow rapidly, it became obvious to Canadian and American intelligence analysts that the Soviet Union was also likely engaged in the use of space for strategic surveillance and reconnaissance. As such, there was a requirement to also look up, identify, and if possible, track foreign satellites passing overhead and determine what they could see and what threat they might pose to North American security.

Shortly after the launch of *Sputnik* in October 1957, the United States Air Force Cambridge Research Laboratory initiated an in-house project to obtain orbital elements on Russian spacecraft. At first the project resembled little more than a quasi-scientific effort, collecting data from a diverse range of telemetry read-out stations, scientific radars, and even amateur astronomers. However, when it became obvious that there was a serious national security requirement to start tracking the ever-increasing number of Soviet satellites and spacecraft launched into orbit (if for no other reason than to determine what sort of threat such satellites might pose to North America), steps were taken to formalize a space detection and tracking system (SPADATS) under the aegis of the newly created NORAD.[32]

In early 1959, the USAF formed an inconspicuously named organization known simply as the 496L System Program Office (SPO) at Hanscom Field, Bedford, Massachusetts, and gave it the responsibility of developing a military satellite tracking system.[33] Initially, resources were extremely limited, and financial support sufficient to undertake expensive sensor developments was not made available until 1961. In June of that year, the data processing center located at Hanscom was transferred to Cheyenne Mountain at Colorado Springs, where Air Defense Command assumed responsibility for its operations and renamed the whole system SPACETRACK.

In turn, the USAF SPACETRACK system was integrated into the NORAD SPADATS system and controlled through the newly created Space Defense Center (SDC), also located within Cheyenne Mountain. SPADATS was then further expanded to include the U.S. Navy Space Surveillance System (NAVSPASUR), and later Canadian contributions as they evolved. Apart from the transfer of the data processing center, the rest of 496L SPO remained at Bedford where it continued its work to improve the overall system architecture.[34] Canada formally joined the American SPADATS effort in late 1960, providing personnel and equipment both in Canada and the United States, including its own Satellite Identification Tracking Unit (SITU) at RCAF Station Cold Lake, Alberta, and liaison officers to 496L SPO at Hanscom in late 1961.[35]

At Cold Lake, the SITU was tasked with tracking designated targets employing a Baker-Nunn optical satellite-tracking camera. This type of camera followed its target by taking advantage of the sunlight that reflected off of the spacecraft. To do this the sensor had to operate in darkness while the target was in daylight, and a suitable angle of reflection had to exist between the two (known as the "look-angle"). The SITU camera crews were given points of reference for the sensor from the SDC at Cheyenne, and then took a series of shots of the satellite against a dark sky background. Once the film was developed, a star atlas transparency marked with a grid reference system was superimposed over the photograph and oriented to the stars on the film. With this done, it was possible to read off the right ascension and declination for any object shown on the film, thus identifying its position in the sky.[36]

The Baker-Nunn camera had a five-degree by 30-degree field of view and the length of exposure was optional, allowing the crew some flexibility in tracking and photographing both stationary and fast moving targets. Once the film was processed and reduced, the satellite position data was sent back to the SDC where it was further processed by a computer and entered into the catalogue. The SDC catalogue grew quickly and the computers computed tirelessly as dozens of space objects became hundreds, then soon after thousands.

The RCAF space agenda reached its zenith in 1963 with the proposal for a Space Defence Program (SDP). The Air Council approved in principle the recommendations of a requirements study for the initiation of a comprehensive program that included the development of co-orbital rendezvous techniques for anti-satellite weapons.[37] Subsequently, $2.2 million was committed to these investigations, aimed at advancing research and development of terminal homing guidance sensors for satellite interceptors. The proposed system was similar to the Exo-Atmospheric Kill Vehicle (EKV) recently under consideration in the United States to support its National Missile Defense (NMD) program today — except that the RCAF was investigating this very means of missile defence over a half century ago. With the approval of Treasury Board funding in principle in July 1963, the RCAF Directorate of Advanced Engineering and Development (DAED) was tasked in August 1963 with the responsibility of initiating the SDP, which would carry a design through its hardware and flight test stages.[38]

The anti-satellite weapons program continued to evolve even after the original parameters were set in mid-1963. In December DAED further advanced the scope of the co-orbital interceptor concept to include inspection sensors and non-nuclear kill mechanisms and negation capabilities. These areas of development were considered favourable because they increased the overall ability of the original technology, and were seen as areas that Canada had investigated and the United States had not. While it was later learned that the United States did have several concurrent investigations into orbital rendezvous, the United States Department of Defense continued to express support for, and interest in, Canadian studies, tests, and evaluations in this field.[39] When RCAF senior personnel met with their American counterparts in the United States Directorate of Defense Research and Engineering (DDR&E) at the Pentagon in March 1964, further discussions concerning options for cooperation and collaboration led Dr. Harold Brown, Director of the DDR&E, to later provide testimony to the United States Senate Committee on Aeronautical and Space Sciences supporting Canadian research into co-orbital rendezvous techniques.[40]

Yet despite these incredible developments, the RCAF program atrophied as quickly as it began. The return of the Liberal Party to power brought considerable changes to Canada's national security policy that in turn affected the country's defence apparatus at every level. Lester ("Mike") Pearson, the new prime minister, had little desire to repeat the defence mistakes of his predecessor and immediately took action to ensure that similar problems would not befall his own Cabinet administration. He appointed his tough-minded defence critic, Paul Hellyer, as the new defence minister and gave him instructions to establish firm control over the Department of National Defence while at the same time quickly but quietly reducing defence expenditures.[41] Hellyer was more than up to the task. His tireless efforts to reshape the department and unify the Canadian Forces (CF) under a single headquarters during the next four years resulted in him becoming one of the most controversial defence ministers in Canadian history.

Nonetheless, within a year of Hellyer's arrival Canada's military space programs (like all CF programs) were in jeopardy. Challenges and obstacles to the formalization of the military space agenda were further exacerbated by competition from the DRB, who preferred programs oriented towards its own pure scientific investigation than to military application such as those of the SDP.

As well, technology, itself, became a problem. The development of electronics, transistors, and miniaturization critical to the design and construction of missiles, rockets, and spacecraft in the 1960s occurred almost exclusively within Canadian defence research establishments. Unlike the United States, where technology was rapidly diffused to the civilian economy making it cheaper to procure such products, the RCAF was forced to manufacture its own specialized components in house at tremendous cost. The Canadian military "technological capability gap" widened each year and only served to further divide political interests within the defence community as the DRB scrambled to protect its much-loved *Alouette*-ISIS satellite program at the expense of all other military efforts.

Further agitated by a dynamic shift in Canadian foreign policy and the reorganization then taking place within the defence and scientific communities DND attention and support for missile and defence space endeavours evaporated. Seen as costly and technologically impossible to develop and sustain, one by one the armed services withdrew their investments in these programs to save others. By the end of the 1960s, Canada's missile and space programs were all but terminated as the last of their military assets were transferred to civilian government sectors, and much needed resources and funds were directed elsewhere.

Technical Demise and Political Change: 1968 to 1986

For the next decade and a half Canadian military space activities fell largely into disarray. None of the SDP initiatives of the 1960s were maintained, and no new champion for missile and space activity appeared within DND during the 1970s. With the disbanding of the DRB in 1974, the Canadian military space program was left as a wanton child, without any well-established, well-supported, and focused organization within DND to direct its development. Programs and initiatives were sporadic and unconnected. It presented a miserable shadow of what was once an impressive undertaking.

As the Canadian Forces (CF) faced tighter defence budgets throughout the 1970s and 1980s, it could afford to invest little in costly and technologically complicated space projects that appeared to generate little interest or application within the Department of National Defence (DND). Interest that did remain was centered around the DRB's successor, the Chief Research and Development (CRAD) branch, in particular, its Director of Communications and Space. In 1974, along with the Defence Management Committee (DMC), the CRAD Branch reiterated the need for a serious interest in military space, but it was some time before their words were transformed into action.

It is difficult to comprehend the bias against military space activity in Canada during this period. Technology, strategic policy, or even defence policy did not drive the anti-sentiment towards military space. In fact, the top priorities in Canada's "1971 Defence White Paper" — Canadian sovereignty and North American security — could easily have been facilitated by the employment of military space-based resources.[42] For example, Canada's expanded claims to Arctic jurisdiction in 1970 could have been more successful if the country had some way of keeping surveillance on its northern territory. Even if Canada lacked the physical means on the ground to arbitrate passage in the north, it could still have the information to seek justice by other means. In addition, space-based assets could have cheaply and effectively assisted with other Canadian concerns such as peacekeeping missions and weapon disarmament verification.

However, Canada's defence space agenda remained dormant until awakened by the strategic defence debates of the 1980s. In 1981 NORAD re-emerged as an influential part of Canada-U.S. space defence cooperation as the organization's role was modified to include detection, tracking, and monitoring of space activities.[43] NORAD's title was even altered from "air" to "aerospace" to reflect this evolution. NORAD clearly demonstrated the evolving dichotomy between Canadian and American space capability in other aspects, as well. By the 1980s, Canadian territory was no longer important for missile and space surveillance functions, and no American Ballistic Missile Early Warning System (BMEWS) radars were built in Canada. As political scientist Joel Sokolsky noted, "Given that only about 11 percent of Soviet warheads were carried by their bomber force, the shift seemed reasonable."[44] Still, NORAD's space functions were almost exclusively the responsibility of the evolving United States Space Command, while Canada's limited roles in this area were phased out.[45] Yet the dramatic attention brought to space weaponization in the mid-1980s practically forced both the Canadian government and DND back into more active roles in defence space programs and issues.

Upon taking office in 1980, Ronald Reagan and his Republican administration immediately made strategic defence a high priority. Within months the United States began a serious overhaul of its military forces by initiating a series of new projects, including several new space programs. The most influential of these programs was the American Strategic Defense Initiative (SDI), a complex and comprehensive space-based weapons platform project designed to protect North America and other American interests from Soviet nuclear ballistic-missile attack. The SDI was an ambitious initiative and its actual construction very unlikely, but the United States forged ahead with examining how it could become a feasible ballistic-missile defence system.

In addition to analyzing their own force capability, the Americans quickly realized that Canada's early-warning capability would require upgrading, if the umbrella over the continent were to be complete. At the time Canada was still against the deployment of Ballistic Missile Defense (BMD) in Canada, even though the 1981 renewal had omitted the anti-ballistic missile (ABM) clause from the agreement. The Right Honourable Joe Clark, then secretary of state for external affairs, explained the removal of the clause was done, "precisely to avoid any suggestion that either Canada or the United States might take actions [that] would breach the ABM Treaty."[46] Others suggested that having no clause would not foreclose any options.

As the SDI project progressed, it captured an incredible amount of media attention, causing it to become popularized as "star wars" because of the conceptualization of the system as huge space stations armed with planet-killing lasers as seen in the famous science fiction film of the same name. The concept generated a general public concern in Canada that through its collective defence arrangements with the United States it may become involved in the potential deployment of weapons in space, as well. The Canadian public had become opposed to any involvement of its country in American BMD programs, violations of the ABM Treaty, and the actual deployment of weapons into space. The American SDI project suggested it would do all these things, causing a great deal of concern in Ottawa when it appeared that NORAD would be involved in some way.

The election of a new Progressive Conservative government in Canada in 1984, as well as the selection the previous year of Canada's first astronauts — a total of seven members being selected to participate in upcoming missions of the Space Transportation System (STS), brought a different approach to the issue. In efforts to further strengthen Canadian-U.S. relations, Prime Minister Brian Mulroney proposed to start a series of civilian and military-related space projects, some of which were confirmed during his first meeting with U.S. President Ronald Reagan in 1985. The defence initiatives were later reinforced by voices raised in two government committees in 1985 calling for a renewed military space program in Canada.[47]

However, the Senate Special Committee on National Defence hearings on air defence was the greater advocate, recommending the establishment of a solid military space program to concentrate on early warning, surveillance, and communication tasks necessary to the protection of national security. The committee concluded that DND required a minimum of eight to 12 dedicated military satellites and should be allocated at least $150 million per year for five years to build and launch these assets.[48] Beginning in 1990 the annual allotment would have to be raised to $350 million. Though unquestionably bold, the government balked at these recommendations and instead sought a less expensive means of officially getting Canada back into the military space business.

In 1985, Prime Minister Mulroney promised the Americans that Canada would proceed with earlier plans to construct a new chain of early-warning radar stations, namely the North Warning System (NWS), across Canada's Arctic to replace the aging Distant Early Warning (DEW) line.[49] Given that neither Canada nor the United States had space-based radar technology yet, Canada restrained its military space commitment to the ground segment only, rather than take the opportunity to advance its space support and control capabilities. However, it did convince the American government to contribute 60 percent of the funds required to update Canada's air defence infrastructure. One could argue that NORAD was providing Canada with the opportunity to meet the other recommendations of the Senate Special Committee on air defence. But realistically, without its own space assets or launch and control facilities Canada was unable to produce the infrastructure required for a truly space-capable state. Avoiding and rejecting offers by the United States to become involved in space defence, as in the case with SDI and other related projects, only encouraged the American inclination to plan for the space future without Canadian involvement. Where the threat of sovereignty protection had often driven Canada to become involved in bilateral defence arrangements with the United States in the past, it appeared that with space defence Ottawa was content to be left out of any consideration whatsoever. By ignoring American offers of space defence cooperation, Canada was ensuring that the United States would be less likely to respect the Canadian sovereignty from space it so loudly demanded.

The 1986 NORAD renewal debate was particularly difficult because of the potential ramifications of the SDI on Canada's continued participation in the bilateral defence of North America. The United States had interpreted that article V of the ABM Treaty, signed between the Soviet Union and the United States on October 3, 1972, limited all SDI work to research, lab work, and tests of sub-components.[50] This limited the primary debate in the United States to what constituted a component or sub-component and what constituted research and development and employment of dual-use technologies.[51] When the United States invited the Canadian government to participate in the SDI in 1985, the debate for

Canadian involvement revolved around the same issues. A special joint committee was assembled and convened in Ottawa in July 1985 to hear evidence for and against the invitation, even though the Conservative government had announced in January that it would support the research and development phase of SDI.

The SDI invitation was a particularly difficult crossroads in Canadian-American space defence cooperation for it exposed how unprepared DND was to deal with space issues and national security. The SDI's magnitude and potential implications for the bilateral defence relationship was overwhelming to the Canadian government, who since Pierre Elliott Trudeau came to power, had given little serious attention to Canadian security policy.[52] Regardless of the outcome resulting from the Canadian decision to participate in, or opt out of, SDI it was clear that the Canadian government lacked any mechanism to seriously deal with space security issues. As a result, the minister of defence (MND) and the chief of defence staff (CDS) tabled and approved National Defence Headquarters (NDHQ) Evaluation Directive E3/86, which led to a study of Canada's future military space requirements.[53] After nearly two decades, the lacuna between space and defence was closed as military space programs were officially put back on the Canadian security agenda.

Returning to Space: 1987 to 1997

In June 1987 Canada issued its first white paper on defence in 16 years. Entitled *Challenge and Commitment: A Defence Policy for Canada*, it was also the first such document to officially recognize space as an area of strategic concern. Although the white paper was widely criticized for its obsolescence, it did acknowledge how the rapid fusion of information and military operations resulting from space technologies created a range of new national security concerns for Canada.[54]

Concurrent with the new defence policy, DND also issued its first official space policy paper authorized by deputy minister of defence D.B. Dewar and General P.D. Manson, then the CDS. Released on July 13, 1987, the brief document gave very loose guidelines for Canada's military application of space and made no mention of any activity in missile defence or related strategic programs. Essentially a bookmark rather than a way ahead, it was a small but encouraging indication that DND was beginning to appreciate the impact of space on military operations once more.

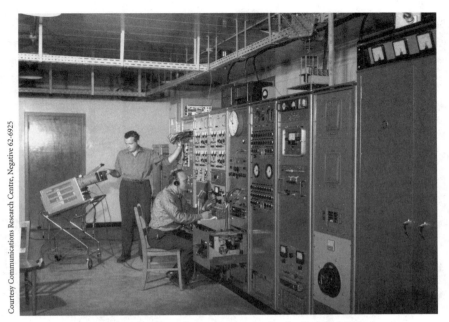

Courtesy Communications Research Centre, Negative 62-6925

Burt Schrieber and Art Hill work on equipment in the Satellite Telemetry Station (Building 14), December 6, 1962.

The adoption of a new defence space program once again took place during a period of considerable political transformation. Drastic changes in the global political situation brought a dramatic and swift end to the Cold War, making Canada's primary defence document all but obsolete. Instead, Canada interpreted the end of the Cold War as an opportunity to conserve on defence spending and initiated the cancellation of many proposals and procurement projects. Once again space-based defence in Canada had its official life cut short. Although space derived data had proven its value in intelligence, planning, and operations, in 1989 the government disbanded the NDHQ Directorate of Space Doctrine and Operations less than two years after it was stood up. This took place at the same time that the chief of review services (CRS) was finalizing a report arguing to increase Canada's military activity in the space field. The CRS report proved to be a comprehensive historical analysis and was formally tabled on July 31, 1989. It was ratified just in time to be shelved. Still, some of the resulting recommendations were approved and implementation of these began within other DND organizations starting in July 1990.[55]

In sum, the 1989 CRS space report consisted of a detailed study of the rapid expansion of space activity and the use of space for military purposes by both the allies and potential adversaries. Even though the report was prepared before the end of the Cold War, and followed the traditional style of Canadian defence documents by making proposals more appropriate to the immediate past than the future, it adequately assessed Canadian needs in a fragmented and unpredictable world. It noted large changes in space activity between 1980 and 1989, as well as the increasing use of space assets in terrestrial military operations. The CRS report made a number of recommendations on Canadian defence policy, plans, projects, and management structure, which were implemented by a newly established Space Defence Working Group (SDWG) in 1991.[56] The first document produced by the SDWG was a Space Appreciation with the purpose "to provide an initial CF space development framework from which subsequent policy and program planning activities may be generated."[57]

Canada witnessed the role space played in warfare first hand within months of issuing its own way ahead. On August 2, 1990, Iraq invaded its neighbour Kuwait, successfully conquering the tiny state in a single day. During the ensuing conflict, American and coalition forces out-manoeuvred and out-fought their Iraqi adversary with the aid of new space-based technologies such as "theatre ballistic missile early warning tactical" satellite imagery, surveillance, and reconnaissance, and the evolving Global Positioning System (GPS) navigation satellite constellation.

Canada was unprepared to take advantage of space in the Gulf War, and the conflict highlighted a number of important areas where knowledge, resources, and assets were lacking within the Canadian Forces. Both the United States and Russia sought to provide a surge capability in war with the rapid launch of additional task oriented satellites that could operate for limited periods of time. Although Canada did have a launch facility in Churchill, it lacked any apparatus or assets to take advantage of such an opportunity to augment its force projection. As such, Canadian space support in Operation Friction was almost entirely American originated or supported.

Going into combat, after decades of peacetime time soldiering and operations in small brushfire type wars, highlighted the glaring technological deficiencies in Canadian command and control and information systems (C2IS). Among those deficiencies was space support, a capability that the Canadian Forces not only did not have but also one that few in its ranks understood in any depth. The quick-fix space support delivered for Operation Friction (Canada's moniker for military operations in the Gulf) came from American sources. Canada carried almost all its communications through American satellites, navigated using American-based commercial satellites, and received a good portion of its intelligence data from American space-based sources. Given the size of the Canadian force in theatre it was not a huge burden on the United States' space resources, but it was a burden nonetheless.

Most important, Canada's Gulf War experience demonstrated the paramount need for indigenous effort in space-related defence planning. The primary stimulus for a revised space policy in the late 1980s was DND's concern about the future of its assured access to American ballistic-missile, early-warning data after the North Warning System (NWS) became obsolete. While the existing NWS ground-based facilities located in Canada guaranteed Canadian access to American generated and controlled data, and a replacement would guarantee similar access, an American satellite-based follow-on system then under consideration by the USAF did not carry the same guarantee. The Gulf War heightened such concerns about access to data when the United States devoted almost its entire space capability to supporting its own forces in theatre. Other coalition allies including Canada, although supported by American space assets, received only the minimum data required to carry out their mission. The privileges of sharing a large amount of space resources in the defence of North America did not apply equally to combat operations in Southwest Asia.

The new reality of warfare provided some focus. Between 1991 and 1996, the Space Defence Working Group implemented the four core items of the CRS report. In 1992, DND tabled its first comprehensive space policy, ratified by the chief of defence staff and the minister of national defence in June 1993. This in itself was something of an accomplishment because the greatest hurdle that defence planners faced during the previous decade was making both the government and the public understand and accept the inherent differences between the militarization and weaponization of space. The new defence space policy was based on national sovereignty and security, the establishment of a national defence presence in space, the possession of a national capability to monitor space activities in areas of interest, and the possession of a proper mechanism to develop appropriate policy and resource responses. The new policy was virtually a conceptual revolution in military space thinking in Canada.

Although the government still advocated against the proliferation of Weapons of Mass Destruction (WMD) and ballistic-missile and orbital technologies associated with the weaponization of space, many other more easily legitimized potential threats were offered to justify its continued support for the militarization of space.[58] Besides the more obvious military and strategic advantages of having such programs, the 1992 defence space policy was also careful to identify domestic sovereignty goals such as economic security, curbing the illegal importation of drugs and refugees, monitoring and ensuring the safety of our fishing zones, search and rescue (SAR), and the prevention of economic exploitation (for example, natural resource exploration). The duality of purpose assuaged those concerned with arms control while maintaining some degree of forward defence capability for the Canadian Forces.

Using the 1992 policy directive as a base, the SDWG submitted proposals to be included in CF development plans and planning guidance documents, which advocated the requirement for an indigenous space-based capability.[59] Within three years some of the recommendations were realized as projects. For example, the SDWG initiated the Canadian Military Satellite Communications (CANMILSATCOM) project, and the Joint Space Project (JSP), which included intelligence collection and space surveillance requirements.[60]

In the spring of 1994, the government began hearings on defence policy through a Special Joint Committee of the House of Commons and the Senate. The hearings were part of an overall review of defence and foreign policy initiated by the newly elected Liberal government. Later that year it released its "1994 Defence White Paper," in which the government produced a reduced yet reasonable and realistic defence policy for its armed forces. The issue of space was again present, demonstrating that it had finally become a permanent fixture of Canadian defence policy decision-making.

Of the traditional roles of the CF, bilateral military cooperation (primarily through NORAD) remained a major aim. This no doubt pleased the United States, which was increasingly concerned about the seriousness of Canada's commitment to cooperative space defence especially after the tribulations of the 1991 NORAD renewal agreement.[61] The white paper's confirmation of Canada's intent to share the space burden was at least a start. It remained to be seen, of course, to what extent Canada would actually be able to contribute to cooperative space defence activities given that the document was often referred to as a plan for "doing less with less."[62]

In 1996, the SDWG implemented the last of the CRS report requirements — management structure. Ironically, this led to the dissolution of the SDWG in December; however, a newly formed Directorate of Space Development (D Space D) replaced it in 1997 under the authority of the deputy chief of the defence staff (DCDS).[63] That same year the DCDS was also designated as the departmental space advocate. A Canadian military space program was finally established after 10 long years and a tenuous journey through government bureaucracy.

Present Problems and Promises: 1997 to 2005

Although the final establishment of a dedicated Canadian military space organization was achieved autonomously, there was no illusion within NDHQ that it could evolve in isolation from United States military space policy and programs. The Policy and Strategy section within D Space D acknowledged that its original focal point was not to attempt the development of an entirely indigenous military space capability for Canada, but to capitalize on the potential benefits of dedicated cooperation with the United States.[64] The intention was made clear in the vision statement of D Space D's first business plan produced in 1997. Given that the organization understood its deficiencies it stated:

> In light of the limited resources allocated to space in the CF Long Term Capital Plan, cooperative participation in US programmes is considered a key component in the development of a modest space capability for the CF. Our partnership in NORAD will be leveraged, where practicable, to provide Canada a conduit into US space programmes and ensure an equitable contribution to burden-sharing in the future. An important enabling mechanism will be a Statement of Intent concerning defence space cooperation to be developed between DND and the US Department of Defence (US DoD).[65]

In July 1996, a Space Cooperation Ad Hoc Working Group (SCWG) was formed under the auspices of the Canada and United States (CANUS) Military Cooperation Committee (MCC) to identify specific mutually beneficial opportunities for increased bi-national space cooperation. A number of major objectives were initiated by the new SCWG including a tentative position on the future cooperation of North American defence. The final report of the group was presented to the MCC in June 1997. The MCC then agreed to disband the SCWG and transfer oversight of future defence space cooperation to the Permanent Joint Board on Defence (PJBD).

The PJBD pursued several initiatives including a Statement of Intent (SOI) between the U.S. Department of Defense and DND to establish the necessary legal and policy framework within which to harmonize the collaborative space-related defence and security efforts of both countries. Following this, Canada hoped to obtain mutual approval of a Memorandum of Understanding (MOU) concerning space defence cooperation by October 1998 and additionally, to develop an Implementing Arrangement (IA) for the surveillance of space by June 1999.

Of the five major initiatives outlined in D Space D's first business plan, four entailed some degree of cooperation with American space programs. Additionally, a USAF officer was brought into the strategy, plans, and coordination section of D Space D to advise on American space doctrine and concepts, to coordinate NORAD issues, and to assist in the definition and implementation of a tactical exploitation of space capability within the CF.[66] More recently American air force officers were also invited to instruct at the Canadian Forces School of Aerospace Studies (CFSAS), lending an extensive range of experience and knowledge to the renewed Canadian space indoctrination courses.

In addition, D Space D identified a number of capability deficiencies within the CF that required immediate attention. These included modernized access to space-derived data, updated ballistic-missile early warning at both the strategic and operational (theatre) level, space-based surveillance and reconnaissance, space weather, geomatics support, navigation and positioning accuracy capabilities, and space support to the war fighter.

Space-based surveillance and reconnaissance, weather, and mapping were critical to the modernization and future effectiveness of deployed operations. Although modern CF space surveillance and reconnaissance activities remain classified, there was a need to monitor and assess the potential uses and impact of commercial satellite imagery. The rapid expansion of this industry within the civilian economy in the 1990s fundamentally reshaped the nature of military operations as highly detailed imagery became commercially available at reasonable prices. Likewise, DND renewed its interest in other space surveillance activities and continues to promote development in this area.

Under the JSP, D Space D planned to acquire guaranteed sources of global meteorological and oceanographic information derived from the remote sensing sources of commercial, allied, or other government departments (OGD). Again the primary source for the CF was the U.S. Defense Meteorological Satellite Program (DMSP), through which it obtained most of its data. To ensure the continuation of access to that data, D Space D also sought to negotiate MOUs with the United States that would allow for Canadian Forces abroad to tap into up-to-date American weather sources. By the end of the 1990s DND hoped to have reached an agreement with DoD for assured access to DMSP classified data.[67] D Space D also planned the same for geomatics support, thereby ensuring that current data was available for planning and operations.

The acquisition of surveillance of space capability rested within the ability of the Directorate of Space Development through the JSP to become a full partner in the U.S. Space Surveillance Network (SSN). In 1998, the concept was put forth that Canada allow the Americans to either deploy or assist in the Canadian deployment of one or more SSN sensors on Canadian soil. By doing so, Canada would be able to demonstrate its intent to share the burden of such assets, while at the same time ensuring access to SSN data. As a first step, D Space D sought to develop some level of expertise in the area through the posting of CF officers to the Millstone Hill space surveillance radar facility at the Lincoln Laboratories of the Massachusetts Institute of Technology (MIT) near Boston.

The Haystack space surveillance high frequency radar housed at Millstone Hill provides high-quality, accurate satellite surveillance and tracking data products that are currently unavailable through Canadian systems. Eventually, however, Canada plans to retrofit some of its existing assets and potentially acquire a new phased array radar system to ensure space surveillance capability in the future.[68] Additionally, Canada would seek to acquire an electro-optical surveillance system based on the American RAVEN technology.

Canada's early-warning and defence capabilities also underwent transformation. According to DND's 1998 military space strategy document the preferred approach "[was] to address this deficiency through the Joint Command and Control Information Systems (JC²IS) project. A candidate system for connection to the JC²IS [was] the U.S. Tactical Information Broadcast System (TIBS)."[69] Other aspects of warning and defence such as that against ICBMs and other WMD were still controlled through NORAD. DND conducted research and modelling simulation dealing with specific areas of interest and D Space D later sponsored studies through its Joint Space Support Project. Additionally, DND posted a military officer and a defence scientist to the U.S. Joint National Test Facility where the two members participated in operations research and the development of operational concepts for missile defence.[70] Such participation seemed highly contradictory to the traditional perception of Canadian ballistic-missile defence abstention, but at the working level, both DND and the government understood the critical necessity of early warning to Canada's defence.

Other capability requirements — navigation, search and rescue, and communications — were also met through joint ventures with the United States. The Search and Rescue Satellite (SARSAT) project has been highly successful since its initiation and the CF plans to continue its participation by providing additional repeaters for American satellites, as well as two additional receiving stations on Canadian soil.

Meanwhile, Canada has also committed to two joint projects to provide satellite-based communications to the DND and CF abroad. The first project aims to gain assured access to the U.S. Military Satellite Communications (MILSATCOM) space segment and to acquire the requisite MILSATCOM terminals and possibly a control segment, as well. The second project identified the requirement to fit Canadian ships with a permanent satellite communications capability to ensure future interoperability with the U.S. Navy (USN) and other allied ships. The Royal Canadian Navy (RCN) planned to continue using the U.S. Fleet Satellite Communications system as part of its primary communications capability.

Photographer: Bernd Horn

This Distant Early Warning site at Gladman Point in the Northwest Territories, photographed in the 1980s, is typical of such installations.

Most recently, D Space D has investigated options for integrating space and missile warning capabilities and systems experts directly into operational and tactical level headquarters, and command and control elements. Over the next few years it is hoped that the injection of space support activities at all service colleges, and at the strategic and operational command levels will result in the integration of missile and space issues into all future CF mission planning and execution. Although the project demonstrates the forward thinking of D Space D, it may be too ambitious given the incredible limitations that small initiatives face within today's armed forces. High operational tempo and ever-shrinking assets and resources within the CF mean little is left to pursue personnel intensive and technologically sophisticated endeavours such as space support. Still, missile and space activities are a fundamental part of the future battle space and as such cannot be ignored by deployed forces in theatres of operations. As such, space support must and will eventually become part of CF operations abroad.

Conclusion: The Politics of Space Security

In responding to questions on the country's official stance towards the proposed American National Missile Defence (NMD) program in February 2002, the Honourable Bill Graham, minister of foreign affairs, replied, "Canada's position has always been against the weaponization of space and we will maintain that position."[71] As this chapter demonstrates, the Canadian government's opposition to the weaponization of space is a more recent phenomenon than previously suggested while its stance on the militarization of space is carefully left out of discussion. Though avoiding public debate where possible, the government does not intend deceit against its population. An examination of the Department of Foreign Affairs and International Trade (DFAIT) website on space and missile defence clearly demonstrates that Canada's position on the militarization of space and the weaponization of space differ from each other.

Global trends clearly indicate that access to, and freedom of, manoeuvre in space will become an area of heightened political concern in the next decade. The United States has readily accepted that control of outer space will be contested by states and has already implemented strategy to ensure American dominance of space well throughout the twenty-first century. By contrast, Canada has developed a modest program, with no independent access to space and only a limited freedom of manoeuvre in space. Ultimately, Canada's defence space capability is dependent on cooperation with the United States, and unless the government adopts a radical alternate approach, it will likely continue to be dependent on the Americans for some time.

Developing space policy and space assets in Canada has always been a challenge for historical, political, and economic reasons. Overcoming that challenge to advance its own national security interests while achieving a balance between its civilian and military roles in space has been a major issue for Canada, made even more complicated by the country's desire to continue its cooperation in this field with the United States. Since the 1986 NORAD agreement renewal, Canada has sporadically developed a civilian and military space policy that is in itself both reasonable and realistic considering the limited space capability of the state. Within NDHQ, the Directorate of Space Development has become a small yet efficient space organization dedicated to monitoring and where possible improving Canada's national security interests in and through space. Though hardly equipped to go it alone in space support and control, D Space D provides a mechanism for developing a modest indigenous capability, as well as acting as the main conduit into American space defence programs.

The present state of Canada's space defence capability and its reliance on American participation for its existence clearly demonstrates the junior role that Ottawa plays in the bilateral space defence relationship. Although Canada has taken significant steps to revitalize its military space effort since 1986, the necessity of American cooperation to achieve any aim is obvious. Of all the major initiatives, only human resources do not depend heavily on assistance from the United States. That being said, however, there is no doubt that Canadian officers are professionally developed through their exposure to their American counterparts and partners. If present efforts are maintained then Canada's recent performance and future potential make it possible to re-establish a reasonable balance in Canadian-American space defence cooperation, but for now it is still a long road back from dependence to alliance.[72]

Since the advent of space flight in the 1950s, the role of outer space in safeguarding Canadian security interests has increased steadily. However, since the 1970s it was evident that the primary objective of Canada's space strategy was not to ensure the satisfactory defence of North America but to augment wherever possible its own defence abilities while making a modest contribution in sharing the burden of North American defence. While at times politically sensitive, the government never swayed from this course of action, and while at times militarily intangible, DND always had access to either space assets or space-derived products to augment military operations. In the end, Canada's position has been, and will most likely continue to be, for the foreseeable future, to support the militarization, and oppose the weaponization, of space.

NOTES

1. Nuclear brinkmanship is described in detail in L. Freedman, *The Evolution of Nuclear Strategy* (New York: St. Martin's Press, 1989). For Canadian perspectives of this period see Andrew Richter, *Avoiding Armageddon: Canadian Military Strategy and Nuclear Weapons, 1950–1963* (Vancouver: University of British Columbia Press, 2002); and Sean Maloney, *Learning to Love the Bomb: Canada's Cold War Strategy and Nuclear Weapons, 1951–1968* (Unpublished Ph.D. Dissertation, Temple University, 1996). Both of these works includes chapters discussing threat assessments, intelligence, strategic thinking, and Canadian national security policy during the early Cold War period.
2. For an example of American perspectives see Stephen B. Johnson, "Bernard Schriever and the Scientific Vision," *Air Power History* (Spring 2002), 30–45.
3. See M.E. Davies and W.R. Harris, *RAND's Role in the Evolution of Balloon and Satellite Observation Systems and Related U.S. Space Technology* (Santa Monica, CA: RAND, 1988); and William A. Ulman, "Russian Planes Are Raiding Canadian Skies: Special Report on U.S. Air Defenses," *Collier's*, October 16, 1953, 33–45.
4. H. Bull, *The Control of the Arms Race: Disarmament and Arms Control in the Missile Age* (London: Weidenfeld and Nicolson, 1961), introduction.
5. For a detailed analysis of the defence origins of the Canadian space program see Andrew B. Godefroy, "Defence and Discovery: Science, the Cold War, and Canada's Rocket and Space Program." Unpublished War Studies Program PhD Dissertation, 2004, Royal Military College of Canada.
6. R.C. Fetherstonhaugh, *McGill University at War, 1914–1918 and 1939–1945* (Montreal: McGill University Press, 1947), 321 and 336.
7. D.H. Avery, *The Science of War* (Toronto: University of Toronto Press, 1998), 248–249.
8. For discussion on Canadian continental air defence during this period see J. Jockel, *No Boundaries Upstairs: Canada, the United States, and the Origins of North American Air Defence, 1945–1958* (Vancouver: University of British Columbia Press, 1987).
9. The Soviet Union had developed a space-based strike weapon known as the Fractional Orbital Bombardment System (FOBS). FOBS worked by lofting a nuclear weapon on a partial orbital trajectory via the South Pole, so that it could circumvent North American strategic early warning and strike with surprise. FOBS was tested but officially never deployed with nuclear warheads.
10. While American national intelligence estimates (NIE) are well known and analyzed, the detailed examination of Canada's strategic assessments during this period have only recently been explored in depth. For further debate and discussion see Richter, *Avoiding Armageddon*; and Maloney, *Learning to Love the Bomb*.
11. Overflights of the Soviet Union and China began in 1949, and eventually included support and participation from the British and the Nationalist Chinese (Taiwan).

For detailed history see Curtis Peebles, *Shadow Flights: America's Secret Air War Against the Soviet Union* (Novato, CA: Presidio Press 2002).

12. *Ibid.*, 261–268.

13. By the time Gary Powers was shot down over the Soviet Union in 1960, the CIA's *Corona* spy satellite program had already begun returning useful imagery. See Peebles, *The Corona Project*, and W.E. Burrows, *Deep Black: Space Espionage and National Security* (New York: Random House, 1986).

14. Library and National Canada (LAC), RG25, DEA. Box 112, File 4145-09-1, Vol. 1.

15. In July 1957, the recently elected Diefenbaker government ratified its decision to share the responsibilities of North America's air defence (NORAD) with the United States. Originally tasked to provide strategic early warning, as well as coordinate armed defence and response to any attack, NORAD soon adopted other roles such as space analysis, satellite tracking, and later anti-ballistic-missile defence. It is not the intent or in the scope of this study to detail the history of Canada and NORAD, as it is well addressed in literature elsewhere. Among others see Jockel, *No Boundaries Upstairs.*

16. On the navy, see J. Vardalas, "From DATAR to the FP-6000 Computer: Technological Change in a Canadian Industrial Context," *IEEE Annals of the History of Computing*, Vol. 16, No. 2 (1994); also "The Navy's Pursuit of Self Reliance in Digital Electronics," in J. Vardalas, *The Computer Revolution in Canada*. On the army, see Sean Maloney, *An Identifiable Cult: The Evolution of Combat Development in the Canadian Army* (Kingston, ON: DND, Directorate of Land Strategic Concepts, August 1999). Both pioneering efforts in the Canadian history of science and technology, these articles introduce often ignored aspects of post-war modernization of the Canadian military.

17. Yet what the RCAF did not expect was an all-out political battle with the DRB to become the office of primary interest (OPI) for the development of Canadian military space applications. Nor did it expect to see the day where the DRB would suggest that its primary function was pure scientific investigation not defence research and development. For more on this debate see further below in this chapter.

18. See below in this chapter. For example, the RCAF Space Development Program proposed an ambitious space-based weapons project that likely would have required the simultaneous development of an indigenous launch capability such as the American Scout rocket then under consideration.

19. Correspondence from Air Marshal Hugh Campbell, chief of air staff, to Air Marshal C.R. Slemon, deputy commander-in-chief of NORAD, dated March 28, 1961, 1. LAC, RG 24, Vol. 17829, File 840-105-001.8.

20. The USAF did start a conceptual study within its Blue Gemini Program for the design of a missile carrying spacecraft.

21. Development and Associated Research Policy Group Paper 12/65 — A Canadian Forces Space Development Program dated May 12, 1965, 2. ATI. LAC, RG 24, Vol. 17973 File 925-121-3. L1150-4110/D8 (Secret).

22. Correspondence from Air Marshal Hugh Campbell, chief of air staff, to Air Marshal C.R. Slemon, deputy commander-in-chief of NORAD, dated March 28, 1961, 2. LAC, RG 24, Vol. 17829, File 840-105-001.8.

23. *Ibid.*, 3.

24. *Ibid.*, 4. While not directly entering the U.S. astronaut corps, RCAF officers did work within NASA. See also the section on the Space Indoctrination Program later in this chapter.

25. These activities included, among others, Projects LOOKOUT and BLIND TWINKLER.

26. J. Starnes, *Closely Guarded: A Life in Canadian Security and Intelligence* (Toronto: University of Toronto Press, 1998), 105–106. Starnes was likely one of very few senior Canadian intelligence officials to have the privilege of visiting the National Photographic Interpretation Center (NPIC) in its well concealed and inconspicuous run-down building on the outskirts of Washington, D.C., sometime during 1961 or 1962.

27. Correspondence from Air Marshal Hugh Campbell, chief of air staff, to Air Marshal C.R. Slemon, deputy commander-in-chief of NORAD, dated March 28, 1961, 3. ATI, LAC, RG 24, Vol. 17829, File 840-105-001.8.

28. For the only known published Canadian source on the SIP see Anon. "Canadian Missile Men," *Sentinel*, September 1969, 32–33. Interviews with RCAF officers in the SIP have revealed that they were never informed that their "loan" to the United States fell under any organized plan, although official documentation and the above-mentioned article make reference to SIP.

29. "Reports and Returns — RCAF Personnel on Exchange Duties — USAF — HQS Air Force Space Systems Division — Los Angeles — Calif. 1963–1965." ATI, LAC, RG 24, File 813-89/3-42.

30. C. Peebles, *The Corona Project: America's First Spy Satellites*, appendix 1 and 2.

31. Archives and research did not reveal any unclassified documentation or personal claim citing how extensively informed senior Canadian officials were of American secret satellite systems such as *Corona*. As detailed above, John Starnes noted in his memoirs visiting the NPIC in 1961–62, but provides little further insight. It is estimated that senior members of joint intelligence communities, and certain members of the CF were likely aware of American photoreconnaissance capabilities to some extent, but only further investigation and declassification of documents will determine the level of awareness that existed.

32. Even four decades later, activities surrounding Canadian-American cooperation in the surveillance of space remain classified. Most of the material available on this section was derived "Telecommunication Services — Data Processing — Ground Environment — Space Detection and Tracking System (SPADATS)." ATI, LAC, RG 24, Vol. 17996, file 947-103–6.

33. Annex A to 947-3-6 (DRDP), Dated November 26, 1964 — "A Report on Exchange Duty with the USAF 496L System Program Office," 2. ATI, LAC, RG 24, Vol. 17996, file 947-103-6.

34. *Ibid.*, 2.

35. Major K. Rodzinyak, "Like a Sapphire in the Sky: Canada's Surveillance of Space Project." Unpublished MA paper, War Studies Program, Royal Military College of Canada, Kingston, Ontario, 2002.

36. Lieutenant-Colonel B. Wooding and Lieutenant-Colonel T.A. Spruston, "The Canadian Armed Forces and the Space Mission," *Canadian Defence Quarterly*, Vol. 5, No. 2 (Winter 1975), 17. For high Earth and geosynchronous orbit satellites this method was particularly effective, allowing for accuracy to 30/3600ths of a degree (30 seconds of arc). It was claimed that the process could be further refined if needed, bringing the accuracy down to two or three seconds of arc.

37. Appendix A to S925-121-3 (Secret) "Recommendations for Future Action on the RCAF Proposal for a Canadian Defence Space Program," dated July 20, 1964. ATI, LAC, RG 24, Vol. 17829, File 840-105-001.8.

38. *Ibid.*, 6.

39. *Ibid.*, 6–7.

40. *Ibid.*, 7–8.

41. *Ibid.*, 58.
42. Kirton, *A Renewed Opportunity*, 117.
43. J. Sokolsky, *Defending Canada: U.S.-Canadian Defense Policies* (New York, 1989), 7.
44. *Ibid.*, 7.
45. The Canadian Baker-Nunn space surveillance cameras were phased out of operation in 1988.
46. Canada, *Hansard*, February 4, 1985, 1961.
47. The first was the Senate Special Committee on National Defence in January 1985, and the second was the House of Commons Standing Committee on External Affairs and National Defence in February 1986.
48. Canada, *Space Indoctrination Handbook: 5th Edition* (Winnipeg: DND,1996), 3–3.
49. The NWS cost approximately U.S. $1.2 billion.
50. Article V essentially stated that neither the United States nor the Soviet Union could develop, test, or deploy ABM systems or components that are sea-based, space-based, or mobile land-based.
51. United States of America, *Space Handbook — A Warfighter's Guide to Space, Volume 1* (Maxwell AFB: DoD, 1993), 33.
52. The consensus of many Canadian strategic thinkers is that the Liberal government maintained a tradition of defence without strategic analysis. See Hare Byers, and Lindsey, *Aerospace Defence: Canada's Future Role?* (Toronto: CIIA, 1985); and D. Leyton-Brown, and M. Slack, eds., *The Canadian Strategic Review, 1984.* (Toronto: CISS, 1985).
53. The results of the study were incorporated first into the 1987 white paper on defence and then later in a 1987 DND space policy paper.
54. The first recommendation came through the Senate Special Committee on National Defence in January 1985. The second came through the House of Commons Standing Committee on External Affairs and National Defence in February 1986.
55. Canada, *A Canadian Military Space Strategy*, 1.
56. The SDWG was formed on June 3, 1991 by NDHQ instruction DCDS 2/91.
57. Canada, *A Canadian Military Space Strategy*, 1.
58. Canada, *Space Policy* (Ottawa, DND, 1992), 1.
59. *Ibid.*, 3.
60. The JSP was designated Defence Services Program (DSP) G2667 on August 17, 1995, following Program Planning Proposal (PPP) approval. In June 1997, the Intelligence Collection element was established as a stand-alone project with the unclassified named TROODOS, with DSP number G2773.
61. For an analysis of the panel review see R. Hill, et al., "The NORAD Renewal Issue," CIIPS Working Paper N0.33, Toronto, March 1991, 53–61.
62. Sokolsky, *Canada, Getting It Right This Time*, 8.
63. D Space D is part of Capability Component 4 (CC4).
64. Interview with Major G. Liddy (D Space D 3-2), March 1998.
65. DND, "D Space D Level 3 Business Plan 1997/98," 4.
66. Major Karl Mickelson, USAF, held this position (designated D Space D 3-3) during 1997–98.
67. DND, "D Space D Level 3 Business Plan FY99/00-03/04," A-1/8.
68. Canada is considering the retrofit of a space surveillance radar into the existing Algonquin Radio Telescope.
69. Canada, *A Canadian Military Space Strategy*, 8–9.
70. *Ibid.*, 8.

71. Canada, *Hansard* Index, 37th Parliament, 1st Session, February 27, 2002, o.q. 9296 (150:14:30). The Honourable Bill Graham, minister of foreign affairs, responding to questions from the Right Honourable Joe Clark on Canadian participation in American National Missile Defence.
72. Canada is perhaps no different from many other countries in NATO that depend heavily on the United States for space support.

CHAPTER 12

Years of Innocence and Drift: The Canadian Way of War in the Post–Cold War Era
by Scot Robertson

Introduction

On the night of November 7, 1989, the Berlin Wall was breached, setting off a wave of informal celebrations that swept across Europe and beyond. The Cold War had ended in a fashion that few had dared to hope possible — peacefully. While it would take several years yet to fully appreciate that the decades long stand-off between NATO and the Warsaw Pact (WP) was indeed a historical relic, it took little time for many NATO member-states to embark upon fanciful planning for a new world order. In doing so, statesmen, politicians and planners were engaging in behaviour with well-established roots, namely wishful thinking. Historically, the end of a major war — hot or cold — often results in the expectation that the settlement will be lasting.

Historically, this expectation is often proven to be false. Armed with this knowledge and understanding, wise statesmen would approach a plan for the future with a degree of circumspection. Expectations for the future, based on shallow and hasty deliberations often sow the seeds for longer-term disappointment.

A sage once commented that the greatest derangement of the human mind is to believe in something because one wishes it to be so. If that is indeed the case, then Canada suffered a surfeit of derangement as it contemplated a future free of the oppressive yoke of the Cold War confrontation. As the Berlin Wall fell, and the Cold War fizzled out, Canadian planning for the future, such as it was, was not based on a sober and cautious understanding of the prospects and pitfalls, but on a mixture of wishful thinking, naïve optimism, and an understandable but reckless rush to slash defence spending.

Perhaps the single best expression of the woolly headed thinking that characterized Canada's hopes for the post–Cold War order can be found in a curious document entitled *Canada and Common Security in the Twenty-First Century*.[1] Authored by a group of eminent Canadians under the moniker of the Canada 21 Committee, this report betrayed a degree of liberal internationalist cant that was to have a pervasive and perfidious influence on Canada's foreign and defence policy in general, and on Canada's military capability in particular. A decade after its release, it is both instructive and illuminating to re-read the report of the Canada 21 Committee. Virtually every prognostication and forecast proved incorrect. Yet because of the committee's considerable influence, the report informed the making of foreign and defence policy at the dawn of the post–Cold War era. More alarmingly, *Canada and Common Security in the Twenty-First Century* cast a long shadow over the execution of foreign and defence policy for nearly a decade, even after all but a few diehards had admitted that the hopeful expectations of the authors were baseless.

Informed by Innocence: Expectations of the Post–Cold War Era

When Canadian historians turn their hand to the period 1989 to 2001, a period that we still persist in calling the post–Cold War era, they will not need to struggle to find a term to characterize those years. For Canada, that period can perhaps best be thought of as years of innocence and drift. Some will argue that the Canadian way of war has always been informed by innocence. In that, they are largely correct. However, it could also be argued that in bygone days this was never a fatal shortcoming. Through much of Canada's existence as an independent nation, Canadian foreign and defence policy have largely been formulated and executed within the context of a relationship with a protector or guarantor. As this book has demonstrated, the Canadian way of war has evolved under an umbrella held first by the United Kingdom, and then by the United States.

Moreover, Canada's existence as an independent nation has overlapped with the great struggles of the twentieth century, namely the struggle between liberal-democratic values on the one hand, and the forces of totalitarianism on the other. In that sense, Canada's policy was largely pre-ordained — it would stand with the forces of liberal democracy against totalitarianism. On the big questions, there was never a choice and never a doubt. When the situation demanded it, Canada would answer the call.

In answering the calls of the twentieth century, Canada, like many other smaller states, contributed to a larger coalition, in which, for the most part, the great powers determined the strategy, the plans, and the force requirements. To the best of their abilities, the smaller powers provided personnel and supplies, and sometimes, larger formations. In some cases, they were invited to participate in the higher planning conferences, but more often than not, the overall direction had already been hammered out. This, from the point of view of the smaller contributors, may not have been an ideal situation, but was, at least to some extent, understandable.

At the onset of the Cold War, Canada demonstrated a nascent strategic culture, one that stood in stark contrast to its recent historical experience. Canada was an early, if somewhat reluctant, proponent of the North Atlantic Alliance. Canada saw the need to provide a shield behind which the shattered states of Europe could rebuild. It saw a need to stand as a bulwark against a third major totalitarian threat to liberal-democratic values. In short, Canada recognized that its traditional approach to foreign and defence policy would need to change somewhat. Yet there were limits, real and perceived, to this newfound strategic culture. Although Canada emerged from World War II as one of the largest military powers, this was always acknowledged to be a temporary phenomenon. In light of this, Canada embarked on a strategy of multilateralism. Informed partly by a realistic appraisal of the transitory nature of Canada's immediate post-war status, and partly by a degree of hope that the future nature of international relations might move beyond the simple calculus of *realpolitik*, Canada was also a strong proponent of the United Nations.

Canada's most fundamental goal in pursuing this multilateral strategy, however, was to find a way to balance its growing complex of ties with the United States. Canada recognized that the United States would be Canada's "protector." It could hardly be otherwise. Canada also recognized that there could be times when the United States might be a reluctant player on the international stage, and that this was a tendency to be discouraged. In short, Canada set out to devise a strategy that would serve on a number of levels. It would seek to encourage multilateral cooperative solutions to international problems when appropriate. It sought a framework within which the compelling and real threat posed by the Soviet Union could be forestalled. It sought a mechanism within which the United States could take up the challenge of "protecting" the free world. And it sought to do so without the need to build large and expensive standing forces. It was, therefore, a vast and ambitious strategy, born partly of hard-headed realism, and partly of naïve optimism. It was, nonetheless, a strategy.

Pursued consistently and with vigour, such a strategy would have served Canada and its allies well. However, to borrow from the title of Jack Granatstein's latest work, something intervened to kill the Canadian military, and by extension, the strategy for navigating the difficult contours of the Cold War.[2] That something, in Granatstein's view, was United Nations peacekeeping, or at the least the mythical version of peacekeeping propagated by the liberal internationalists in Canada beginning in the late 1960s. As historian Sean Maloney has so painstakingly revealed, the idea and practice of peacekeeping as conceived of by Lester Pearson in 1956, has been so misconstrued and misrepresented by successive generations of Canadian myth-makers, that it supplanted virtually every other consideration with respect to foreign and defence policy for many years.[3]

The extent to which Canadians have lost touch with the reality of our nascent strategic culture only became clear as we confronted the need to plan for the post–Cold War era. What would we do? What were our goals? How could they best be achieved? These were all questions that deserved some clear thinking in the early 1990s. Instead, what passed for strategic thinking was the report of the Canada 21 Committee. Read in 1992, when it was first issued, the report seemed remarkably naïve and optimistic. Read in 2004, the report seems downright silly. On virtually every count and recommendation, the Canada 21 Committee was flat out wrong. In many cases, these shortcomings stemmed from faulty or shaky analysis. In other cases, they emerged from wishful thinking born of the myths of liberal internationalism.

A report such as that of the Canada 21 Committee often makes for interesting reading, and provides considerable fodder for the chattering classes and policy communities. In most instances, however, that is as far as their influence extends. However, in this case, the reach was considerably greater, and the effect considerably more devastating. The report contained not only faulty analysis of the coming future, but faulty recommendations concerning the size and shape of the armed forces necessary to meet that future.[4] Upon close examination, the force model recommended by the Canada 21 Committee, and that delivered by the government after the issuance of the "1994 Defence White Paper" are remarkably similar. In addition, they were remarkably incapable of meeting the needs of the post–Cold War period to say nothing of the period we find ourselves in following September 11, 2001 (9/11). In

Photographer: Bernd Horn

Declining defence budgets commenced in the 1960s but began a spiralling free-fall in the 1980s and 1990s when military spending was dramatically pared as one measure to combat a looming national financial crisis.

answer to Granatstein's question, "Who killed the Canadian military?" one could readily point an accusing finger at the Canada 21 Committee.

A Policy of Drift: Canada in the Post–Cold War Years

In the immediate aftermath of the Cold War, there was little under-standing or comprehension of what lay ahead. Although the fall of the Berlin Wall would mark the de facto conclusion of a 40-year con-frontation between the members of the North Atlantic Treaty Organisation (NATO) and the Warsaw Pact (WP), it would take a few years for it to be universally recognized that the Cold War was, for all intents and purposes, over. There was even a brief period of wondering whether the collapse of the Warsaw Pact was an elaborate hoax engi-neered by the Soviet Union — a *maskirovka* — before it became clear that the long and dangerous stand-off was indeed over.[5] This end of the Cold War was not even marked by a treaty or peace settlement. Nor was it marked by serious considerations of what might follow. Rather, it seemed to simply pass into the shadows of history.

On one level, it appeared as though people were relieved that the Cold War was over, and simply desired to move on. On another level, however, some held that it was time to consider new vistas and new possibilities. During the first few years of the last decade of the twentieth century, numerous articles and books purported to describe what the new world might look like. For instance, Francis Fukuyama penned his infamous "end of history" thesis, for which he has been roundly excoriated. Charles Krauthammer coined the term *unipolar moment* to describe the new world strategic geometry, in which the United States remained the sole super-power. President George H.W. Bush, who often mocked his own inelegant use of language, simply referred to the "new world order." Samuel Huntington posited a "clash of civilizations." While Joseph Nye held that the United States would be "bound to lead," some neo-isolationists thought that the United States should return to North America and be content in Fortress America. Liberal internationalists, the Canada 21 Committee included, felt that the time was ripe to embark on a grand venture of institution building, giving free rein to the United Nations to carry out the good works intended by the founders. In short, there was no agreement on what the future might hold, or how it should be approached.[6]

All, however, did agree on one thing, namely a desire to reap the peace dividend. In this, Canada was perhaps the leader in NATO, one of the few times Canada could make a legitimate claim to leading in anything, even though this might not be something to celebrate. The Conservative government of Prime Minister Brian Mulroney, faced with a looming financial crisis, desperately needed to slash spending. Its budget-cutters first recourse was to the defence portfolio. Even though the Mulroney government had come to power with grand designs to rebuild Canada's military capacity, it delivered little in this regard, confronted as it was with the reality of domestic spending. So when the Berlin Wall fell, so did the Mulroney government's resolve on defence. Budgets were slashed. Programs were cancelled, and force levels were slated for reduction.[7] For the Canadian Armed Forces, the death spiral had begun.

Yet, at the same time, the Mulroney government initiated a number of deployments that would continue unabated for very nearly 10 years. These deployments were, perhaps ironically, book-ended by two dangerous and significant operations — the Persian Gulf War in 1991, and deployments to Afghanistan following the events of the terrorist attacks on the World Trade Center towers, in New York, on 9/11. Between those two missions, the Canadian Forces (CF) was sent across the globe to do all manner of things.

Looked at with the aid of hindsight, the 1990s can rightly be characterized as a decade of drift. Successive governments, prime ministers, ministers of national defence, and elite opinion makers increasingly saw the Canadian Armed Forces as an instrument of a perhaps well-intentioned, but ultimately ill-considered and futile pursuit of what the Canada 21 Committee referred to as "common security."

So, very early in the post–Cold War period, Canada's military found itself confronted with two diametrically opposed and irreconcilable demands. On the one hand, the military was compelled to live with ever-shrinking budgets; fewer soldiers, sailors, and airmen, and aging and increasingly ineffective and dangerous equipment. On the other hand, they were faced with a seemingly rapacious and never-ending appetite on the part of successive governments to join every possible mission on offer. The Canadian way of war in the post–Cold War era, then, was characterized by a policy of innocence and drift. Innocence, in the view of the world that predominated for many of those years, and drift in that the Canadian military was largely left to find its own way once the strategy was found to be wanting.

What are the consequences of more than a decade of innocence and drift? These are not difficult to ascertain. One need only consider the virtual flood of reports and studies pertaining to the woeful state of the Canadian Armed Forces to gain a sense of the problem. Each draws attention to the parlous state of the military, and each calls for spending more money on the armed forces.[8] In that sense, however, they are merely another voice in the chorus calling for greater government spending on a wide range of social programs. Politicians know that in Canada, there are few votes in defence, and when it is contrasted with public policy issues such as health care and education, defence is something that can be safely ignored. If this is a fair characterization of the state of national security and defence policy thinking in this country, the real challenge is to understand why this situation has arisen, what the risks and consequences of this might be, and what, if anything, can be done to remedy the situation.

Why Innocence and Why Drift? An Immature Strategic Culture

Our traditional approach to matters of national security — especially between the fall of the Berlin Wall and the terror attacks on the United States in 2001, what we might call the post–Cold War years, revealed the inadequacies of the Canadian defence and security approach. More important, left unaddressed, this approach will continue to fall short in the face of the complexities and problems in the world today. A foreign policy built on platitudes, or Canadian conceits may be comforting, but it will not, as recent events have manifestly made clear, ensure the protection and promotion of our strategic interests. Similarly, a defence policy based on the myth of peacekeeping will be equally insufficient, particularly since the gap between the pervasive cliché and the reality of peace enforcement operations of the past decade has become an unbridgeable chasm.

Perhaps most discomfiting, Canada's ad hoc national security policy-making apparatus seems unable to bring policy coherence to the various departments and agencies with an interest in security affairs. Nor is this ad hoc approach able to mobilize the country's disparate elements of national power in ways appropriate for new circumstances. What is necessary is a fundamental rethinking of how Canada will go about securing its national interests and pursuing its national objectives. Anything short of that will be a major disappointment, and will run the risk of courting irrelevance in the twenty-first century.

Canada confronts an uncomfortable situation in the aftermath of the U.S. action against Iraq in 2003. We find ourselves standing at one of those proverbial forks in the road. How we reached this point is less important than decisions we face about the direction we must now take. Sadly, it is not clear that Canada, as a nation, as a people, and as a government, is able to make a clear and forthright decision on the best direction to take, and how we will get there. The inability to consider something as basic as our strategic interests reflects a lack of strategic culture — or at the least an immaturity in strategic culture — that has plagued this country for much of the past decade, if not longer.[9]

Historian and essayist Sean Maloney has endeavoured to address this shortcoming in some of his recent work. He has, for instance begun to explore what he terms the Canadian strategic tradition. In Maloney's view, this consists of four inter-related elements: (1) forward security; (2) coalition warfare; (3) operational influence; and (4) saliency. Taken together, Maloney argues, these four elements represent a strategic tradition that has served Canada well in the past.[10] However, by 1970 or so, that strategic tradition was, if not repudiated, then at the least allowed to wither and die, and was not formally replaced by anything that could serve in its stead. All that was left was a series of government policy statements, which, as every first year civics student knows, are malleable and changeable.[11]

Photographer: Corporal S.M. Kent, Department of National Defence

In the war against terrorism, Task Force 151 (HMCS Fredericton, *right; HMCS* Iroquois, *centre; HMCS* Regina, *left; and HMNZS* Te Mana) *sails in diamond formation in the Arabian Gulf in May 2003. The warships were responsible for escorting ships, boarding suspect vessels, and guarding against attacks on shipping in support of Operation Apollo and Operation Freedom.*

Although that situation may not have been ideal, it was not overly damaging throughout the 1970s and 1980s. Canadian defence policy of that period was still tied inextricably to NATO and the Cold War confrontation with the Warsaw Pact. In that sense, Canadian defence policy could not stray too far from the strategic tradition. While there were efforts to break free — perhaps most infamously those of Pierre Trudeau and Ivan Head to repudiate what they saw as the unduly constraining nature of our NATO-centric policy — *realpolitik* often intervened to drag us back. So although our strategic tradition was supplanted by a series of vague and amorphous policy statements, circumstances dictated, at least to a large extent, that Canada would continue to meet its obligations, even if only minimally.

Now that the period termed, for want of a better description, the post–Cold War era has ended, we stand at the threshold of a new security environment. The contours of this new security environment have only begun to emerge, but it seems probable that this will portend significant implications for our long-term strategic interests. At root, the challenge that the country faces is far more complex than finding additional resources, even though additional resources are sorely needed. The real challenge involves re-structuring the national security policy making apparatus of government, or perhaps more appropriately, creating a national security apparatus.

In doing so, the government will be able draw on an emerging consensus that a clear understanding of strategic interests and a more coherent national security strategy are essential preconditions for success and relevance in the twenty-first century security environment. This consensus is strongest on a number of key points. First governments will need to address the basic, but by no means straightforward matter of identifying strategic interests or national interests. Then there will need to be a general discussion of national security policy planning, with a view to implementing a more comprehensive and responsive apparatus. Finally, it will be necessary to overcome a strong and pervasive overhang that makes discussing national security policy difficult and challenging. Desmond Morton, in his recent book, *Understanding Canadian Defence*, captures neatly the challenge. While Morton provides a broad and by and large accurate reading of how we reached our current nadir, he then basically shrugs his shoulders and suggests that we are condemned to continue down the same path. This attitude is representative of a school of thought that could be best characterized as the "historical drag school." While it is important to understand how we reached the point we are at, it is equally important to look to alternate paths for the future. This will be the test. Only if Canada is able to contemplate a different path to the future, and begin down that path, can it overcome a policy of innocence and drift.

An End to Innocence and Drift: Crafting a New Canadian Way of War

If the post–Cold War years taught Canadians one thing, it should have been that the greatest derangement of the human mind is to believe in something because we wish it to be so. This could characterize much of Canadian thinking and policy during the age of innocence and drift. A Canadian way of war during those years might best be described as one of tactical proficiency, operational credibility, and strategic incredulousness. No one can question the tactical expertise and facility of the

Canadian military. They demonstrated time and time again that they are second to none in terms of competence at the individual and small-unit level. At the next level up, the operational level, one could argue that over the post–Cold War period, the Canadian military demonstrated a degree of credibility, although arguably this was a wasting asset as the effects of overstretch, exhaustion, downsizing, and parsimony began to take hold. Finally, the strategic level was marked by incredulousness, confusion, and chaos. Perhaps this should not be surprising. Consciously or not, a sound Canadian strategic tradition had been allowed to wither on the vine, and was not replaced by anything of substance. The Canadian military was simply conceived of as a tool in the pursuit of common or cooperative security, with little or no appreciation of the need to ensure that soft power needed to be supported by some measure of hard power — the iron fist in the velvet glove. Without a realization of this underlying verity, the Canadian military became a simple contributor to many United Nations sponsored peace or stabilization missions. It seemed to have lost the capacity to think strategically.

In a sense, we seemed to be returning to an earlier pattern of behaviour marked in which we would shelter behind the shield of a protector or guarantor, and generate forces if and when necessary and turn them over to a higher command. Strategic thought was left to others. While this

Photographer: Master-Corporal Frank Hudec, Department of National Defence

During the ongoing war against terrorism, a boarding party of ordinary seamen from HMCS Iroquois *searches a suspect tanker in the Gulf of Oman in April 2003.*

may have been both necessary and understandable in an earlier era, it is far from clear that it is appropriate today. The post–Cold War period of innocence and drift is over. It ended, whether we like it or not, with the attacks on the World Trade Center and the Pentagon on September 11, 2001. While there were earlier indications that a policy based on the naïve and optimistic thinking along the lines of the Canada 21 Committee had reached its nadir, this was confirmed by the events of 9/11. Not everyone was prepared to embrace the ideals posited by liberal internationalism. In fact, some were obviously prepared to reject it in a violent fashion.

Whatever the causality, it has become all too apparent that notions of common or cooperative security are not universally shared. Hence, a strategic policy based on innocence will no longer suffice. It will need to be replaced by one that considers national interests and sets out to secure those interests with military power when necessary. That will necessitate an end to the drift that has plagued the armed forces during the post–Cold War period.

New Directions

Undeniably, in the decade since the 1993–94 defence and foreign policy reviews that culminated in the current white paper for defence and guidance for Foreign Affairs, a number of issues have emerged that have added to the defence-related lexicon, but not necessarily the defence budget. A decade ago *peace enforcement, asymmetric war, terror with a global reach, globalization,* and *human security* were terms not to be found in common use. Equally absent were considerations of NATO's "26" nations, or the Office of Homeland Defense. Part of the process of considering new directions involves taking stock of many of these new developments, emerging threats, opportunities, and risks while weighing old and enduring challenges among the newly emergent.

Major Themes

A wide range of important topics will need to be addressed if the post–Cold War policy of innocence and drift is to be overcome in the conduct of any future reviews of defence policy, foreign policy, and perhaps national security policy. Although it is impossible to cover the full range of themes in detail, the major points include the following:

Confronting New Threats

The broad range new threats and challenges must be considered.

National Security Architecture

The need for new ways and means for dealing with these threats and challenges, including a new national security architecture for effective intelligence and interagency cooperation. There was a profound sense that our national security architecture, based as it is on a nineteenth-century model, is woefully inadequate in the twenty-first century.

Force Structure

The critical role of task-tailored forces ranging from platoon to larger formations for the land elements, single ships to task forces for the maritime elements, and a range of reconfigurable air elements.

Canada-U.S. Relations

The overarching importance of our relationship with the United States cannot be overstated, but we also have fundamental differences and the fine balance between managing both demands careful, concerted attention.

Confronting New Threats and Challenges

Perhaps it is a blinding flash of the obvious, but the twenty-first century will test Canada and the Canadian Forces with a number of new and very difficult challenges. First and foremost, the spectre of the "new" terrorism evidenced most spectacularly in the attacks of 9/11, but followed up by the attacks in Bali, and those that will no doubt come in the days and years ahead, will require a degree of fortitude and effort that may mirror the type of commitment called for during the Cold War. In contemplating this future, there should be considerable discussion of the role of military forces, and whether they should be front and centre in this endeavour. While armed forces will have a key role, they will be largely supportive. Intelligence services and special operations forces will be called on to take point. In addition, foreign aid and international development assistance will be instrumental in draining the swamps. Finally, models of intervention will need to be amended. UN-sponsored intervention may become less relevant, replaced by regionally sponsored interventions and coalitions of the willing.

In short, the government will need to bring more coherence to how we deal with emerging problem areas. Rather than operating in splendid isolation, a more coordinated, cooperative approach should be brought to the full range of issues that constitute Canadian international policy. For instance, there is an emerging awareness that development issues, latent and nascent crises, and crisis intervention should not be thought of as the sole prerogative of the Canadian International Development Agency (CIDA), or the Foreign Affairs Canada (FAC), or the Department of National Defence (DND). Rather Canada's response should be thought of as involving all the instruments of international policy in some measure or another, and working relationships between these and other agencies need to be hammered out and thought through in a more concerted manner, so as to avoid problems such as those experienced by FAC in contributing to the CF mission in Afghanistan. More to the point, there is a growing recognition that the pace at which situations can change from relatively benign to a full-blown crisis will necessitate more nimble, responsive, and considered government action than we have heretofore seen.

National Security Architecture

An issue that has pervaded many discussions of defence issues of late has been the adequacy of the current Canadian national security policy-making architecture. Many of the emerging challenges will be of a dynamic and fast emerging nature. Many expert commentators question the responsiveness of the national security architecture, in particular the analytical and forecasting ability of national level intelligence bodies and the coordination of national security policy. We have a system that at the least makes it difficult to know what has been done. Moreover, existing ad hoc coordinating arrangements have been deemed "dysfunctional" and in urgent need of reform. Because they are too ad hoc in their structure, there is considerable doubt as to their ability to cope with the nature and pace of the new threats, many of which resemble network structures, rather than traditional state based hierarchical, bureaucratically structured threats.

Some suggestions for remedying these deficiencies have been forthcoming. One such recommendation highlights the need for a more permanent inter-departmental planning body with responsibility for assessment, strategic planning, and coordination of national efforts somewhat akin to the U.S. National Security Council, or the Australian Office of National Assessment. There have been calls by Canadian commentators and experts for just such a body, yet little apparent action has been observed.[12]

Force Structure

Rather than engage in prosaic questions of force structure it is perhaps of greater importance to consider broad themes that should be addressed in any future review of defence and security policy. The armed forces will need to focus on the following key requirements: readiness, sustainability, jointness, reorganization, modern high-tech equipment, and international cooperation. Most defence experts and analysts in this country seem in broad agreement that these are the very issues that the CF will need to address in the future.[13]

Canada-U.S. Relations

The Canada-U.S. relationship has been cast in a stark light of late. The new demands of dealing with North American security, which range well beyond the mandate of national defence, let alone keeping abreast of operational methods for cooperating with U.S. forces in expeditionary operations, is a tall order, and one that may be beyond our modest reach. Before 9/11, concern in Ottawa hinged on the apparent rise in unilateralism by the White House. Cancellation of the Anti-Ballistic Missile (ABM) Treaty, withdrawal from Kyoto, tensions with China, softwood lumber, and a number of other issues, left the Ottawa mandarins lamenting the breakdown of the "special relationship" and the faltering of the intricate multilateral matrix within which Ottawa enjoyed entangling Washington for the stabilization of the international status quo. How will this affect Canada as we look out to a confused and uncertain future?

At the risk of stating the obvious, one of the most important requirements that will face the government and the nation is that of managing the relationship with the United States. Generally, we as a nation have not thought through all the implications of (1) U.S. predominance in the world, (2) American determination to transform the Middle East and elsewhere to deal with terrorists and their sponsors, and (3) the realities of our economic dependence on the U.S. economy and geographical proximity to the United States. These are not issues to be resolved, rather they require perpetual management.

Defence Budgets and Resources

It should come as no surprise that the issue of the inadequacies of the defence budget will feature prominently in any discussions. This note has been sounded by virtually every study of defence in Canada over the past half decade. While it is one thing to simply call for additional spending on defence, it is quite another to determine where existing and new resources should be allocated at a time of significant change. Hence, the question of resource allocation will feature prominently in the months ahead. In this regard, several areas will require concerted attention. First, the Canadian Forces must confront the transformation agenda. For too long, modernization and transformation have been neglected. The result of this neglect is that the Canadian forces lack the breadth and depth of capability to confront the broad range of challenges that the future will hold. Recognizing that over the short term, and barring a major calamity, any additional money made available will be short of what is required, choices will have to be made. Having said that, however, guidance and direction will be necessary, and this should form the basis of a meaningful defence review.

All in all, the path to a new policy, one radically different and more appropriate than the policy of innocence and drift of the post–Cold War era, will be long and difficult. A number of general conclusions are possible as the CF and DND move forward. First, strategists must reconsider their preconceptions and embrace a more comprehensive definition of security. Second, they must take note of a range of nontraditional security threats that demand the attention of the CF (for example, terrorism, weapons of mass destruction, narcotics, transnational crime, people smuggling). Third, they need to acknowledge in a clearer fashion than heretofore that the defence of Canada will be

Photographer: Sergeant Frank Hudec, Department of National Defence

To meet coalition demands, a 3rd Battalion, Royal Canadian Regiment Battle Group Light Armoured Vehicle III patrols in Kabul, Afghanistan, in June 2003 as part of Operation Athena, Canada's contribution to the International Security Assistance Force.

much more complex because of the "globalization of security." Fourth, they will need to question the contemporary relevance of some of the long-standing underpinnings of strategic policy, that challenges to Canadian security are only found in far away places, and that we always have a choice about how we respond.

The effort to break with the past will be difficult because one cannot escape it. However, for the purposes of contemplating a new Canadian way of war, the national security and defence community in Canada should consider the following issues.

First, and foremost, we need to contemplate whether there is in fact a new reality emerging in which threats arise from non-traditional sources in non-traditional ways, and that this requires an ability to conduct short or no-warning crisis response operations in a timely fashion. Second, and flowing from the first, is the notion that territorial defence will take on a broader meaning, and that this might entail contributions to offshore collective defence (for example, permanent treaty arrangements or coalitions of the willing). Third, that joint and combined operations will become the rule rather than the exception, and that in many instances other government departments and non-state actors will be an integral part of any response. Hence, adjustments to the national security apparatus and structure will need to be made. Fourth, transparency in defence, foreign, and national security policy will be critical to building understanding and support among Canadians. Too often, defence and security matters in Canada have remained shrouded in secrecy, and have been seen as the purview of elites. If Canada is to move beyond innocence and drift, to craft a policy based on a realistic consideration of national interests, then a meaningful and open debate will be critical. Finally, there is the undeniable fact that additional defence spending will be necessary in areas that support transformation to ensure short, medium, and long-term relevance. This is a tall order, made all the more difficult by the fact that the armed forces and the defence establishment DND have suffered from a decade of downsizing and fiscal retrenchment. The journey will be arduous, and will demand hard thinking by all those with an interest in national security policy. A decade and a half after the Cold War ended, a period that was marked by innocence and drift, it is time for Canada to craft a strategy and policy that will help guide us in the difficult years ahead.

NOTES

1. The publication *Canada 21: Canada and Common Security in the Twenty-First Century* was produced by the Centre for International Studies, University of Toronto, in 1992. The chair of the council was Ivan Head, a professor of law and political science at the University of British Columbia; former foreign policy adviser to Prime Minister Pierre Elliott Trudeau, 1968–1978; and the president of the International Development Research Centre, 1978–1991. In essence the Canada 21 Council argued for a reordering of priorities and a reallocation of resources to better defend Canadian sovereignty and contribute to common security. Their recommendations rested on four principles: (1) common security does not depend on cultural homogeneity, but on the ability to create the conditions of tolerance and respect where a multiplicity of cultures and communities can flourish; (2) cooperation with other nations and people is the only way Canada can protect its sovereignty and enhance its security; (3) challenges to common security are likely to arise from conflict triggered by involuntary migration, resource scarcities, and ethnic clashes; and (4) Canada must develop policies that address the underlying causes of conflict through preventive action, and those policies must draw on a wide range of instruments and resources if they are to be effective in defending sovereignty and contributing to common security. *Ibid.*, 12.

2. Jack Granatstein, *Who Killed the Canadian Military?* (Toronto: Harper Flamingo Canada, 2004).

3. Readers seeking a sustained and thorough critique of this interpretation of Canada's long record with peace missions led or sponsored by the United Nations should consult the various works of Sean Maloney. Maloney has virtually single-handedly endeavoured to balance the myth of the Canadian peacekeeper and Canada as a peacekeeping nation generated by Canadian liberal internationalists, with a more realistic — indeed

more *realpolitik* — treatment. His point is made most forcefully in *Canada and UN Peacekeeping: Cold War by Other Means, 1945–1970* (St. Catharines, ON: Vanwell, 2002).

4. A searing analysis of the Canada 21 Committee Report can be found in John Cartier, "Critique of Canada 21: Canada and Common Security in the Twenty-first Century," (unpublished paper issued under a nom de plume, no date). Extensive digging has not revealed the author of this essay, although it is clear that the author had extensive experience in strategic analysis, military force structuring and modelling, and budget analysis.

5. Historians and veterans of the Cold War will remember this term fondly. It was often thought that the Soviets would engage in elaborate deception operations to entice NATO to let its guard down.

6. See "Selected Bibliography, Part IV — Brave New World," in this volume for sources that cover this material in more detail.

7. Between 1993 and 1998, the DND budget fell by 23 percent, and the real purchasing power of the department fell by more than 30 percent. Despite up-ticks beginning in 1998, the decline in purchasing power for the Canadian Forces has amounted to something in the order of $32 billion FY03/04 dollars. (Source ADM (Fin CS)/DB — FINSTAT, 31 January 2004).

8. For instance, see Granatstein, *Who Killed the Canadian Military?* 163–198; Joseph Jockel, *The Canadian Forces: Hard Choices, Soft Power* (Toronto: Canadian Institute of Strategic Studies, 1999), 9–34; Tim Naumetz, "Recall Troops for Total Overhaul: Senators," *Kingston Whig-Standard*, November 13, 2002, 1 and 10; Sheldon Alberts, "No Increase for Military, Manley Says," *National Post*, September 5, 2002, *http://www.canada.com/trail.story*, accessed September 5, 2002; and David Rudd, "The Centre Cannot Hold," *esprit de corps*, Vol. 9, No. 4 (February 2002), 6.

9. The term *strategic culture* has been much abused of late. Arguably, it has been stretched and broadened to such an extent that it has become overgeneralized. For the purposes of this essay, the term *strategic culture* as defined by Alastair Johnston will be used. Johnston defines strategic culture as a "system of symbols (e.g., argumentation structures, languages, analogies, metaphors), which acts to establish pervasive and long-lasting strategic preferences by formulating concepts of the role and efficacy of military force in interstate political affairs ..." See Alastair Iain Johnston, "Thinking About Strategic Culture," *International Security*, Vol. 19, No. 4 (Spring 1995).

10. See Maloney, *Canada and UN Peacekeeping*; and Sean Maloney, "Canada and the Cold War: The Maturation and Decline of a Nation," in Bernd Horn, ed., *Forging a Nation: Perspectives on the Canadian Military Experience* (St. Catharines, ON: Vanwell, 2002), 353–366.

11. See for instance, Colin S. Gray, *Modern Strategy* (New York: Oxford University Press, 1999); and Richard K. Betts, "Is Strategy an Illusion?" *International Security*, Vol. 25, No. 2 (Fall 2000), 5–50.

12. For example see the *Report of the Auditor General of Canada to the House of Commons, Chapter 3, National Security in Canada — The 2001 Anti-Terrorism Initiative* (Ottawa: Office of the Auditor General of Canada, March 2004).

13. For example, see Major-General Robert H. Scales, Jr., *Yellow Smoke: The Future of Land Warfare for America's Military* (New York: Rowman & Littlefield Publishers, 2003); Colin Gray, "Thinking Asymmetrically in Times of Terror," *Parameters*, Vol. 32, No. 1 (Spring 2002); Ministry of Defence, *The Strategic Defence Review: A New Chapter* (London: Ministry of Defence, 2002); Canada, *Future Force: Concepts of Future Army Capabilities* (Kingston, ON: DND, 2003).

AFTERWORD
by Bernd Horn

In examining the Canadian military experience, many have difficulty in accepting the premise that Canada, the "peaceable kingdom," has a distinct "way of war," or in simpler, more accurate terms, a conscious methodology of how it uses armed force or military to support its national interest. Nevertheless, military force has always been a distinct policy tool that all states have used in one manner or another to achieve political purpose. Canada has been no different. The government has consistently used its armed forces to achieve political ends. More often than not, the Canadian way of war has been a direct reflection of circumstance and political will. It has never been a doctrinal treatise or a formal carefully detailed Jominian exposition that has been passed on over time. Rather, it is a pragmatic and philosophical methodology of how our country structures and uses its military potential to further its national interests. This has developed over time and is based on the country's needs, capability, economic capacity, and the temperament of its people.

Although an evolutionary process was unavoidable as Canada matured and the world around it grew more complex, clear components of the Canadian way of war have always permeated our military experience. The nation's soldiers, whether volunteer or conscript, have created a legacy of competence, courage, stamina, and tenacity. Through blood, they have earned the respect of their allies and foes alike. And, despite the continual assertions by historians that Canadians are an "unmilitary" people, the truth of the matter is we have continually proven in conflict and war, at home, and abroad, that Canadians as soldiers, sailors, and airmen are second to none.

But the essence of a Canadian way of war is more than just pride in the martial spirit, willingness, and capability of our people when required for military service. Quite simply, to recognize a Canadian way of war does not imply an existence of, or attempt at militaristic jingoism.

Rather, it is, as already mentioned, the acknowledgement of a conscious, pragmatic, and philosophical approach to how the country structures and uses its military forces to further its national interests. As such, historically there have been several key themes that have permeated our military experience, namely, a reliance on alliances and coalitions, and an aversion to risk — if not a deferment of immediate action and decision making. In addition, this experience has included an effort at functionalism and saliency; a dependence on tactical expertise (with little experience or ability at the operational or strategic level of war); a dedication to defence "on the cheap;" as well as a focus on limiting commitment to potentially hazardous, costly (in terms of both money and casualties), and politically dangerous ventures overseas.

As such, the various authors have examined the Canadian military experience and have directly or indirectly touched on the tenets of the Canadian way of war. As described in the first chapter, *la petite guerre* became a strategy of survival based on the circumstances, geography, and political will of its leaders. New France as a distant and largely untamed colony, with a small population base and an extremely large frontier to defend against a numerically and militarily superior neighbour, was from its beginnings in a position of relative weakness. As a result, military operations had to be limited and in consonance with the colony's strengths and capabilities. As such, *les canadiens* developed a reliance on alliances with a number of First Nations, an active role for citizen soldiers (militia), a manner of warfare that depended on a very offensive — defensive strategy (i.e., an active policy of raids and ambushes in enemy territory that terrorized their enemies and kept them off balance by pre-empting their offensive plans and/or forcing them to focus on defending their own territory). In essence, it was a form of forward defence, a fight-away policy, choosing to solve potential problems or conflict elsewhere to protect the homeland and provide stability for economic growth and prosperity. But more importantly, this tactical approach was cost effective, low on casualties, and tailored to the strength and temperament of *les canadiens*. In the end, it allowed New France an influence and power greater than its economic or military strength should have allowed.

Many of these themes are continued in John Grodzinski's examination of the Great War of 1783 to 1815. As he explains, many of the strategic, economic, political, and military problems remained the same. Not surprisingly, so did many of the solutions. Once again, alliances and a forward defence strategy (i.e., vigorous offensive activities in enemy territory to pre-empt his ability to concentrate forces elsewhere) were undertaken. In this chapter, Grodzinski tackles conventional wisdom, and while acknowledging that the war was fought largely by British regulars, he argues that the Canadian soldier did make a significant contribution to the defence of Canada during the war.

Similarly, Grodzinski's examination of the 1800s, as well as Horn and Haycock's chapter on the Boer War experience, begins to shed light on the evolution of the Canadian military establishment. Not surprisingly, echoes of many of the same concerns and solutions of the earlier years were once again present. However, what becomes clearly apparent is the perennial concern and practice of defence on the cheap — the desire for security but at someone else's expense. In addition, the economic, political, and social costs of military commitment become omnipresent, a trend that grows ever more visible as the nation matures.

Nonetheless, during this period the effectiveness and contribution of Canadian soldiers, whether militia or regular, became more fully realized by political and military leaders, as well as the public at large. Military force became an essential tool domestically for national survival and political stability. Additionally, it contributed to national pride, international recognition, and political relevance. Importantly, these concepts for a sovereign nation have serious economic and political ramifications. As Canada soon learned, a seat at the international table required an ante, a contribution to the global community, or at a minimum, to the alliance one wished to be a member of.

As such, Canada reluctantly became a global player with its precedent-setting deployment of troops overseas, to South Africa, in 1899. It was a learning experience, but it was also in keeping with the tenets of the Canadian way of war. The deployment supported national interests (i.e., helping to maintain political power at home by placating the pro-imperialist voters in, largely, English Canada, without alienating French Canada). And it was seen as an opportunity to leverage imperial support for defence of Canadian interests in North America (particularly in light of the Alaska Panhandle dispute), as well as an obvious economic opportunity. All pragmatic reasons why the government chose to support the deployment of Canadian troops.

The First World War, as Andrew Godefroy explains, was no different. Although the Boer War lesson of national command and control of one's troops was well learned and practised, Canadian political leaders were content to contribute tactically to the alliance and leave the larger operational and strategic questions to their imperial protector. Again, Canadian soldiers stood out for their courage, innovative abilities, and tactical prowess on the battlefield. But the enormous butcher's bill that became synonymous with the stagnant deadly combat of the Western Front confirmed the fear of overseas commitment that Canadian politicians have always tried to avoid. Their aversion to such risk seemed validated. After all, supporting military endeavour almost always proved to be costly, in terms of national treasure, casualties and, potentially, political power.

In the inter-war years, as Stephen Harris articulates, a debate arose in the Canadian military regarding its ongoing strategy. Its exemplary legacy of courage, and uniquely Canadian innovation and tactical proficiency from the First World War was quickly lost. Ideas for the defence of Canada against the American bogeyman were based on an offensive forward strategy that harkened back to Vaudreuil and Brock. Others called for functionalism, suggesting the Canadian military should be optimized for cold weather operations or motor guerrilla swarms. However, all these ideas were quickly quashed in favour of the security of imperial uniformity and the ruling belief that the senior partner will determine the doctrine for the army and the strategy for the defence of Canada. Although the author clearly states that there was no Canadian way of war at this time, arguably this approach was very much in keeping with the Canadian approach — namely, an aversion to risk; a functional and tactical focus that allows participation in potential operations as a sub-component that can readily be plugged into a larger formation; a reliance on an alliance where the senior partner, as guarantor and protector, determines strategy (which limits commitment and allows the flexibility to opt out if the strategy or parts thereof fail to resonate with voters at home); and of course defence on the cheap (i.e., reliance on imperial doctrine, structures, and defence plans that eliminate the need and enormous cost of a self-defence capability).

The Second World War reinforced many of the themes already discussed. Douglas Delaney, using the Montgomery/Crerar command relationship, addresses the alliance focus and tactical orientation, focusing in on the question of national politics and the quintessential Canadian concern for command and control. Not surprisingly, the consistent theme of the "splendid" Canadian soldier remains clearly visible.

Canada's contribution to the Second World War, just as in the First, was impressive and the nation emerged as an industrially and militarily strong and vibrant country. As such, it was not lost on the country's political and military leaders in the post-war years that only a peaceful and stable world would keep Canadian prosperity possible and the nation safe from the ravages of war. Peace and stability were not easy to maintain in a world that was becoming increasingly dangerous with the ever-widening gulf between East and West, further complicated by Canada's strategic position between the two arch rivals — the Soviet Union and the United States of America. Moreover, recent experience had clearly demonstrated that the Americans, now Canada's closest ally and neighbour, viewed Canada as an exposed flank. Therefore, to the Americans, defence of the United States implied continental defence, with or without Canadian agreement.

Not surprisingly, the post-war period that developed into the Cold War between the Soviet Bloc and the NATO alliance, created additional challenges for Canada. To establish and retain relevancy on the international stage, given its position in the shadow of its superpower neighbour, meant Canada needed to participate in constructive international initiatives. This more often than not meant military contributions to alliance, coalition, or international organizations or actions. In essence, the currency of association, membership, and recognition was military participation.

As such, the array of chapters that deal with the Cold War and related activities clearly articulate the adherence to a consistent Canadian approach. Alliance membership was key throughout. Once again, Canadians were content to derive the maximum amount of global and continental defence and security at someone else's expense. The requirement for participation was always understood, but within a collective security umbrella it was easy to limit one's effort. Furthermore, within an alliance structure, doctrine, and strategy were largely determined by others and the national approach was again one of functionalism and saliency — provide an effective, credible contribution that is valued by alliance partners at the cheapest possible price. This consistently came in the form of military contributions. And, contrary to the mythology of Canadian "do-gooding," peacekeeping operations throughout the Cold War, as described by Sean Maloney, were a reflection of a Canadian way of war — the use of its military to serve pragmatic national self-interest (i.e., economic, political, and security). In essence, it was also an adherence to the tried and true principle of forward defence — the art of containing violence and instability as far away from North America as possible to ensure the continued affluence and security of Canada and its people.

This reality did not change with the fall of the wall or the post–Cold War era. The stabilization campaigns around the world were again undertaken to serve the national interest. The Canadian military has once again been used to support alliance and coalition initiatives and rather than determine an independent strategy the nation has stuck to its traditional way of war. Despite criticisms from within and outside, the Canadian government has steered a predictable course based on its tolerance for risk and its comprehension of what Canadians will accept, in terms of cost, casualties, and national commitment to conflicts that cannot be readily cloaked in a UN or "peace" operations mantle.

And so, the nation has consciously and consistently utilized military force in support of the national interest to further its security, as well as its economic and political well-being. But it has done so in a deliberate manner to reduce its costs, liabilities, commitments, and risks to the lowest possible level. Nonetheless, Canada's leadership has very rarely failed to comprehend that the use of military force is a critical implement in an unforgiving global environment where *realpolitik* is the real foundation of action. Despite the best of intentions to aid others, the reality is that military force has most often served the national interest by achieving practical political purposes, rather than altruistic deeds.

In the final analysis, the Canadian military experience and national way of war has been integral to creating the advanced, affluent, and vibrant nation that exists today. Undoubtedly, in spite of the popular mythology of Canadian humanitarianism, the national interest has always been best served by the hard edge of military participation in alliance and coalition operations. In so doing, despite its limited resources and small military establishment, Canada has consistently achieved, for the most part, its strategic goals by practising its own distinct way of war.

GLOSSARY OF ABBREVIATIONS

ABC	American — British — Canadian
ABCA	American — British — Canadian — Australian
ABM	Anti-Ballistic Missile
ADC	Air Defence Command
AFHQ	Air Force Headquarters
AMC	Air Material Command
ANZUS	Australia — New Zealand — United States
APC	Armoured Personnel Carriers
ASW	Anti-Submarine Warfare
ATEP	Advanced Technology Evaluation Program
ATI	Access to Information
BCATP	British Commonwealth Air Training Plan
Bde	Brigade
BEF	British Expeditionary Corps
BMD	Ballistic Missile Defence
BMEWS	Ballistic Missile Early Warning System
C2IS	Command, Control, and Information Systems
CAF	Canadian Armed Forces
CANMILSATCOM	Canadian Military Satellite Communications
CANUS	Canada — United States
CAS	Chief of the Air Staff
Cdn	Canadian
CDQ	*Canadian Defence Quarterly*
CDS	Chief of the Defence Staff
CEF	Canadian Expeditionary Force
CF	Canadian Forces
CFSAS	Canadian Forces School of Aerospace Studies
CGS	Chief of the General Staff
CIA	Central Intelligence Agency
CIBG	Canadian Infantry Brigade Group
CIDA	Canadian International Development Agency
CIGS	Chief of the Imperial General Staff
CinC	Commander-in-Chief
CMHQ	Canadian Military Headquarters
CMR	Canadian Mounted Rifles

CO	Commanding Officer [or Colonial Office]
COHQ	Combined Operations Headquarters
COR	Chief of Operational Requirements
COS	Chief(s) of Staff
COTC	Canadian Officers' Training Corps
Coy	Company
CP	Command Post
CRAD	Chief Research and Development
CRS	Chief Review Services
CSCE	Conference for Security and Cooperation in Europe
CSM	Company Sergeant Major
CWAC	Canadian Women's Army Corps
CWM	Canadian War Museum
DAED	Directorate of Advanced Engineering and Development
DCDS	Deputy Chief of the Defence Staff
DCGS	Deputy Chief of the General Staff
DCO	Deputy Commanding Officer
DDR&E	Directorate of Defense Research and Engineering [U.S.]
DEW	Distant Early Warning
DFAIT	Department of Foreign Affairs and International Trade
DHH	[DND] Directorate of History and Heritage
Div	Division
DLO	Director of Land Operations
DMC	Defence Management Committee
DMO & P	Director Military Operations and Plans
DMSP	Defence Meteorological Satellite Program
DMT	Directorate of Military Training
DND	Department of National Defence [Canada]
DoD	Department of Defense [U.S.]
DRB	Defence Research Board
DRTE	Defence Research Telecommunications Establishment
DSE	Director Systems Evaluation
DSP	Defence Support Program
D SPACE D	Directorate of Space Development
ECMM	European Community Monitor Mission
EKV	Exo-Atmospheric Kill Vehicle
Engr	Engineer
EU	European Union
Ex	Exercise
FAAA	First Allied Airborne Army
FAC	Forward Air Controller
Fd	Field
FLQ	Front de Libération du Québec
FOO	Forward Observation Officer
FSSF	First Special Service Force
GDP	Gross Domestic Product

GHQ	General Headquarters
Gp	Group
GPS	Global Positioning System
GOC	General Officer Commanding
GS	General Staff
HD	Home Defence
HQ	Headquarters
hrs	Hours
IA	Implementing Arrangements
ICBM	Intercontinental Ballistic Missile
ICCS	International Commission for Control and Supervision
ICSC	International Commission for Supervision and Control
IFOR	Implementation Force
ISAF	International Security Assistance Force [Afghanistan]
IWM	Imperial War Museum
JAG	Judge Advocate General
JIMPC	Joint [U.S.-Canadian] Industrial Mobilization Planning Committee
JNA	Jugoslav National Army
JSP	Joint Space Project
KFOR	Kosovo Force
LAC	Library and Archives Canada
MCC	Military Cooperation Committee
MFO	Multinational Force Observers
MG	Machine Gun
MHQ	Military Headquarters
MIDAS	Missile Detection Alarm System
MILSATCOM	Military Satellite Communications
MIT	Massachusetts Institute of Technology
MND	Minister of National Defence
MOU	Memorandum of Understanding
MP	Member of Parliament
NATO	North Atlantic Treaty Organisation
NAVSPASUR	Navy Space Surveillance System [U.S.]
NCO	Non-Commissioned Officer
NDHQ	National Defence Headquarters
NORAD	North American Air [Aerospace] Defense Command
NPIC	National Photographic Interpretation Center
NRC	National Research Council
NRMA	National Resources Mobilization Act
NWMP	North-West Mounted Police
NWS	North Warning System
OGD	Other Government Departments

OMFC	[Ministry for] Overseas Military Forces of Canada
ONUC	Organisation Nations Unies au Congo
ONUSAL	Observer Mission in El Salvador [UN]
OP	Operation or Observation Post [Depending on Context]
PGM	Precision Guided Munition
PJBD	Permanent Joint Board of Defence
PLO	Palestinian Liberation Organization
PoW	Prisoner of War
PPCLI	Princess Patricia's Canadian Light Infantry
PRO	Public Record Office [U.K.]
QMG	Quartermaster General
RA	Royal Artillery
RAF	Royal Air Force
R22eR	Royal 22 Regiment
RCA	Royal Canadian Artillery
RCAF	Royal Canadian Air Force
RCAMC	Royal Canadian Army Medical Corps
RCASC	Royal Canadian Army Service Corps
RCD	Royal Canadian Dragoons
RCE	Royal Canadian Engineers
RCHA	Royal Canadian Horse Artillery
RCIC	Royal Canadian Infantry Corps
RCN	Royal Canadian Navy
RCR	Royal Canadian Regiment
RE	Royal Engineers
Recce	Reconnaissance
Regt	Regiment
RHQ	Regimental Headquarters
RMA	Revolution in Military Affairs
RMC	Royal Military College of Canada
RN	Royal Navy
RSM	Regimental Sergeant Major
RTU	Return to Unit
RV	Rendevous Point
SAC	Strategic Air Command
SACEUR	Supreme Allied Commander, Europe
SAR	Search and Rescue
SARSAT	Search and Rescue Satellite
SAS	Special Air Service [British]
SDC	Space Defense Center
SDI	Strategic Defence Initiative
SDWG	Space Defence Working Group
SF	Special Forces
SFOR	Stabilization Force
SIC	Space Indoctrination Course
SIP	Space Indoctrination Program

SITU	Satellite Identification Tracking Unit
SOI	Statement of Intent
SOP	Standard Operating Procedure
SPADATS	Space Detection and Tracking System
SPO	System Program Office
SSD	Space System Division
SSN	Space Satellite Network
STS	Space Transportation System
TIBS	Tactical Information Broadcast System
TOW	Tube Launched, Optically Tracked, Wire Guided
UN	United Nations
UNAMIR	United Nations Assistance Mission in Rwanda
UNAVEM	United Nations Angola Verification Mission
UNDOF	United Nations Disengagement Observer Force
UNEF	United Nations Emergency Force
UNFICYP	United Nations Force in Cyprus
UNIFIL	United Nations Interim Force in Lebanon
UNITAF	Unified Task Force [Somalia]
UNIKOM	United Nations Iraq Kuwait Observation Mission
UNMOGIIP	United Nations Military Observer Group in India — Pakistan
UNOMIL	United Nations Observer Mission in Liberia
UNPREDEP	United Nations Preventive Deployment
UNPROFOR	United Nations Protection Force
UNTAC	United Nations Transition Authority in Cambodia
UNTAG	United Nations Transition Assistance Group
UNTEA	United Nations Temporary Executive Authority in New Guinea
UNTSO	United Nations Truce Supervision Organization
UNYOM	United Nations Yemen Observation Mission
USAF	United States Air Force
USAAF	United States Army Air Force
USN	United States Navy
VC	Victoria Cross
VCDS	Vice Chief of the Defence Staff
VCGS	Vice Chief of the General Staff
WCTU	Women's Christian Temperance Union
WO	War Office [U.K.]
WP	Warsaw Pact
WMD	Weapons of Mass Destruction
2 PPCLI	2 Battalion, Princess Patricia's Canadian Light Infantry
9/11	September 11, 2001 (Terrorist Attack on the World Trade Center, New York City)
25 CIBG	25 Canadian Infantry Brigade Group
82 AB Div	82 Airborne Division [U.S.]

SELECTED BIBLIOGRAPHY

INTRODUCTION

Goodspeed, D.J., ed. *The Armed Forces of Canada, 1867–1967: A Century of Achievement.* Ottawa: Canadian Forces Headquarters, 1967.

Granatstein, J.L. *Canada's Army.* Toronto: University of Toronto Press, 2002.

Horn, Bernd, ed. *Forging a Nation: Perspectives on the Canadian Military Experience.* St. Catharines, ON: Vanwell, 2002.

Morton, Desmond. *A Military History of Canada From Champlain to Kosovo,* 4th ed. Toronto: McClelland & Stewart, 1999.

_____. *Canada and War: A Military and Political History.* Toronto: Butterworth's, 1981.

Stanley, George F. *Canada's Soldiers: The Military History of an Unmilitary People.* Toronto: Macmillan of Canada, 1960.

PART I — ESTABLISHING A DISTINCT CANADIAN WAY OF WAR

Allen, Robert S. *His Majesty's Indian Allies: British Indian Policy in the Defence of Canada.* Toronto: Dundurn Press, 1993.

Anderson, Fred. *Crucible of War.* New York: Vintage Books, 2001.

Benn, Carl. *The Iroquois in the War of 1812.* Toronto: University of Toronto Press, 1998.

Brumwell, Stephen. *Redcoat: British Soldiers and War in the Americas, 1755–63.* Cambridge, Eng.: University of Cambridge Press, 2002.

Chartrand, René. *Canadian Military Heritage, Volume 2, 1755–1871.* Montreal: Art Global, 1995.

Graham, Gerald S. *Sea Power and British North America, 1783–1820.* London: Cambridge-Harvard University Press, 1941.

Gray, William. *Soldiers of the Kings: The Upper Canadian Militia, 1812–1815*. Toronto: Stoddart, 1995.

Graves, Donald E. *Field of Glory: The Battle of Crysler's Farm, 1813*. Toronto: Robin Brass Studio, 1999.

Harris, Stephen. *Canadian Brass: The Making of a Professional Army 1860–1890*. Toronto: University of Toronto Press, 1988.

Hitsman, J. Mackay. (Updated by Donald E. Graves). *The Incredible War of 1812*. Toronto: Robin Brass Studio, 1999.

Lepine, Luc, *Les officier de milice du Bas-Canada, 1812–1815/Lower Canada's Militia Officer's, 1812–1815*. Montreal: Société Génélogique Canadienne-Française, 1996.

Miller, Carman. *Painting the Map Red: Canada and the South African War 1899–1902*. Montreal: Canadian War Museum and McGill-Queen's University Press, 1993.

Miller, I.H.M. *Our Glory and Our Grief: Torontonians and the Great War*. Toronto: University of Toronto Press, 2002.

Morton, Desmond. *The Last War Drum*. Toronto: Hakkert, 1972.

Parkman, Francis. *Montcalm and Wolfe*. New York: The Modern Library, 1999 (reprint).

Reid, Brian. *Our Little Army in the Field: The Canadians in South Africa 1899–1902*. St. Catharines, ON: Vanwell, 1996.

Steele, Ian K. *Guerillas and Grenadiers*. Toronto: Ryerson Press, 1969.

Thwaites, Reuben Gold, ed. *The Jesuit Relations and Allied Documents: Travels and Explorations of the Jesuit Missionaries in New France, 1610–1791*. Vol. 1–70. New York: Pageant Book Company, 1959.

Verney, Jack. *The Good Regiment: The Carignan-Salières Regiment in Canada, 1665-1668*. Montreal: McGill-Queen's University Press, 1991.

Part II — Fighting Abroad

Dancocks, Daniel G. *Spearhead to Victory: Canada and the Great War*. Edmonton, AB: Hurtig, 1987.

Eayrs, James. *In Defence of Canada, Vol. 1: From the Great War to the Great Depression*. Toronto: University of Toronto Press, 1964.

English, John A. *Failure in High Command: The Canadian Army and the Normandy Campaign*. Ottawa: Golden Dog Press, 1995.

Granatstein, J.L. *The Generals: The Canadian Army's Senior Commanders in the Second World War*. Toronto: Stoddart, 1993.

_____. *Canada's War: The Politics of the Mackenzie King Government, 1939–1945*. Toronto: Oxford University Press, 1975.

Granatstein, J.L., and Desmond Morton. *Canada and the Two World Wars*. Toronto: Key Porter Books, 2003.

Haycock, Ronald G. *Sam Hughes*. Waterloo, ON: Wilfrid Laurier Press, 1986.

Horn, Bernd, and Stephen J. Harris, eds. *Warrior Chiefs: Perspectives on Senior Canadian Military Leaders*. Toronto: Dundurn Press, 2001.

Hyatt, A.M.J. *General Sir Arthur Currie: A Military Biography*. Toronto: University of Toronto Press, 1987.

Morton, Desmond. *When Your Number Is Up: The Canadian Soldier in the First World War*. Toronto: Random House Canada, 1993.

_____. *A Peculiar Kind of Politics: Canada's Overseas Ministry in the First World War*. Toronto: University of Toronto Press, 1982.

Nicholson, Colonel G.W.L. *Official History of the Canadian Army in the First World War: Canadian Expeditionary Force, 1914–1919*. Ottawa: Queen's Printer, 1964.

Schreiber, Shane B. *Shock Army of the British Empire: The Canadian Corps in the Last 100 Days of the Great War*. New York: Praeger, 1997.

Stacey, C.P. *Six Years of War: The Army in Canada, Britain and the Pacific*. Ottawa: Queen's Printer, 1966.

Rawling, Bill. *Surviving Trench Warfare: Technology and the Canadian Corps, 1914–1918*. Toronto: University of Toronto Press, 1992.

Part III — Assuring Global Stability

Bercuson, David J. *Blood on the Hills: The Canadian Army in the Korean War*. Toronto: University of Toronto Press, 1999.

Bland, Douglas. *Canada's National Defence, Vol. 1: Defence Policy*. Kingston, ON: Queen's School of Policy Studies, 1997.

_____. *Canada's National Defence, Vol. 2: Defence Organization*. Kingston, ON: Queen's School of Policy Studies, 1998.

_____. *The Administration of Defence Policy in Canada 1947–1985*. Kingston, ON: Ronald P.Frye & Company, 1987.

Clearwater, John. U.S. Nuclear Weapons in Canada. Toronto: Dundurn Press, 1999.

____. *Canadian Nuclear Weapons: The Untold Story of Canada's Cold War Arsenal.* Toronto: Dundurn Press, 1998.

Eayrs, James. *In Defence of Canada, Vol. 3: Peacemaking and Deterrence.* Toronto: University of Toronto Press, 1972.

____. *In Defence of Canada, Vol. 4: Growing Up Allied.* Toronto: University of Toronto Press, 1980.

____. *In Defence of Canada, Vol. 5: Indochina: Roots of Complicity.* Toronto: University of Toronto Press, 1983.

English, John A. *Lament for an Army: The Decline of Military Professionalism.* Concord, ON: Irwin, 1998.

Haglund, David G. *The North Atlantic Triangle Revisited: Canadian Grand Strategy at Century's End.* Toronto: Irwin, 2000.

Haydon, Peter T. *The 1962 Cuban Missile Crisis: Canadian Involvement Reconsidered.* Toronto: Canadian Institute of Strategic Studies, 1993.

Hilliker, John, and Donald Barry. *Canada's Department of External Affairs: Volume 2 Coming of Age, 1946–1968.* Canadian Public Administration Series. Kingston, ON: McGill-Queen's University Press, 1995.

Jockel, Joseph T. *No Boundaries Upstairs: Canada, the United States and the Origins of North American Air Defence, 1945–1958.* Vancouver: University of British Columbia Press, 1987.

Johnston, William. *A War of Patrols: Canadian Army Operations in Korea.* Vancouver: University of British Columbia Press, 2003.

Maloney, Sean M. *Canada and UN Peacekeeping: Cold War by Other Means 1945–1970.* St. Catharines, ON: Vanwell, 2002.

____. *War Without Battles: Canada's NATO Brigade in Germany 1951–1993.* Whitby, ON: McGraw-Hill Ryerson Limited, 1997.

Middlemiss, D.W., and J.J. Sokolsky. *Canadian Defence: Decisions and Determinants.* Toronto: Harcourt Brace Jovanovich, 1989.

Milner, Marc. *Canada's Navy: The First Century.* Toronto: University of Toronto Press, 1999.

Richter, Andrew. *Avoiding Armageddon: Canadian Military Strategy and Nuclear Weapons, 1950–63.* Vancouver: University of British Columbia Press, 2002.

Sokolsky, Joel, and Joseph Jockel, eds. *Fifty Years of Canada–United States Defence Co-operation: The Road from Ogdensburg.* Lewiston, NY: Mellon Press, 1992.

Willett, J.C. *A Heritage at Risk: The Canadian Militia as a Social Institution*. Boulder, CO: Westview Press, 1987.

Wood, Lieutenant-Colonel Herbert Fairlie. *Strange Battleground: The Operations in Korea and Their Effects on the Defence Policy of Canada*. Ottawa: Queen's Printer, 1966.

PART IV — BRAVE NEW WORLD: AFTER THE FALL OF THE WALL

Carment, David, et al., eds. *Coping with the American Colossus: Canada Among Nations 2003*. Toronto: Oxford University Press, 2003.

Cohen, Andrew. *While Canada Slept: How We Lost Our Place in the World*. Toronto: McClelland & Stewart, 2003.

Granatstein, J.L. *Who Killed the Canadian Military?* Toronto: Harper Flamingo Canada, 2004.

____. *Yankee Go Home? Canadians and Anti-Americanism*. Toronto: HarperCollins Canada, 1996.

Horn, Bernd, and Stephen J. Harris, eds. *Generalship and the Art of the Admiral*. St. Catharines, ON: Vanwell, 2001.

Jockel, Joseph. *The Canadian Forces: Hard Choices, Soft Power*. Toronto: Canadian Institute of Strategic Studies, 1999.

Morton, Desmond. *Understanding Canadian Defence*. Toronto: Penguin Canada, 2003.

Contributors

Lieutenant-Colonel Howard G. Coombs is the commanding officer of the Prince of Wales Own Regiment in Kingston and a PhD candidate in history at Queen's University.

Major Douglas E. Delaney, PhD, is a serving officer in the Canadian Forces who is currently an assistant professor of history at the Royal Military College of Canada in Kingston, Ontario.

Dr. Andrew B. Godefroy is currently a policy and operations analyst with the Directorate of Land Strategic Concepts in Kingston, Ontario.

Richard Goette is an air force historian and a PhD candidate in history at Queen's University.

Major John R. Grodzinski, MA, is a serving officer in the Canadian Forces and the former managing editor of *The Army Training and Doctrine Bulletin*.

Dr. Stephen J. Harris is the chief historian at the Directorate of History and Heritage, National Defence Headquarters.

Dr. Ronald G. Haycock is a professor of history and war studies, as well as a former dean of arts, at the Royal Military College of Canada.

Dr. Michael A. Hennessy is an associate professor of history and war studies and the chair of the History Department at the Royal Military College of Canada.

Colonel Bernd Horn, PhD, is a serving officer in the Canadian Forces who is currently the director of the Canadian Forces Leadership Institute and an adjunct associate professor of history at the Royal Military College of Canada.

Dr. Sean M. Maloney is an associate professor of history at the Royal Military College of Canada.

Dr. Scot Robertson is a former associate professor in the Department of Politics and Economics and a former associate chair of the Graduate Program in War Studies at the Royal Military College of Canada. He is currently an associate professor of history at the University of Alberta.

INDEX